PLAY/WRITE

ELECTRACY AND TRANSMEDIA STUDIES
Series Editors: Jan Rune Holmevik and Cynthia Haynes

The Electracy and Transmedia Studies Series publishes research that examines the mixed realities that emerge through electracy, play, rhetorical knowledge, game design, community, code, and transmedia artifacts. This book series aims to augment traditional artistic and literate forms with examinations of electrate and literate play in the age of transmedia. Writing about play should, in other words, be grounded in playing with writing. The distinction between play and reflection, as Stuart Moulthrop argues, is a false dichotomy. Cultural transmedia artifacts that are interactive, that move, that are situated in real time, call for inventive/electrate means of creating new scholarly traction in transdisciplinary fields. The series publishes research that produces such traction through innovative processes that move research forward across its own limiting surfaces (surfaces that create static friction). The series exemplifies extreme points of contact where increased electrate traction might occur. The series also aims to broaden how scholarly treatments of electracy and transmedia can include both academic and general audiences in an effort to create points of contact between a wide range of readers. The Electracy and Transmedia Series follows what Gregory Ulmer calls an image logic based upon a wide scope— "an aesthetic embodiment of one's attunement with the world."

BOOKS IN THE SERIES

Future Texts: Subversive Performance and Feminist Bodies, edited by Vicki Callahan and Virginia Kuhn (2016)

Play/Write: Digital Rhetoric, Writing, Games, edited by Douglas Eyman and Andréa D. Davis (2016)

PLAY/WRITE

DIGITAL RHETORIC, WRITING, GAMES

Douglas Eyman and Andréa D. Davis

Parlor Press
Anderson, South Carolina
www.parlorpress.com

Parlor Press LLC, Anderson, South Carolina, USA
© 2016 by Parlor Press
All rights reserved.
Printed in the United States of America on acid-free paper.

S A N: 2 5 4 - 8 8 7 9

Library of Congress Cataloging-in-Publication Data

Names: Eyman, Douglas, editor. | Davis, Andréa D., 1969- editor.
Title: Play/write : digital rhetoric, writing games / [edited by] Douglas
    Eyman and Andréa D. Davis.
Description: Anderson, South Carolina : Parlor Press, [2016] | Series:
    Electracy and transmedia studies | Includes bibliographical references and
    index.
Identifiers: LCCN 2016010313 (print) | LCCN 2016024402 (ebook) | ISBN
    9781602357310 (pbk. : alk. paper) | ISBN 9781602357327 (hardcover : alk.
    paper) | ISBN 9781602357334 (pdf) | ISBN 9781602357341 (epub) | ISBN
    9781602357358 (iBook) | ISBN 9781602357365 (Kindle)
Subjects: LCSH: English language--Composition and
    exercises--Computer-assisted instruction. | English
    language--Rhetoric--Computer-assisted instruction. | Video games in
    education.
Classification: LCC LB1576.7 .P53 2016 (print) | LCC LB1576.7 (ebook) |
    DDC
    808/.0420285--dc23
LC record available at https://lccn.loc.gov/2016010313

2 3 4 5
Electracy and Transmedia Studies
Series Editors: Jan Rune Holmevik and Cynthia Haynes

Cover image: © 2016 by nadla. iStockphoto ID:87033821. Used by
    permission.
Copyeditor: Jared Jameson.
Cover design: Christopher A. Clements and David Blakesley

Parlor Press, LLC is an independent publisher of scholarly and trade titles
in print and multimedia formats. This book is available in paper, cloth and
eBook formats from Parlor Press on the World Wide Web at http://www.
parlorpress.com or through online and brick-and-mortar bookstores. For
submission information or to find out about Parlor Press publications, write
to Parlor Press, 3015 Brackenberry Drive, Anderson, South Carolina, 29621,
or email editor@parlorpress.com.

Contents

1 Introduction: Networks of Gaming and Writing   *3*
       Douglas Eyman

**Part I: Game Rhetorics and Gaming Pedagogies
   (or, Writing About Games)**   19

2 Aleatory Invention and Glorious Trainwrecks'
   Accursed Share   *21*
       Steven Holmes

3 "What Do You Mean None of My Choices Mattered?":
   Collaborative Composition and the Ethics of Ownership
   in Games—A Case Study of *Mass Effect 3*   *42*
       Jessica Masri Eberhard

4 The Composing Practices and Rhetorical Acumen of MMORPG
   Players: What *City of Heroes* Means for Writing Instruction   *74*
       Phill Alexander

5 Procedurality as Play: Movement in Games and Composition   *97*
       Grace Hagood

**Part II: Game Ecologies and Networks (or,
   Writing Around Games)**   115

6 Who's That Walking on My Bridge? Transmedia
   Shifts and Trolling in Game Forums   *117*
       Richard Colby and Rebekah Shultz Colby

7 Data vs. Play: The Digital Rhetorics of Theorycrafting   *140*
       Lee Sherlock

8 Intellectual Property Pong: Three Classic Matches
   That Affect Your Play Today   *159*
       Scott Nelson

Part III: Games and/as Rhetorical Production (or, Writing In or Through Games)   179

9 "Leeroy Jenkins!" What Computer Gamers Can Teach Us about Visual Arguments   *181*
    Andréa Davis

10 Playing with Play: Machinima in the Classroom   *196*
    Wendi Sierra

11 VoIP, Composition, and Membership: Constructing Working Identities through Collaborative Play   *218*
    Emily Stuemke

12 Gaming Between Civic Knowledge and Civic Know-How: Direct Engagement and the Simulated City   *234*
    Sean Conrey

Part IV: Composing Games in Industry and Classroom Contexts (or, Writing Games)   253

13 Narrative Realities and Alternate Zombies: A Student-Centered Alternate Reality Game   *255*
    Jill Morris

14 Procedural Rhetoric, Proairesis, Game Design, and the Revaluing of Invention   *270*
    James J. Brown, Jr. and Eric Alexander

15 Games and the Search for "Contextually Valid Settings" in the Writing Classroom   *288*
    David M. Sheridan and Kym Buchanan

16 Programming, Pedagogy, Play   *309*
    Brian Ladd

17 Writing for Games   *339*
    Brandes Stoddard

18 Game Writing in Practice—MMORPG Quests   *347*
    Joshua Peery

Contributors   *363*
Index   *367*

Play/Write

1 Introduction: Networks of Gaming and Writing

Douglas Eyman

This collection originally began as a conversation with a group of colleagues at Michigan State University that were either interested in games as part of their own research agenda or had begun using games in their writing classes. James Gee's (2003) *What Videogames Can Teach Us about Learning and Literacy* had recently been published, providing a solid pedagogical foundation for thinking about games, learning, and literacy across a broad range of classes and contexts, but there seemed to be few instances of games and gaming being used in writing classes, either as cultural artifacts that could be investigated and reported on (much like film, television, and advertising has been used as objects of critique for cultural-studies influenced composition courses) or as new media writing spaces themselves. A review of handbooks and readers for writing courses published between 2005 and 2007 showed only two mentions of videogames, both of which were readings that examined the relationship between videogames and violent behavior in game players.

We appear to be at a cultural moment that recalls the resistance of the humanities to the introduction of computer and networked technologies that writing teachers faced in the early 1990s—at that time, teachers who were interested in how writing technologies could be leveraged to teach and research composition practices fought for the validity and relevance of computers in writing classrooms; just as computers as writing tools have become essentially ubiquitous both in higher education and in the culture at large, we are now facing a similar task in arguing for the relevance of games and game studies to the goals and methods of writing studies, including both teaching and research practices. Scholars of writing and rhetoric are not the only academics arguing for the value of videogames as teaching and research spaces; in the field of Cultural Studies, for instance, Matthew Southern (2001) notes that "if there is one cultural form that is subjected to this debate, it is the often-despised phenomenon of videogames. Almost since their inception, videogames have been met with rampant prejudice, legislation and stigma. Indeed, they are often 'beneath popular culture'" (n.p.).

It is important, however, that we learn from the history of computers and writing as we make arguments for the importance of computer games. Early technology evangelists sometimes deployed an overly-enthusiastic and largely uncritical approach to their arguments for the inclusion of computers in English studies, countering an extreme distrust of technology on the part of the humanities with an over-compensation of positive marketing. This approach gradually shifted to a more nuanced, critical approach to technology use in teaching and research, but the earlier approach may have done more harm than good through its insistence on the value of the computer as a writing tool. In this collection, we want to avoid being simply evangelistic— we will not simply advocate for games in the writing classroom based on our students' enthusiasm or our own interests in new technologies, but will provide both example uses and critical commentary on the possibilities and problems that arise when bringing videogames into writing classrooms.

A starting point for nearly all arguments for the relevance of games is the economic and cultural impact of the videogame industry: as part of the fabric of the ubiquitous technology space, we need to pay attention to games in the same way that we teach students to become critical consumers of other media (print, television, film, audio). Video and computer games are gaining influence, both economically and culturally; accordingly, scholarly examinations of videogames and computer-game research are beginning to appear with greater frequency. There is no doubt that gaming is economically important: as a case in point, the release of *Halo 3* in October of 2007 brought in $170 million in sales in one day (which is more than opening day receipts for any film up to that date.) In 2001, economist Edward Castronova calculated the GDP of virtual game economies at $135 million per year, and estimates of the impact of the gaming industry on real-world economies indicate that as much as $880 million annually is spent on the purchase of virtual goods and in-game currency. More recently, the Entertainment Software Association released "Videogames in the 21st Century: The 2014 Report," which claimed that between 2009 and 2012, the video game industry as a whole grew by nine percent (more than four times greater than the US economic growth during that time) and that the entertainment software industry added over $6.2 billion to US Gross Domestic Product (Siwek, 2014, p. 1).

In addition to purely economic metrics, there is evidence that video and computer games are increasingly visible in American popular culture, showing up in television shows such as *South Park* and *CSI:Miami*; in movies based on games including *Doom, Tomb Raider, Alone in the Dark, Silent Hill* (among many others); and in advertising—perhaps the most recognizable example of which is the 2007 Coca Cola spoof of *Grand Theft Auto* that aired during the Super Bowl. News media are increasingly paying attention to both the economic power of games and questions of sociocultural effects, with a particular focus on the question of whether videogames, like other forms of popular entertainment, may be contributing to social ills.

In the past several years, there has been a dramatic increase in research related to video and computer games: psychologists are studying the transferability of leadership skills and examining interpersonal communication and relationship issues related to online games (Yee 2014); sociologists are examining games as sites of social practice through ethnographic research (Yee 2009; Harrelson 2006); scholars in cultural studies are exploring the intersections of games and identity formation (Filiciak, 2003; Griebel 2006); and computer games for education and training have a long history of research (although this trend became more visible with the publication of James Gee's *What Video Games Have to Teach Us About Learning and Literacy* in 2003). In 2002, Kurt Squire argued that

> What's missing from contemporary debate on gaming and culture is any naturalistic study of what game-playing experiences are like, how gaming fits into people's lives, and the kinds of practices people are engaged in while gaming. Few, if any researchers have studied how and why people play games, and what gaming environments are like. . . . (n.p.)

In 2007, Selfe and Hawisher's *Gaming Lives in the Twenty-First Century* took up that challenge by examining video games within the context of a range of case studies of gamers' lived experience. Just as

Squire called for a research agenda that examines video game literacy practices in context, this collection argues for a rhetoric-based research approach to the study of game-based literacies as they relate to the teaching of composition and to research methods in writing studies. Computer games, particularly those games that support multi-player environments, are complex rhetorical spaces where both players and designers engage in the solving of rhetorical problems through the exercise of gaming literacies.

This collection aims to continue a new approach to examining video games as rhetorical ecologies and writing platforms, following the trajectory of two groundbreaking collections: *Rhetoric/Composition/Play Through Video Games* (2013), edited by Richard Colby, Matthew S. S. Johnson, and Rebekah Shultz Colby, and *Computer Games and Technical Communication* (2014), edited by Jennifer deWinter and Ryan Moeller. This collection should both complement these collections and extend our views of how we can teach with, research, and even produce scholarship with and through games.

DIGITAL LITERACY AND DIGITAL RHETORIC

Gunther Kress argues that "Language-as-speech will remain the major mode of communication; language-as-writing will increasingly be displaced by image in many domains of public communication, though writing will remain the preferred mode of the political and cultural elites. The combined effects on writing of the dominance of the mode of image and of the medium of the screen will produce deep changes in the forms and functions of writing" (2005, p. 1). However, in both literacy studies and composition studies, examinations of genre and media for composing have looked not just to the visual, but at a variety of modes and media—thus prompting a move toward a vision of composition as multimodal and multimedia:

> Increasingly, the literacies practiced by individuals who communicate primarily in online environments exist within a dynamic cultural ecology influenced by expanding global markets and computer networks that stretch across language barriers, cultural groupings, and geopolitical borders. Within this ecology, as the New London Group [1996] and Kress [2003] have explained, new-media literacies—which rely as much on images, video clips, animation, sound, and

still-photography as on words—have begun to emerge and compete vigorously with more traditional alphabetic print texts for readers' attention. (DeVoss *et al.*, 2003, p. 168).

Lester Faigley (2001), in fact, contends that "we have no justification aside from disciplinary baggage to restrict our conception of rhetoric to words alone. More important, this expansion is necessary if we are to make good on our claims of preparing students to engage in public discourse" (p. 187). DeVoss et al. (2003), drawing on case studies that problematize a lack of teacher training, argue that "English-composition teachers and programs must be willing to address an increasingly broad range of literacies—emerging, competing, and fading—if they want their instruction to remain relevant to students' changing communication needs and experiences within the contemporary cultural ecology" (p. 169).

Digital composition practices are changing the traditional emphases of classical rhetoric: as I have argued elsewhere, digital rhetoric "shifts the productive technē of the rhetorical process (as typically instantiated in composition and other writing courses) from primarily invention-driven to a broader rhetorical approach that privileges arrangement as a focal activity and reclaims the importance of delivery and memory as key areas of rhetorical practice" (DigiRhet.Net, 2006, pp. 242–243). Additionally, in classical rhetoric, the audience—the living component in what might be considered a communication ecology—has always been assumed to have greater agency (and is therefore of greater concern to the rhetor) than the nonliving components such as the medium of delivery and the immediate context of the rhetorical act (although these elements do play an important role; rhetoric derives a great deal of its power from the fact that it engages medium, mode, and context). Digital rhetoric sees agency in the interactions and interrelationships of any of the components of a given ecosystem. This is particularly important for digital game spaces, which feature both users and system-agents (including non-player characters, the environments in which the actions take place, and the rules that govern in-game interactions).

To date, the most explicit application of a digital rhetoric approach to computer games is Ian Bogost's work in *Persuasive Games* (2007). Bogost identifies procedurality as a rhetorical practice specific to computer programming—one through which, he contends, videogames open a new domain for persuasion by mounting arguments and influencing players. Procedural rhetoric, he says,

> is a practice of using processes persuasively. More specifically, procedural rhetoric is the practice of persuading through processes in general and computational processes in particular. Just as verbal rhetoric is useful for both the orator and the audience, and just as written rhetoric is useful for both the writer and the reader, so procedural rhetoric is useful for both the programmer and the user, the game designer and the player. (p. ix)

While Bogost's procedural rhetoric focuses on the internal logic of the game construction, it is also possible to develop digital rhetoric approaches to the contexts of game playing that extend beyond the player-game interaction. Games do not exist in isolation from other contexts; in fact, we can identify a series of contexts that highlight the interactions of gameplay and composition. These relationships develop in particular locales and support a wide range of rhetorical activity, but also provide boundaries that help us to taxonomize the genres of writing that take place in different contexts. Considering relationships between computer gaming and writing within these contexts suggests the possibility of an ecological approach to teaching and researching video games and writing activities.

WRITING ECOLOGIES AND COMPUTER GAME CONTEXTS

This collection, therefore, is loosely framed by an ecological framework through which we can organize the activities, both textual and transtextual, that work in, through, and around computer games. We can see a series of discrete contexts and relationships that arise from the activities within these specific contexts; thus, we divide our approach to writing and games by specifying the relationship between game, writing, and context. Research, theory, and pedagogical approaches can be divided into four ecosystems defined by the location and relationship between writing and gaming activities:

- Writing about Games
- Writing around Games
- Writing inside Games
- Writing Games

Using rhetoric as both analytic method and productive heuristic, we can develop writing pedagogies that engage each of these locales as either providing *texts* for reading, response, and critique, or for providing *contexts* for writing and reflection.

WRITING ABOUT GAMES

Much of the current research and academic work that addresses computer games focuses on how to read the games as texts or examining the effects of games on game players. Scholars who take these approaches are primarily writing *about* games as viewed from a variety of contexts. Most writing about games draws on one of three main approaches: psychological effects, literacies of/and gaming, or a cultural studies examination of the social and institutional structures at play in various games and game worlds. This third approach—cultural studies of computer and video games—is the most prevalent form of games research in rhetoric/composition and related fields (although Selfe and Hawisher's [2007] collection of ethnographies of game players has spurred an interest in the examination of gaming and literacy). In the cultural studies approach, research has included considerations of gender ("girl" games vs. "boy" games; gender representations in games), race (representation and stereotyping in games), labor conditions and globalization (the work of "gold farmers" in massive multiplayer online games), and economics (particularly in terms of the videogame and computer game industry). Games provide a fruitful research location for cultural studies because they can also be used to show the effect of institutional structure (the designed worlds) on the available actions of the players, thus foregrounding power relationships as delineated in simulated social spaces.

Only recently has there been a turn to rhetorical analysis as an approach to writing about games (this is most evident with Ian Bogost's [2007] work, mentioned above); in 2008, Bill Blake argued for an ethical criticism of computer gaming, suggesting that "we need a more socially aware form of ethical reasoning capable of framing our critical response to media content" (p. B6). This collection continues the move toward rhetorical analysis of games as well as a rhetorical approach to teaching writing through gaming media.

Writing Around Games

Although much academic writing treats games as objects of critique or analysis, there is a great deal of nonacademic writing that has more direct connections to the games and gameplay. Much of this writing is produced by game players and represents a rich corpus of texts that are ripe for rhetorical analyses. We identify this kind of writing as writing *around* games because the games are not the objects of research but are instead subjects and frameworks that support the various related writing genres. Examples include game-based fan fiction (in which players appropriate the worlds, histories, myths, and characters of the game and apply them to their personal writing), personal diaries written by an individual's in-game persona, websites created by gaming guilds (serving as social network sites that both support and promote specific game-paying communities), and sites that provide information about how to play a specific game (such as wowwiki.com, which provides a comprehensive guide to *World of Warcraft* that is composed of player-contributed texts).

Writing Inside Games

Very little work has focused on video games as writing spaces, despite the fact that there is an abundance of in-game textual communication (particularly for multi-player games) as well as a number of "static" texts (books, messages, monuments, etc.) that play pivotal roles in a wide variety of game types. Text-based communication between and among players can include problem-solving activities (such as coordinating a team's actions when working toward a common goal), role-playing, and persuasive appeals (requests for help, signing guild charters, sales of goods and services). Game designers also use texts with particular rhetorical functions: in-game documents might include guild charters, books, storylines, and information delivered by non-player characters (NPCs). In addition to player-produced and designer-produced texts, game interfaces can also be viewed as multimodal texts that require specific literacies for effective utilization; these interfaces are often player-modifiable—in other words, they can be both read and written by both game players and game designers.

WRITING GAMES

Finally, writing studies scholars can examine and participate in the writing of the games themselves. Quite a bit of writing takes place at the design phase, including development of narrative arcs for the games' stories, character development (for both players and NPCs), documentation and technical specifications (particularly appropriate genres for technical and professional writing courses), and the interaction design of the game interfaces (and the development of interfaces as multimodal texts to which digital rhetoric analyses may be applied). Although there is some work in this area (notably Alice Robison's studies of video game designers), there is a great unfulfilled opportunity to bring rhetoric and writing scholars together with computer scientists and game designers in order to make explicit connections between computer game production and writing. Brian Ladd's chapter on writing (and) games in a computer programming course represents one such connection, but there is certainly room for significant growth in this area.

In each of these four contexts where gaming and writing activities intersect, we suggest that there are opportunities for teaching and research that will benefit writing studies scholars, game designers, game studies theorists, and students. If, as Selfe, Mareck, and Gardiner (2007) suggest, "success in a world of rapid technological change may well depend on the ability to develop new literacy practices that prove increasingly effective in transnational digital landscapes like gaming environments" (p.33), then it behooves us as writing teachers to consider how we can engage and leverage these new literacy practices in light of what we know about how to teach effective written (and, increasingly, multimedia) communication. We see the work of this collection as primarily focusing on pedagogy, but there is also a great deal of research about the intersections of gaming and rhetoric that we should begin to explore as well. As Dmitri Williams (2007) notes, while it is "still fair to ask about what games are doing *to* us . . . it is equally important to ask what they are doing *for* us" (p. 253).

Thus the goals of this collection are two-fold: to present an argument for the inclusion of game studies in teaching, research, and theory-building within the fields of writing and rhetoric and to provide a series of models that move the current approach to games in the writing classroom from a cultural-studies based view of games as objects of cultural critique to a view of games as rhetorically-rich compositional spaces.

PLAY/WRITE: THE COLLECTION

Part I: Game Rhetorics and Gaming Pedagogies (or, Writing *About* Games)

In the opening section, Game Rhetorics and Gaming Pedagogies, we present four works that write *about* games from a rhetorical perspective (that is, not primarily via narrative analysis or cultural criticism).

The first entry is an example of theorizing digital modes of invention through a consideration of DIY game production. In "Aleatory Invention and Glorious Trainwrecks' Accursed Share," Steven Holmes uses the "Glorious Trainwrecks" (GT) video game design community and the games produced by GT members to theorize the effect of restricted economies on multimodal invention, arguing that composition teachers should "think carefully about the questions of invention that surround the relationship between rhetoric and videogames as a compositional medium." This deep dive into theories of gift economies, surplus energy, and aleatory procedures of invention exemplifies an approach to games in writing studies that ventures beyond an expression of utility or pedagogical value and demonstrates the kind of sophisticated approach to games and writing this collection aims to showcase.

Jessica Eberhard's case study of the controversy surrounding the ending of *Mass Effect 3* (which disregarded all player choices leading to the conclusion of the game) examines the disconnect between games as stories (with attendant artistic integrity) and games as co-created, interactive events. Writing about games—and specifically game writing—and their effect on a range of interested communities blurs the line between writing about games and a focus on the paratexts of games and gaming, but we include it in this section because the focus is on a particular game-derived event (and what that can show us about tensions between traditional and new digital economies), rather than an analysis of extended game ecologies.

While Holmes's chapter theorizes game economies and Eberhard's contribution focuses on the interrelationships among games, writing, and game players, our third contribution focuses on writing about gameplay itself and makes an explicit connection between the practice of gaming and writing pedagogies. In "The Composing Practices and Rhetorical Acumen of MMORPG Players: What *City of Heroes* Means for Writing Instruction," Phill Alexander constructs a theoretical model by focusing on literacy practices of game players. Alexander uses interviews with gamers and his own extensive personal experience to sketch out a game-based literacy framework, followed by a series of concrete suggestions for teaching that arise from the results of his research.

Finally, in "Procedurality as Play: Movement in Games and Composition," Grace Hagood returns us to theories of invention in relation to procedural rhetorics. Her chapter considers two games, *Passage* and *Skyrim*, in terms of procedurality and then argues for a reconsideration of how procedurality functions in relation to play and purpose if the focus of gaming is shifted to an embodied rhetoric of movement. She concludes by demonstrating how this shift in focus can be used in composition pedagogy.

Part II: Game Ecologies and Networks (or, Writing *Around* Games)

The second part of the collection focuses on the larger networks and extensive ecologies inhabited by games. Rather than focusing on the game itself, the next three chapters examine a wide range of contexts and paratexts where games and gaming play a pivotal role.

The first chapter in this section, "Who's that Walking on my Bridge? The Transmedia Rhetorics of Trolling on Video Game Forums" by Richard Colby and Rebekah Schultz Colby, focuses on online forums for game players and the participatory literacies enacted in those spaces. Their chapter looks specifically at trolling as a rhetorical practice in gaming communities that extends the interaction of the game itself to its external, networked ecologies.

In the second chapter, Lee Sherlock examines the practice of "theorycrafting"–using data and analytics to make arguments about how to optimize the relationship between player and designed system in order to achieve the highest levels of proficiency in the game. While the results of theorycrafting take place in the game, the data-driven arguments about what constitutes best practices play out in external forums and websites. "Data vs. Play: The Digital Rhetorics of Theorycrafting" first defines and explicates theorycrafting before using a series of examples from *World of Warcraft* to demonstrate theorycrafting as a rhetorical practice in action.

While the preceding two chapters focused on the activities of players, the final chapter in this section focuses on the corporations that produce games and the intellectual property decisions that have been driven by industry-based lawsuits. Scott Nelson's "Intellectual Property Pong: Three Classic Matches that Affect Your Play Today" places the rhetorics of gaming into the larger network where game economies of production and legal considerations of copyright and patents play out in the courts. While not as directly connected to gaming practice, these legal considerations constitute writing around games that has a significant impact and, we would argue, is of critical consideration for the field of writing studies.

Part III: Games and/as Rhetorical Production (or, Writing *In* or *Through* Games)

Relatively little work, to date, has focused on the idea of games as compositional media—that is, media that can serve as a platform for writing, a mode of composing, and the product of composition processes. This third section of the collection presents examples of writing that happens inside game contexts or that uses games (or game content) to drive new forms of composition (indeed, this section could have been subtitled "Writing With Games" as well).

In the first chapter, Andréa Davis leads the reader into the complex multimodal environment of *World of Warcraft* as a site of production and composition in "'Leeroy Jenkins!' What Computer Gamers Can Teach Us about Visual Arguments." Davis considers the pedagogical implications of seeing game spaces as composing environments, and then provides a case study of a player-produced multimedia composition, unpacking the arguments and embedded rhetorical moves of the "Leeroy Jenkins" video. She concludes her chapter with a consideration of the implications for incorporating gaming-based student-composed multimedia arguments in writing instruction.

The second chapter in this section demonstrates similar methods of composing using in-game content as the primary content. In "Playing with Play: Machinima in the Composition Classroom," Wendi Sierra makes a distinction between games as content systems and games as authoring systems and shows how to make use of the latter approach in writing classes. She argues that composing through/with games allows students to directly experience and explore how rhetorical and new media theory can be embodied in the multimodal works they create.

In "Embodiment, Materiality, and Rehabilitative Composition: VoIP Gameplay as Writing," Emily Stuemke takes a different approach to multimodal composition by focusing on sound-as-writing that uses the game as the compositional medium. Rather than recording game elements and remixing compositions from them, Stuemke looks at how in-game activities construct a link between digital identity and material body and how gameplay and game chat co-write the gaming experience.

Finally, in "Gaming Between Civic Knowledge and Civic Know-How: Direct Engagement and the Simulated City," Sean Conrey provides a detailed account of a writing course assignment that asked students to play *SimCity*. Conrey saw the game as "a springboard for recognition, reflection and theorizing of actual civic and environmental systems, so that the knowledge and know-how the students acquired by playing the game could be brought into real, lived fruition in their daily lives." By composing urban spaces within the game, the students gain forms of knowledge that can be leveraged into a more critical consideration for the possibilities of civic engagement beyond the confines of the game, although making these connections must be facilitated by reflection and writing. In this case, the composing happens both within the game and outside of it (as prompted by the in-game activity).

Part IV—Composing Games in Industry and Classroom Contexts (or, Writing Games)

The last part of the collection focuses on creating and deploying games in the classroom and in more public contexts. The first three chapters specifically address game design and implementation in writing classes; the fourth looks at games-as-writing (in the Writing Across the Curriculum tradition) in a computer science class; and the final entries present the voices of game designers as they consider the role of writing in designing commercial games.

The first chapter in this section begins not with video games per se, but with the creating of an alternative reality game (or ARG) across several writing courses in multiple institutions. In "Narrative Realities and Alternate Zombies: A Student-Centered Alternate Reality Game," Jill Morris recounts the creation of an ARG that took place during one semester of coursework. Students in one class served as game designers and puppet-masters, while students in other courses took on the role of ARG players. In this case, not only did the students co-write the game, but the game became a way of writing the curriculum as well.

The second chapter also looks at designing games as a writing class activity, but in this case, the students both played and created digital games. The students were introduced to the notion of "procedural rhetoric" and asked to compose games intended to craft procedural arguments about local state politics. In "Procedural Rhetoric, *Proairesis*, Game Design, and the Revaluing of Invention," James J. Brown Jr. and Eric Alexander use their classroom experience to further arguments about the ways in which games can help rhetoricians to reconceptualize their approaches to invention as a mode that may need to resist closure or remain open ended (that is, *proairetic* invention). This chapter's explicit connection of game design and rhetorical theorization is echoed in the following chapter as well.

In "Games and the Search for 'Contextually Valid Settings' in the Writing Classroom," David Sheridan and Kym Buchanan provide a rich description of the theoretical models they developed as they sought to create a game whose central activity would be writing itself. In this game, *Ink*, players are asked to perform a variety of writing and editing tasks in order to acquire resources and allow their characters to progress; the game is designed to "provide contexts that allow for several fundamental rhetorical practices that are notoriously difficult to capture in the writing classroom." Sheridan and Buchanan thus show what writing and rhetoric scholars can bring as much to computer games as they can bring to our classes.

In "Programming, Pedagogy, Play," Bran Ladd provides a model for writing-across-the curriculum that features games, but "rather than discussing games that are assigned by teachers and *played* by learners, it focuses on games that are *built* by the learners." Ladd teaches computer science courses that make explicit connections between best practices in composition and best practices in programming—as he argues, it's "all writing." In this chapter, he provides a description of how he makes those connections in a course that features a game design project, hinting at some intriguing possibilities for linked composition and computer science courses.

In the final two chapters of this section, we asked working game designers to talk about their understanding of writing for games. Our first entry, "Writing for Games" by Brandes Stoddard, considers the role of writing in game development, broadly-writ. In the second entry, Joshua Peery presents an example of the specific gaming genre of MMORPG Quests. These direct narratives give some insight into the role that writing plays in commercial game design, but we would encourage more work on the roles and practices of writers in the game design world as a fruitful area of continued scholarly work at the intersections of game studies and digital rhetoric.

REFERENCES

Blake, B. (July 27, 2008). Go ahead, steal my car. *The Chronicle of Higher Education*, p. B6.

Bogost, I. (2007). *Persuasive games: The expressive power of videogames.* Boston, MA: MIT Press.

Castronova, E. (2001). Virtual worlds: A first-hand account of market and society on the cyberian frontier. CESifo Working Paper Series No. 618. Retrieved from http://ssrn.com/abstract=294828

Colby, R., Johnson, M. S. S., & Colby, R. S., (Eds.). (2013). Rhetoric/composition/play through video games: Reshaping theory and practice of writing. New York: Palgrave Macmillan.

DeVoss, D., Johansen, J., Selfe, C., & Williams, J. (2003). Under the radar of composition programs: Glimpsing the future through case studies of literacy in electronic contexts. In Lynn Z. Bloom, Donald A. Daiker, & Edward M. White, (Eds.), *Composition studies in the new millennium: Rereading the past, rewriting the future* (157–173). Carbondale, IL: Southern Illinois UP.

DeWinter, J., & Moeller, R. M., (Eds.). (2014). Computer games and technical communication: Critical methods and applications at the intersection. Burlington, VT: Ashgate.

DigiRhet.net. (2006). Teaching digital rhetoric: Community, critical engagement, and application. *Pedagogy, 6*(2), 231–259.

Faigley, L. (2001). They are already in it. In John F. Barber & Dene Grigar, (Eds.), *New worlds, new words: Exploring pathways for writing about and in electronic environments* (417–420). Cresskill, NJ: Hampton Press.

Faigley, L. (2003). The challenge of the multimedia essay. In Lynn Z. Bloom, Donald A. Daiker, & Edward M. White, (Eds.), *Composition studies in the new millennium: Rereading the past, rewriting the future* (174–187). Carbondale, IL: Southern Illinois UP.

Gee, J. P. (2003). *What videogames have to teach us about learning and literacy.* New York: Palgrave Macmillan.

Kress, G. (2003). *Literacy in the new media age.* London: Routledge.

McKee, H., & Porter, J. (2008). The ethics of digital writing research: A rhetorical approach. *College Composition and Communication, 59*(4), 711–749.

New London Group. (1996). A pedagogy of multiliteracies: Designing social futures. *Harvard Educational Review, 66*(1), 60–92.

Neuwirth, C. M. (2003). Multimedia literacy: Confessions of a nonmajor. In Lynn Z. Bloom, Donald A. Daiker, & Edward M. White, (Eds.), *Composition studies in the new millennium: Rereading the past, rewriting the future* (188–190). Carbondale, IL: Southern Illinois UP.

Selfe, C., & Hawisher, G. (2007). *Gaming lives in the 21st century: Literate connections*. New York: Palgrave.

Selfe, C., Mareck, A., & Gardiner, J. (2007). Computer *gaming* as literacy. In Cynthia *Selfe* & Gail Hawisher (Eds.), *Gaming lives in the 21st century: Literate connections* (21–36). New York: Palgrave.

Siwek, S. (2014). Video games in the 21st century: The 2014 report. Entertainment Software Association. Retrieved from http://www.theesa.com/article/u-s-video-game-industrys-economic-impact/

Southern, M. (2001). The cultural study of games: More than just games. International Game Developer's Association. http://www.igda.org/articles/msouthern_culture.php

Squire, K. (2002). Cultural framing of computer/video games. *Game Studies, 2*(1): http://www.gamestudies.org/0102/squire/

Williams, D. (2007). Afterword: The return of the player. In Cynthia *Selfe* & Gail Hawisher (Eds.), *Gaming lives in the 21st century: Literate connections* (253–260). New York: Palgrave.

Yee, N. (2014) *The Proteus Paradox: How Online Games and Virtual Worlds Change Us--And How They Don't*. Yale University Press.

Yee, N. (2009). Befriending ogres and wood-elves: Relationship formation and the social architecture of norrath. *Game Studies, 9*(1): http://gamestudies.org/0901/articles/yee

PART I: GAME RHETORICS AND GAMING

PEDAGOGIES (OR, WRITING *ABOUT* GAMES)

2 Aleatory Invention and Glorious Trainwrecks' Accursed Share

Steven Holmes

PRETEXT: GIFT GIVING

y motivation for writing this essay stems from a desire to think through videogames, digital rhetoric, and writing in relationship to the philosopher George Bataille's notion of "the accursed share." Bataille (2008) was interested in exploring gift economies and the practice of potlatch in order to recast human motivations for production and exchange.[1] To offer an impossibly brief introduction, the anthropologist Marcel Mauss's comparative cultural analyses of social practices in early human civilizations helped to establish the idea of a "gift economy." Beyond our commonsense associations of selfless generosity, early forms of gift giving placed an obligation upon the giftee to receive the gift while simultaneously showing the giftee's respect to the giver's status and ability to give a gift. Bataille comments, "Hence giving must become acquiring a power. . . . He [the gift giver] regards his virtue, that which he had the capacity for, as an asset, as a power that he now possesses. He enriches himself with a contempt for riches, and what he proves to be miserly of is in fact his generosity" (2008, p. 375). The obligation of the giftee to return the gift functioned to create and maintain existing social hierarchies.

Bataille found particular value in Mauss's description of "potlatch" in certain Northwest Native American gift-giving contests. In these contests, a host would lavish excessive gifts upon guests, often to the point of incredible material and economic waste. Guests (rival chieftains) were consequently obligated to reciprocate with gifts of a similar magnitude and exchange. Those of us raised in capitalist countries would likely view potlatch as an irrational practice because we customarily equate acquiring things and commodities with "wealth" and social power. Most neoliberal economic theories presuppose what Bataille called "restricted economies": production and exchange processes regulated by utility, bourgeois morality, need, and, especially, economic scarcity. A restricted economy pushes all forms of production and exchange to sustain the general needs of a society as part of a naturalized process of growth and expansion through the efficient management of finite natural resources.

By contrast, Bataille's theory of production and exchange began not with an assumption of *scarcity* but with potlatch's more primordial relationship to *excess* and material energy—a "general economy." He argues, "On the surface of the globe, *for living matter in general*, energy is always in excess; the question is always posed in terms of extravagance. The choice is limited to how the wealth is to be squandered" (1988, p. 23, emphasis original). Bataille offered the example of solar energy from the sun. The sun gives its energy without reckoning. As plants capture the sun's light and convert this light into energy to survive, plants are left with an excess of energy that they can channel into growth and reproduction or expend on comparatively useless activities such as improving the beauty of their leaves. According to Bataille (1988), human societies are no different from plants with regard to the need to expend excess biological energy:

> On the whole, a society always produces more than is necessary for its survival; it has a surplus at its disposal. It is precisely the use it makes of this surplus that determines it: the surplus is the cause of the agitation, of the structural changes, and of the entire history of society. But this surplus has more than one outlet, the most common of which is growth. And growth itself has many forms, each one of which eventually comes up against some limit. Thwarted demographic growth becomes military; it is forced to engage in conquest. Once the military limits is reached, the surplus has the sumptuary forms of religion as an outlet, along with games and spectacles that derive therefrom, or personal luxury. (p. 106)

As a result, societies are truly differentiated by the ways that a given society encourages its citizens to channel or expend their idle capacities—their *accursed share*.[2] After any expenditure, humans are left with ever-greater excesses that can be spent either "*gloriously*" or "*catastrophi-*

cally" (see Vitanza, 1997, p. 90–112). If humans attempt to emulate the sun's excessive giving without recognition or reciprocity, then we engage in war, economic or territorial expansion, or potlatch (rivalry, resentment) on the road to catastrophe such as war or killing. By contrast, glorious expenditure could take non-utilitarian forms of a general economy such as subversive forms of potlatch like the "transfer of American wealth to India without reciprocation" (Bataille, 2008, p. 100). As an ethical practice, Bataille encouraged us to expend surplus through "a margin of profitless operations," including surrealist spectacle, art (or, the making of life into art), and sexuality (p. 100).

Digital Rhetoric and the Accursed Share

While Bataille's thinking may seem far removed from the immediate interests of composition teachers and digital rhetoric scholars, the accursed share offers an increasingly important metaphor for the teaching of writing and videogame rhetorics. As composition studies has begun to explore videogames and procedural literacies and rhetorics (Gee 2007; Losh, 2009; Bogost, 2010), I suggest that we should be increasingly aware of the forms of composition that would align student or scholarly videogame projects exclusively within restricted economies. I have two distinct aspects in mind: restricted economies of circulation and invention. I want to re-envision these two aspects by articulating a method of "aleatory invention" that can offer an alternative general economy for videogame design in the composition classroom. As theorized by Richard Young (1980), most contemporary forms of rhetorical invention are heuristic. Heuristic approaches include previous paradigms such as neo-Aristotelian formalism (current-traditional rhetoric), Flowers and Hayes' cognitivism, and rule-based approaches to writing. These paradigms examine inventional elements such as experience, intuition, ideology, common knowledge, and disciplinary knowledge. While descriptive in many respects, Victor J. Vitanza (2000) counters that heuristic forms of invention still presuppose a negated creative subject who writes, thinks, produces, and exchanges within restricted economies. In contrast, Vitanza encourages us to experiment with aleatory procedures of invention to include factors such as the unconscious, random chance, libidinal economies, nonconscious affect, and Bataille's general economy of surplus energy.

In what follows, I extend discussions of aleatory invention through videogames by exploring Jeremy Penner's *Glorious Trainwrecks* (GT) videogame design community. Penner directly engages potlatch and spectacle. His metaphor for invention—the trainwreck—comes from the staged trainwrecks of empty trains (potlatch) for spectators' entertainment in the early twentieth century. GT is an online gallery for "do-it-yourself" (DIY) game creation and features an "anything goes" grab-bag game design aesthetic. Among DIY communities, GT's explicit non-commercial orientation is unique in that it does not seek to produce only good or commercially viable designs. GT accepts all games—good, bad, spectacular, or monstrous—and seeks only to inculcate an aleatory sensibility toward productive freedom and chance hazard. As a collaborative design community, GT thereby offers digital rhetoric and multimodal composition scholars a *para-method* (defined below) to theorize and practice the glorious expenditure of potlatch and the networked accursed share through DIY game design.

VIDEO GAMES AND RESTRICTED ECONOMIES OF CIRCULATION

A quick examination of the contemporary videogame landscape unsurprisingly reveals a pervasive emphasis on restricted economies: creation (gift exchange) for purposes of profit. Videogame sales now rival and often surpass opening-weekend film box office returns. In 2011, Activision's *Call of Duty: Black Ops* made $650 million in sales in the first five days (Cross, 2011, p. 1). In what can only be labeled as a lavish expenditure of excess, graphic design teams can spend months working on a single avatar's face for a large commercial series such as Bethesda's *Skyrim IV: The Elder Scrolls* (2012) or, more recently, Bungie and Activision's *Destiny* (2014). Despite the growing number of indie, activist, artistic, and independent designers, it is still not inaccurate to characterize the current commercial videogame design moment as being dominated by complex, labor-intensive, and expensive design software that create a *de facto* divide between commercial game designers and non-game designers.

Some might point to DIY or "prosumer-friendly" programs (Game Maker; GameSalad; Scalpel), the app market, and casual gaming as evidence of a general economy for productive energy. In another story from 2011, one easily recalls the sensation of Owen Voorhees, the eleven-year-old designer of the (then) bestselling iPhone app *Math Time*. Furthermore, the dominance and popularity of commercial games does not in any way mean that independent designers, artists, and activists are not active or that their designs have had no impact. Newsgames (Bogost, Ferari, & Schweizer, 2010), videogame zines (Anthropy, 2012), alternate reality gaming (McGonigal, 2011; Flanagan, 2009) and persuasive games have all emerged as viable expressive forms.

At the same time, restricted economies of circulation work to appropriate many of these forms of distributed creativity. Lowering the barriers to game design enables Apple and many other companies to harness the creative efforts of thousands of non-salary earning potential creators. Indie game designer Anna Anthropy (2012) argues that independent creators often end up with a difficult choice. While videogame and app developers may enable solitary designers and non-experts like Voorhees a chance to make a living outside of a company space, their creations generally gain popularity only if they are willing to work through corporate distributors. Anthropy laments, "[Major companies such as Apple, Android, Steam, and the Xbox Live Marketplace] are all digital distribution stores tied to specific technologies, and each is run by a corporation that exercises total control over what content is available on which device. It's a situation that leaves creators at the mercy of corporations . . ." (p. 108). Distributors can eliminate games without notice or consent for any content that is deemed too sexual or politically radical. In a related event, *Wired* magazine reported in August, 2013 that Android will allow Amazon to market actual non-game items within developers' videogames (Rigney, 2008, p. 1). Much of DIY game and app design platforms, in other words, are not encouraged to be gifts that are given without the expectation of return.

In the continental philosophers Gilles Deleuze and Felix Guattari's terms, if prosumer creativity and Internet platforms for user-generated content, the Internet, and distributed prosumer software "de-territorialized" a mode of production historically limited to corporatized mass media production facilities, then companies have become equally as adept at "re-territorializing" prosumer cultures and harnessing the potential creative energy (idle capacities) of consumers and designers. For example, *Skyrim IV*'s creation kit offers streamlined methods to create and share new content, utilizing user-initiative, collective intelligence, and crowdsourcing techniques to aid in development and production. While player mods and user-generated paratexts or "ecologies of practice" (Brooke, 2009) can certainly operate at a level of egalitarian gift-giving in the level of intention, these acts are frequently bound up in the perpetuation of the catastrophic expenditures of the restricted economy. Mods in *Skyrim* or *The World of Warcraft*, after all, inevitably sustain Bethesda and Blizzard's respective bottom lines, and neither company publically offers its source code for as genuinely creative repurposing as potlatch. As critics such as David Harvey and Frederic Jameson have repeatedly observed, this late stage of flexible neo-liberal capitalism is excellent at co-opting cultural practices of the production and distribution of content (e.g., gift giving).

Many would no doubt point to open source and freeware gaming movements built on Linux or other open-source platforms as a route to realizing general economies of production so that student videogame writers do not serve as pseudo-developers for Apple or Android. Again, I do not wish to overstate my claim, and I readily affirm that a great deal of productive non-restricted practices of circulation occur in open source and freeware movements. However, Wendy Chun (2012) causes us to question whether open source and freeware markets have truly escaped restricted economies. Speaking of software in general, Chun maintains,

> Software, free or not, is embedded and participates in structures of knowledge-power. For instance, using free software does not mean escaping from power, but rather engaging it differently, for free and open source software profoundly privatizes the public domain: GNU copyleft—which allows one to use, modify, and redistribute source code and derived programs, but only if the original distribution terms are maintained—seeks to fight copyright by spreading licenses everywhere. More subtly, the free software movement, by linking freedom and freely accessible source code, amplifies the power of source code both politically and technically. (2012, p. 21)

Following from Chun's observations, even if writing teachers were to embrace Collin Gifford Brooke's (2009) call to study and create videogames through "code" as part of new media (or videogame) rhetorics by turning to open source gaming development platforms and independent networks of circulation, open source in and itself is neither a necessary nor sufficient condition for avoiding restricted economies. Digital writing, code, and its circulation are always materializable activities bound up with labor (Trimbur, 2002; Sheridan, Ridolfo, & Michel, 2012) and "transsituational" rhetorical relations of space, power, place, and matter (Edbauer, 2005).

Specifically related to the local situatedness of many composition teachers, a potential turn to open source and DIY software also present formidable obstacles in the classroom. Shareware and freeware production suites can be comparatively less user friendly. Commercial browsers such as Layar, for example, a point-and-click DIY augmented reality app development tool that could be used to create a variety of alternate/augmented reality games, requires very little technical training. By comparison, Junaio—a less commercial creation and distribution platform—requires considerable knowledge of formal coding techniques. In a typical composition classroom that can only devote so much time to technical training for multimodal editing alongside traditional print-based rhetorical production, it is unsurprising that one hears more about multimedia productions through "prosumer-ready" software like Apple's iLife Suite than through teaching students coding skills. I have little doubt that many writing teachers (including myself) have and will turn away from the more complex DIY programs such as GameMaker or commercial grade 3-D modeling languages for player builds like Maya and toward distribution-ready, user-friendly, and streamlined programs such as Game Salad, Scalpel, and the potential restricted economies of circulation that these programs enact.

RESTRICTED ECONOMIES OF MULTIMODAL INVENTION

My observations about certain trends within the current state of videogame design are not intended in any way to suggest that videogames and distributed development systems produced by large corporations or corporatized distribution systems are either *a priori* good or bad. Rather, my larger goal has been to establish some of the dominant social and economic forces that seek to confine and harness creators' excess—their accursed share—and to channel these energies within restricted economies of distribution at various levels under the discourses of DIY, open source, and app design. At the same time, even if student videogame compositions do ultimately avoid restricted economies of circulation, there is the related problem of restricted economies of rhetorical invention to contend with. In the passage quoted above, Chun's criticism is specifically targeted not only toward restricted economies of production and exchange, but also the unexamined presumption of a human agent specifically instrumentalizing code for a specific rhetorical outcome. In her reading, the open source code movement's mistake was to conflate the rejection of a restricted economy of exchange and production with the (implicit) realization of a general, profitless economy. Open source has yet to actually challenge a crypto-humanist instrumental view of rhetoric, intentionality, and agency. This crypto-humanist view enables restricted economies to come into play regardless of "control" over processes of production, circulation, and exchange. Chun's comments additionally illustrate why avoiding restricted economies of distribution are not sufficient. There is always the need to theorize rhetorical *invention* and its corresponding conditions of agency—the politics of invention with code or game design—as part of the formation of restricted economies of videogame design.

Outside of composition scholarship, an instrumental view of rhetoric and agency is pervasive within the utopian rhetoric surrounding the persuasive power of videogames. Bogost (2010) suggests that a videogame "makes a claim about how something works by modeling its processes" (p. 29). While Bogost acknowledges a gap between the algorithm and the production of the user's subjectivity, he also proposes a fairly narrow Aristotelian view of rhetorical *techne* as a means-ends function of the programmer's conscious and discrete aims. Along similar lines, Jane McGonigal (2011) has strongly suggested that games can "save the world" by promoting progressive or educational interventions into political issues. Such claims are undeniably the result of the strategic need to strengthen videogames' value as a cultural, aesthetic, persuasive, educational, and artistic medium in the public eye beyond their still-pervasive connotations of mindless entertainment or inculcators of violence. I firmly support this project and have asked my students to compose persuasive games in the past. However, one does not have to look far to see the instrumental form of agency and intervention within these definitions. McGonigal and Bogost idealize a designer who is interested in a videogame-specific continuation of liberal democratic debate wherein deliberative citizens manifest specific rhetorical ends to achieve non-coercive forms of persuasion.

As Vitanza (2000) argues, the main problem is that rhetoric cannot be reduced to instrumental aims and the purposeful use of coding and procedures without reinscribing an intentional humanist rhetor at some level, thereby reproducing restricted economies of invention. Any time we ask students to write in a given medium, we are not merely teaching them neutral *techne* divorced from any social or economic contexts. Simply put, a designer does not merely learn formal production techniques in videogames, such as how to locate and size a "health bar" relative to the screen action or to time the re-spawning of zombie mobs. It is also not sufficient for beginning designers to incorporate well-worn commercial design *topoi* alone, such as "if you make your character in a first-person shooter game die with one bullet, then no one will play your game." Rather, game design engages a host of assumptions about the ontology, agency, and ethics of writing and rhetoric, including a consideration of the restricted economies of gaming.

From this perspective, instrumental views of rhetoric are not strictly related to the profit/gift-exchange problem that Bataille has identified. Rather, they are related to problems of heuristics and negation that aleatory forms of invention and the general economy work against. In Young's (1980) famous division between "knack" and "craft," rhetorical *techne* in the twentieth-century should be aligned with instrumental rhetorical agent. He suggests that *techne* as "craft" is "knowledge necessary for producing preconceived results by conscious directed action" (p.168). "Knack," by contrast, represents the realm of intuition, non-conscious, or unknowable processes. Many theories of rhetoric tend to default to craft and consciousness. Hal Rivers Weidner (1975) claims, "If one wants a theory of rhetoric to be useful to a practitioner, then it must be formulated at the level of *awareness* at which he perceives the fundamental relationships of rhetoric, i.e., at the level of social interaction and opinion" (p. 72). This claim to "awareness" and intentionality is at heart of the videogame-persuasion nexus. A programmer manifests his specific awareness of a known and relatable social end into the videogame medium for persuasive effect. Anything that results from nonconscious motivations or that is not bound up with instrumental persuasion is *a priori* non-rhetorical.

Vitanza (2000) claims that an instrumental view of rhetoric is often related to algorithmic and heuristic forms of invention. Early twentieth-century rhetoric took on a formalist (algorithmic) bent: identify the rules of writing/rhetoric, memorize them, and apply them. Heuristic forms of invention offered a more expansive view of invention/writing than algorithmic *techne* by considering rhetoric and writing as productive of and responsive to social constructivist dialectics. For example, James Berlin's social-epistemic heuristics incorporated aspects such as experience, ideology, epistemology, structuralism, and cognitive psychology.

Heuristics—aids to invention—are *topoi* generated from previous experiences and socially-formed knowledge. Vitanza nevertheless maintains that heuristics still presuppose an intentional agent who works through an expanded yet knowable and teachable set of rhetorical aims. Vitanza groups algorithmic and heuristic thinking as proceeding through the identical process of negation: claiming knowledge by "negating"—not including and excluding—other sources of affect and 'suasion. Vitanza (2000) writes, "From Plato to the present, one of the invidious tests for whether a notion or a practice has any value is to determine whether it can be generalized (is generic) and whether it is transferable (codifiable, teachable)" (p. 193). For many in rhetoric and composition studies in recent decades, *topoi* and probable arguments won the day over forms of invention that did not operate according to rules, discrete audiences, and specific instrumental aims. As many advocates of the "post-process" movement in rhetoric and composition studies have argued, the issue is not that one can do away with the rules; rather, a strict focus on systematizeable knowledge may exclude sources of affectivity present at the scene of writing that could not be directly accounted for by either algorithmic or heuristic forms.

The general economy of writing then tries to reinclude these excluded sources of affect. For example, Byron Hawk (2007), via Martin Heidegger, reads Aristotle not as separating *techne* into art (craft/rationality) and intuition (or, knack)—knowledge and non-knowledge). He reads Aristotle as supporting a vitalist combination of the two: "*techne* is both a rational, conscious capacity to produce and an intuitive, unconscious ability to make" (2007, p. 168). Post-*techne* identifies a view of persuasion and composition that will register both what is accountable and what is unaccountable—algorithmic and heuristic modes of invention alongside aleatory invention. If *techne* aligns with the rational and the knowable, then aleatory procedures do not start with the knowable, but by proceeding in a way analogous to the French symbolist poet Stéphane Mallarmé's "a throw of the dice": "aleatory procedures are chance procedures" (Vitanza, 2000, p. 187).

In Young's terms, the aleatory opens a space where the divide between knack (irrationality) and craft (knowable/teachable) cannot be sustained. This division is important to consider because a worldview of knack versus craft separates rational (those capable of rhetoric) from irrational (those incapable) and producers of "real" videogames (artists) from non-artists by virtue of having a prior definition of what constitutes a "proper" (persuasive) videogame. According to Vitanza, aleatory procedures refuse binaries between artistic/non-artistic, real/actual, or fantasy/reality and work instead toward something "hyperreal, giving us new conditions" for invention (2000, p.187). Similar to Hawk, Vitanza's point is that there are always nonconscious or nonlogical forces, elements, components, and networks that are responsible for co-producing what we conceive of after the fact as an intentional and conscious act of persuasion. These aspects include processes of the general economy, libidinal drives and investments, affect, emotion, and, more importantly, the accursed share. The accursed share is the surplus that every creator must expend in either glorious or catastrophic expenditure.

From this vantage point, our stance on rhetorical invention (algorithmic, heuristic, or aleatory) presupposes an understanding of production and exchange and the operation of restricted or general economies. Elsewhere, Vitanza (1997) identifies Bataille's economy of excess as a challenge to the restricted economy of capitalism/negation. If knowledge proceeds from negation, then it is, as Vitanza quotes Bataille, "Non-knowledge [that] communicates ecstasy—but only if the possibility (the movement) of ecstasy already belonged, to some degree, to one who disrobes himself of knowledge" (1997, p. 81). If we begin with the accursed share, rhetoric does not begin with the known and the rational or serious, but with acts of "desire, poetry, laughter" that "unceasingly cause life to slip in the opposite direction, moving from the known to the unknown" (p. 10).

Gifts that Keep on Giving: Videogames as Receivable Texts

The aleatory is not a "solution" to the problems of excess and surplus in the sense of eliminating the cycle of potlatch once and for all. Bataille is very clear that humans will always possess an accursed share to expend. Along different lines, Vitanza is also clear in that the aleatory is not an endorsement of an "anything goes" nihilism. The aleatory does not function as a justification to engage in more negation or violence. As I prefer to think through this issue, the aleatory functions instead as a reinclusion of what is expunged by the structures that produce negativity and restricted economies, but does not necessarily entail a positive valuation of *everything* (violence). In fact, the very move to declare negation and restricted economies a problem is an ethical valuation of general economies. Yet, if it is clear why one might want to avoid restricted economies of circulation and invention, then it is still not clear how we might instruct our students (and ourselves) to compose the unknown (videogame) through aleatory methods? While there are a variety of ways that scholars like Vitanza, Hawk, and Gregory Ulmer have sought to answer this question, I believe that Penner's GT design community offers one such approach in the specific context of videogames and rhetorical invention.

GT's primary point of existence is to encourage the process of rhetorical invention among interested designers, but in a very particular sense. On GT's website, Penner (2008) declares a desire to "[bring] back the spirit of postcardware, circa 1993. It's about throwing a bunch of random crap into your game and keeping whatever sticks . . . [it is] the true spirit of Indie gaming" (p. 109). For such a concise and informal description of the GT's collective invention strategy, there is a rich amount of suggestive detail packed into these lines. *Postcardware* is an idiosyncratic form of 1990s shareware, where authors would distribute games/programs only on the condition that users would send the author a postcard. Simply put, "pure invention" coincides with a circulatory motivation—mimicking capitalist cycles of commodity exchange but with products that have only sentimental but not exchange value. This reference to sentimentality may sound like an obvious point, but it is one worth stressing. In GT, anyone and everyone, *especially* those who wish to expend their accursed share outside of a restricted gift economy, are welcome to participate.

We can find an analogy for postcardware in Roland Barthes's (1975) *Pleasure of the Text.* He discusses three categories of texts: writerly (realist), readerly (modern), and receivable. He references a hypothetical "society of friends of the text" in which individuals would participate in *ad hoc* reading groups without any pre-determined texts, methods, or agendas. Akin to a surrealist happening, the friends of the text would read and discuss any passages of interest and allow meaning to emerge from chance associations—"I read on, I skip, I look up, I dip in again"—and the immediate experience of communal participation is, in itself, under the absence of conditions for production (1975, p. 12). Receivable texts designate texts that Barthes receives unconditionally—without assessing a participant or writer's worthiness to write or produce texts (gifts)—and that he does not know how to categorize. Receivable texts function through an aleatory process that Craig Saper (2001) calls "networked composition." In a networked composition of receivable texts, the goal of maintaining a network and system of exchange serves as the *primary* motivation and outcome of an individual act of composition. In terms more familiar to composition theorists, GT's networked compositions radically elevate the process of invention over the finished product but with the condition that the process cannot be understood in terms of algorithmic, cognitive, or heuristic forms alone. The motivation for post-cardware or trainwrecks is not "gift," but anti-gift: a "receivable text" that affirms one's participation within a network of a certain type of reciprocity governed by a general economy.

GT's aleatory methods offer an unconditional circulatory outlet for the production of receivable videogame artifacts (texts). In the "Klik of the Month Klub," for instance, there are no rules about tools or specified types of games that participants should make (e.g., first-person shooters or space invaders). The value of production for exchange is not reducible to any specific rhetorical intention or effect and can only refer to maintaining certain aleatory (non-restricted) forms of distribution and invention. GT imposes only a single constraint: a participant should make the game in two hours. Having participated in some of these marathons, Anthropy (2012) writes, "The experience forces participants to get past their egos and their meticulous plans for future epic games, to stop focusing on details and CREATE" (p. 110, emphasis original). For Klik of the Month Klub #74 in 2013, a user named Leon Arnott created a game called *Show Yourself*. The player is confronted with 10 small avatars on a checkerboard floor with multiple rotating spotlights. The only instructions read: "These minor characters are trying to be you, the protagonist! Move yourself with the arrow keys or WASD keys, and they'll all imitate you! They're good—but not perfect! Click on you!" (Penner, 2008, p. 1). Each time the player hits the "up" or "down" keys, all of the avatars move in parallel fashion. The player has to move a mouse-controlled spotlight to locate a tiny difference in appearance/movement on one avatar and the game is over.

After playing *Show Yourself* or any other Klik of the Month Klub gift, the incorrect question to ask is whether or not the game was a success or a failure in terms of whether it persuaded an audience or resembled something commercially viable. Success and failure are conditions that all too often reflect values of utility, heuristics, and monetization in the commercial design community. There are no incentives for production and exchange in GT other than the glorious expenditure of surplus to produce trainwrecks. In terms of being hospitable to receivable texts, GT monumentalizes both successes and failures (variously understood). In GT's "Breathtaking Triumphs," award section, Penner writes, "And then there are those games whose releases were singular, seismic events.

Ordinary men would never expect such results from a bunch of random people on the Internet noodling around with Klik & Play, and yet, it is undeniable that these games provided a glimpse of genius" (p. 1). GT's "Trainwrecks Gallery" makes no essential distinction or value differential between success and failure. It is clear that breathtaking triumphs and glorious trainswrecks are both accidents (but not catastrophes). Given that triumphs and trainwrecks are subject to the same aleatory constraints, the production of a breathtaking triumph will not inscribe any distinction between designers/non-designers and affirm only the non-restricted expenditure of creative potentiality (*dynamis*). It is undeniably true that a breathtaking triumph might go on to have economic value and enter into circulation on in the Android or Apple casual gaming market. However, any product for the immediate act of expending the accursed share in GT will only ever have the same non-restricted value at the moment of its originary production and exchange.

In her brief discussion of GT, Anthropy offers a descriptive analogy for GT in a footnote to "crap art" at crapart.spacebar.org, a (then) self-described "new art movement." In the tradition of Fluxus and many other artists, crap art seeks to eliminate any pairing of art with "elitism," which reinforces strict divisions between artists (game designers) and non-artists (players/consumers; knack/craft). Instead, the authors of crapart.org (2001) declare, "We hope that everyone can make art" (p. 5). This manifesto is quite radical in this context despite its simplicity. For crap artists, "The creation of art is more important than its consumption," maintaining that "aesthetics (except in the biased eye/ear of the creator) are overrated as a judgment of the worth of art" (p. 2). Given this perspective, it is entirely possible to read their claims as a romantic valorization of subjectivity. However, I believe that their larger point, like GT's overall orientation, is simply to encourage experimentation with trainwrecks. These processes and compositional forms push against the false dichotomy between romanticism and "serious" art forms in a way that parallels Young's craft/knack distinction. The only criteria for participation in crap art is that the "attempt is honest" (p. 5). Crap art offers excellent advice for the inculcation of the aleatory: "Try to forget your conceptions of what a 'painting' or 'drawing' looks like, or what a 'song' sounds like, and make lots and lots. Don't spend too long on any one item. Afterwards, look or listen and discover what you've done. Perhaps you'll find something that appeals to you? If you do, you've won! If you don't, open your mind and try again!" (p. 6). "For this site is about nothing," Penner similarly declares on GT's home page—that is, nothing but receivable texts and the inculcation of a certain method of being-in-the-world.

From these requirements of Young's knowable/instrumental *techne*, GT's methods of invention—aleatory—can only be deemed an abject rhetorical failure. A two-hour limit does not allow for a fully conscious design process to manifest a specific rhetorical object for a discrete audience. Most theories of communication, writing, and rhetoric operate according to some manner of intentionality. "I don't have to tell you," Diane Davis (2010) reminds us, "that the specter of the intentional agent is alive and well in rhetorical studies" (p. 108). Furthermore, even shifts in theories of invention from so-called product to process theory nevertheless expect, in the end, students to demonstrate some sort of mastery over argumentation, reasoning, and the commonplaces. GT implicitly challenges these sorts of assumptions by making creativity a faculty (*dynamis*) that everyone always already possesses. Game creation for a networked general economy of composition becomes a primary means of invention in and of itself. Responsibility—individualized and conscious—is impossible. What Davis calls "response*ability*"—the "voluntary" removal of intentional agency for the purposes of opening a designers' invention process to the more authentic or primordial play of intuition, hazard, and affect—is all that is possible as a form of exchange and ciruclation in GT. The goal is to expend a designer's productive surplus for potlatch—trainwrecks. If Erasmus recommended an aleatory assignment of *copia*—writing the same sentence numerous different ways to plume the depths of style, then GT is interested in *copia* that only participates in general economies. The goal is not perfection of a single sentence or videogame genre for improved instrumental persuasion, but strictly for engagement with the accident that may accidentally result in a breathtaking triumph as determined by the community's general economy alone.

Some might object that time constraints may sound like an algorithmic form of composition. However, Vitanza (2010) indicates that algorithmic *generators*—not algorithmic *techne*—can be productive of aleatory outcomes. He writes, "computers paradoxically are entirely suitable for the introduction of randomness" (p. 189). Contrary to popular mythology of computers where a user encounters a precise and inflexible Turing machine, machines can actually introduce randomness and aleatory procedures into composing. Computers' random generation capacities simulate the absence of authorial intent. Analogously, we see the time constraints of *GT* as a similar attempt to simulate the absence of the author by introducing randomness while prohibiting the imposition of a fully intentional (restricted economy) creator. Such aleatory constraints, Vitanza maintains, "work to dispel mystery as a mere vitalism and romantic fantasy" (p. 190).

Vitanza offers a detailed discussion of aleatory computer invention by foregrounding Gregory Ulmer's (1994) "heuretic" forms of invention. Heuretics, similar to Penner's goal for GT, is interested in "a rhetoric/ poetics leading to the production of a new work" (p. 94). Heuretics is not an inductive, deductive, or abductive, but a *conductive* (hyper-linked, free associational) logic specific to electronic literacies (electracy). Like the logic of hypertext linking (but on a much grander scale), conduction does not work within clearly defined wholes and parts of *techne* and *topoi*, but instead engages fragments and affectivity of *post-techne* and the aleatory. Ulmer writes, "[Heuretics] is a new rhetoric . . . that does not argue but that replaces the logic governing argumentative writing with associational networks" (p. 18). Intuition—rhetoric—is co-produced by the medium and constraints and excessed of cognition specific to a given medium.

Unlike methods of invention grounded in heuristics or algorithms, Ulmer wants to take stock of something that exists (a theory or an object) and build something new through it to the extent that the final product cannot follow algorithmic or heuristic means. For instance, Ulmer offers the heuretic generator of CATTt: A writer chooses idiosyncratic and personal elements to plug into ratios of Contrast, Analogy, Theory, Target, and tale.[3] Ulmer's method includes instrumental aims, as CATTt ultimately points toward a specific Target, but the overall invention itself emerges from affective complexes and aleatory procedures outside of the rhetor's conscious control. These elements help to guide conductive relays and do not actually provide *topoi* or heuristics to guide invention. Invention becomes an aleatory process of "Inventing [the method] while [we are] inventing it" (p. 17). As many in rhetoric who have dealt with Ulmer's thinking have noted, it is *chora*—Plato's affective/material "before space" of conscious action and meaning formation in the *Timaeus*—and not *topoi* that heuretics engages (Arroyo, 2013; Rickert 2013). Analogous to how videogames themselves simulate or model real life processes, heuretics *models* or *simulates* the aleatory—the actual conductive processes of writing and thinking out of the general economy.

On GT's homepage, Penner links to a Wikipedia page that describes an era when trainwrecks of empty trains were staged (sacrificed) by entertainment companies for the amusement of interested spectators. In GT, he has reconfigured the trainwrecks' restricted economies into a conductive relay—a heuretic generator—to appropriate an interactive spectacle as the mundane acts of electronic reasoning through general economies in videogame production and circulation. Heuretics and the aleatory enable writing teachers to avoid copying GT's aims and structures. After all, I could easily require my students to participate in a Klik of the Month Klub gathering. Ulmer's greater lesson would be to convert GT into a conductive relay useful to my class's own purposes—our own "tale"—as teachers and students interested in videogames and general economies.

To offer one example of CATTt in action, we could use GT as a conductive relay while substituting a new point of Contrast (general/restricted economies) and new Targets. What if we took "first-person shooters and violence" as a Target and imposed not a two-hour production limit but a goal to re-think the first-person shooter into something ethically affirmative of life? What if we incorporated Bogost's phenomenological speculations about the inner lives of things and nonhuman objects in *Alien Phenomenology* (2013) as a Theory and designed games from the gun's point of view? The point of addressing aleatory invention in relationship to videogames is to examine the ways in which writing, technology, and surpluses can exceed any narrow instrumental view of rhetoric or reduction of rhetoric to formalist *techne*. The aleatory heuretic does not seek to affirm (or deny) instrumental mastery but to pursue the more important task of activating creative/rhetorical *dynamis* in the service of glorious expenditure. For those who wonder if any form of (ethical) value can emerge from relinquishing rhetorical and writerly autonomy in experiments like GT, the aleatory demonstrates the political value of what Jesper Juul calls "paragames"—games like glorious trainwrecks or "Crap Art" that make no sense or are unreasonably bad (e.g., fail to fit into our conventional or traditional understanding of games) (Sample, 2014). Paragames teach us more about our standard *topoi* regarding and regulating tasting and playing habit and thereby offer ways of diagnosing the limitations of these tastes in a way similar to how Bataille's privilege of excess demonstrates the societal limitations of thinking of creativity in terms of economic utility and rationality alone.

Conclusion: Receivable Video Games

GT usefully serves as a call for composition teachers to consider the complex role of invention that informs the nascent relationship between rhetoric and videogames as a compositional medium. Such considerations are increasingly important as a growing number in our field like Richard Colby (2014) begin to ask digital writing students to compose videogames. As with any medium, we need to teach them about the role of the aleatory. Years ago, Ann E. Berthoff wisely wrote in "Learning the Uses of Chaos," "[C]haos is scary: the meanings which can emerge from it, which can be discerned taking shape within it, can be discovered only if students who are learning to write can learn to tolerate ambiguity" (p. 77). In particular, this toleration can take the form of renewed support for new, monstrous, or emerging DIY videogame genres as a whole. Anthropy (2012) cites an observation from Bogost regarding how the DIY videogames are analogous to the emergence of photographic snapshots like Polaroids. Instantly developed snapshots allowed nonprofessionals to design and create in ways that had previously been limited only to professional photographers with expensive equipment. Bogost offers the example of a videogame, *You're Invited to Go to Heaven.* The videogame poses one question to players, "Who is the Lord of your life?" with four possible answers: Chris Brown, Orlando Bloom, Jesus Christ, and Zac Effron." Hard core and commercial gamers would surely cringe at the idea of millions of these games being enacted in spaces such as GT.

According to Anthropy, Bogost argues that the emergence of DIY paragames and the expanded means of production do not *a priori* make for better or worse videogames. Rather, games, like snapshots, "are created for different purposes" (p. 114). He claims, "The future of video game snapshots will require platform creators to show their potential users how to incorporate games into their individual lives" (p. 114). By blurring the boundaries between professional and amateurs or ideal marketability standards and glorious trainwreck amateurism, digital rhetoric and writing teachers can analogously help students actively develop and participate in general economic spaces of production and exchange. The point of considering aleatory rhetorics in relationship to videogames is to affirm a general economy of exchange and not to relocate hermeneutic and rhetorical power within algorithmic or heuristic forms of invention or circulation. A deceptively simple task for the aleatory in the multimodal composition classroom is to promote the production and exchange of receivable videogame compositions in order to encourage the glorious expenditure of our accursed share.

Notes

1. See Nick Land (2011) for a detailed explanation of Bataille's relationship to gift economies and potlatch.

2. It cannot be overstated enough that Bataille's model dramatically challenges most conventional understandings of societal motivation, from historical assumptions that war is a competition among nation states over scarce resources to Hobbesian political philosophy. Excess, as Jurgen Habermas commented of Bataille, "is literally the transgression of those boundaries drawn by [capitalist] individuation" (230).

3. C = Contrast (opposition, inversion, differentiation); A = Analogy (figuration, displacement); T = Theory (repetition, literalization); T = Target (application, purpose); and t = tale (secondary elaboration, representatibility)

References

Anthropy, A. (2012). *Rise of the videogame zinesters*. New York: Seven Series Press.

The Arcade Wire (2009). *Oil gods*. Persuasive Games.Org [videogame].

Arroyo, S. J. (2013). *Participatory composition: Video culture, writing, and electracy*. Carbondale, Ill.: Southern Illinois UP.

Barthes, R. (1975). *The pleasure of the text* (Trans. R. Howard, Trans). New York: Hill and Wang.

Bataille, G. (1988). *The accursed share: An essay on general economy* (Vol. 1, R. Hurley., Trans). New York: Zone.

Bethesda Software. (2012). *Skyrim IV: The elder scrolls* [video game].

Bogost, I. (2012). *Alien phenomenology, or what it's like to be a thing*. Minneapolis, Minn.: U of Minnesota P.

Bogost, I. (2010). *Persuasive games: The expressive power of videogames*. Cambridge: The MIT Press.

Bogost, I., Ferrari, S., & Schweizer, B. (2010). *Newsgames: Journalism at play*. Cambridge, Mass: The MIT Press.

Brooke, C. (2009). *Lingua fracta: Toward a rhetoric of new media*. Cresskill, NJ: Hampton Press.

Chun, W. (2012). *Programmed visions*. Cambridge, Mass: The MIT Press.

Colby, R. (2014. Writing and assessing procedural phetoric in student-produced video games. *Computers and Composition, 31*, 43–52.

Crapart.org. (2001, July 6). Crap art. Retrieved from http://crapart.spacebar.org/

Cross, T. (2011, Dec. 12). All the world's a game. *The Economist*. Retrieved from http://www.economist.com/node/21541164

Davis, D. (2010). *Inessential solidarity: Rhetoric and foreigner relations*. Pittsburgh: U of Pittsburgh P.

Edbauer, J. H. (2005). Unframing models of public distribution: From rhetorical situation to rhetorical ecologies. *Rhetoric Society Quarterly 35*(4), 5–24.

Flanagan, M. (2009). *Critical play radical game design*. Cambridge, MA: MIT Press.

Gee, J.P. (2007). *What video games have to teach us about learning and literacy* (2nd ed.). New York: Palgrave MacMillan.

Hawk, B. (2007). A counter-history of composition: Toward methodologies of complexity. Pittsburgh, PA: U of Pittsburgh P.

Katz, S.B. (1992, March). The ethic of expediency: Classical rhetoric, technology, and the holocaust. *College English, 54*(3), 255–275.

Land, N. (1991). *The thirst for annihilation: Georges bataille and virulent nihilism*. New York: Routledge.

Losh, E. (2009). *Virtualpolitik an electronic history of government media-making in a*
time of war, scandal, disaster, miscommunication, and mistakes. Cambridge, MA: MIT Press.

McGonigal, J. (2011). *Reality is broken: Why games make us better and how they can change the world*. New York: Penguin.

Mead, C. (2013). *War play: Video games and the future of armed conflict*. New York: Eamon Dolan/Houghton Mifflin Harcourt.

Penner, J. (2008). *Glorious Trainwrecks*. Retrieved from http://www.glorious-trainwrecks.com/

Rigney, R. (2013, August 8). Amazon infiltrates android games to sell to you while you play. *Wired*. Retrieved from http://www.wired.com/2013/08/amazon-mobile-associates/

Rickert, T. (2013). *Ambient rhetoric: The attunements of rhetorical being*. Pittsburgh, PA: U of Pittsburgh P.

Sample, M. (2013). Criminal code: Procedural logic and rhetorical excess in videogames. *Digital Humanities Quarterly, 7*(1). Retrieved from http://www.digitalhumanities.org/dhq/vol/7/1/000153/000153.html

Saper, C. J. (2001). *Networked art*. Minneapolis: U of Minnesota P.

Sheridan, D.M., Ridolfo, J., & Michel, A. (2012). *The available means of persuasion: Mapping a theory and pedagogy of multimodal public discourse*. Anderson, SC: Parlor Press

Sicart, M. (2011). Against procedurality. *Games Studies: The International Journal of Computer Game Research, 11*(3). Retrieved from http://gamestudies.org/1103/articles/sicart_ap

Weidner, H. R. (1975). *Three models of rhetoric: Traditional, mechanical and vital*. (Unpublished doctoral dissertation). Ann Arbor, MI: U of Michigan P.

Trimbur, J. (2002). Delivering the message: Typography and the materiality of writing. In Gary Olson (Ed.), *Rhetoric and composition as intellectual work* (pp. 188–202). Carbondale: Southern Illinois UP.

Ulmer, G. (1994). Heuretics: The logic of invention. Baltimore: Johns Hopkins UP.

Vitanza, V. J. (2000). From heuristic to aleatory procedures; or, towards "writing the accident." In Maureen Daly Goggin (Ed.), *Essays for richard young* (pp. 185–206.) Urbana, IL: NCTE.

—. (1997). *Negation, subjectivity, and the history of rhetoric*. Albany: State U of New York P.

Young, R. E. (1980). Arts, crafts, gifts, and knacks: Some disharmonies in the new rhetoric. *Visible Language, 14*(4), 341–50.

3 "What Do You Mean None of My Choices Mattered?": Collaborative Composition and the Ethics of Ownership in Games—A Case Study of *Mass Effect 3*

Jessica Masri Eberhard

THE WORST COMPANY IN AMERICA

When *The Consumerist* (2012) published the results of their annual poll designating the "Worst Company in America" in April 2012, the results were met with disbelief. In the midst of an economic crisis made up of bank bailouts and scandals, a collapsed housing industry, and vehement protests of Wall Street, the number-one most hated entity in corporate America, according to the poll of 250,000 people, was Electronic Arts, or EA Games, a large video game corporation infamous in the game world for its ruthless buy outs, corporate greed, and eye-gouging profit margins. Bank of America was the runner up for second. Many people were outraged: "People are losing their homes to mortgage companies. People are losing their lives trying to get healthcare. And you choose a company that made poor Johnny frustrated because they deleted his World of Warcraft account? Really?" (JGKojak). "Does this mean Consumerist voters are idiots? BofA actually ruins people's lives, EA only ruins people's video gaming" (dush). Some even called foul, claiming there had been a mistake, but *The Consumerist* assured people the results were legitimate: EA Games had been voted the most hated company in America. What the average middle-aged individuals struggling with unemployment and credit card debt did not know was that this was a long time coming. The nomination was not only an unexpected testament to the growing strength and influence of the gaming community that for so long had been considered a marginalized, narrowly defined sub-culture; it was also the result of a highly kairotic string of events. Although the vote may seem petty when seen from a national perspective, it also stands as a sign of the times, revealing major changes in fundamental American values surrounding cultural production, specifically as it relates to authorship, ownership, and composition practices.

The growing popularity of the video game industry, added to the growing threat of pirating and the growing availability of high-quality free/online games, has spurred companies like EA to spend the last several years coming up with strategies for increasing profit margins and controlling intellectual property rights. Asking players to pay for post-purchase downloadable game content (DLC) bit by bit, stretching out the transaction for years, is one major practice for which EA is famous. In the end, a single game could ultimately cost anywhere from $300-$870, all said and done (Carter, 2012). Few people would in fact buy all the expansions and add-ons available; however, after a $60 initial purchase, consumers still feel nickel and dimed to death. Additionally, due to the high cost of game production and the difficulty of start-up, EA has a history of buying out smaller but high-quality game companies, to the chagrin of indie-game supporters. But all these details were not, ultimately, the reason why thousands voted EA the worst company in America. There was a reason why the gaming community showed up in unexpected numbers to the *Consumerist* poll and why they had chosen this month to express their disdain for EA—it was because of the release, and subsequent controversy, surrounding *Mass Effect 3*, the final installment of a game trilogy which had gained international attention for its groundbreaking narrative play style. The game failed grossly to live up to its own claims of collaborative creation and violated the very philosophy that had made the series famous—that of individual choice and relational bonding, culminating in a totally individualized story. Consumers were left betrayed and outraged and quickly demanded that the production company, BioWare (which had recently been bought out by Electronic Arts), recreate the ending. The story of how the mega-corporation (seemingly) agreed to meet consumer demands, and the reason for the poor quality release in the first place, sheds interesting light on the changing definition of narrative, creative control, authorship, and the ethics of the producer-consumer relationship.

GAMING 2.0—A NEW ERA OF ENTERTAINMENT

As Martin Weller, Laurence Lessig, Yochai Benkler, and Clay Shirkey point out, major cultural and knowledge-making industries such as journalism, music, and print have been transformed in the last two decades by the advent of digital culture. Media's multi-modality, its accessibility, and its capacity for social networking have created the potential for traditional production processes to take on whole new forms. Industries no longer depend on the sale of physical objects—such as daily papers, CD albums, and how-to manuals. Rather, the bulk of transactions are digital (taking place electronically), more granular (e.g. songs, vs. albums), and gain popularity based on their networked presence within social networks due to the Power Law (e.g., news articles with the most Facebook "likes," shares, and lively forum discussions are the most widely read) (see Shirkey, 2003). Similarly, companies depend heavily on digital tools such as online reviews, discussion forums, and multi-media help tools (such as video tutorials, instant chat, and online downloads and instructions) to gather information on, communicate with, and offer services to their users/consumers (Porter, 2010). These patterns have also proven true in the ever-growing digital entertainment industry—usually referred to as the gaming industry—whose production processes have morphed to accommodate and make use of their consumers' digital network connections.

Over the past six years, the game industry has exploded, transforming from a quasi-marginal market to a mainstream entertainment genre rivaling the newspaper and film industries in revenue (Cross, 2011). As video games' demographic demand grows, controlling the product availability and copyright of games has become a bigger concern for producers. With the advent of cloud-based systems like *Steam* (wherein players have to log in with a username to access games), the purchase, ownership and playing of games has become even more fully digital as opposed to hardware-dependent. The shift has allowed for more company-control of products, limiting pirating and protecting copyrights. While connectivity posed some threats to the economic gain of game companies, it has also allowed the industry to flourish. Message boards, chat features, and wikis play an increasingly crucial part in game play and participation (e.g.: search for "Skyrim wiki"). Multi-player and single-player gam-ers alike rely on these online venues to discuss strategies and character builds, to share valuable information about story and combat, and to share in-game items and objects (legally and illegally). Game producers have wisely tapped into these social media as a way of interacting with and inviting the feedback of their consumers, making game develop-ment more collaborative by nature. While the ability to modify games has existed for several decades, allowing users to create and share their own additional game content, over time, the industry has evolved to the point that some developers adopt user ideas, implementing them for the benefit of the entire community. For example,user-created maps and themes for *Left4Dead* were adopted by its producers, Valve, and released in *Left4Dead 2*. And, Valve as well as Bethesda—the creators of *Halflife* and *The Elder Scrolls* respectively—provide free creation kits that allow users to compose new in-game maps and to change skins, textures, and weapons for their games. Then, the creators of the "mods" (modifica-tions) share their work freely with the community, posting the patches to online wikis and forums, increasingly hosted by cloud-sourced game platforms (e.g. *Steam*).

Similar to other industries, the game industries' harnessing of cloud and social networking technology has led to more interactive, commu-nication-rich, responsive, and collaborative communities of consumers (Cain, 2011; Lehdonvirta, 2010). Gaming is no longer an isolated expe-rience—something that un-socialized men do alone, in a cave, because they don't have other inter-personal skills. It is a highly interactive, social experience which is growing to include larger and larger swaths of soci-ety. For example, as of 2011 approximately forty-two percent of gamers were women (Cross, 2011). Designers have a richer data pool of consum-er feedback to pull from and respond to. Gamers have more collective agency and group-think capability to problem-solve and create within the game worlds. As a result, the genre of the game itself has changed remarkably.

Many of these changes have been discussed by researchers and schol-ars in education, English, and economics. In 2001, Giesler et al. dis-cussed the fact that a videogame becomes a new "text" each time the player inter-acts with it, noting the collaborative nature of this creative endeavor. Massive Multiplayer Online games (MMOs) and MMO Role Playing Games (MMORPGs) are often discussed as revolutionary ven-ues within the gaming world and society at large for the way that they connect people around the world in the context of a fictional, narrative universe of cooperative play where writing is a chief form of communication (Paul, 2010; Lehdonvirta, 2010; Remley, 2010; Steinkuehler, 2007; Wiley, 2007; Swalwell, 2006; Williams, 2006; Smith, 2006). Jackson (2002), Gee (2004), Kitchens (2006), McKenny (2007), Robinson (2011), and others have specifically discussed the use of narrative-based games for improving literacy, writing, and rhetoric in the classroom, and a vast amount of literature in marketing and economics considers the impact of game theory on other industries—a field that fits under the broad designation of "gamification" studies (see Burke, 2011). This chapter will build on these studies, taking a broader social approach in order to look at how the game industry, collaborative composition practices, social networking, and narrative evolution are converging with serious implications for the next generation of producer-consumer ethics. By considering specific events surrounding the 2012 release of the third-person shooter/role-playing game, *Mass Effect 3*, this paper will demonstrate that, like multiplayer genres, post-Web 2.0 single-player game genres are also being revolutionized—and *revolutionizing*—the entertainment world, challenging and reformulating some of our most basic ideological values, power relations, and social constructs within creative culture—constructs such as the Author function, audience, producer/consumer, and the ethics of narrative ownership.

First I will outline the content of *Mass Effect 1* (*ME1*), its play-style, reception, and the subsequent success of its sequel, *Mass Effect 2* (*ME2*), with the goal of elucidating why the series holds such grand potential for the future of narrative. Then, I will describe the events leading up to and surrounding the release of *Mass Effect 3* (*ME3*), the fallout that ensued, the compositional reason behind the failure, and BioWare's response to these events. Finally, I will provide an analysis investigating the implications of these events for both the rhetoric of technology, writing and gaming, and the ethics of the industry.

Mass Effect—What It Is and Why It Matters

One of the most acclaimed RPGs on the market, noted for its sophisticated ethical themes, deeply complex dialogue trees, and fully voice-recorded cast, *Mass Effect,* released in 2007, was revolutionary primarily because it allowed players to choose the micro-level actions and reactions of their characters. As a combination third-person shooter/role-playing game (TPS/RPG), you the player create an avatar for your main character—who can be either male or female—and then begin a storyline set in deep space during a war and colonization era in the future. However, rather than simply providing a linear storyline that the character plays through with a few optional quests on the side, as is true with most role-playing games, *Mass Effect* allows players to choose every relationship, substantial line of dialogue, and character response in the game. Each time you encounter another character you have the option of forming a relationship with him or her based on intimidation, subtle coercion, or heroic leadership. The way you choose to speak, act, and respond to other characters' words and deeds changes the way that your character develops over time, which in turn, drastically changes the narrative events in the future of the game. You may be able to persuade, ally with, or kill a character later in the game, based on how you interact with them in the present, and their life or death could change the outcomes of major events. This makes the player's particular choices, rhetorical as well as material, incredibly crucial to the outcome of the story, and according to BioWare, no two players' stories will be exactly alike.

What constitutes "rhetorical action" in a video game? Essentially, in *ME,* it comprises communicative choices made by the player's main character that have a material effect on the action and narrative of the game—a design principle reflecting J.L. Austin's concept of *speech-acts,* wherein words are not merely the communication of abstract ideas but actions with direct consequences. In *Mass Effect,* you move through a storyline, interacting with major and minor (even optional) characters along the way. Each time you engage in dialogue with a character (all of which is voice acted), the player *chooses* how they will respond by picking what they will say to a character, which highlights nuanced attitudes, vocabulary, and meanings. There are always at least three types of responses in the main dialogue, before your character shifts into investigation mode (where you simply ask questions in order to gather information): you may engage in dialogue based on a) aggression and intimidation, which gains you "Renegade" points; b) carful diplomacy; or c) generous heroism, which gains you "Paragon" points.

To illustrate this process, there is a scene in the beginning of the game when you discover, while speaking with the spaceship's navigator, that the vessel has a Turian Spector commanding the mission. The navigator is not happy about this. You have the option of a) displaying disdain for the alien race (showing solidarity with the navigator); b) of dissuading his prejudice (through gentle but clear correction); or c) simply stating that the alien's presence doesn't matter as long as you all stick to business and follow orders. As you make these rhetorical choices, over time, your patterns aggregate points that develop your character either as a "Renegade" or "Paragon" hero. Each style of leadership comes with particular powers and narrative opportunities as the game progresses. So, if you successfully win the trust of a particular soldier, either by allowing her to confide in you or by helping her in a time of need, you may be able to persuade her later in the game to do you a favor or to be on your squad. On the other hand, if you successfully intimidate certain characters, and have a high enough "Renegade" score, you may be able to force information out of a man who later proves crucial to other relationships. So your actions and abilities as a commander directly depend on aggregate rhetorical moves you choose to make as you move through the role-playing component of the story.

As the game goes on, the stakes are raised regarding the choices you make. At one point in *ME1*, a fight breaks out in your squad between two major characters. A Krogan, whose race has been sterilized by another race to prevent reproduction and dominance, finds out that a cure for his people's malady has been discovered, but the facility where it is being held is about to be destroyed. As the Krogan becomes dangerously aggressive in his fury toward your character, you have the option, in the heat of the moment and based on the points you've gathered, to either talk the Krogan down or allow the other squad member to shoot and kill him. If you choose to kill him, the Krogan will effectively disappear from the game, along with any future dialogue or narrative options accompanying him. If, however, you do not choose to kill him, the Krogan will provide opportunities for you to ally with his race in the following *two* games. Neither choice is presented as the "right" or "wrong" choice for the player—it all just depends on the type of character the player is building, their feelings toward the other characters, and the types of alliances they desire to make. That being said, the game quickly gained a reputation for being a highly personal game, in which individual players made these choices very conscientiously and developed deep emotional bonds with those they chose to surround themselves with throughout the trilogy.

This brings us to the most revolutionary aspect of *Mass Effect*'s game design: all the choices that you make as a player in *Mass Effect 1* transfer into and seriously impact *Mass Effect 2*'s storyline. In other words, that person you killed in game one is still dead. That other person you made an alliance with: you can call on them for help when you need them. In fact, seven hundred different plot points and their accompanying choices in *ME1* are specifically logged and carried over to the second *and* third game (Bui, 2011). Additionally, your "Renegade" and "Paragon" score, with all the options that they unlock, are also transferred to the next game, impacting your potential choices and actions. The same is true for the transition from *Mass Effect 2* to the highly anticipated *Mass Effect 3*. So, not only is the gamer playing a major role in the micro-level choices of a single story's plot—they are helping to write a story which spans an entire *trilogy*. Such a thing had never been done, and it won the production company, BioWare, a lot of attention.

When *Mass Effect 2* was released in 2010, it became one of the most highly acclaimed games in history. Exceeding market expectations, the RPG won numerous awards for "Best Game" and "Best Writing" in countries such as America, Britain, Australia, and Canada. Some critics even claimed it was the best game ever made because it set a new horizon of possibility for interactive digital media. The art from *Mass Effect 2* was also included in the special exhibit for video game art featured at the Smithsonian Museum from March to September of 2012. BioWare advertised *Mass Effect* as an RPG in which no two player's games could be alike—a tall claim indeed for a game. After the release of *Mass Effect 2*, the players believed it. Players claimed they had never felt so directly, psychologically, and emotionally connected to a story or its characters as they did to Commander Shepherd and his/her companions. Players raved about the game's immersive qualities, its deep characters, and their own ability to *choose* how they'd like to develop their own character and his or her relationship to their team.

Here are some examples from metacritic.com (2011) of players' responses to the game. The user-name of each writer is noted after the quotations. The same themes occur again and again, revolving around three primary observations. The first is the quality and captivation of the story, including a sincere adoration for the characters: "One of the best games I've ever played, the story traps you from first to last minute" (dantexr); "This is easily one of the best games I have ever played. . . . probably one of the greatest and most intriguing story lines ever. As someone who never played the first ME i still had an immediate attachment to shepherd right from the first moving scene (Deadeagle); "This is one of the rare franchises where I feel a connection to the characters and want to know more about them" (Coverton); "The romances add depth to the characters in the game and make the party feel alive" (tsavostfu); "the best cast of characters from any game i've played" (Even365).

The second major theme is an appreciation for the player's ability to choose narrative actions and relationships, which seems to go hand in hand with an emotional investment in the game: "I especially love the many choices you can make. A-ma-zing. Good or bad Shepard? Choice is yours!" (Lluminari); "you actually get to make decision which will affect the game . . . Every minute I spent with it it grabs me emotionally on every decision I make. It make[s] you believe that the characters are real people thanks to the marvellous acting and amazing dialogue" (Tetsuo); "I can't wait for Mass Effect 3 to come out. I am really interested to see how the choices I made in ME2 are going to affect the final chapter" (baalsoptio); "I loved every second of it. Had never played ME 1 before trying this. After my heart settled down after first playthrough I rushed out to buy ME1 before playing them both twice back to back. I now have two different stories to continue when ME 3 comes out . . . and I cant wait!" (Zokopops); "oh my god the story is just amazing, you really get caught up in it. The replayabillety is good, because you have so many different choices to make and different classes to use on commander Shepard" (TheAllmighty).

Finally, the immersive experience of the story as a whole is often compared to other well established narrative genres, and players express a desire to see even more of this style of story-telling: "the games final hours you can't help but feel that you are an integral part of the action as you battle your way towards ME2's epic conclusion" (johnnypopular); "throughout the game felt like I was in a film" (Starlet025); "Beautiful, balanced and beyond awe inspiring . . . It reminds me of a very good book, you wont put it down until you have finished and you will yearn for the sequel" (Giar); "Phenomenal game. I've never been more invested in a game than I was with Mass Effect 2. The last mission is one of the greatest endings I have ever seen in a video game" (xPyroMatt); "you get sucked into the storyline . . . The tension builds throughout and I can honestly say I have never been so nervous going into a final battle—I mean, it's a video game for goodness sake but I was so involved, it had that affect on me !!" (Kwaker76); "No review would be fair to this game. Mass Effect 2 is not a game, it is an experience. It must not be 'played,' this is too mundane. It must be lived" (GrumpyReviewer).

In their feedback to BioWare, via social networks, commentary, and discussion boards, players requested the ability to make even more choices, in particular regarding their relationships to other characters: "The romances add depth to the characters in the game and make the party feel alive. Having said that I didn't like being railroaded into helping Cerberus do anything—it should have been a choice" (tsavostfu); "I would have liked to have been able to talk to my romance option much more than I could. I enjoy the romance aspect of bioware games and it's nice to be able to have chats and cut scenes with your chosen love interest sometimes for a bit of light relief from the main campaign so I felt this could have been fleshed out a bit more" (Starlet025).

According to BioWare, these requests made by consumers (among others) were taken very seriously in the game development process because BioWare saw the players/users as integral contributors, even "collaborators" with them in the creative process. As executive producer, Cacey Hudson (Priestly, 2012) boasts:

> Over the course of the series, Mass Effect has been a shared experience between the development team and our fans—not just of shared experience in playing the game, but in designing and developing them. An outpouring of love for Garrus and Tali led to their inclusion as love interests in Mass Effect 2. A request for deeper RPG systems led to key design changes in Mass Effect 3. . . . Mass Effect is a collaboration between developers and players, and we continue to listen.

The company prides itself on its flexibility and its responsiveness to fan feed-back. Indeed, BioWare was known in the gaming community for its ethical practices and quality products. In an age when many corporations are simply out to make a buck, or nickel-and-dime the consumer to death, gamers recognized that BioWare was committed to real artistic production: "BioWare deserve a medal, because this is how games should be made and they know how to look after the people that pay their wages . . . that[']s you and me" (Metacritic, 2011, [Madmaz]).

Fans were also excited to see how the choices, characters, and relationships they had carefully constructed since *ME1* would carry over to *Mass Effect 3*. In fact, players reported playing the games many times over, in an effort to construct their "perfect commander Shepard" (Burney, 2012), so that when the final game appeared, they could act out their ideal story. Interestingly, this pattern was not one of isolated individualism; rather, it was innately social:

> I have been observing the frantic rush of replays by people in various communities. There is definitely a sense of a communal effort; people relating their plans for their 'perfect' Commander Shepard and what kind of universe they want to forge with his or her decisions, as well as providing each other with tips on how to tackle certain spots, things to look out for and optimal strategies for keeping companions alive. Moreover, at this level of fandom, there is much at stake, and therefore much speculation and hope that the game lives up to its hype (Burney, 2012).

And there were good indications that it would. In an interview, gameplay designer Christina Noman assured audiences that their choices would play an integral role in an exciting and meaningful way:

> I can't talk about any of the specific decisions or what they actually do. But what I can say is that decisions through all of the Mass Effect games, including the DLC, will matter for Mass Effect 3. And it's not just like decisions that carried over from ME1 to ME2 will matter in ME3, they'll be decisions in ME1 that did not visibly impact ME2 that will have an impact in ME3. What we looked at is the total story, everything that happened in Mass Effect 1 and Mass Effect 2 is real and matters, we let the writers draw on that as much as they want to customize the experience and to be pretty much without limits (Bui, 2011).

As if these promises weren't enough, BioWare made an announcement at the 2011 E3 press conference, unveiling the Xbox Kinect implementation of *ME3*, which would feature the ability for players to use voice commands to choose their rhetorical responses to other characters (Macllem, 2011). This final development really did take the game to the most advanced stage of immersive play available in that system generation. With so much artistic promise, as well as the internationally acclaimed status of BioWare as a production company and its strong ethos with the gaming community itself, fans had substantial reason to expect great things from the final chapter of the *Mass Effect* trilogy. And so, the world waited in eager expectation for the conclusion of this historically significant and beloved saga.

THE SCANDAL

Between 2010 and 2012, fans waited expectantly for the final installment of the *Mass Effect* trilogy. In fact, the pre-order of the collector's
edition of the game was a number one best seller on Amazon in the USA
and Germany. BioWare's Executive Producer, Casey Hudson, boasted
that this would be the greatest game yet and promised it would "excee[d]
everyone's expectations" (BioWare, 2011b). Critics who reviewed the
game before its release praised it as a triumph, an epic ending to a his-
toric series. It was nominated for several awards at E3 (BioWare, 2011c),
the *New York Times* hailed the game as a masterpiece, and a motion
picture was even announced. Unfortunately, as BioWare hurried to meet
its March deadline for the release, no one saw the chaos that was about
to ensue, all thanks to an unfortunate call regarding the writing process.

When the game was released on March 6, 2012, community members were in for a major disappointment. The endings were terrible. Not
simply from a plot and narrative standpoint, but mainly because the development and content of the endings was in no way consistent with the
themes, messages, and philosophy behind the entire series. At the final
moment, when the main character must decide the fate of the human
and non-human universe, almost none of the choices the player has
made in the entire three-game series make even a fraction of an ounce of
difference. Additionally, no matter what ending you choose, the graphics
are virtually the same, with little more than lighting and color defining
the different outcomes. People were enraged.

Where the critics had given the game an average 8.5 out of 10 on
Metacritic (2012) (lower than *ME2's* average rating), players rated the
game at a whopping 4.3 (based on 3,620 reviews). Users said it best:

> Ending killed it, completely, 1000% nuked it to jesus's 8th com-
> ing, killed it. The good: Combat, . . . Melee . . . Customizing
> my guns . . . The Bad: . . . the ending just sucked. Great, 3 dif-
> ferent colors, and for some reason all the relays are blown up
> although only one of the options was supposed to destroy em [in
> other words: all the endings are the same regardless of choice].
> . . . for some reason Joker wasn't on planet earth, wtf? Story, i
> honestly felt 0 connection. [In] ME1 I wanted to kill sarin, I was
> sad that i had to let my crew mate die back there . . . [In] ME2,
> Collectors must die! killed [my] crew, blew up my old ship, de-
> stroyed my relationship with Ashley. Must die! . . . And the

ending was influenced by how well you maintained re[la]tion-
ships with your crew. Mass Effect 3 had none of that. You['re]
standing with the crew doesn't matter, [a particular character]
got removed, [and] who comes with you on the final mission is
also pointless. All your decisions are meaningless in the end. So,
would i recommend it? . . . i would not. Worst 60 dollars i have
ever spent. (Metacritic, 2012, [Ageoffan])

The above reviewer gave the game a 6/10, generous compared to another
reviewer who only managed 4/10—a score closer to the representative
average. Their words sum up the collective pain of players, particularly
regarding not just the game's plot failures, but why the failure mattered
so much to those who were dedicated to the series:

Possibly the most disappointing release I've ever played. I will,
in all honesty, never forgive the developer for taking narrative
control away from a character I'd spent _years_ with and forcing her to engage in the least satisfying ending- and least in-
character actions- imaginable. . . . Regardless of how many new
'cool' weapons and commendation packs they throw at me, the
game is dead to me. I paid for it and have no interest in ever
going back. And all those "critics" who gave the game a 10/10 . .
. I doubt I'll be trusting your opinions from here on out. (Meta-
crtic, 2012, [kyrgsh])

These sentiments were echoed by thousands on channels across the Web.
The last sentence highlights the major breach of trust that the game's
release embodied for those supporting the industry; in many ways, this
was the straw that broke the camel's back. BioWare had been the surviv-
ing hero of the game industry—representing ethical employment practices, quality products, world-class craftsmanship, and costumer value
despite it's absorption into the devil of the gaming world, Electronic
Arts. Although the reason behind the finale's breach of continuity was
unclear, the apparent rush to complete a product within a multi-million
dollar franchise at the expense of the game's climax simply reeked of
the typical corporate-American corruption that the country as a whole
was completely exasperated with in early 2012. Game critics had long
been accused of pandering to their financial backers, but this particular
discrepancy between professional and user evaluation of the game was
honestly outrageous. While any number of anticipated games in the past
several years had proven less than satisfying to expectant fans, *Mass Ef-*

fect was a totally new type of game, which had a totally different psychological effect on those who engaged with it—different than anything which had come before, and the producers were simply not prepared for how strongly fans would react to an ending that suddenly ejected them from the position of creative control that they had inhabited for half a decade. As a result, BioWare's once pristine ethos with the community was also shot.

The Internet quickly flooded with expressions of disappointment and disbelief in all manner of media: blogs, videos, memes, news, reviews. Seemingly overnight, BioWare was transformed from prodigy to betrayer. Figure 1 shows just one of hundreds that circulated in the days following the game's release ("Mass Effect 3," 2012).

The emotional turmoil and anger of players who had deeply invested themselves in the game is captured well in a Hitler video meme uploaded by IAmRodyle (2012). The meme synchs English captions to a clip from the famous German film *Der Untergang* (*Downfall*), in which Hitler explodes at chief officials after being informed of a major military defeat. Having been told, in the meme, that the game's ending comes down to a photoshopped cut-scene in three different colors, Hitler dismisses all those in the room "who have not emotionally invested themselves in these games since the first installment;" then, he unleashes an Academy Award-worthy performance (thanks to the film's actors), denouncing the ending:

> [screaming:] Are you telling me that absolutely NOTHING I've done over all 3 games factors into the ending? I was not expecting a perfect ending. . . . The whole reason I loved these games is because your choices felt REAL. And they give us an ending that we have no control over and is so ridden with plot holes it doesn't even make sense! . . . Five years! I've spent god knows how many hours playing and replaying the first two games, tweaking every part of the story the way I wanted! I loved these games because they made me feel like I was part of the story! I learned about the world, fell in love with its characters, and poured every ounce of myself into its narrative. But none of it ever mattered . . . Every hour of time invested in this story this series is rendered wasted by this shitfuck of an ending! [pause; in a more gentle tone:] All I wanted was a little closure.

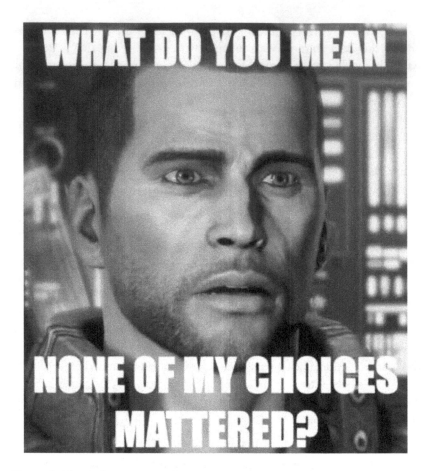

Figure 1. Gamers' response to the controversy.

I went into this game knowing that Shepard was likely going to die. But his legacy was suppose to be your own. I feel like such an idiot. . . . all the alternate characters I made over the past month aren't even worth importing anymore. It would just be too painful to go through. . . . [Two women are shown crying outside of the room. One comforts the other]: Don't worry, we'll make up our own ending. [Back to Hitler; quietly:] I just wanted to be with Tali in the end. If not, at least just being able to talk to her without her mask on. Just once. . . . Dicks.

Not only did players create artistic representations like this one of user resistance, but organizations and serious activist groups quickly sprung up, arguing that the trilogy was too historically significant to allow a horrible choice on BioWare's part to ruin the series forever. People began to demand a remake of the final game. For those not familiar with the game community, players are especially known for their particularly bombastic whining and bad attitudes; they often complain about even the highest-quality game, and of course there are always "haters" who demand their money back. However, it is *not* common for gamers to demand that a product—something that takes millions of dollars and usually several years of complex creative process to make—be completely remade. In fact, this is no doubt the first time in the industry's history that a significant number of people have seriously suggested it. They did an excellent job of making their voices heard.

Child's Play, a charity that donates game-related merchandise to kids suffering from cancer, ended up becoming one of the chaotic epicenters of the online *Mass Effect 3* protests. Founded by well-known game-based web comic, *Penny Arcade*, the charity foundation was one of the many communication forums where fans were passionately discussing the failed release of *ME3*. At some point, an initiative formed that suggested combining Child's Play donations with a fund to get BioWare to remake the ending of *ME3*. In a mixture of what Penny Arcade later called "a grassroots effort . . . part community, part online petition, and part . . . Donation Drive," confusion ensued (Tycho, 2012). Although Child's Play had made no such call to action, the misunderstanding caused a ripple effect in the highly networked gaming community, and Penny Arcade's donor site was suddenly flooded with thousands of dollars ($67,000 to be exact), purportedly given as part of the "Retake Mass Effect" cause. Flooded with emails and seeing the legal ramification of what was going on, Penny Arcade quickly shut down its donor site with declarations that their collections were not meant to fund major art and entertainment projects, but to help children who were sick—in case there was any confusion. Those who had supported the digital rally quickly moved over to Facebook, where they started the "Demand A Better Ending to Mass Effect 3" page, which now enjoys the support of about 56,000 "likes" (*Retake*, 2012).

BioWare's immediate response to their followers' outrage was decidedly diplomatic. First, they tried to reassure consumers by announcing the release of some new components of the game as "downloadable content" (DLC)—which could be purchased for a small fee, of course. These additions, they promised, would make the game better. Of course, this did not make players happy; in fact, it made the situation significantly worse, further damaging BioWare's already fragile ethos within the community. Users responded, arguing that the game was innately flawed and could not be fixed with simple add-ons and patches; they demanded a serious *revision*. They even expressed the hope that the game's current ending was no more than a "dream sequence" invented by the story's villain—a final attempt to brainwash the hero, and from which the hero would awake and defy the claim of impotence. After having to shut down various social-media hubs to stem the malignant barrage of criticism, BioWare's executive producer released a post saying that BioWare would work with the game community to improve components of the game, but defended BioWare's artistic choices (Gaudiosi, 2012; Priestly, 2012). This stance elicited yet more backlash on Twitter, Facebook, and social media forums. Online commentator Doyce Testerman (2012) demonstrates that users are too well-educated about the nature of creative process to buy such a defense:

> This isn't about a bunch of privileged gamers complaining about a sad ending, because there are well-done sad endings that make contextual sense. . . . Maybe you say "this is art, and it is inviolate and immutable in the face of outside forces," . . . Name me a story that saw print, or a movie that saw the Big Screen, and I'll show you art that changed because of input from someone other than the original creator. . . . Hiding behind some kind of "but it's art, so we're not changing it" defense is insulting, disingenuous, and flat-out stupid. Worse, it perpetuates the idea that the creator's output is in some stupid way sacrosanct and, as art, cannot *be* "wrong" or "bad." If you as a creator imagine that to be the case—if you think that kind of argument is going defend your right to never do a rewrite or a revision or line edits or to ever alter, in any way, your precious Artistic Process—discard that notion. Or become accustomed to a long life as an "undiscovered talent."

In other words, the community saw the disastrous ending of the trilogy as a fundamental problem with the creative composition of the work, grounded in the production process itself. Furthermore, the game community held BioWare to a standard of quality that they claimed was not determined by the company's "privileged" eye, but by those experiencing the game. Some community members went so far as to report the game to the Federal Trade Commission and the Better Business Bureau for false advertising (Alex, 2012).

Amidst all the demonstrations, protests, and digital rallies, people were desperately searching for the culprit behind this epic, creative, and communal catastrophe. Who was to blame for the greatest let down in gaming history? Lots of names and accusations were flying around the forums—the writing team responsible for all the dialogue and overall plot of the games were obviously under fire, but other major executives were being implicated too. Rumors even circulated that the original writer of the series had left BioWare, and that his detailed outline and explanation of the ending—which had been leaked the previous year—had been scrapped and replaced by a brand new (read, inexperienced) author's ending (Doyce, 2012).

Finally, after these rumors circulated, a post appeared on the *Penny Arcade* forums, written by "Takyris," a well-known community member whose profile linked to the Live Journal of Patrick Weekes—one of the authors on the *Mass Effect* writing team. A well-known blogger for the BioWare team, Takyris' post was the first insider statement explaining what had happened to the ending. In it, Takyris provides a detailed analysis of the game's strengths and weaknesses, his role in each of these creative decisions, and then claims that, while the entire series had been composed via a collaborative, peer-review process in which the whole team vetted each narrative decision, the final ending of the games had been solely authored by the executive producer, Cacey Hudson, and the head of the writing team, Mac Walters, who had openly bypassed the collaborative process:

> The ending . . . was entirely the work of our lead and Casey himself, sitting in a room and going through draft after draft. And honestly, it kind of shows. Every other mission in the game had to be held up to the rest of the writing team, and the writing team then picked it apart and made suggestions and pointed out the parts that made no sense. This mission? Casey and our lead decided that they didn't need to be peer-reviewed (as cited in Armstrong, 2012).

Takyris goes on to argue that, while the entire game had been written with the overall themes and targets of the mission driving the message, the endgame did not do so: "You have to understand. Casey is really smart and really analytical. And the problem is that when he's not checked, he will assume that other people are him, and will really appreciate an almost completely unemotional intellectual ending" (As cited in Armstrong, 2012). Takyris also adds that he does not know why the final cut scenes are all virtually the same: "Maybe they were cut for budget reasons at the last minute. I don't know. But holy crap, yeah, I can see how incredibly disappointing it'd be . . . to have it break down to 'which color is stuff glowing?'" He made it clear he would be deleting his post in an hour and that his complaint was *not* that Shepard sacrificed himself in the end, but rather that he expected "a stronger tie to the core themes": "I still teared up at the ending myself, but really, I was tearing up for the quick flashbacks to old friends and the death of Anderson. I wasn't tearing up over making a choice."

Just hours after the post appeared, true to his promise, the writer deleted his statement, requesting community members to spread the information without reference to his name or identity. Takyris/Weekes, in fact, denies authorship of the post to this day—an issue that has sparked major discussion regarding corporate and journalistic ethics for those that chose to save/screen-shot and republish his deleted post with his name attached (see Armstrong, 2012). When the news of the circulating post reached BioWare, the company claimed (on their own forums) that it was a hoax, and dismissed the explanation—although they did not correct or rebut it. However, there was also speculation that this was a merciful act, since admitting that Weekes had posted the statement might have meant his dismissal from the team. Takyris also disappeared from the *Penny Arcade* forums—ironic, since he had used the venue as a place to "bounce light ideas" about his writing off of the gaming community (Armstrong, 2012). Players point to the incident as yet another betrayal of trust in the relationship between BioWare and the community. The significance of the post, however, remained fairly uncontested: a member of BioWare's own writing team had validated one of the primary claims of the "Retake Mass Effect" movement: that the ending had not lived up to what had been promised, and that this was a result of poor internal decision making.

"Mass Effect of the People"

Finally, after fifteen days of constant criticism, Dr. Ray Muzyka, co-founder of BioWare came out with an official statement of grievance expressing the company's care for players' emotions, admitting the seriousness of the complaints and promising to seek resolution, all while still maintaining the "right to artistic integrity" perspective held by the game producers:

> Our first instinct is to defend our work and point to the high ratings offered by critics—but out of respect to our fans, we need to accept the criticism and feedback with humility. . . . Mass Effect 3 concludes a trilogy with so much player control and ownership of the story that it was hard for us to predict the range of emotions players would feel when they finished playing through it. The journey you undertake in Mass Effect provokes an intense range of highly personal emotions in the player; even so, the passionate reaction of some of our most loyal players to the current endings in Mass Effect 3 is something that has genuinely surprised us. This is an issue we care about deeply, and we will respond to it in a fair and timely way. We're already working hard to do that. . . . *We're working hard to maintain the right to balance between the artistic integrity of the original story while addressing the fan feedback we've received* (Darklarke, 2012, emphasis added).

Something worth noting in this statement is Muzyka's reference to the question of artistic integrity, which he refers to earlier in the statement as the company's "right to balance" their vision for the narrative with the experiential creativity of the players. This line of argument, along with the actions that stem from it, begs the question: Who owns *Mass Effect?* The current consensus in this discourse community seems to imply, *we all do.* True, according to traditional economic definitions, the originating producer has creative rights over his product, but as this situation proved, the traditional roles may not apply so much in such a distributed creative process. There is strong evidence to suggest, for example, that part of the writing team takes no ownership of the story's ending. On the other hand, the players, who were invited to become a part of the story's creation by the producers, do claim that ownership—even, if it's necessary to say so—because they paid for it. Perhaps a violation of a social contract has occurred, but it is not the consumer's breaching the rights of their producers. Rather, it might be that the executive producer breached the rights of creative control that were distributed to the writing team, in turn, violating the creative rights of the game players that had been invited to take part in the story's collaborative creation. Obviously we don't know what happened in the final production, but we do know that EA decided it would be more advisable and likely, more lucrative, to give the fans what they wanted: a new ending to their stories. As *Forbes* writer, Erik Kain (2012b) says, "the BioWare and *Mass Effect* Franchise may very well go down in history if they release a *free* 'real' ending to the third game sometime soon."

Although BioWare released a series of extended epilogues and cut scenes, they ultimately did not provide any alternative endings, and as a result, the parent corporation, EA, won *Consumerist's* title of "Worst Company in America, 2012." Although there is no direct reference in *The Consumerist's* announcement of the winner, the last line of the declaration reads as follows: "All that's left to do is send off the Golden Poo to EA. Traditionally, the Poo has been delivered on its little red pillow. But this year, we'll give EA three different color options for its pillow, though in the end it's still the same old Poo" (Morran, 2012).

AUTHORITY, OWNERSHIP, AND ETHICS—
WHEN TWO ECONOMIES COLLIDE

As you may recall, voters in *The Consumerist's* worst company contest of 2012 were fairly disgusted that hundreds of thousands of people had voted EA as the worst company over its competing finalist, Bank of America. Although gamers had some fair defenses against this claim—such as the fact that BoA had won the contest for the past two years and didn't need any help drawing public attention to their unethical practices—this did not keep other voters from sneering at a generation of "Johnny's" who saw their sense of entitlement over "their World of Warcraft account" as more important than foreclosures and "ruined lives." (The irony in the parallel between "Johnny wants his video game" and "Johnny can't write" is of course, fabulous here). However, as is probably clear by now, there is a lot more going on in this public controversy than would be apparent to outsiders.

Ultimately, what we are seeing in the *ME3* scandal is an ethical battle surrounding the clash of two powerful systems of economy and the rhetorical values associated with them—specifically the categories of authorship/authority, ownership, and art, or in this case, narrative. The massive online debate that has been birthed from this kairotic event constitutes a collective deliberation in which the two parties—BioWare/EA Games/Video Game Companies and Players/Users/Consumers—defend their positions using appeals to social values, derived from two different economic and community systems: the traditional economy (that of consumer capitalism) and the new digital economy.

In *Wealth of Networks,* Benkler (2007) first outlined the major differences between the "old" and "new" cultural economies. Economics before the digital revolution was built on private, rival (competing) goods with significant marginal costs accompanying production, while the economics of the new digital culture are largely based on non-rival, peer-produced, public goods with low or no marginal costs associated with production. As Porter (2010) notes, these differences invoke a necessarily different rhetorical situation for writers and composers of digital texts, and a different rhetorical economy of values. Similarly, Benkler and Nissenbaum (2006) have argued that with the new digital economy and production processes, come innately new ethical systems in which particular moral values are both required and encouraged through participation with peers for the purpose of achieving greater goals than any one person could aspire to on their own. Virtues such as benevolence, generosity, charity, altruism, camaraderie, and friendship, which hold little or limited practical value within a traditional market (due to the nature of rival goods), have great *measurable worth,* as well as direct personal benefit and reward within the new digital economy. Gamers' willingness to create elaborate new game modifications on their own time and then share them for free with the community is one example of this virtue system. More importantly for this discussion, individual credibility, value, authority, and trustworthiness—that is, *ethos*—within these new communities is largely determined by the ethics of contribution and one's willingness to share freely with the larger group. Without displaying and enacting these virtues, one holds little to no sway with the crowd, politically, rhetorically, or practically.

The "Retake *Mass Effect*" movement represents a monumental clash in the old and new economies and their corresponding value systems. Although the video-game world still operates within a traditional market industry, based on rival-goods and high initial production costs, its user/consumer base of players exists and operates *primarily* in a digital economy on a daily basis, espousing values and rhetorical constraints more attuned to collective, peer production and collaborative creation. Over the past decade, the game industry has worked hard to appeal to the values of, and therefore reap the benefits of, both worlds. Companies try to accommodate the expectations and tap into the conveniences afforded by new digital technologies and information economies, by offering things such as online forums, free software for "modding" games, and cloud-sourcing, so that games can be played from any location. At the same time, companies have also been maneuvering to maintain their singular control over the traditional economics of what Foucault (2007) calls the "Author-function" and all that it entails: individual, elitist identity of the author; singular, unique, unified, and original status of the text; cultural authority over and credit for said text; and at least nominal legal priv-ileges regarding its intellectual property rights, including production, distribution, and revenues. A certain level of said control is necessary in order for artisans and entrepreneurs to maintain economic stability and incentive for production. However, As Boyle (2008) notes in *The Public Domain: Enclosing the Commons of the Mind*, a limit on those controls encourages and enables cultural creativity and production to flourish.

> In the case of the game industry, we have a situation in which companies have tried their best to straddle both worlds—that of intellectual control and open peer production. By accepting and appealing to the values of the digital economy, BioWare/EA Games (and perhaps the game industry as a whole) were unable to hold their ground within the values of traditional economy. In order to open their product up to the collaborative poten-tial offered by social media and the new composition and gam-ing technologies, they were forced to relinquish at least some of the rights associated with the traditional economy and the Author-function. Specifically, they had to relinquish, what Al-berti (2008) would call, their uncontested and singular "author-ity" over a unified text. BioWare could not both invite gamers to become collaborative authors of the creative experience of *Mass Effect* and maintain their absolute ownership and exclusive in-tellectual rights over the story. By opening up narrative control, they also opened up ownership, author-ity, and ethical rights over the game and its total content—including its ending. To gamers, this compositional reality is obvious:
>
>> The idea that players should just deal with the ending, be-cause it's BioWare's ending and not theirs is one of the interest-ing points of this debate, simply because it rides this weird line where we don't really have a cultural context for what the Mass Effect series *is*: Is it a game? Is it a story? If it's a game, then who cares about the story, and if it's a story, then treat it like a

> book and stop pretending you get to influence it, stupid con-
> sumer. The answer is more complicated: Is it a game or story?
> Yes. Moreover, it's a game that's welcomed player input into the
> narrative from the first moment, and as such should be commit-
> ted to honoring that input throughout. It's a story, but it belongs
> to everyone telling it. (Testerman, 2012).

This quotation demonstrates an awareness on the critic's part that the "old" rules of authorship, which applied to the print genres such as novels, do not hold within our current cultural context. And, for what it's worth, this fact is not new news, even in rhetoric and composition studies. Giesler, Bazerman, Doheny-Farina, Gurak, Hass, and Johnson-Eilola took note of the collaborative nature of video-game texts as early as 2001. In 2008, Alberti pointed out that notions such as "author," "audience," and "the useful fiction . . . of the stable text, the 'product' of the process/product model" are completely destabilized by video games (p. 266). Furthermore, game designers and theorists *themselves* discuss this complex phenomenology of textual experience in their own work: "The more progressive developers in the industry are similarly aware that because games are interactive, player-driven experiences, they are unique media that require wholly new methods for development, inter-pretation, and analysis" (Robinson, 2011, p. 362). The fact that BioWare themselves openly ascribe to this philosophy—even boasting about it on a regular basis—makes their decision to appeal to new-critical values of the stable text, authorship, and artistry in an attempt to cover their mistakes, all the more weak and disappointing in their audiences' eyes. Once again, citing from Testerman (2012):

> There's a recurring tune being played by BioWare in response to
> this outcry, and it goes something like this: "We might respond
> to these complaints, and we might flesh out the ending we pre-
> sented, but we're not going to *change* anything, because this is
> **art**—this is the product of artists—and as such it is inviolate
> and immutable in the face of outside forces." Which is, speaking
> as a working artist, complete and utter horseshit.

BioWare's continued insistence on their creative rights and intellectual control over the game's ending was in many ways an attempt to rhetori-cally reinforce their traditional economic position by appealing to the code of the Author-function: art is a unified whole; the author is a single individual with full rights over their creation. On the one hand, by continually choosing to use the word "we" and "our" in reference to creative choices about the game's composition ("our first instinct is to defend our work"; "it was hard for us to predict"; "we're already working hard to" etc.)—emphasizing the singularity of the design team—BioWare was emphasizing their solidarity to protect individuals under attack within the corporation. On the other hand, they were *also* reinforcing the idea of the author as a single, unified entity—not a group of authors with various roles and often divergent opinions. The rhetoric tends to mask the reality of collaborative writing and normalizes the concept of the unified creative mind that produces a wholly seamless object, internally consistent, understandable, and interpretable by the "ideal audience." Certain commentators and BioWare employees' suggestions (on blogs and forums) that gamers simply did not *appreciate* their "artwork" was an insinuation that such players were *not* the ideal audience and were thus uneducated, unsophisticated, and/or unworthy of "high culture" to begin with.

This position, in turn, also presents an *economic justification* of Bio-Ware's choices because within a traditional author-function print economy, the producer is under no obligation whatsoever to revise their product because it displeases consumers—the consumer made the choice to buy the object; if they don't like it, too bad. Don't recommend it to others. After all, production companies don't re-make movies because of bad ratings. Sure, some series are completely re-made—take *Spider Man* as a recent example—but in those cases we are talking about completely new directors, actors, writers, etc, all of whom stand to gain a profit where the earlier producers missed out. In the case of *Mass Effect*, why should the production company spend time and money on something that a) they already spent years and millions of dollars creating and b) that has generated a multi-million dollar, world-wide, award-winning franchise? All loss and no gain. To expect otherwise, under traditional circumstances, would literally be seen as outrageous and quite frankly, petty.

This point leads to another major trope BioWare rhetorically invoked in their defense against "Retake *Mass Effect*": the claim that the protesters were just your typical, "entitled" group of spoiled-brat consumers who didn't understand the hard work of real life. This argument cleverly coupled two already popular ethical attacks of our time: first, anti-consumerist/capitalist rhetoric that bemoans the typical American consumer's ingratitude and obliviousness, and second, classic anti-gamer rhetoric which depicts the player as the anti-social, lazy, fat, and unproductive member of society, out of touch with the real world, with no appreciation for real work—the "Johnny" that's angry about his *World of Warcraft* account. Put together, these tropes created a substantial attack on the credibility of the "Retake" movement. The Child's Play donation drive went a long way in combating these accusations. Luckily, even outside observers saw the ad-hominem flaws in EA/BioWare's argument. *Forbes* author, Erik Kain (2012a) posted an article criticizing BioWare, and the game industry as a whole, for this very issue:

> [T]he game industry, and gaming media, is wrong to label upset consumers as "entitled" or ignore the investment of fans beyond simply spending their hard-earned cash . . . What [critics are] really saying is that gamers have no *investment* in the games they play and love (or hate.) It's the same attitude you hear in politics when someone says 'If you don't love America, why don't you go somewhere else?' But gamers really *do* have investment . . . The relationship between gamer and developer, and across the entire community, is a social and participatory relationship. (Kain, 2012)

Quotations like these, from (or at least supported by) entities who would not even be considered "insiders" of the game community, demonstrate the heavy sway of public opinion against BioWare—and more broadly, EA and the game industry as a whole—regarding their ethical framework for relating to customers and collaborative consumers.

The final outcome of the "Retake Mass Effect 3" event—BioWare's succumbing to the demand to recreate the end-game content—demonstrates the fact that, while the old economy is still up and running, the new economy is powerful and alive, and with the help of its host of 2.0 technologies, it cannot be ignored. On the *BioWare Social Network,* previous PR specialist, atghunter (his screen name) would provide the *ME* community with regular analyses of BioWare's response to consumers during the "Take Back" movement. While he supported a continued trust in BioWare's ability to respond to user concerns, he also pointed out BioWare's inability to combat the movement, due to the overwhelming tide of digital media feedback. While in the past, traditional methods of damage control would have sufficed—black outs, stalling, and faux olive branches, all of which are meant to buy time while consumers cool off—this was one of the first outcries on record in which the corporate entity under attack did not have the ability to dampen consumers emotions fast enough because of their ability to network:

> Here's the part that amazes me . . . The disenfranchised base here is changing the old methodology. . . . social media and the 24 hour news cycle have simply changed everything. Twenty years ago, you could not mass 30,000 protesters into a networked base without . . . money, a GREAT cause and (most importantly) time. . . . Groups like Take Back have altered the landscape and suddenly the contest is taken from the old paradigm to a crazy new (and wonderful IMO) place. Preorder sales took away customers biggest weapon in the past (i.e. don't buy the product). Now customers who feel they have received poor value have been potentially re-empowered by the internet. (anghunter, 2012)

Furthermore, the old economy cannot participate in the new digital one without being effected—without being dialogically transformed by the rhetoric and values embodied in digital communities, activity groups, and artifacts. That which is produced within the new networks of digital collaborative culture is indelibly inscribed with meaning-making practices, economic values, and ethical imperatives of that network. Increasingly, very little can be created that is not somehow articulated to those networks. The implication is that we are no doubt going to see many more situations like the *Mass Effect* 3 uprising in the near future, wherein the composition of the old network economies are re-composed (Latour, 2010) by the rhetorical values of new media.

As Latour (1999) would point out—all agencies are a collective, and "modern" society is in a continual state of hybridization, even while we verbally reinforce its "purification"—the segregation of entities into verbal categories like "old" and "new" (Latour, 1993). Although I have continually referred in this chapter to *traditional* and *digital* economies, the truth is that these are simply useful verbal categories that do not exist in the praxis of real material life. In reality, these economic systems, values, processes, and expectations are all intricately and indelibly interwoven and continue to become more so over time. An event like the "Retake Mass Effect" only draws attention to the reality of this process, and acts as a litmus test of the developments, via rhetorical appeals, arguments, and deliberative outcomes. The only question that really remains to be seen is that of power and agentive distribution: how will the values be woven together, who will attain the greatest sway through connective mass, and what new norms and practices will evolve out of these distributed powers and expectations? As of right now, the "mass effect" of connectivity, if you will, is on the side of the networked community of players and consumers, championing an ethic of communal composition and shared ownership over texts and narrative experiences.

CONCLUSION

The events surrounding *Mass Effect 3* offer us excellent insights into the ways that cultural production landscape is changing, even as we speak. My husband, a life-long gamer, said it best: "the moment BioWare opened up the story to their audience and invited them to take part in the creation and ownership of the narrative, offering them intimate relationships with characters of their choosing, they became indebted to that other party and responsible to honor their vision and desires for the outcome of the plot." Some commentators have warned *Mass Effect* fans, pointing out that a fickle audience is a greedy company's delight: if their consumers want changes, they will give them gladly, as long as there is a source of revenue: "If people are dissatisfied with art, better to make their own rather than force other artists to change their work" (Angello, 2012). There is certainly wisdom in this statement. On the other hand, these events are one more piece of evidence that the digital revolution really has shifted us from a highly individualistic society where the author/artist function rules the market as a singular entity, to a more collective age of society where authorship and ownership are more distributed. The ethos of artistry depends upon the good-faith belief that all those involved in the creative process remain included in that process—in some way, shape, or form—through its completion. Globalization, social networks, and the Internet allow for more connected community communication, stronger rallying forces, and a more cooperative control over the creation of cultural artifacts. No one wants the rule of the mob. But everyone appreciates it when they find that many others share their experiences, concerns, and passions. The world is changed because of *Mass Effect*, and it is even further changed by its supporters' successful demands for a quality of closure that does the series justice. And, as the "worst company in America" reminds us, the alternative to an unruly crowd is often an established order of greed and self-interest. Despite the disparaging remarks of those on *The Consumerist*, who did not understand why anyone would vote for EA Games over Bank of America, they may in fact share much more in common with the gaming community than they realized.

References

Alberti, J. (2008). The game of reading and writing: How video games reframe our understanding of literacy. *Computers and Composition, 25*(3), 258–269.

Alex. (2012, March 16). Fan filing FTC complaints against EA after Mass Effect 3 ending. *GamePur.* Retrieved from http://www.gamepur.com/news/7426-fans-filing-ftc-complaints-against-ea-after-mass-effect-3-ending.html

Angello, A.J. (2012, March 21). Mass Effect of the people: BioWare makes new Mass Effect 3 ending. *Digital Trends.* Retrieved From http://www.digitaltrends.com/gaming/mass-effect-of-the-people-bioware-makes-new-mass-effect-3-ending/

Atghunter. (2012, Mar. 22). EA/BioWare in full PR damage control mode [pp. 6]. Message posted to http://social.bioware.com/forum/1/topic/355/index/10084349/6

Armstrong, J. (2012, March 22). Controversy erupts over Mass Effect 3 writer's forum post, name released. *PikiGeek.* Retrieved from https://web.archive.org/web/20120327045321/http://geek.pikimal.com/2012/03/22/controversy-erupts-over-mass-effect-3-writers-forum-post-name-release/

Benkler, Y. (2006). *The wealth of networks: how social production transforms markets and freedom.* New Haven: Yale UP.

Benkler, Y. and Nissenbaum, H. (2006). Commons-based peer production and virtue. *The journal of political philosophy, 14*(4), 394–419.

BioWare Team. (2011). *News archive: Mass Effect 2.* Retrieved from http://www.bioware.com/archive/mass-effect-2

BioWare Team. (2011, May 5). New Mass Effect 3 Screenshots and Release Date information. *News achive: Mass Effect 3.* Retrieved from http://www.bioware.com/archive/mass-effect-3

BioWare Team. (2011, June 9). Mass Effect 3 Earns Multiple E3 Nominations. *News archive: Mass Effect 3.* Retrieved from http://www.bioware.com/archive/mass-effect-3

Boyle, J. (2008). *The public domain, enclosing the commons of the mind.* Creative Commons and Yale UP. Retrieved from http://www.thepublicdomain.org/

Bui, T. (Interviewer) & Norman, C. (Interviewee) (2011, March 7). GDC 2011: Interview with Mass Effect 3 gameplay deigner Christina Norman. *Game Rant.* Retrieved from http://gamerant.com/mass-effect-3-interview-bioware-christina-norman-gdc-trung-71733/

Burke, B. (2011, Dec. 20). Innovation insight: Gamification adds fun and innovation to inspire engagement. *Gartner ID: G00226393.*

Burney, N. (2012, April 4). Prepare the Canons. *The Slow Down!* Retrieved from http://www.slowdown.vg/2012/03/04/prepare-the-canons/

Cain, M. W., Mann, J.M., Silver, M.A., Basso, M. (2012, Aug. 3). *Gartner ID G00226087.* Retrieved from http://my.gartner.com/portal/server.pt?open=512&objID=260&mode=2&PageID=3460702&resId=1732315&ref=QuickSearch&sthkw=%22video+games%22+2010.

Carter, C. (2012, Feb 17). It will cost you around $870 to get Mass Effect 3's DLC." Retrieved from http://www.destructoid.com/it-will-cost-you-around-870-to-get-mass-effect-3-s-dlc-222045.phtml

Colby, R.S. and Colby, R. (2008). A Pedagogy of play: Integrating computer games into the writing classroom. *Computers and Composition, 25*(3), 300–312.

Cross, T. (2012, Aug. 3). *Special Report: Video Games: All the World's a Game. The Economist.* Retrieved from http://www.economist.com/node/21541164

Darklarke. (2012, March 21). To Mass Effect 3 players, from Dr. Ray Muzyka, co-founder of BioWare. *BioWare Blog.* Retrieved from http://blog.bioware.com/2012/03/21/4108/

Davidson, C. (2012, Spring). Cyborg literacy aquisition through Second Life: Contesting "old" school spaces with vPortfolios. *Computers & Composition Online.* Retrieved from http://www2.bgsu.edu/departments/english/cconline/cconline_Sp_2012/cyborgliteracy/index.htm

dush. (2012, April 4). [6:48pm]. message posted to http://consumerist.com/2012/04/congratulations-ea-you-are-the-worst-company-in-america-for-2012.html

Foucault, M. (2007). What is an author? In D. H. Richter (Ed.), *The critical tradition: Classic texts and contemporary trends* (3rd ed., pp. 904–914). New York: Bedford/St Martin's.

Gartner Report. (2011, Nov. 28). *Predicts 2012: The Rising Force of Social Networking and Collaboration Services.* Stamford, CT: Gartner.

Gaudiosi, J. (2012, March 13). Exclusive: Mass Effect 3's director addresses the game's controversies (Updated!). *Digital Trends.* Retrieved from http://www.digitaltrends.com/gaming/exclusive-mass-effect-3s-director-addresses-the-games-controversies/

Gee, J.P. (2003). *What video games have to teach us about learning and literacy.* New York: Palgrave Macmillan.

IAmRodyle. (2012, March 9). Hitler finds out about Mass Effect 3's ending [Video file]. Retrieved from http://www.youtube.com/watch?v=b33tJx8iy0A&feature=player_embedded

Jackson, Z.A. (2002). Connecting video games and storytelling to teach narratives in first-year composition. *Kairos, 7*(3). Retrieved from http://kairos.technorhetoric.net/7.3/coverweb/jackson/index.htm

JGKojak. (2012, April 5). [10:40 AM]. Message posted to http://consumerist. com/2012/04/congratulations-ea-you-are-the-worst-company-in-america-for-2012.html

Kain, E. (2012, March 13). Mass Effect 3 and the pernicious myth of gamer "entitlement." *Forbes: Tech.* Retrieved from http://www.forbes.com/sites/ erikkain/2012/03/13/mass-effect-3-and-the-pernicious-myth-of-gamer-entitlement/

Kain, E. (2012, March 17). Former BioWare designer Brent Knowles on day-one DLC and the Mass Effect of public relations. *Forbes: Tech.* Retrieved from   http://www.forbes.com/sites/erikkain/2012/03/17/former-bioware-designer-brent-knowles-on-day-one-dlc-and-the-mass-effect-of-public-relations/

Kain, E. (2012, March 21). BioWare co-founder apologizes to fans for the Mass Effect 3 Ending—sort of. *Forbes: Tech.* Retrieved from http://www.forbes. com/sites/erikkain/2012/03/21/bioware-co-founder-apologizes-to-fans-for-the-mass-effect-3-ending-sort-of/

Kitchens, M.W. (2006, Spring). Student inquiry in new media: Critical media literacy and video games. *Kairos*, 10.2. Retrieved from http://kairos.tech-norhetoric.net/10.2/binder2.html?coverweb/kitchens/index.html

Latour, B. (1993). *We have never been modern.* (Catherine Porter, Trans.). Cambridge, MA: Harvard UP.

Latour, B. (1999). *Pandora's Hope.* Cambidge, MA: Harvard UP.

Latour, B. (2010). An attempt at a "compositionist manifesto." *New Literary History*, 41, pp. 474–490.

Lehdonvirta, V. (2010, April). Virtual worlds don't exist: questioning the dichotomous approach in MMO studies. *The International Journal of Computer Game Research*, *10.2.* Retrieved from http://gamestudies.org/1001/ articles/lehdonvirta

Mark11em. (2011, June 6). Mass Effect 3—Kinect implementation—Microsoft Press Conference E3 2011 [Video file}. Retrieved from http://www. youtube.com/watch?v=gesJDORzfoI

Mass Effect 3 ending reception. (2012, April). *Know Your Meme.* Retrieved from   http://knowyourmeme.com/memes/events/mass-effect-3-endings-reception

McKenny, C. (2008, Fall). Building the labyrinth: Adapting video game design concepts for writing course design. *Computers & Composition Online 2008.* Retrieved from http://www2.bgsu.edu/departments/english/cconline/gaming_issue_2008/McKenney_Building/

Metacritic. (2011). Mass Effect 2 PlayStation 3: User reviews. *Metacritic.* Retrieved from http://www.metacritic.com/game/playstation-3/mass-effect-2/ user-reviews

Metacritic. (2012). Mass Effect 3 PC: Summary. *Metacritic.* Retrieved from http://www.metacritic.com/game/pc/mass-effect-3

Mallory, J. (2012, March 24). Child's play shuts down fundraiser aimed at changing Mass Effect 3's ending. *Joystiq*. Retrieved from http://www. joystiq.com/2012/03/24/childs-play-shuts-down-fundraiser-to-change-mass-effect-3s-end/

Morran, C. (2012, April 4). The voters have spoken: EA is your worst company in America for 2012! *The Consumerist*. Retrieved from http://consumerist. com/2012/04/congratulations-ea-you-are-the-worst-company-in-america-for-2012.html

Paul, C.A. (2010). Process, paratexts, and texts: Rhetorical analysis and virtual worlds." *Journal of Virtual Worlds Research, 3*(1). Retrieved from http://journals.tdl.org/jvwr/article/viewArticle/804

Porter, J.E. (2010). Rhetoric in (as) a digital economy. In S.A. Selber (Ed.), *Rhetorics and technologies: New directions in writing and communication.* (pp. 173–97). Columbia, SC: U of South Carolina P.

Priestly, C. (2012, March 17). Casey Hudson on the conclusion of Mass Effect 3 [blog post]. *BioWare Social Network*. Retrieved from http://social.bioware. com/forum/1/topic/324/index/10089946

Remley, D. (2010, Spring). SecondLife literacies: critiquing writing technologies of SecondLife. *Computers & Composition Online*. Retrieved from http:// www2.bgsu.edu/departments/english/cconline/Remley/

Shirky, C. (2003, Feb. 8). Power laws, weblogs, and inequality. *Clay Shirky's writings about the internet: Economics & culture, media & community, open source.* Retrieved from http://www.shirky.com/writings/powerlaw_weblog. html

Smith, C. J. (2006). Body matters in massively multiplayer online role-playing games. *Reconstruction, 6*(1). Retrieved from http://reconstruction.eserver. org/issues/061/smith.shtml

Steinkuehler, C. (2007). Massive multiplayer online gaming as a constellation of literacy practices. *E-learning, 4.* 297–318. doi: 10.234/elea.2007.4.3.297.

Swalwell, M. (2006). Multi-player computer gaming: "Better than playing (pc games) with yourself." *Reconstruction, 6*(1). Retrieved from http://reconstruction.eserver.org/Issues/061/swalwell.shtml

Testerman, D. (2012, Mar 26). Mass Effect, Tolkien, and your bullshit artistic process. *Doyce Testerman: Perpetual projects and daily obsessions.* Retrieved from http://doycetesterman.com/index.php/2012/03/mass-effect-tolkein-and-your-bullshit-artistic-process/

Tycho. (2012, March 22). Child's play and "retake Mass Effect." *Penny Arcade.* Retrieved from: http://penny-arcade.com/2012/03/21/childs-play-and-retake-mass-effect

Wiley, Steve & Root-Wiley, Mark. (2007). Identification, please: Communication and control in an online learning environment. *Kairos: A Journal of Rhetoric, Technology, and Pedagogy, 11*(2). Retrieved from http://kairos. technorhetoric.net/11.2/binder.html?topoi/wiley/index.html

4 The Composing Practices and Rhetorical Acumen of MMORPG Players: What *City of Heroes* Means for Writing Instruction

Phill Alexander

A BRIEF INTERLUDE: PORTRAIT OF THE RESEARCHER AS A YOUNG NOOB

"Are you clicking?" Ryan asked me.

"Um . . . clicking?"

"The icons in your tray, are you clicking them?" He asked amid a quick flurry of text amid a series of attacks on a clutch of trolls.

"Yeah," I typed, then quickly clicked across a series of four attacks (click, click, click, click) as the digital brute dishing out damage lurched left and right, knocking trolls to the ground in response to my input.

"Just hit your number keys," Ryan said, still systematically dismantling the troll gang.

I made another pair of clumsy swings, staring intently at my screen and trying to figure out what he'd just told me. Then I saw them. Next to each icon on the tray there were tiny little numbers. Instead of clicking on an icon to launch a mace attack, for example, I could hit the corresponding number on my keyboard. Then another. I pulled off what I would call an impressive combination attack as I moved to meet Ryan in the middle of the battlefield.

"Didn't know about the numbers did you?" he asked, typing quickly amid attacks. "Noob."

It was my second week as a player/researcher in the NCSoft MMOR-PG (Massively Multiplayer Online Role Playing Game) *City of Heroes* (hereafter *CoH*). As a life-long gamer, I was able to leap in and hold my own, but as the exchange above illustrates, I didn't *really* know what I was doing. The *CoH* manual is sparse, and in classic gamer style I chose not to read it anyway. The tutorial stage at the beginning of the game showed me how to speak to other players, find teams, and take on tasks from the various NPC (non-player character) "contacts," but at no point did it mention that the attack icon control panel was pre-mapped to my number pad. In roughly thirty seconds, Ryan—the first interviewee in my research project—had transformed my gaming practices.

James Paul Gee (2003) would refer to the piece of information that Ryan gave me as shared game knowledge—dispersed by Ryan to a researcher who was, at the time, knocking on the door to his affinity group but didn't yet know the codeword. The exchange also brings to mind Johndan Johnson-Eilola's (1998) "Living on the Surface" that was written because of conversations Johnson-Eilola had with his eight-year-old daughter Carolyn. Johnson-Eilola utilized a transcript of a discussion he had with Carolyn about a game called *Per.Oxyd*. It contains a telling exchange (one that has deep implications for other video game scholarship):

> C: Yeah. But this is . . . this is just the first level. They're all different.
> J: Wow . . . So how do you figure out what the rules are?
> C: Just play.
> J: Just play? And then what happens?
> C: You just . . . play. (p. 187)

As Johnson-Eilola exhibited with the example, the method of thinking encouraged by video games ("just play") can appear to be random or even worrisome to someone familiar with linear, traditional learning. This method of learning—akin to foreign language immersion—values learning as a hands-on experience over previous memorization followed by the application of a set of rules. Gamers know the importance of immersion on an almost instinctive level, and a wanna-be gamer who insists on learning *about* the game before learning *within* the game will find gaming incredibly inorganic and infuriating. And while I was actually learning from Ryan, he himself discovered this method of attacking by "accidentally" hitting a number key and realizing that the attacks were mapped to the number keys (and that the key strokes resulted in faster responses than his mouse clicks).

Unlike students who are charged with academic work, gamers aren't keenly aware that they are engaging in the development and implementation of a literacy, but they devote a great deal of time, contemplation, and energy to their gaming practices just the same. In order to better understand the gaming literacy shaping many young adults' experiences and expectations for learning, I conducted a person-based study of *City of Heroes* gamers. Researching primarily through the game's interface itself and in the spaces where my study participants "expanded" the game (blogs, message boards, and other Web spaces), my primary goal was to find out exactly how the gamers themselves viewed the process of learning within the game, the development of skills to then play the game "better" (be that more efficiently, to better fit the character, or both), and developing their character narratives. In this chapter I explore how two gamers, Sarah (a thirty-something female) and Jared (a thirty-something male) develop their characters both within the *CoH* interface and through writing they do in other places.

PLAYING WITH LITERACY ONLINE

It is important to create a working definition for the word *literacy* in this instance. Scholars must be ever-cautious of the pitfalls the word implies; if placed in a binary, the opposite is "illiteracy," a term that carries a great deal of emotional baggage for many, particularly those caught in the various "wars on illiteracy." Stuart Selber (2004) claims that literacy is "not a monolithic or static phenomenon with predictable consequences," hinting that scholars must avoid the desire to convert literacy into something concrete (p. 4). For my purposes, I am referring to literacy not simply as the ability to "read" a game but rather as careful, critical reading, composing, and interacting. As Gee (2003) wrote, "when you read [think], you are always reading [thinking about] something in some way. You are never just reading 'in general' but not reading anything in particular" (p. 1). And as Elizabeth Tebeaux (1996) asserts, "Literacy is no longer just the ability to read and write, but the ability to grasp intellectually and then link concepts, to turn data into information and information into knowledge that can be communicated in a variety of textual forms" (p. 40). In that spirit I approach gaming literacy as the learning and practicing of everything a gamer must *do* in order to "play" the game in question.

In *Multiliteracies for a Digital Age*, Selber (2004) asserts that there are three computer literacies: functional, critical, and rhetorical. Paralleling Selber's triad, I believe there are three types of online gaming literacy that I identify and describe below (see Figures 1 and 2).

Category	Metaphor	Subject position	Objective
Functional literacy	Computers as tools	Students as users of technology	Effective employment
Critical literacy	Computers as cultural artifacts	Students as questioners of technology	Informed critique
Rhetorical literacy	Computers as hypertextual media	Students as producers of technology	Reflective praxis

Figure 1. Selber's (2004) Conceptual Landscape of Computer Multiliteracies (p. 25)

Category	Metaphor	Subject Position	Objective
Mechanical Literacy	Video game as rule set	Gamer as educated player	Mastery of interface
Character Literacy	"Masked player" as element of game	Gamer as protagonist/ hero	Understanding as player's in game environment
Social/Interaction Literacy	Character as part of collaborative community	Gamer as member of larger gaming culture	Membership in a complex discourse community

Figure 2. Concept Map of Online Gaming Literacies

While I could have borrowed Selber's "functional," I prefer to refer to the first gaming literacy as *mechanical*. I make this distinction because Selber's term "functional" indicates that the user is capable of doing work with the computer, but in the case of mechanical online gaming literacy one can function as an end user, but one cannot yet truly *play* the game. Mechanical literacy is understanding the game's interface, menu systems, and other strictly technical/mechanical issues so that the player gains *agency* in the gaming world. Mechanical literacy allows the gamer to interface with the game and use the input device(s) to accomplish basic in-game tasks. Ryan was helping me to attain mechanical literacy by assisting me in refining my method of input. I already knew one way to launch an in-game attack, but my "point and click" method wasn't an efficient, or the most common, way of engaging in combat and thus it appeared "clumsy" to other players. The knowledge that the keypad was pre-mapped to the attack icons made a dramatic change in the speed with which I could attack while in battle, making me a more proficient player.

I refer to the second form of gaming literacy as *character* literacy. Character literacy is learning/knowing one's own in-game strengths and weaknesses, understanding ones in-game character, and attaining some level of mastery over that character in order to successfully "play" *as* the in-game character. This literacy, at least initially, is developed while the gamer gains mechanical literacy, but it is recursive. With each new character the gamer must return to a previous stage of character development and once again recall character literacy.

The final form of gaming literacy I am developing is *social/interaction* literacy. Richard Smith and Pamela Curtain (1998) suggest that video gamers form "symbolic communities" (p. 214), noting that video games and the communities that their players form spawn jargon, styles, and attitudes. Because MMOPRGs are nearly impossible to play alone, the final stage of understanding comes through knowing both how to interact and what the social norms are for the gaming world or "symbolic community." In *City of Heroes*, all of the heroes live in Paragon City, a virtual cityscape that grows with each of the game's regular updates or "expansions." Within Paragon City, heroes have different home neighborhoods, though, and spend significant amounts of time campaigning in specific areas. Beyond the level of city and neighborhood, there are also eleven servers, each with a distinct social reality, and a whole host of supergroups (SG)–or "clans" or "guilds" as they are also known—or teams on each server. Players must learn to navigate these various social networks, knowing at first the bedrock principles of life in Paragon City, then learning about the culture of the specific server one is playing on, then the neighborhood, the social role of the type of character chosen, and finally the personality make-up and discourse patterns of the super-group or team with which the player is campaigning.

In reality, almost every game involves these three literacies to one degree or another. To successfully play soccer, for example, the player must know that one cannot grab the soccer ball and run with it or that one will not score points if the ball is shot into the incorrect goal. That is *mechanical* literacy. In soccer, *character* literacy would involve learning to play a specific position and learning that one has strengths and weaknesses within the game. For example, if the player was assigned to play goalie, one gains the right to physically "handle" the ball frequently, but unlike all the other players, that would mean that the goalie must stay positioned in front of the goal itself, inside a box, essentially tethered to the goal. Instead of scoring, the goalie's job is to stop other players from scoring. In choosing or being assigned the position of goalie, the player takes on special duties that are critical to the success of the other players on his or her team. The realization of how those duties and rights involve other players is the soccer version of *social/interaction* literacy. A player must understand where he or she is being sent as the goalie and what the goalie does, but he/she must also know how to communicate and work with the other players in order to actually be "playing" soccer.

In my example above, Ryan was "teaching" me a bit of mechanical literacy, but he was teaching it through the use of social/interaction literacy. Because a game like *City of Heroes* involves so much of what Gee (2003) calls "probing" the environment, players are frequently learning new bits of mechanical literacy as they play. For example, during one of my interview sessions my computer crashed. When I rebooted and logged back into the server, I found that I'd lost several lines of interview text. My interviewee had been playing *CoH* for years, but she didn't know the command to copy the chat log and paste it into an outside application. She learned that from me, and in the process she helped me recover that missing portion of our interview.

CHARACTER LITERACY: "I HOPE YOU DON'T GET ATTACHED TO THAT FIRST TOON . . ."

Character literacy in the case of a game like *City of Heroes* is present in every aspect of "playing." One must develop a character—or toon, as gamers call them—the first time he or she logs into *City of Heroes*. As one of my interviewees said "I hope you didn't get *attached* to that first toon . . . once you learn to play, you have to go back and create one that *fits* you."[1] The process of creating a toon is involved and engaging. One of my participants claimed that the character design process of *City of Heroes* could be a game all by itself. Sarah, an enthusiastic thirty-something female gamer, has many characters, including Hugs, a member of a supergroup called The St. Joseph's School (a group modeled after a private Catholic high school with a passing resemblance to the Xavier Institute of the famed *X-Men* comics, cartoons, toys, and movies). Hugs is involved in the St. Joseph's "student council"—doing work outside the game interface—and she has a secondary outfit that conforms to the school's highly specific dress code (a virtual school uniform). Sarah describes her experience learning the St. Joseph's School character development expectations:

Sarah: I made pretty costumes, decided what looked fun to play and went for it. Well, I never considered character design at all until I got into this supergroup and I HAD to.

Phill: Did it feel at all like a writing assignment? Like hero homework?

Sarah laughs suddenly[2]

Sarah: Oh, you have no idea! I was standing in Atlas [Park—a character meeting place], minding my own business when Miranda [supergroup leader] charged up, gave me the once over and said "Nice boots! Now write me a bio!" . . . Grin. Mimi doesn't much care for public opinion I guess. She can be kind of autocratic. She is very passionate about RPing and characters and writing stories. She really wants to build a world for people here.

In this explanation of how Sarah's character Hugs[3] came to be part of the St. Joseph's School, she explains both the writing she had to do and the importance of her character's appearance. She gave specific consideration to utilizing a power called "ice armor," not because it was particularly useful but because it "looks like Hugs is covered in big, shimmering diamonds" and adds a layer of individuality to a character that is wearing a "school uniform."

The creation process, then, becomes a moment where the player must balance three motivations. One must first know what one can do/wishes to do as a player, one must know the story one wants to tell with the character, and the player must know how well he or she will be able to play the character from a mechanical literacy perspective, as each type of character calls for a different style of play with different powers and different modes of input. A character created without careful attention—and even those with considerable thought—will be taken to task by other players and could ultimately fail.

After my experience with Ryan (where without realizing it I dove head-first into hardcore role-playing with a character I set up as a former bouncer who was created to smash things, which was well outside of any culture I understood) I decided to create a new character for my interview with Sarah. I wanted to play on some existing mythology, so I created a teenage hero called Anguta, an Alaskan nerd-turned-hero who claimed to be the shepherd of the dead. I wrote a bio for him (I consider this writing, though gamers would refer to it as part of playing the game). When it came time to design him, I wanted to incorporate both elements that would make him seem "contemporary" but at the same time bring to mind something "ghostly." He ended up in baggy cargo pants with a sleek leather padded top and a stylized skull mask (see figure 3).

I carefully considered how the character should "act tough" while simultaneously having no idea how to handle being in "the big city" and how I would slowly reveal his status as a naïve teenager by crafting a narrative where his youthful side bled through his carefully crafted appearance.[4] His "powers" are based on distance attacks, but I equipped him with an ice sword so that he could "act" the role of a "warrior" and engage in close quarters combat. I did some brief research on "goth" culture to get a sense of what this sort of character would be interested in, and I set his powers to be a mix of energy blasts and weapons made from ice to reflect both the supernatural and his ties to his cold native Alaskan climate.

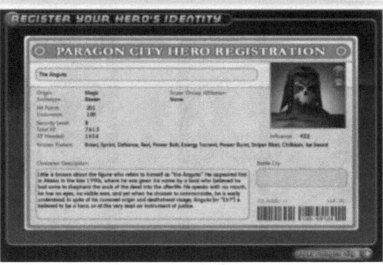

Figure 3. Anguta.

Anguta is not nearly as complicated as many of my research participant's toons. It still took nearly an hour just to create him and move him into the game world. Others have professed to spending as many as three hours perfecting a toon's visual design before moving on to establishing powers for the character or a biography. Active players also talk about modifying their toon's look to match up to how the character is evolving through game play. The game has built-in stages where players can add a second, third, and fourth costume[5] and many players utilize these benchmarks as points where they change their toon's look to better match the character's persona. One of my participants role plays a character who wears a suit of mechanical armor like Marvel's famous *Iron Man*. He would often refer to opportunities to "tweak his armor" when adding new powers or changing appearance, using changes in his costume and the abilities that he could anchor to the costume as an extension of his character's story.

Once Anguta was prepared and I met up with Sarah's character, our initial interview started on an interesting note:

Sarah: Zo. Tell me about yourself Anguta.

Phill: I'm just a guy who plans to do big things. I come from a much smaller area than this . . .

[at this point I had to pause to kill a robot]

Phill: Used to be able to get by on the menacing look and the ice sword.

Sarah: I think we all plan for big things! I think I just plan to live through this warehouse . . . Paragon, she is a much bigger place . . .

[more robot killing]

Sarah: You make my heart hurt! Ouch, Ang! Whyfore did you charge them? They were BIGGER than us!

Whereas when I met up with Ryan we had a few moments of casual chat before he asked if I was comfortable role-playing, Sarah approached me from the onset *in character*. While there was no direct implication that were I not to role play I would be branded "outsider," our interview didn't start with Sarah talking to me; it started with *Sarah's character talking to Anguta*, with the two of us as interviewer and interviewee virtually invisible. As is also evident in the above excerpt, Sarah was trying to project a French accent. She maintained that—and maintained her character meticulously—until we both code switched when I said "((Okay to break character?))."[6] Sarah actually responded:

Sarah: ((I think so. for one thing, my grasp of her[Sarah's character] is not well centered yet. I don't know who she is! . . . she is still in malleable frosh stage, and I'd hate to mess you up further as I waffle amongst responses))

Sarah's response here is telling. As a gamer, she treated me as a fellow gamer instead of as an academic who was "watching" her play. She was concerned that her unsteady understanding of her own new toon would "mess [me] up," as a role-player since I, too, was establishing a character. I learned through playing Anguta—and talking to Sarah about him— that he simply looked too "evil" for many players to accept him as a hero. While mainstream popular culture may have embraced the anti-hero, the *City of Heroes* discourse community has different standards for what is or is not "heroic." Anguta was essentially a failure, in spite of all my efforts and other player's attempts to help me make him work.

Sarah's stance on character creation reflects the sort of character literacy that helps one to avoid the mistakes I made with Anguta:

Sarah: Hmm. Well, there is the proper way and then there is my way. To be honest, I start with the costume. Then I figure out a name that seems to fit. Then I start thinking about a back story that works with both. I start with the look, most certainly. [I draw inspiration] from books of course, and from talking to others in the SG that are inspirations in themselves. Some of the stories people come up with are just fantastic. It makes you reach for something a little deeper than you might normally go for.

Sarah's character creation practices are consistent—or at least compatible—with most of the other participants in my study. While the priority between appearance and story shifts from gamer to gamer (and for some from toon concept to toon concept), the same basic considerations arise. Players draw from the popular culture around them (particularly movies and comic books), from classic literature and from their fellow teammates/super-group members when developing new characters. Ryan, for example, had a character who had to be of a certain "type" (a "blaster" who uses a bow and arrow) because his supergroup was a guild of archers. In the case of Sarah's characters, the unifying element for each was that they were all designed to be students at the St. Joseph's School (her supergroup).

Of the particular character she chose for our gaming session, Sarah said:

So far, I know that [this character] comes from a French Canadian background and travels with a circus with her family. Due to her power manifestation and the unfortunate destruction of the big top one night, she's been enrolled in St. Joes [the super hero high school supergroup] for her family's sanity. She was a high wire artist, or starting to be one. Mostly one of those girls that spins on the rope and things like that. She was studying to be trapeze though before her fire skills decided to manifest.

Sarah's French Canadian, former circus-performing toon was visually interesting. She looked like a mime, but instead of hair she had violet leaves (sort of like a fern) on the top of her head. The character's powers and accent bear a passing resemblance to the X-man Gambit, but the premise also draws heavily from Robin, the famous Batman sidekick. Sarah also mentioned during the interview that of late she'd been fascinated with Cirque Du Soleil. All of these elements mix in the French accent, the mutant energy blast power, the role of young hero, and the circus performer back story. The finishing touches that make the toon unique come from Sarah, and as she professed, the fashioning of that aspect of the character—the glue that holds the visuals and the biographical bits together—was incomplete at the time of our interactions.

SOCIAL/INTERACTION LITERACY: BUILDING PARAGON CITY, BRICK BY ROLE PLAY BRICK

Sarah's character literacy bleeds heavily into her social/interaction literacy. As you can see above, she takes great pains to maintain her character, even lamenting that she feared she was damaging the character—and my gaming experience—by reacting at times without *thinking like the character*. She also posts to the message board at SuperHighSchool.com in character, expanding her character's story outside of the game itself, or as she and other players would say "taking the game somewhere else." In those posts she fleshes out her character's back story in ways that one simply couldn't within the game (through writing essays, diary entries, re-telling the story of a battle from her point of view, etc.). (see Figure 4)

Figure 4: A screen capture of one of Sarah's posts written in character on the St. Joseph's School's message board and the St. Joseph's School uniform template

Like Sarah, the majority of Heroes in the *CoH* community are "role players," who role play to varying degrees from the casual player, slipping from behaving in character to simply talking to another player or making jokes as a form of meta-discourse at will, to the hardcore role player who will actually make in-character comments to those who break role-play conventions essentially "policing" through treating the "real" comments (out of character) as the "imaginary" or "ridiculous" within the role play construct. For those that are hardcore role players, it is important that other players in their groups and on their teams stay in character. More importantly, it matters that other players *know* their characters and behave *as their characters would* in the online community. During my early sessions in the game, I found that when I was in a large group with an interviewee and someone asked me a question, any answer from Phill was singled out. Each of the characters I created during the process of my research have at least one unique quirk, and other players could sense when I slid out of character by abandoning those elements. People wanted to hear from my character, and they were perceptive enough to know which of us was speaking in a given situation. For example, Anguta rarely knows what he's doing (he frequently asks questions and acts tentative; he is, after all, in over his head). In one case, Anguta was in a small group that rushed into a task and got lost on the mission map. I took the lead because I (Phill) knew the area. Anguta had already professed to being unfamiliar with the area and the mission, so when I took the lead, one of the other players pointed out to me, via private message, that I (Anguta) shouldn't know what to do next. It turns out he or she, too, knew the mission and the map from playing with another character. Using that knowledge, however, violates character literacy. Anguta (the toon) didn't know the map, so while I (Phill, the player) knew it, that knowledge was socially "off limits."

The importance of the role play tradition was a key factor in my discussions with Jared, another avid role player. Jared maintains a MySpace blog for his character Kitten (see figure 5). Though Jared is a thirty-something, married professional, Kitten is a sixteen-year-old hero, and she takes things like her MySpace page seriously. Jared's ability to maintain a character that is so different from his own persona illustrates the level of critical thought and rhetorical consideration *City of Heroes* players devote to their toons.

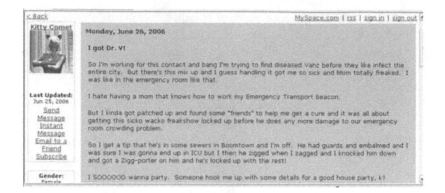

Figure 5. A screen capture of Jared's Kitten MySpace page.

The first time I talked to Jared, he was posting in character on a super-group message board. While scheduling an interview session, he mentioned that he and his wife had a "standing" gaming date every Monday night wherein they sit at their respective computers and role play (speaking to each other in the room out of character but never breaking character on screen). In addition to being an avid gamer, Jared also teaches computer programming and has created his own levels and other content for games such as *Neverwinter Nights* and *Maximum Force*. He approaches his toons as characters he will write for both in the game and on supergroup message boards:

> . . . I think about what kind of character might be interesting to do [write]. My highest [level] character came from the idea of "what if my hero was indeed a fallen arc[h]angel and didn't know it?" So from there I built her up as a storm defender, an angel of vengeance "trapped" in the body of a pious woman . . . made for fun playing as the "demon" (as she thought it) started to exert itself over her more and more . . . I was lucky enough to be in a good Role Play SG at the time, so I was able to develop her slowly with other people.

It was apparent during our conversations that Jared was devoted to carefully and creatively role-playing his characters. During exchanges like the one that resulted in the long quote above, he responded quickly and was more than willing to volunteer details. The character he describes, which sadly I wasn't able to observe because he's since lost that account, shows the level of complexity he puts into each of his designs. It is also telling that Jared approaches his character from the point of view of what sort of character would be fun to write about/play (the exact word he used in the sentence was "do," and when I asked him to clarify, he said "write role-plays for and stuff").

Jared is also careful to maintain his character—not just in the game and while role-playing on other boards, but also when confronted by players who refuse to role-play:

> In a group that's mixed of RPer's and "gamers" I just RP, and if I have to put nearly every comment in (())'s I do . . . I don't often enter the city unless I know what kind of person my character is . . . [role-playing] is getting harder to do in some games. [In] DDO [Dungeons and Dragons Online] it's nearly impossible, but I'm an actor at heart.

The quotation above not only shares Jared's thoughts but shows what conversations within the community start to look like when the player becomes an "insider." I didn't realize just now bizarre it read until I showed the quote to someone else and had to translate, as I developed deep *CoH* literacy while researching. I knew what it meant for his text to appear in the meta-comment double parentheses, and it wasn't at all odd for him to refer to playing the game as "entering the city" because role-players wouldn't say "logged into the game;" that isn't what their toons are doing. What Jared is saying is that if he ends up on a team that is a mix of players who role-play and those who break character, he maintains his role-playing persona (and doesn't break character), using the accepted *CoH* social code of meta-commenting (surrounding a statement in double parentheses to indicate that he is speaking out-of-character).

While I would separate the "Kitten" MySpace blog from *the City of Heroes* game, Jared would not. His view is indicative of the community in general:

Phil: Would you consider that—the blog—a part of the game experience?

Jared: Yeah . . . usually once I get active in a supergroup they have an in-character board I post on as my character, and it's a way to flesh the game out a little, give you a way to play on your lunch hour or when you don't have time for a mission.

Phil: So would you consider that playing or writing?

Jared: I consider it part of the overall role-playing game . . . writing itself is a game.

Jared's opinion of game-related writing strikes me in many ways as the critical disconnect between gamers and those who consider gaming to be "a waste of time." Gamers who consider role-playing and writing in other spaces to be a part of their gaming experience, that create characters and vivid back stories or that create instructional or social websites, are doing a great deal of what some would consider "work" as part of the practice of gaming.

Jared's reflections on the way he plays illustrates the importance of social/interaction literacy. Jared's characters, like Kitty Comet, are forged through a process that shows his understanding of character literacy, but he then practices social/interaction literacy with an unwavering devotion to the social nature of the game. He takes this so far as to follow the meta-commentary conventions even when most of the rest of his team abandon the convention.[7] He also described creating characters that depended upon the actions of others, such as the archangel character. This character eventually became a "guardian angel" that Jared role-played as a sort of "neighborhood defender." She took new toons under her wing and served as a leader of sorts for a ragtag supergroup.

GAME OVER? IMPLICATIONS FOR COMPOSITION PEDAGOGY

At Miami University, we ask our students to begin the second semester of first year composition by creating an "inventory" of their reading and writing habits. The first time I assigned this activity, two students told me, "Phill . . . um . . . we don't . . . um . . . read." I asked "so what do you do in your free time?" These two—who lived across the hall from each other in the dorms—were "obsessed" with *Halo 2*, an FPS (first person shooter) and war game. They had a clan, and their clan had a webpage with forums where they shared strategies, planned battles, etc. One of them also spent hours playing a game called *Elder Scrolls III: Morrowind*, an RPG (role-playing game) that requires the same sort of character creation and "in character" play present in *City of Heroes*. The other played *Madden* football regularly and maintained "virtual" franchise web pages that tracked the progress of his team throughout the season(s) he played. Both talked of hours of playing, hours of reading message boards, and all the reading activities that went into finding solutions to their gaming problems. In five minutes of banter these two young men who claimed to "not read" described their roles as highly literate participants in a set of gamer discourse communities.

As scholars of composition, we have much to learn from the way gamers interact and what they *claim* is gaming. From the careful rhetorical positioning of their characters to the ways they interact with other players within the game space (and in other spaces where the game extends beyond its perceived borders) they are utilizing the critical thinking and rhetorical awareness that some claim video games, television, and popular culture hinder. As Cindy Selfe, Anne Mareck, and Josh Gardner (2007) recently asserted, "Young people . . . and the adults in their worlds do not necessarily share a common understanding of and appreciation for gaming as literacy." Later in the same piece Selfe, Marcck, and Gardner argued: "Perhaps in our well-intended concern for our youth, we have been inclined to overlook or dismiss the positive, exciting, socially transformative developments in computer gaming—or the skillful, tactical agency that young people, themselves, can enact (n.p.)."

While many of the gamers I met while researching/playing *City of Heroes* were twenty- or thirty-somethings, all of them "grew up" as gamers. For most of them, games are equated with television, comic books, and movies with an added interactive element. Traditionalists with a deep reverence for the canon might dispute the belief that games are "literature," but understanding how *gamers* view games opens an interesting new avenue for academia. Many of them don't use the language scholars use, but gamers consider games to be multi-modal texts and cultural artifacts. Further understanding of the games leads to further understanding of the gamers themselves. And further understanding of gaming cultures will reveal ways that Sarah and Jared can apply their extra-gaming practices to other textual or multi-modal composing.

Sarah is part of a virtual student council, coordinating school events and helping with "new student orientation" in a world that exists only because she and the other "students" at St. Joseph's School have written it. Kitten has both "virtual" and "real" friends who visit her MySpace page because Jared has composed a life for Kitten that extends beyond the game itself. Gamers consider writing several pages of coherent, themed text to be "playing." Knowing that, it's difficult to see how video games could be treated as anything other than a blessing for composition and rhetoric scholars. We ask our students to learn to read critically, to learn to address the world from multiple perspectives in multiple modes, and we fear that our students will lack technical proficiency—and comfort—when placed in front of a computer. Through their pre-existing gaming practices, gamers are utilizing computer literacies, rhetorical analysis, and composition skills in their free time. And they *enjoy* it; some spend massive amounts of money for the technology and games just so they can continue to contribute to these communities by playing.

At this point it is unclear exactly what impact bringing video games into the composition classroom might have, but each of the following seems to be a logical progression from what students are already doing as gamers:

1. *Video games could easily be used as a front door to computer literacy.* Students who are intimidated by the prospects of using a computer could benefit greatly from the "jump in and play around" concept that defines the video game as a genre. While asking a student to create a video in *Macromedia's Flash* might be intimidating on the first day of class, it seems reasonable to assume that students—due to previous experiences—would be willing to jump into a video game. An instructor could then design a course where students begin the semester by playing *City of Heroes*, discussing what it would mean to create a hero then jumping in and creating the character and navigating Paragon City. The mentality, and the skills developed through "prodding" the game environment and using the character creation tool and gaming interface can then be transferred to software like *Flash* or *Adobe Photoshop*. Once the students have latched onto that bedrock concept of "you can't really break it, so play around," learning new software is less intimidating and more enjoyable.

2. *Gamers can use their pre-existing extra-gaming reading and writing to better understand the Internet as a collection of discourse communities.* Even students who aren't gamers are highly likely to have encountered online chat interfaces like those used in games, and they may have extensive experience blogging, writing on message boards, or creating their own Web-based projects. All of these practices are modeled by gamers, making a gaming community an ideal model of online recreational writing. If composition instructors can stress that these casual gaming acts are composition, it will make students aware of skills they already have and open the door to "new" composition practices by re-classifying something students do for fun as something they will use academically and professionally.

3. *Avid gamers can be pulled into careful consideration of complex top-*
    ics by being introduced to them through games. A game like *City of*
    Heroes can be used as a sort of social life simulator. While it takes
    effort on the part of a player, a toon could "turn to the dark side,"
    as one of my participants referred to the process, and become a
    villain, leaping from *City of Heroes* to *City of Villains*. Players can
    form social cliques and can make conscious choices to enforce a
    specific moral code. There is, however, a layer of separation with-
    in the game similar to what many scholars have noticed in online
    discussion forums. If gamers cannot see the person on the other
    side of the exchange, there is freedom to take risks one might not
    take in a face-to-face encounter. Used for academic purposes, a
    teacher could construct discussions on race, the concepts of law,
    morality, or practically any social issue by inciting an incident in
    the gaming world, asking students to react/interact, then discuss-
    ing the events either within the game or outside "in real life."
    With a game like *City of Heroes*, there's the added element of the
    superhero genre and its tendency to grapple with issues of moral-
    ity due to the inherent nature of what heroes "do."

4. *Students can experience multi-modality through gaming and under-*
    standing gaming practices. Games themselves are like videos, with
    soundtracks and in some cases voice acting or actual vocal inter-
    action. Most games still utilize text as well. More importantly
    the blogs, message boards, and supergroup pages that players
    create include sound, images, text, and animation. Students are
    already working in the age of digital multi-modality; they just
    don't *call* it what we call it. If students were given access to some
    of these existing fansites as models, instructors could ask them
    to compose multi-modal texts about their gaming experiences or
    other hobbies. If students were to use other gamers as resources,
    they would discover that these practices that they might view as
    homework are actually a part of regular game play.

5. *Students can be inspired to experiment with their writing through*
    writing documents to accompany their gaming. Those biographical
    entries and role plays from *City of Heroes* are often long, complex
    documents. Players create them without a groan, without a sigh,
    and they relish the chance to receive feedback from others so that
    they can revise. That same passion can be harnessed in the class-

room by bringing in the things that students love. Students could rhetorically analyze games, create characters, or even design their own games as assignments in the composition classroom. These documents also exist largely outside the bounds of defined academic genres; because there is no standard way to compose a character biography or to role-play, students have the freedom to experiment without believing there is an "expected" outcome.

6. *Students can learn to compose biographical and ethnographical texts through their video game characters.* Current first year "autobiographical" or "autoethnographical" writing often faces two major pitfalls: students are hesitant to see and, specifically, to label, themselves as "different," and students are often uncomfortable sharing secrets they consider intimate or simply have no experience turning the lens on themselves as they write. Going through the process of creating and playing a toon in City of Heroes (or a character in any of a number of other MMORPGs) and then writing a rich, engaging biography for the character would allow students to learn how to work with biographical and ethnographical genres without the "risks" they feel when trying to reflect on their own identities. Students are also less likely to make assumptions about what the audience does or does not know when writing about a character, as the students are in the process of learning everything about their characters for the first time instead of attempting to summarize their own lives.

Video games currently occupy an interesting position in American society. The video gaming marketplace accounts for nearly \$100 billion, [8] with the target demographic centered on children and college-age young adults. Every year more students arrive on college campuses with personal computers, laptops, Xboxes, Playstations and Nintendos. They play games to relax, to spend time with friends, and to experience popular culture. They have mechanical, character, and social/interaction gaming literacies, even if they don't realize they are utilizing critical thinking skills, rhetorical strategies, and composing well-crafted texts as a part of their hobby. They're constantly networking with new people, composing rich multi-modal texts that most academics may never see. There are thousands of Kitty Comets, thousands of toons like Hugs, and sitting behind keyboards there are thousands of Sarahs and Jareds practicing literacies that have gone largely ignored for decades.

At the end of their days, many of our students trek back to their dorm rooms to play games. Whether we embrace or alienate video games as a potential academic genre, they continue to thrive as one of the most popular hobbies among students. And while our students are playing, they will use some variation of all the skills we hope to teach them in first year composition. We should be playing with them. They should be playing with us. We should all be using video games as the complex social and intellectual environment that the gamers of *City of Heroes* do. We should experiment. We should try new things in our composition classrooms, knowing that if they don't go exactly as we hoped they would we can still continue the game. I guess what I'm trying to say is that it wouldn't hurt us to stop occasionally to destroy a few robots if it opens the door to new understanding.

NOTES

1. This quote came from Mike, a participant that doesn't appear elsewhere in this chapter.

2. Any time an action appears within one of the quotes from my interviews, they indicate in game "emotes" by the interviewee's player character (or my own character, if it's Phill committing the action). While the characters literally act out these emotes on-screen, a textual note of what the player has done on-screen appears in the chat. So while Sarah's character engaged in a belly laugh on screen at this point in the interview, the textual label for her laugh appears in the transcript as well.

3. Sarah's character's name is not actually "Hugs," but due to the highly personal nature of online identities, I've given my interviewee's toons pseudonyms, too.

4. Readers familiar with Spiderman will realize that this was a case of hero emulation on my part. I grew up with Spiderman, but I didn't realize as I was crafting my character that I had lifted that aspect of Peter Parker's personality for my own use.

5. The most important costume to most toons is the second, as it comes at the end of a "trial" that results in the player having access to capes. The cape is a point of pride for players; it proves that one has the staying power to get to level 20 and complete the difficult trial. During my research I managed to take two toons on the cape trial, and each was showered in congratulations from other players upon arrival in the public square with his cape flapping in the wind.

6. Any time a player wants to break character his or her dialogue must appear within two sets of parenthesis ((like this))—I refer to these comments as "meta-dialogue."

7. Jared and I spent a portion of our first interaction in a group of eight "leveling" on a sewer map that exists only for characters to rapidly kill enemies so as to raise their levels. Of the eight members of the team, only he and I remained in character, but he still separated his in-character and out-of-character comments. I did, as well, out of respect for Jared's devotion to the social norms even when we were in a group that obviously didn't share his feelings.

8. See http://www.gartner.com/newsroom/id/2614915

REFERENCES

Gee, J. (2003). *What video games have to teach us about learning and literacy.* New York: Palgrave.

Johnson-Eilola, J. (1998). Living on the surface: Learning in the age of global communication networks. In Ilana Snyder (Ed.), *Page to screen: Taking literacy into the electronic era* (pp. 185–209). London: Routledge.

Selber, S. (2004). *Multiliteracies for a digital age.* Carbondale: Southern Illinois UP.

Selfe, C. L., Mareck, A. F., & Gardiner, J. (2007). "Computer Gaming as Literacy." In Cindy Selfe &Gail Hawisher (Eds.), *Gaming Lives in the 21st Century: Literate Connections* (pp. 21–35). New York: Palgrave Macmillan

Smith, R. & Curtin, P. (1998). Children, computers and life online: Education in a cyber world. In Ilana Snyder (Ed.), *Page to screen: Taking literacy into the electronic era* (pp. 211–233). London: Routledge.

Tebeaux, E. (1996). Nonacademic writing into the 21st century: Achieving and sustaining relevance in research and curricula. In Ann Hill Duin & Craig Hansen (Eds.), *Nonacademic writing: Social theory and technology* (pp. 35–55). Mahwah: Lawrence Erlbaum.

5 Procedurality as Play: Movement in Games and Composition

Grace Hagood

In the foundational composition studies text, *Composition-Rhetoric*, Robert Connors (1997) succinctly identifies the promise of the writing process movement to emphasize "becoming over being, process over product, and thus continuing experience over final judgment" (p. 67).[1] However, despite the best intentions of process theory enthusiasts, the pedagogical practices associated with the movement quickly became concretized. As early as 1994, Lad Tobin noted that "the writing process has become an entity, even an industry, with a life of its own, certainly a life apart from its first theorists" (p. 8).

As writing process theory has arguably developed from an open system of invention to a calcified set of practices, academics have looked for less systematized models of composition to explore. From Geoffrey Sirc's (2002) use of avant-garde art practices for composition, to Alex Reid's (2007) theorization of composition and the virtual spaces of philosophy and networked media, scholars are engaging new avenues for writing pedagogy. Games are one such avenue, and a popular one at that, as evidenced by the abundance of books and articles published over the past few years such as: Jonathan Alexander's 2009 *College Composition and Communication* article, "Gaming, Student Literacies, and the Composition Classroom: Some Possibilities for Transformation," which tantalizes readers by touting games as "juicier thinking about *literacy*" (p. 53); and Rebekah Shultz Colby's 2012 article in *Computers and Composition Online*, "Gender and Games in a First-Year Writing Classroom," which theorizes digital and academic literacies through six case studies of female *World of Warcraft* players.

In the past fifteen years, scholars have approached the study of digital games through a wide variety of lenses, from the application of cultural studies in Mary Flanagan's (2009) *Critical Play* to the extrapolation of pedagogical practices from games in James Paul Gee's (2003) *What Video Games Have to Teach Us About Learning and Literacy*. However, since the publication of Ian Bogost's *Persuasive Games* in 2007, rhetorical criticism of games has been dominated by a focus on procedurality, or how the rhetorical and computational structures of games create procedures through which meaning is made. Bogost takes particular care in *Persuasive Games* to show how computation functions as the representational medium of games and how procedurality produces expression through representation—a model that composition scholars may find familiar if we consider language our representational medium and writing processes as the means of expression.

Bogost (2007) is quick to point out that procedurality is not limited to computation; procedural structures can be found in "literature, art, film, and daily life" (p. 5). Further, he notes that procedures both limit and allow action, are not necessarily linear, and can hold unexpected consequences in the meaning-making process. However, the popularity of procedural rhetoric may be leading to a use of procedurality as a reductive, concretized method of game design rather than as a way of viewing games in terms of the full range of possibilities enabled and precluded by their structures. As such, procedural rhetoric may be facing a characterization similar to that which writing process theory faced in the 1990s: a potentially useful but restrictive heuristic that often limits the inventive power it intends to support.

In this moment when games seem to offer a fruitful new way to consider composition, the current deployment of procedurality risks undermining these exciting possibilities. Just as the classroom use of writing process theory attempted to account for every step of the meaning-making process—despite the fact that composition is much messier than such a model would posit—the use of procedural rhetoric seems to be poised for a similarly reductive path. All too often, procedurality is linked solely to computational processes, as Miguel Sicart (2011) argues in "Against Procedurality," and this limited view of procedure risks excludes the unpredictable multitude of choices that a player brings to bear upon the structures of games. If games are to serve as a useful model for traditional print composition, we should reconsider how procedure functions in relation to play and purpose.

Rather than exploring invention in games and composition via their procedural nature, I suggest that the inventive power of games lies in movement. Such movement can be seen in the oscillation between free-play and procedural structures, or to use Roger Caillois's (1961) binary, the movement between *paidia* and *ludus*. Further, a number of scholars have argued for a method of invention that takes movement into account, such as John Muckelbauer's (2008) sophistic itineration and Samuel Taylor Coleridge's (1818) "s'orienter." After exploring these theories through two games—*Passage* (Rohrer, 2007), a highly-regarded independent game, and *The Elder Scrolls V: Skyrim* (2011), a well-known commercial game—I turn to new theories in social science on mobile methods of research that ground epistemology in ontologies of movement. By showing how embodied movement functions as an epistemic method, I reconsider how procedurality functions in relation to play and purpose, how this emergent ecology makes movement and invention possible rather than determines thinking, and how such procedural strategies play out in composition classes.

PAIDIA, LUDUS, PURPOSE

In *Man, Play and Games*, Roger Caillois (1961) articulates a continuum of *paidia* and *ludus* that helps clarify the relation between procedure and play. *Paidia*, for Caillois, is spontaneous, unstructured playfulness while *ludus* includes highly structured, rules-based games. This distinction is important to note because both humans and animals begin their play-experience through *paidia*. Caillois explains, "I shall define [*paidia*], for my purpose, as a word covering the spontaneous manifestations of the play instinct: a cat entangled in a ball of wool, a dog sniffing, and an infant laughing at his rattle represent the first identifiable examples of this type of activity" (pp. 27–28). As a further example, the child playing with its toes does so spontaneously as he or she begins to explore the boundaries of the body, and this exploratory play is unstructured. The child may wiggle its toes, grab its toes, put its toes in its mouth; the only rules are those imposed by the limits of the child's own body.

Caillois argues that such *paidiac* play quickly evolves, however, to become more *ludic* (p. 28). That same child soon begins to self-impose rules or seek pre-determined rules for play, giving rise to a host of games from hopscotch to *Twister*. In *Twister*, the player must spin a plastic arrow pinned on a color-coded board to determine which hand or foot must be placed in a corresponding colored circle on a floor mat. Such a game still involves the exploration and playful use of one's body, just as grabbing one's toes does, but *Twister* is much more structured and governed by preset rules. However, Caillois does not see this movement as unidirectional. Once the rules of a game become fixed, players then will find ways to make the game more *paidiac*. House rules and the re-purposing of established game objects for new games offer two ways that *ludic* games can be revised toward more spontaneous games. This oscillation between spontaneous, unstructured exploration and rules-based, structured games shows that play is an emergent process. We use *paidiac* exploration to create *ludic* games, which then serve as a basis for further *paidiac* exploration.

It is important to note that reaching either a purely *paidiac* or purely *ludic* method is impossible: taking either orientation to its exclusionary conclusion would produce only stasis. Pure *paidia* would be completely unstructured, unbounded chaos. Devoid of a structuring force, pure *paidia* would always remain an inchoate field of possibilities from which nothing could be generated. Similarly, pure *ludus* would be so bounded by rules that all movement would be constrained. We might liken these extremes to perfect order and utter chaos. We need never fear reaching such static null points, however. Callois identifies the tension between structure and freedom as intrinsic to play. This tension is also inherent in language itself, as Derrida explains in reference to the play of sign substitution. Derrida eschews the possibility of static totalization:

> If totalization no longer has any meaning, it is not because the infinity of a field cannot be covered by a finite glance or a finite discourse, but because the nature of the field—that is, language and a finite language—excludes totalization. This field is in fact that of freeplay, that is to say, a field of infinite substitutions in the closure of a finite ensemble. This field permits these infinite substitutions only because it is finite, that is to say, because instead of being an inexhaustible field, as in the classical hypothesis, instead of being too large, there is something missing from it: a center which arrests and founds the freeplay of substitutions. (1961, p. 289)

Thus, the material and semiotic ecologies of our world seem mutually dependent on both rules-bound order and generative spontaneity. The productive, inventive space of play is necessarily located between the two end points of the spectrum and invention is enabled through the oscilla-tion from *paidiac* to *ludic* and back.

Further, I would argue that this interplay between *paidia* and *ludus* makes a renewed, emergent purpose possible, and disrupts stasis and a pre-determined line of procedural development. This dynamic is similar to Richard Lanham's (2006) description of attention economies as "ir-remediably and self-consciously dramatic" (p. 10). In *The Economics of Attention*, he argues that in such a theatrical ecology, the roles of partici-pants become conflated. Actor, author, audience, operator: we refuse to be bounded by any one orientation. Lanham specifically identifies video games as digital dramas that can train participants to become econo-mists of attention through such conflation:

> The video gamer acts in his world. It is participatory theater par excellence. But he must also, to improve his performance, be-come a student of his own attention and the attention structure designed into the game. He must become, that is, an econo-mist of attention, studying his performance even while he is im-mersed in it or in a high-frequency oscillation between the two states. (p. 17)

This is the world of Lanham's play, game, and purpose, and ultimately Coleridge's "s'orienter." In *The Electronic Word*, Lanham (1993) argues that the oscillation of play and game produces an insistent purpose, or a continually reoriented goal. Play remains internalized without the ex-ternal problem situation made possible in games, and, as we will see later, in embodied research. For Lanham, the mixture of the three mo-tives—pleasure in play, competition in game, and problem solving in purpose—produces an emergent ecology where one motive is continu-ally modified by the others. This ecology disrupts a linear model of con-trol and an isolated model of procedurality (pp. 187–89).

SOPHISTIC ITINERATION IN *PASSAGE*

More attention to movements between play and game, then, is required to better understand the inventive force of play as a compositional meth-od. Play is often characterized as sophistic. In *The Future of Invention*, John Muckelbauer (2008) offers a performative analysis of Plato's *Sophist* to seek out "novel relations between the philosopher and the sophist" (p. 82) through the movement of the search itself and thereby articulate an itinerant style of invention. In *Homo Ludens*, Johan Huizinga (1955) explains that play occupies a liminal space between instinct and will: "If we call the active principle that makes up the essence of play, 'instinct,' we explain nothing; if we call it 'mind' or 'will' we say too much" (p. 1). It is this locating of play in contingency that links it to the sophists. Further, Huizinga claims that the sophists were "perfectly well aware of the playful character of their art" (p. 147). In *Sophist*, Plato invokes the notion of *paidia* to define sophists as the sort "who give themselves up to play" (p. 235a). This description characterizes the sophists as those who function in a spontaneous, unbounded way, which is unsurprising considering that Jacqueline de Romilly identifies the sophists as "professional itinerant teachers" (qtd. in Muckelbauer, p. 80). Itineration, moving from place to place in order to teach or preach, provides the sophist ever new rhetorical situations that require the invention of newer rules or heuristics. Ironically, heuristic constraints emerge from itinerant movement, a hallmark of the sophist himself.

Muckelbauer (2008) brings to bear considerable scholarship on the importance of itineration as an inventive and epistemic process. He notes, "this itinerant following points toward an affirmative sense of repetition that indicates, in Derrida's (1978) terms, a 'strategy without finality,' an inventive strategy that does not have a predetermined goal, but does not proceed blindly" (p. 80). In seeking out the sophist, Socrates must rely upon a seemingly sophistic stranger to guide him. Muckelbauer highlights parallels between the sophists and the stranger, positing, "It may be the case that, through such overt parallels, Plato is indicating that in order to track down the sophist, we must retain a guide who is himself a sophist" (p. 83). The movement toward a bounded understanding of the sophist is made possible through the figure of the unbounded sophist; similarly, the sophist is constituted as such through the itinerant act of being located. Muckelbauer explains the constitutive nature of itineration when he claims that "the sophist . . . is less a determinate identity than a differential movement of the encounter in which the subject itself must be at stake. In other words, the sophist is itinerant travel itself, the very movement through which, for Plato, one comes into true contact with reality (by becoming other)" (p. 97). In this case, itinerant invention does not just create the conditions of possibility for an object of study but also for a subject; Muckelbauer characterizes itinerant invention as "a very precise and demanding mode of self-transformation" (p. 98).

Muckelbauer's analysis is useful to game scholars in showing how itinerant movement constitutes a subject through the act of being located. This constitutive process can be seen in a game like Jason Rohrer's 2007 independent work, *Passage*. Created for Kokoromi's *Gamma 256* show, *Passage* features an 8x8 pixel man based on the designer himself. The game is freely available on the Internet and lasts only five minutes. The gameplay is simple. The character begins at the left edge of the game field, and the player can move the character forward, backward, up, or down across a landscape littered with obstacles. The player can also meet a romantic partner who will travel with his character, and the character can open treasure chests that sometimes contain loot. Exploring and looting chests earn points; you can earn more points if you travel with a partner, but navigating the obstacles along the way to reach treasure chests is more difficult. However, none of these actions are required.

The central procedure of the game is one that the player cannot control—time, or the necessary forward movement of life.

> *Passage* is a *memento mori* game. It presents an entire life, from young adulthood through old age and death, in the span of five minutes. Of course, it's a *game*, not a painting or a film, so the choices that you make as the player are crucial. There's no "right" way to play *Passage*, just as there's no right way to interpret it. . . . So what can you do with your life?" (Rohrer, 2007)

Over time, the character will move closer to the right edge of the game field regardless of the player's actions. At the end of five minutes, the character dies, represented by the avatar being replaced by a tombstone. As a persuasive game, *Passage*'s argument is clear: do what you will, we all die in the end. It creates its argument by the forcible movement of the player character along what can be read as a timeline. Time is the primary rule of the game that cannot be avoided, and it is time that puts the subject at stake. Within that temporal structure, the player is able to constitute the self solely by movement.

I often use *Passage* as an example of a gamic argument in first-year English classes. Students sometimes watch and emulate each other while playing since they may miss the romantic partner at the beginning or fail to notice the treasure chests. In the first two minutes of play, many of the students feel an impulse to compete with their peers, calling out their scores or noting which treasure chests held loot. Then it hits them— their characters are aging. Some try to run back toward the starting point of the game; others are so stunned they stop moving entirely. They usually express some disappointment when their partner dies and even more when their own character dies. It always surprises me how quickly they relate to their pixelated character, how quickly they refer to it in the first person.

The players' decisions about how, where, or even if they move their characters work to articulate the character as a subject. As such, their choices of movement and the forced itineration of the gamic procedures function together to create the character. Even though the character's movement over time appears visually linear, the process of movement is iterative, changing the appearance of the character over time to represent aging. Muckelbauer (2008) explains that "unlike habits . . . repetition is a differential kind of movement, the movement of difference itself. . . . It is characterized by the very movement of differential repetition . . ." (pp. 92–93). This differential repetition, created by the game's designer and enacted jointly by the computing processes and the player, constitutes the character in *Passage*. Further, returning to Caillois (1961), when we speak of the oscillation between *paidia* and *ludus*, we are, in fact, speaking of this iterative, differential repetition.

Purpose as Recursive Self-Orientation in *Skyrim*

In "Treatise on Method," Samuel Taylor Coleridge (1818) espouses an inventive method that includes differential repetition and oscillation as well, but also includes the role of purpose in the process. This is, perhaps, not so surprising, given that the word *method* itself denotes a mode or way of proceeding, implicitly containing movement as its condition of possibility. Coleridge's views on method have long been taken up by compositionists, as Byron Hawk (2007) traces in *A Counter-History of Composition*. In his teasing out of the role of vitalism and complexity in composition, Hawk analyzes the ways Coleridge has been used by James Berlin, Seamus Perry, John Beer, and Paul Kameen, among others. In each case, Hawk notes how Coleridge's theory of method functions to engender movement. For example, according to Hawk, Berlin emphasizes the importance of Coleridge's "polarities," which "produces a dialectical movement toward more understanding" by "placing things or ideas in relation to other things or ideas" with a preference for the process in poetic form (p. 53). Hawk highlights views of Coleridge's dialectical movement as an oscillation between the subject and object (p.

53), the poetic and the rhetorical (p. 53), the mind and the world (p. 95). However, Coleridge's dialectic functions differently from the kind of differential repetition evident in Plato's *Sophist*. Berlin's argument points out that while "Plato's dialectic is primarily dialogue," "Coleridge's is primarily polarity"—the productive tension of opposing forces in the world and dialectical oppositions in the mind (p. 57). This distinction allows Hawk to emphasize Berlin's reading of Coleridge's method as "generative of reality," rather than expressive of an *a priori* reality (p. 57).

Coleridge's method is one of such continual, recursive movement, which he characterizes using a nautical metaphor:

> [Method] requires, in short, a constant wakefulness of mind; so that if we wander but in a single instance from our path, we cannot reach the goal, but by retracing our steps to the point of divergency, and thence beginning our progress anew. Thus, a ship beating off and on an unknown coast, often takes, in nautical phrase, "a new departure:" and thus it is necessary often to recur to that regulating process, which the French language so happily expresses by the word *s'orienter*, i.e. to find out the east for ourselves, and so to put to rights our faulty reckoning. (pp. 633–634)

While compositionists tend to use the term "recursion" rather loosely to describe any iterative process, in mathematics, recursion specifically denotes a process in which the application of a function is part of the definition of that function (Gauld, 2007). In other words, if Method is recursive, then employing a method is necessarily constitutive of that method, and we can only fully identify our method after the fact. This mathematical definition is particularly useful since it addresses the constitutive nature of the subject similarly to Muckelbauer's (2008) work on the sophist and the constitutive nature of Coleridge's self-orienting method.

Unlike Muckelbauer's sophistic itineration, Coleridge's method includes purpose or a goal. However, we should not think of this goal as particularly limited or limiting. In "Toward a Rhetoric of Network (Media) Culture: Notes on Polarities and Potentiality," Hawk (2004) notes that Kameen argues against goal-oriented, problem-solving models of composition that reduce invention to "only finding the solution that is already predetermined often by the teacher or the structure established via heuristics" (p. 845). Kameen sees an alternative in Coleridge's method because "it reveals its pattern as exploration proceeds, each step preparing the ground for its (often unanticipated) successor; and because methodical thinking is spontaneously self-questioning, it is more nearly subversive than recursive in its capacity to adjust to the unexpected" (qtd. in Hawk p. 845). Rather than viewing Coleridge's goal as typical of process writing models, we might view the goal as constantly negotiable. As such, Coleridge's method is goal-oriented, but with a fluid goal.

A continual self-orienting toward an open goal such as Coleridge seems to propose is often found in sandbox games, or games that offer a space of self-directed play. In recent years, the *Fallout* series, the *Grand Theft Auto* series, and the *Elder Scrolls* series have consistently offered some of the more innovative play elements of this genre, which is characterized by non-linear gameplay and vast play spaces for exploration. *Skyrim*, a 2011 release from Bethesda Game Studios and the fifth installment of the *Elder Scrolls* series, offers a popular example. The player begins the game in a village that quickly falls to a dragon attack. After the encounter, which cannot be avoided, the player may engage the world in a number of ways. Players can take part in a lengthy overarching story in which the protagonist can defeat a Dragon-god, or not. They are under no obligation to follow this main story, and with a number of other interesting means of character development, they can feel free to develop other goals.

Traveling from one area to another in the world of *Skyrim*, it's easy to understand why Coleridge would advise his readers that only a "constant wakefulness of mind" (p. 633) can lead us to our goals. I have not completed the main story yet; I keep finding myself taking seemingly tangential trips to new areas, which lead me to new possibilities, which lead me to more new areas. During one game session, I began collecting ingredients like flowers and mushrooms to make alchemical potions, and by the time my bags were full, I was three hamlets away from where I intended to be.

The wandering my character engages in acts as both an epistemic and ontological activity. My character has stabbed her way into joining a guild of assassins, become a werewolf as part of an inner circle of rather goodly mercenaries, and has trained as both a proficient alchemist and blacksmith. She is often noted as an "adventurer" by non-player characters in the game, and her mobility is a key component of her ability to adventure. Town guards will sometimes exclaim in passing, "I used to be an adventurer like you, but then I took an arrow in the knee!" (*Skyrim*,

2011). My character has been constituted through these experiences, which are made visible through procedures or the game mechanics of gaining levels, earning rewards, and increasing ability scores. Through side quests—which often require traversing large sections of the game map—my character has learned much of the history, lore, and secrets of that world, and more importantly, has both shaped the world and been shaped by it. The main quest, however, continues to sit in my character's journal, and in order to complete it, my character must take a tip from Coleridge (1995) and literally retrace her steps back to "the point of divergency" (p. 633) to resume her progress. Further, while I would have been unable to complete the main quest without developing the character first, the particular development I chose is not implicit in the goal of fulfilling the main quest.

Coleridge claims that purposeful wandering is not only critical to reaching one's goal, but unavoidable: "From the first, or initiative idea, as from a seed, successive ideas germinate. . . . This is the *principle* of an indefinite, not to say infinite, *progression*; but this progression, which is truly Method, requires not only the proper choice of an initiative, but also the following it out through all its ramifications" (p. 633). In playing *Skyrim*, I am following the ramifications of the opening encounter by guiding my character through experiences that will teach her what she needs to know and support her as she becomes powerful enough to defeat the Dragon-god. While games like *Passage* and *Skyrim* seem to give primacy to physical wandering as a self-constitutive force, such embodied movement is clearly tied to mental itineration as well, as Muckelbauer and Coleridge's works show.

This open, goal-oriented recursion differs from the kind of unavoidable itineration seen in *Passage* (2007). In *Passage*, the constraints of time and forced movement create a defined end point to the process. While the procedures might seem to stifle the player, it is possible to read the game as a space in which the character can act freely without consequences precisely because the end is pre-determined. In other words, while the game is designed to be mercilessly bounded by its simple rules, offering typically *ludic* restrictions, it is those same constraints that allow the *paidiac* play of character development. Conversely, Coleridge (1995) offers a model in which a negotiable goal, even when chosen, is not assured. Itineration in Coleridge's method is, therefore, a potentially more dangerous and certainly more difficult way of constructing the self than that in *Passage*. The *paidiac* affordances of Coleridge's view seem to require that one creates his or her own restrictions to keep from falling off course.

MOBILE RESEARCH AND THE PRACTICE OF PROCEDURALITY

Procedurality, as something that grounds practice but is continually re-addressed and remade, functions in both research and pedagogy. While Muckelbauer (2008) and Coleridge (1995) develop theories of method as movement, other scholars offer enactments of movement as research methods. In a recent anthology, *Mobile Methodologies*, Ben Fincham, Mark McGuinness, and Lesley Murray (2010) compile ten studies that utilize a number of traditional methods—from discourse analysis and diaries to ethnographies and interviews—but all in the context of a methodology of movement. As such, the methods employed not only function as a means of keeping up with moving, material research objects but also address the challenges of mobile research configured by time and space, digital networks, and the human imagination. Despite differences in methods, objects of study, and fields of study, the common thread among these essays is their concern with the ways movement and mobility function ontologically as well as epistemologically.

For example, Nick Clarke's essay, "Writing Mobility: Australia's Working Holiday Programme," shows how British working holiday participants are configured by their travel, how the author's expectations of the participants were changed though his knowledge of them, and how the author's experience with movement changed the composition he created. Clarke notes, " . . . the mobilities I encountered in the field provoked me to think more carefully about the writing part of my project. I did this in the knowledge that writing not only attempts to mirror reality, but also helps to construct reality—that writing involves both *de*scription and *in*scription" (p. 122). As another example, Lesley Murray's chapter, "Contextualizing and Mobilising Research," outlines her work on children's journeys to school. Murray had the children videotape and narrate their journeys, watch the videos with her and talk about the journeys, and then answer a follow-up survey two years later. Her conclusion explicitly argues that embodied movement produces knowledge and constructs locations: "Mobile research can enhance knowledge about how we 'do' and how we experience what we do in different contexts. At the same time, such research demonstrates how mobility is productive of space and place, and how space and place are productive of mobilities" (p. 24).

Each of these projects starts with traditional research methods, enacts them in material contexts, and allows the methods to co-produce or in- scribe events. In "Growing Routes," Ilene Whitney Crawford (2010) takes a similar, open approach to research procedures to enact a version of Viet- nam. She uses mind, body, and emotion as three locations through which she constructs rhetoric as movement in order to study how gendered sub- jects are constituted: "I began theorizing rhetoric as the study and prac- tice of movement, rather than the study and practice of how language achieves its effects, i.e., persuasion. What moves us through time and space—physically, emotionally, and intellectually? How are these three registers of movement connected and interdependent?" (p. 76). Using partial, fragmentary, multimodal literacy narratives, Crawford constructs a complex topography of Vietnam, exploring how multiple contradictory forces, from free speech restrictions and cultural imperialism to ossified political infrastructures and free market imperatives, "move human be- ings physically, emotionally, and intellectually" (p. 77).

To consider movement as a methodology, Crawford needed to reframe her understanding of research methods. Crawford began with traditional research methods such as interviewing subjects and researching previously published narratives and photographs, well-established methods I would place at the rules-based, *ludic* end of the *paidia-ludus* spectrum. However, stationary observation did not afford her enough affective engagement. Instead, she felt it necessary to reproduce the embodied movements of her object of study to access the affective force of Vietnam. By later including travel and personal experience as moving modes of research, she oscillated toward a more *paidiac* method. Her practices involved documenting the material and semiotic ecologies of Vietnam: the routes or spaces of Ho Chi Minh City as well as the roots or lives and relationships among the Vietnamese. She attributes her ability to generate the emotionally affec- tive content for her work—which she then transformed back into a tradi- tional print text—to this moving method.

Though her overarching goal to collect literacy narratives was pre- determined, these physical, mental, emotional, and digital wanderings were not part of her plan. Her method speaks to the same kind of itinera- tion that Coleridge and Muckelbauer explicate. To understand Vietnam, she self-oriented through itineration toward a becoming-Vietnamese. Crawford (2010) had to give up not only the image of Vietnam she held before her research, but also her rooted stasis as the researcher-subject who perceives the image. In her routes, she herself became a subject-object complex, whose differential movement was the epistemic wandering that enabled her research and writing. If, in Muckelbauer and Coleridge's works, we are offered a theory of movement as a method for constituting the self and constructing knowledge, in Crawford's work and *Mobile Methodologies*, we are able to see how such a theory is enacted in practice to upend a strict model of procedurality.

It is this current work on mobile methods that I think best holds promise for rethinking the role of procedure in games and composition.[2] As part of an undergraduate writing class, I asked forty-two students to design games. We spent time reading and discussing critical and/or theoretical texts, including Bogost's (2007) *Persuasive Games* and Mary Flanagan's (2009) *Critical Play*. We also spent time playing and analyzing games: subversive games, activist games, educational games, "pink" games, and serious games. Students developed their own game designs working individually or in pairs. Though the students did not create working prototypes of their games, our compositional goal was to produce comprehensive design documents.[3]

I did not push notions of itineration or wandering as important to either the students' writing processes or in the development of their games, yet most students created games in which the protagonist must explore and engage with a virtual world in order to progress in the game. For example, for the game "Ricochet Reporter," Journalism major Stephanie drew upon her experience to create a game in which a reporter must garner interviews with sports figures after a football game. The player must think and act quickly, moving efficiently across the field to snag interviews with star players and coaches while avoiding obstacles like cheerleaders and other reporters. Movement is, therefore, the initial challenge of the game.

The overall purpose of the game remains to garner interviews, but the enacted practice toward this goal requires constantly renewed smaller purposes in response to emergent changes as the game progresses. In contrast, in Laura's game, "Scramble for Literacy," movement functions in multiple ways: players must both navigate the game space and move letters around to form words. The player begins in First grade and must unscramble words, which provide clues to various tasks that must be accomplished to move to the next level. These words and tasks are provided by NPCs that the player must find in the virtual world setting. The initial purpose, simply to unscramble words, opened up multiple, emergent procedures for enacting or moving through the game.

Of course, movement is not important only to game play. Many of the students remarked in their reflections that their writing processes for the games relied on more "planning" than most of their writing. As they developed their game designs, they had to continually trace out possibilities, question the rhetorical efficacy of their choices, retrace, reexamine, and set forth again. In the students' itineration towards creating a game design, they were required to take on multiple roles: visual artist, creative writer, procedural architect, rhetorician, researcher, and player. Like Plato's sophist, the designer is difficult to pin down because she is always moving among a network of functions. She enacts Coleridge's (1995) movement toward understanding through her writing. She collects her data through her embodied experience of the world that she simulates in her design. She attends to procedures as the rhetorical building blocks of her craft. The designer writes through the game, mobilizing the power of play, not as a concretized process, but as a constantly moving, evolving field of possibilities developed through itinerant invention.

NOTES

1. Grace Hagood Downs passed away unexpectedly as this volume was in production. This chapter has been posthumously edited and revised by her dissertation chair Byron Hawk, with advice from fellow students and friends Mary Fratini and Stephanie Boone-Mosher, who worked in a writing group with the author on the chapter, and feedback from volume editor Douglas Eyman.

2. I have had the good fortune to design games in commercial and academic settings. I have worked in the commercial games industry as a content developer for the post-apocalyptic MMORPG *Fallen Earth* and in academia as a scholar-practitioner for the NEH-funded game prototype *Desperate Fishwives* and *Ghosts of Carolina College*.

3. For teachers of composition, this distinction is, perhaps, both necessary and heartening. While there are many merits to having students create playable versions of the games they design, it is not always feasible or even preferable; limits of technology, expertise, and time may mean that a solid articulation of a design is more pedagogically effective and coherent than the game itself would be.

REFERENCES

Alexander, J. (2009). Gaming, student literacies, and the composition classroom: Some possibilities for transformation. *College Composition and Communication, 61*(1), 35–63.

Bogost, I. (2007). *Persuasive games: The expressive power of videogames.* Cambridge, MA: MIT Press.

Caillois, R. (1961). *Man, play, and games.* (Meyer Barah, Trans.). New York: Free of Glencoe.

Clarke, N. (2010). Writing mobility: Australia's working holiday programme. In Benjamin Fincham, Mark McGuinness, & Lesley Murray, (Eds.), *Mobile methodologies* (pp. 118–129). Basingstoke, Hampshire: Palgrave Macmillan.

Colby, R. S. (2012). Gender and gaming in a first year writing class. *Computers and Composition Online.* Retrieved from http://www2.bgsu.edu/departments/english/cconline/cconline_Sp_2012/shultzcolby_girlgamers_cnc/

Coleridge, S. T.(1995). Treatise on method. In H. J. Jackson and James Robert de Jager Jackson (Eds.), *The collected works of Samuel Taylor Coleridge: Shorter works and fragments* (pp. 625–687). Princeton: Princeton UP.

Connors, R. J. (1997). *Composition-Rhetoric: Backgrounds, theory, and pedagogy.* Pittsburgh, PA: U of Pittsburgh P.

Crawford, I. W. (2010). Growing routes. In Eileen E. Schell and K. J. Rawson, (Eds.), *Rhetorica in motion: Feminist rhetorical methods & methodologies* (pp. 71–85). Pittsburgh, PA: U of Pittsburgh P.

Derrida, J. (1978). *Writing and difference.* (Alan Bass,Trans.). Chicago: U of Chicago P.

The Elder Scrolls V: Skyrim. (2011). [video game]. Rockville, MD: Bethesda Softworks.

Fincham, B., McGuinness, M., & Murray, L., (Eds.). (2010). *Mobile methodologies.* Basingstoke, Hampshire: Palgrave Macmillan.

Flanagan, M. (2009). *Critical play: Radical game design.* Cambridge, MA: MIT Press.

Gauld, A. (2007). Recursion. *Learning to Program.* Retrieved from http://alan-g.me.uk/tutor/index.htm

Gee, J. (2003). *What video games have to teach us about learning and literacy.* New York: Palgrave Macmillan.

Hawk, B. (2007). *A Counter-history of composition: Toward methodologies of complexity.* Pittsburgh, PA: U of Pittsburgh P.

Hawk, B. (2004). Toward a rhetoric of network (media) culture: Notes on polarities and potentiality. *JAC, 24*(4), 831–50.

Huizinga, J. (1955). *Homo Ludens: A study of the play-element in culture.* Boston: Beacon.

Lanham, R. (2006). *The economics of attention: Style and substance in the age of information.* Chicago: U of Chicago P.

Lanham, R. (1993). *The electronic word: Democracy, technology, and the arts.* Chicago: U of Chicago P.

Muckelbauer, J. (2008). *The future of invention: Rhetoric, postmodernism, and the problem of change.* Albany: State U of New York P.

Murray, L. (2010). Contextualising and mobilising research. In Benjamin Fincham, Mark McGuinness, and Lesley Murray, (Eds.), *Mobile methodologies* (pp. 13–24). Basingstoke, Hampshire: Palgrave Macmillan.

Plato. (1997). Sophist. In John M. Cooper, (Ed.), *Plato: Complete works* (Nicholas P. White, Trans.). (pp. 235–293). Indianapolis: Hutchinson.

Reid, A. (2007). *The two virtuals: New media and composition*. West Lafayette, IN: Parlor Press.

Rohrer, J. (2007). *Passage*. [video game].

Rohrer, J. (2007). What I was trying to do with *Passage*. Retrieved from http://hcsoftware.sourceforge.net/passage/statement.html

Shipka, Jody. (2011). *Toward a composition made whole*. Pittsburgh, PA: U of Pittsburgh P.

Sicart, Miguel. (2011). Against procedurality. *Games Studies*, 11(3). Retrieved from http://gamestudies.org/1103/articles/sicart_ap

Sirc, G. (2002). *English composition as a happening*. Logan, UT: Utah State UP.

Tobin, Lad. (1994). Introduction: How the writing process was born—and other conversion narratives. In Lad Tobin and Thomas Newkirk, (Eds.). *Taking stock: The writing process movement in the '90s* (pp. 1–14). Portsmouth, NH: Boynton/Cook.

PART II: GAME ECOLOGIES AND NETWORKS

(OR, WRITING AROUND GAMES)

6 Who's That Walking on My Bridge? Transmedia Shifts and Trolling in Game Forums

Richard Colby and Rebekah Shultz Colby

Computer game scholarship often focuses on the game as object, and when it does move beyond the game as object, it does so still within the immediate context of the game's virtual world. This is partly understandable because many games are plentiful in content to study on their own. Simply considering genres such as massively multi-player online games (MMOGs) add to these analyses additional cultural, social, and gameplay interactions. Ethnographic studies in MMORPGs in particular (Nardi, 2010; Pearce, 2009; Taylor, 2006) have focused almost exclusively on player-player discourse or player-game interaction and yet have still presented rich cultural portraits of those games and of those gamers in general. However, as we continue to study gamer culture and practice, we should take care to expand textual study of games to not only the *what* of games as ojects of study, but also *how* we study games and gaming. For one, ignoring the often expansive ecosystem of texts surrounding gaming, texts that often directly influence gaming, atomizes games as an object with only transactional qualities that diminishes the artistic and rhetorical possibilities of those games.

This edited collection exemplifies some of the complexity of gaming ecosystems, so we will not belabor the point here, but we want to address an important second item in expanding our study of games—the ecological layers of texts beyond the immediate game itself. Eyman (2008) has defined five elements or layers of gaming ecologies that he names as follows:

- Environmental action (what happens in the game)
- Para-textual development (game interfaces)

- Documentation (user and developer created texts about games)
- Infrastructural processes (the game design itself)
- Research (critical commentary and scholarly investigation of games and their relationship to "real life") (p. 246)

As game studies has and continues to enrich our understanding of the environmental action and infrastructural processes, we would like to turn our attention to the layer of paratexts that often surrounds gaming. We are referring here to game forums, fansites, guild websites, strategy guides, and a myriad of other participatory texts that augment games and the gaming community. These texts are usually self-sponsored and, when looking at FAQs or strategy guides, can often be quite elaborate. For example, Bkstunt_31's (2013) FAQ for Skyrim is about six hundred pages long and took a little over a year to complete.

Obviously, we do not intend to cover the entirety of paratexts here, but we do intend to confirm empirically how gaming as an ecology operates through one class of participatory paratexts, that of online gaming forums. Our current study focuses on the official forums of the MMORPG *World of Warcraft*, and specifically, certain online rhetorical behaviors including trolling and participatory literacies.

Paratexts and Participatory Culture

Gerard Genette (1987/1997) defines paratexts as "thresholds" (p. 2) to the main text, "the heterogeneous group of practices and discourses" that present a text (p. 2). As a literary scholar, his examples involve the presentation of literary texts through their covers, titles, and prefaces, but they also extend beyond the immediate text and include author interviews and reviews. These latter texts, coming after or external to the original text, Genette defines as epitexts (p. 344). If we turn our attention to computer games, we can see many similarities—games, at least those still purchased in physical form, have cover art. They have titles and designers, prefaces and documentation. Although most current games provide paratexts in digital formats, games in the past routinely would come with print artifacts such as maps, decoder wheels, and strategy guides. These static paratexts still exist, but we have introduced a new set of paratexts partly as a result of changes in media and partly as a result of continued cultural shifts. Genette (1987/1997) remarks that "our 'media' age has seen the proliferation of a type of discourse around texts that was unknown in the classical world" (p. 3); obviously, since 1987, we have seen continued proliferation and evolution of these paratexts, especially with the addition of directly participatory paratexts online: the mass involvement of an audience in commenting, analyzing, and extending the original game text on game forums.

As paratexts, game forums are often split into sections that invite discussion on topics ranging from technical issues, advice for future versions of the game, general discussion of the game, off-topic forums, and even focused forums on specific class or features of a game. However, the discourse on gaming forums is often fraught. Gamers can be mean. They can be competitive. They leverage memes with precision just as they perpetuate arguments long ago lost or won. And they can be sarcastic. Of course, gamers can also be helpful, collaborative, and selfless. Many recognize that they are part of a community of practice, and as such, maintain a certain responsibility and ethos. As Matthew S. S. Johnson (2008) argues,

> Gaming environments are enabling spaces that create an opportunity for their participants to write publicly to real, responsive audiences to establish communities that can ultimately have a significant effect on games and those who produce them. In short, gamer authors realize that through their writing and civic participation they can help to shape a larger culture. (p. 282)

We contend that the relationship here, between the game and the gamer participant, is a significant part of game ecology because how the game is played, or how the game is read as a text and then enacted, is often directly influenced by the paratext of the forums. It is not surprising then that participants often treat the forums as another domain of the game that they are playing—a rhetorical game with similar cooperative or competitive motives.

To further analyze the way that these cooperative or competitive motives appear, we are invoking another lens to literate practices within the ecology. Henry Jenkins et al. (2009) in "Confronting the Challenges of Participatory Culture" argue that we should address new literacies to account for changes in media landscapes. They write that today's youth are part of a participatory culture that enacts the following eleven skills or literacies[1] in order to navigate those media landscapes: play, performance, simulation, appropriation, multitasking, distributed cognition, collective intelligence, judgment, transmedia navigation, networking, and negotiation. Jenkins and his coauthors argue that many will acquire these literacies, but because of issues of access and a lack of opportunities for critical awareness, they might not be fully enacted.

Obviously, much within those eleven literacies is inherent in games. As its very frame, part of participatory culture is inhabiting online affinity spaces, and gamers or even gamers of one particular game inhabit such spaces (see also Gee, 2005). However, we want to draw attention to one particular literacy and its application in game forums—transmedia navigation:

Transmedia navigation involves both processing new types of stories and arguments that are emerging within a convergence culture and expressing ideas in ways that exploit the opportunities and affordances represented by the new media landscape. In other words, it involves the ability to both read and write across all available modes of expression (p. 89)

Jenkins et al. see in this literacy a participant who can expertly read the rhetorical situation within a medium and pick the most appropriate means of composing in that medium, transporting knowledge across those mediums, while also enacting new literacies for new situations. We propose that although transmedia navigation might be the ideal, the real is more like transmedia shift—that is, along with the narratives and arguments, come residual practices connected to those sites. More fully, we might say that transmedia shift is a transporting, or rather a transferring of both knowledge *and* literacies from one mode to the next.

Determining the types of literacy practices and knowledge shifted is our primary research question. We conducted a rhetorical analysis of the posts in context, considering then how some of the eleven participatory culture literacies might shift media—from the game to the forums. In doing this, we argue that such shifting is a quality of any communication ecology, gaming or not. Ecologies are interrelated and reciprocal processes. Actions or effects in one layer of the ecology can, and often do, activate or affect another layer within the ecology. Beyond shifting technical discourse from interactions in the game to interactions on the forum, we theorize that we might see gaming literacies of more play, performance, appropriation, or collective intelligence in forum posts about games that require such literacy. In contrast, we would expect to see literacies on a professional listserv or forum that might originate from that group's practice (e.g., collective intelligence, networking, negotiation for a discourse community of academics). Such shifts become clear evidence for the interdependencies that different layers of a communication eco-system exhibit.

Before describing our study, we want to address an important assumption about who participates on online gaming forums. As the focus of the MacArthur Foundation grant that led to the Jenkins et al. (2009) report was on youth education, they name today's youth as a participatory culture. However, the Entertainment Software Association (ESA) and Pew Internet & American Life have both shown that video gamers are a far more diverse group than just the exemplar teens that Jenkins et al. defines. The ESA claims the average age of video game players is 30, and that 45% are female (2013, p. 3). The Pew data shows game players as a sample of the total US population; it identifies that 55% of men and 50% of women are video game players, and it also shows that "younger generations tend to dominate the gaming world; however, older respondents who do play games are more avid players" (Lenhart, Jones, & Macgill, 2008, p. 3). Our assumption, however, is that such a demographic is not the primary participant on online forums. While there is very little data or scholarship on the demographics of forum participants, we have been teaching a *World of Warcraft* first-year writing course since 2008, and based on pre-course surveys from this very limited dataset (N = 128), very few of the students who sign up for this course indicated that they regularly read (32.58%) or write (7.27%) on gamer forums. Consequently, while video games are played by a diverse audience, those who post on online gaming forums are probably a very small subset of those gamers.

Even if only a small percentage of gamers write participatory paratexts, based on our experiences with various online gaming communities, we have noted some rhetorical moves made in video gaming discussion forums that appear in multiple ecological layers. Many of us are familiar with the transfer of internet acronyms across domains, from Usenet and text messaging with its spatial constraints (i.e., limited bandwidth and storage necessitates typing fewer characters) into gaming with its temporal constraints (i.e., intense interactive play necessitates fast, abbreviated typing). We see these same abbreviations enter game forums. Of course, this is not wholly a gaming phenomenon. All discourse communities "possesses an inbuilt dynamic towards an increasingly shared and specialized terminology" through developing shorthand and technical abbreviations (Swales, 1988, 212). What we are arguing is that more of a shift of rhetorical features embedded in the nature of the game appear in the forum posts, not that they are somehow unique to gamers. In this article, we examine how the game literacies of competition and cooperative collaboration extend themselves rhetorically onto gaming forums with the arguments that gamers choose to make. We also examine trolling as a type of playful rhetorical behavior that is encouraged from the transmedia shift from the playful competition and collaboration within online games onto the rhetorical space of gaming forums.

TROLLS AND THEIR BEHAVIOR

A common definition for an Internet troll is a "person who interrupts communications on the Internet, especially in the online discussion forum" (Shin, 2008). Although there is surprisingly little scholarship on trolls, some work has assigned motives to the troll, the most prevalent focusing on identity. For example, Dahlberg defines trolling as "identity deception in cyberspace [aiming] to embarrass, anger, and disrupt" and Hardaker, through a 172-million-word corpus analysis, defines the troll as a "user who constructs the identity of sincerely wishing to be part of the group in question, including professing, or conveying pseudo-sincere intentions, but whose real intention(s) is/are to cause disruption and/or to trigger or exacerbate conflict for the purposes of their own amusement" (Hardaker, p. 237). Additional studies have also looked at other types of disruptive communication, such as flaming, as also intent on causing a disruption (Moor, Heuvelman, & Verleur, 2010; Lapidot-Lefler & Barak, 2012). In the Internet wilds of computer mediated communication, we might more readily see these examples of participants disrupting conversations to feel that they have a place—an identity—within a group, but doing so anonymously; one notable example is Mr. Bungle as described by Julian Dibbell (1993/1998) in "A Rape in Cyberspace."

At issue, however, is when trolling or troll-like behavior is not attached to a particular and often anonymous identity, that of a troll. In other words, rather than consider the troll as an identity, we might complicate the definition and consider trolling as a series of rhetorical actions that often do not make up a stable rhetorical identity. For instance, what might we make of a gamer forum participant who describes in great and helpful detail how to perform some game function in one post, then on another post drops in the O RLY? Owl to mock what he or she just posted?

Rather than simply defining trolls as a singular identity of those desperate for attention, we contend that trolling behavior is a more apt description, and these behaviors might appear from just about anybody. Herring et al. (2002) define trolling as "luring others into pointless and time-consuming discussions" (p. 372) that often has three qualities: it appears sincere but is also controversial and futile. Rather than labeling a troll, we want to consider a post as evidence for trolling behaviors.

Our study consists of a rhetorical analysis of a series of threads from a gamer forum that clearly operates as a significant interaction paratext layer that is just as complex as the environmental action layer—*World of Warcraft (WoW)*, developed by Blizzard Entertainment. Because *WoW* is a game that can be played individually or with a group and has a variety of competitive components including player vs. player battles (PvP) and an achievement system that often leads to competitive comparison among players, as well as cooperative components including large-scale raiding and smaller group encounters, the forum participants are more apt to display an equally complex series of rhetorical and argumentative moves on the forums. Through forum analyses, we intend to show how gaming literacies shift into the rhetorical strategies that forum participants use when posting to online gamer forums.

METHOD

All threads we examined are from the official Blizzard *World of Warcraft* Battle.net forums. We selected the official Blizzard forums because they are closest to the threshold of the environmental action layer of the *WoW* gaming ecosystem and most likely to be read by the developers of the game as well as the majority of players who read forums about *WoW*. If enough players complain about some aspect of the game, Blizzard often changes the game to address their concerns. Consequently, forum participants have quite a bit of rhetorical agency to change and improve the game. We have kept all quoted examples from the posts uncorrected so as to preserve the precise language used. Where explanation of game-specific discourse was required, we indicated the translation in brackets.

We further limited our scope to how players respond to changes in the game, either from additions made by expansion packs or through patches. We elected to look at these threads for a few reasons. For one, such changes are disruptive to the gameplay familiar to the players. A great deal of effort and player feedback goes into making changes to any game, but such changes also ask players to learn to play the game anew, even if they were experts at the game before the patch.

For our corpus, we selected three controversial threads and one non-controversial thread. The controversial threads were all a result of changes to the game that came from a patch. We qualitatively coded rhetorical features in the threads using a coding scheme derived from Walker et al.'s (2012) Internet Argument Corpus project. We revised the coding scheme for our study because we were doing all the coding ourselves (Walker et al. used Amazon's Mechanical Turk to code 390,704 posts), we preferred an ordinal Likert-type scale rather than their negative/positive rhetorical features scale, and we coded for context, something they did not do. For example, we determined whether the poster was addressing the topic or another poster (or both), and we also coded for the audience of the post (some posters address a particular poster, others address the topic for the forum audience). We also coded for whether forum posters were agreeing or disagreeing with each other specifically to examine the level of competition vs. cooperation posters evidenced toward each other. We further coded for whether or not posters were forming more logical arguments or emotional ones, and the level of respect, niceness, and sarcasm posters showed each other. Evidence of trolling was examined on a qualitative, contextual level. Any instances of posters identifying troll-like behaviors were also noted. Once we coded these posts, we computed measures of central tendency to show empirically some patterns in those posts, but also to determine if certain literacies shifted from the environmental action layer of the gaming ecology to the interaction paratext layer.

FORUM ANALYSIS: PARTICIPATORY CULTURE IN ACTION

"Looks like its the end of wow multiboxing"

The thread, "Looks like its the end of wow multiboxing" argues that the game will lose subscribers because the developers removed the /follow feature from Battlegrounds (Darktide, 2013) in patch 5.2, "The Thunder King." Multiboxing is the process of one player controlling multiple characters, done so that the player always has a "group" to do multiplayer content with, and this is facilitated by a command in the game that allows the player to set his or her twenty-seven characters to follow another character. Battlegrounds are places in the game where groups of players fight against other groups of players.

The thread is interesting for a number of reasons. For one, when we scraped it two days after the patch, it had already generated 540 posts. The second reason is that multiboxing is a rare thing in *WoW* for both skill and financial reasons (i.e., 27 characters would mean $400/month in subscription costs to say nothing of the computer setup required and the skill/dedication used to run the setup), so it is interesting that so many weighed in on so limiting a topic. Third, the removal of the /follow feature was added at the last minute, so a good number of posts were debating whether it was a bug before an official word from Blizzard actually explained the change. Finally, the Original Poster (OP) was clearly trolling. The OP specifically admits as much 114 posts into the thread, writing, "Out of all the threads a blue [Blizzard forum administrator] could respond on . . . my troll thread was the choice" (Darktide, 2013). To say nothing of the fact that debates about game features changed to curb cheating are often futile.

Of the 540 posts, ten posters (n = 241) wrote 30.93 percent of the posts. Table 3 indicates that, based on the 4-point Likert scale we used, the posts were more likely to be insulting (M = 2.43, SD = 0.89) and nasty (M = 2.42, SD = 0.83), with 1 indicating respect and niceness respectively and 4 indicating the opposite of both. However, posters also used more factual/logical arguments than emotional ones (M = 2.46, SD = 1.01), with 1 indicating a strictly emotional argument and 4 indicating an strictly logical one, and agreed more than disagreed with each other (M = 2.63, SD = 1.15), with 1 indicating strong disagreement and 4 indicating strong agreement.

As for markers of competition, agreement was more the norm. However, at least with the top ten posters (the repeat posters), there was a sense of defending attacks on their posts. For example, a Subsequent Poster (SP) writes, "ROFL, you really are ignorant. You are extremely over estimating this. Maybe get your facts straight" (Foomz, 2013) to which the OP replies, "like I said I found ONE online community for boxing with 44k followers, I also say I might have over estimated on how many box since no one really knows. had you finished the 3rd grade maybe you could READ? must be a mad boxer" (Darktide, 2013). There is a sense of defending a post through negotiation, but determining a winner in a debate like this is difficult, if not impossible because of the trolling origins of the post. In other words, the only winner is the one who escapes unscathed from this fray. It is trolling, after all.

For markers of appropriation, or "the ability to meaningfully sample and remix media content" (Jenkins et al., 2009, p. 32) the debate was very focused on whether multiboxers were a good or bad thing, even though the OP and Blizzard posts were about the /follow change. This binary debate, good or bad, was repeated consistently throughout the posts, 12 posters writing "good riddance" 41 mentioning the "skill" or challenge of multiboxing as a quality of respect. In an argument such as this, we might imagine more variation, but instead, posters often just appropriated another's ideas or, if nothing else, appropriated an internet meme to flame or defend against flaming.

Lastly, there was performance, defined by Jenkins et al. (2009) as "the ability to adopt alternative identities for the purpose of improvisation and discovery" (p. 28). Trolling itself is a type of performance, as maybe a display of skill, a game, or sophistry in that pejorative sense of the word. As the debate was instigated as trolling, the outcome is not as important as the performances. This is particularly interesting in the use of sarcasm that was sometimes not understood (55.96% of the posts had some sarcasm in them). For example, one SP wrote of the change to a Previous Poster (PP) who was complaining, "Don't worry. Since you pay more, they will revert the change. Just give it a week or two" (Hixson, 2013). The PP replied, "Then wouldn't this mean Blizzard would have never implemented something like this? Use your head" (Xanzül, 2013), missing the sarcasm from the SP. Performance through sarcasm was also demonstrated through jokes. One poster wrote /fallow rather than /follow to which a SP wrote, "I think that any multiboxers who were using '/fallow' will be just as effective as they were before" (Snowfox, 2013).

"(•_•) (•_•)>⌐■-■ (⌐■_■) DEAL WITH IT"

A public test realm (PTR) patch, version 5.4, led to the second and third posts. PTR patches allow players to experience changes to the game and provide feedback to Blizzard before the changes actually are applied to the "live" version of the game. This post from Wiw (2013) uses the "deal with it" meme, ASCII art and all, to argue that Warlock players should learn to deal with a change to one of their high level talents. Kil'jaden's Cunning (KJC) allowed the warlocks to cast spells while moving; Wiw responded to a change to KJC that made this talent something the player had to activate for a fifteen-second duration if he or she wanted to cast a spell while moving. Wiw (2013) writes, "A ton of you have played for years without KJC and locks [are] better off than they were in previous expansions without it." The poster seems to argue on behalf of Blizzard using an appeal to tradition, and by siding with Blizzard, maintains a particular agency, as if speaking for the company and the change to the game. Of course, the poster fails to see how performing the "deal with it" meme disrupts his or her ethos; after all, Blizzard would never say this to its players. Blizzard is extremely responsive to their gaming audience and, in fact, uses the Battle.net forum as a way of responding to their audience both rhetorically on the forums and through changes that they make to the game through patches.

The discussion that follows plays with the "deal with it" meme. The meme is repeated in 19 of the 44 posts of this thread, sometimes as ad hominem attacks—"You are a tool, deal wit it . . ." (Dazaral, 2013)—but sometimes within more rational arguments. For example, in a lengthy post, Aesica (2013) writes, "Just sitting down and 'dealing with it' isn't how you get positive change to happen." Aesica recognizes her role in the forum ecology providing feedback to Blizzard about the change (see Johnson, 2008).

There is also discussion about the OP's appeal to tradition, which undermines the OP's ethos even further. One poster writes simply, "so game mechanics and balance was the same in vanilla, TBC and WotLK and they didn't have that ability therefore it doesn't matter now. You are some kind of stupid" (Uiharu, 2013). Icedlight writes a similar but lengthier response, describing fights previous to the introduction of the KJC ability and then after:

> Essentially earlier game design took into account that some classes needed opportunities to "turret" unleash or they could not compete, most (not all) of the current content has medium to high movement where either stuff is landing on the ground, your character is targeted and must move, the fight revolves around constant movement. (Icedlight, 2013).

In these cases, the OP, speaking with the aligned agency of Blizzard, still fails to be persuasive. The OP is sincere, but the futility of the post is in siding with a position that he or she feels cannot be changed—hence, the use of "deal with it." Maebd (2013) even accuses the OP of trolling because of this stance: "So, you hop on the lock you never play just to create a troll topic? 0/10 Too obvious."

The data show similar features to the "Multiboxing" thread (see table 3). Of the 44 posts, 7 posters wrote 37.21 percent of the posts. Of the controversial threads, "Deal With It" had the least amount of sarcasm (17.06 percent) and the most disagreement with the OP (M = 1.46).

The participatory culture literacies include a few types of appropriation that occur in this thread. For one, as we indicated, the OP is seemingly aligning with Blizzard, appropriating the agency of the company to give the OP authority. Of course, as shown by our coding, this also led to a great amount of disagreement. This could be that the community sees the OP as a weak representative of the company line, and thus, attacks the change. Besides appropriating agency, similar to "the end of multiboxing," there is a similar repeat of previous posts (M = 15.70 quoted words) and ideas as we indicated (19 of the 44 posts use the "deal with it" phrase).

Despite the OP's trolling behaviors, we also see collective intelligence, "the ability to pool knowledge and compare notes with others toward a common goal" (Jenkins et al., 2009, p. 39) and negotiation, "the ability to travel across diverse communities, discerning and respecting multiple perspectives, and grasping and following alternative norms" (Jenkins et al., 2009, p. 52), here as well. The high amount of disagreement can actually be coded as high agreement if posts from the OP are removed. Compared to the multibox thread, rather than a change that has already occurred and is meant to combat cheating, this change on the PTR is still open to feedback. Lockpower (2013) is the first to attempt negotiation with a non-participating but nevertheless present design team by writing, "There is a balance that can be met with KJC; having all 3 specs with their filler spells being castable while moving at all times seems reasonable to me. So MG [Malefic Grasp] for Aff, Shadow bolt for Demo, and incinerate for destro." Similarly, Grimsrock (2013) agrees with Lockpower's compromise, as does Aesica (2013), who originally questioned the OP's "deal with it" response if they wanted positive change to happen. Collective intelligence and negotiation are noteworthy in MMOGs due to the very nature of the game being social in nature, enacting a collective agency in both the ecological layers of gameplay and the culture of the game. Although the effects of this are never absolutely clear, the developers without comment changed the talent in the patch yet again so that the Warlock can "cast Incinerate, Malefic Grasp, and Shadow Bolt while moving" (Rygarius, 2013)—the very spells that Lockpower suggested.

"Frost Mage Master 5.4 Not A Nerf"

Snarful (2013), the OP, is also responding to a PTR patch, this one about a change to Mages in the game. The talent, called Frostburn, provides the Mage with 16 percent increased damage to a target if that target was frozen by the mage's frost spells. The proposed change would remove the frozen requirement, but instead, give the Mage only a flat 2 percent increase to damage from three of the mage's spells. Snarful's post neither aligns with Blizzard nor seems to exhibit troll-like behaviors; the OP asks, "Don't see how this is a nerf. Would like someone to explain. I take it as our fingers of frost and brainfreeze get a buff. The master affects them not change them [mastery affects the talent damage]. It says an additional. Am I getting this wrong?"

One would think that such an honest question would not entail much disagreement. However, the OP, Snarful, seems to want to continue to argue that the change is not a nerf. In other words, the OP was not a question and seemingly turns into a defense. The majority of posts (52 percent) attempt to correct the OP and explain the change as a nerf, indicating that the change would decrease Mage damage to targets that could be frozen but have no effect on those targets that could not be frozen (e.g., raid bosses or other special characters in the game). Lhivera (2013) states it succinctly: "You're not understanding it right. Damage vs targets that cannot be frozen (bosses): unchanged. Damage vs targets that can be frozen (some adds/spawns/packs): reduced." The argument is perpetuated by the OP and another SP, who both continue to counter the evidence that is presented to them. Three posts even share experiences from the PTR (they actually played with the new changes) and eight posts even engage in some theorycrafting (performing theoretical calculations to demonstrate a gameplay mechanic). For example, Lhivera explains it as follows:

> To lay out the numbers, let's say you've got 30,000 spell power and +30% Mastery.
>
> [patch] 5.3
> Ice Lance vs frozen target, no FOF [fingers of frost]: (260 + 0.25 * 30000) * 4 * 1.3 = 40,352
> Ice Lance with FOF: (260 + 0.25 * 30000) * 4 * 1.3 = 40,352
>
> [patch] 5.4
> Ice Lance vs frozen target, no FOF: (260 + 0.25 * 30000) * 4 = 31,040 (reduced, no mastery benefit)
> Ice Lance with FOF: (260 + 0.25 * 30000) * 4 * 1.3 = 40,352 (unchanged, still gets mastery benefit)

This type of evidence is plentiful in the discussion.

At one point, at post #72, the OP writes, "Last post for me," (Snarful, 2013) but goes on to post 15 more times in the thread. As with the "Deal With It" thread, the level of disagreement (M = 1.89) would be completely reversed if the OP posts were removed. Even at post #131, Snarful admits to being confused and that the change is, in fact, a nerf to the Mage damage. However, subsequent posters seem to perpetuate the argument, like Abracadaver (2013) writing, "And as for Snarful getting confused about something so basic requiring 7 pages just to set you straight, all I can say is wow. You know a lot less about this class than you think you do." This creates a war of "words" between Snarful and Abracadaver:

Abracadaver: "It appears I am confusing poor Snarful with my use of the term shatter, replace shatter with the words "spell hitting frozen target" throughout my posts and it might not be so confusing for you."

Snarful "Love how you change your words. When your wrong YOU'RE WRONG. I'm living proof on this thread there is nothing wrong with admitting it."

Abracadaver: "lol what was I wrong about? I'm changing my TERMINOLOGY, not IDEA because you get confused about every single thing."

Snarful: "Who are you to judge. Please stop playing goody goody. Yes thank you for your help but to blast me for something then not the other is absurd . . . A mistake is a mistake. That's what I'm pointing out. Up to you guys to take the higher road. This thread is now dead for me."

Abracadaver: "Please don't insult my intelligence over semantics. Nothing I said was "incorrect," my wording could have been clearer though."

In this post, participatory culture literacies include judgment, "the ability to evaluate the reliability and credibility of different information" (Jenkins et al., 2009, p. 43), is the most apparent. However, as players compare their theorycrafting, collective intelligence is also apparent. Players seem to respect theorycrafting more than examples written only in words. Those who engage in theorycrafting, theorizing the change using quantitative examples, are not countered in the thread—those who actually tested the changes quantitatively on the PTR and then supported with a screenshot are held in the most esteem; in fact, the OP refers to these posts as evidence for him or her understanding the change as a nerf. What perpetuates the argument is words, namely, differences in specific words as applied to the change. In a social game, where there are multiple semiotic levels, numbers, images, and actions seem to be more persuasive than just words. There is a real sense of competition here, with posters saying they give up only to reenter the discussion later, as if leaving would signal some sort of defeat. We are not arguing that this phenomenon is native or particular to game forums, only that games themselves are situated in a larger culture of practice with additional ecological layers that impact the layers manifested in the game and its virtual space.

"Celestial Blessing for Hunters Strategy!"

We wanted to end with a brief analysis of a thread as evidence for a non-controversial thread. In patch 5.2, "The Thunder King," Blizzard added the reward phase of a legendary quest line that began with the release of the Mists of Pandaria expansion. The final phase to earn a legendary cloak, the best and rarest of items in the game, involves completing a final battle without the help of other players. The Celestial Blessing quest is fairly difficult to complete with over 200 videos on YouTube detailing strategies (and failures). The OP of the thread, "Celestial Blessing for Hunters Strategy!," (Jinza, 2013) volunteers a strategy that worked for him or her, and what follows are additional strategies, with very little disagreement (M = 3.53), but even then, the disagreement is respectful and nice (See tables 1–3).

Table 1. Average total words / quoted words per post by thread.

Thread	Total Words	Quoted Words
Looks like its the end of wow multiboxing.	73.24	32.17
Frost Mage Master 5.4 Not A Nerf	75.68	17.92
Deal With It	66.65	15.70
Celestial Blessing	162.60	47.80

Table 2. Apparent audience of post by thread.

Row Labels	(1) Specific Poster	(2) Both	(3) Forum
Looks like its the end of wow multiboxing.	35.25%	8.20%	56.56%
Frost Mage Master 5.4 Not A Nerf	37.31%	47.76%	11.94%
Deal With It	48.84%	44.19%	6.98%
Celestial Blessing	60.00%	35.00%	5.00%

Table 3. Argumentative features of posts by thread. Means for Likert scale used to determine range of each criteria.

Thread	(4) Insult (1) Respect	(4) Nasty (1) Nice	(4) Agree (1) Disagree	(4) Rational (1) Emotion	Sarcasm
wow multiboxing.	2.43 (0.89)	2.42 (0.83)	2.63 (1.15)	2.46 (1.01)	48.41%
Frost Mage Master 5.4	2.56 (0.90)	2.53 (0.88)	1.89 (1.01)	2.94 (1.08)	26.59%
Deal With It	2.57 (0.97)	2.50 (0.94)	1.46 (0.78)	2.33 (0.95)	17.06%
Celestial Blessing	1.00 (0.00)	1.00 (0.00)	3.53 (0.80)	2.75 (0.97)	0.00%

This thread is an example of cooperative collaboration in the game. In contrast to the last three threads that were highly contentious and the first two, which showed evidence of trolling, this thread demonstrates players working earnestly together on a task that they cannot play together. It shows how the paratext layer of the ecology extends the collaboration inherent in a social game in a positive way beyond the environmental action layer of the game itself. In this thread, the OP explains in a step-by-step way how to complete the quest with a Hunter. A SP explains trying the strategy but it not working, so another post explains a new strategy. In fact, of the 20 posts in this thread, the OP writes 8 of them, working with the other players to perfect the strategy. Participatory culture literacies exhibited include some negotiation, but mainly collective intelligence as the players of the thread compare their strategies for success to create new strategies and networking.

TRANSMEDIA SHIFT

Our analysis suggests partly that posters in these ecologies, a part of a participatory culture, are competitive, and certain topics invite confrontation in which players take verbal jabs at the other participants. We argue that this focus on rhetorical competition in the form of jabs, sarcasm, and a continual focus on agonistic argumentation on the forums is part of the transmedia shift from competing in the game to competing through writing. However, players also exhibit instances of collaboration, earnestly helping each other with play strategies, which also seems to be a shift from the collaborative play available in the *WoW* gameworld to the rhetorical space of the forums. Finally, forum posters exhibit instances of trolling, which does not seem to fall into either categories of collaboration or competition. Rather, trolling is often a playful act of disruption, one in which the poster seems to flout the rules of forum posting in which the post is both sincere and acts with some rhetorical purpose. However, the act of trolling, especially, can be seen as a transmedia shift that transports the act of play from the game space onto the purely rhetorical space of the forums.

In instances of rhetorical competition, forum posters not only exhibited more disagreement but were also more insulting, nastier, and relied more on sarcasm than more collaborative posts. For instance, the "Deal With It" and "Frost Mage" threads had the highest level of disagreement. With a 1 indicating extreme disagreement, they were coded at 1.46 and 1.89 respectively. The most collaborative thread, "Celestial Blessing," had a score of 3.53 in contrast, indicating high levels of agreement. For levels of respect, "Deal With It" and "Frost Mage" also had scores of 2.57 and 2.56, with 4 indicating a high degree of insult, while "Celestial Blessing had a score of 1 as not one of the posters on that thread were insulting in tone. And, not that surprisingly, "Deal With It" and "Frost Mage" were much more sarcastic in tone: 45% of the "Deal With It" thread was sarcastic while the "Celestial Blessing" thread exhibited no sarcasm at all.

Both the competitive argumentation and the more cooperative collaboration on the forums show a transmedia shift from the competitive and collaborative play styles of the *WoW* game space to the rhetorical space of the forums. For instance, in the game, player vs. player (PvP) battles are intensely competitive—one player loses (and dies) at the hand of another player who thus wins. Rhetorically, this winner-take-all attitude is manifested on the forums with often agonistic forms of argumentation. Within these types of arguments, posters often do not concede or admit they are wrong even when they have been shown by several other posters that their argument is flawed. For instance, in the "Frost Mage" thread, after over seven pages of insistently arguing that he or she is correct, the OP does eventually admit that his or her math for the effectiveness to the new frost mage spells was incorrect. The OP writes, "No I have no problem admitting when I'm wrong and there was no reason why I was holding out. I really thought I was reading something right. I give credit where credit is due." However, as if the OP cannot yet admit defeat, in the very next post, he or she starts yelling in all caps about another poster being wrong: "Again. . . . YOU HAVE NO IDEA WHAT YOU ARE TALKING ABOUT. You will ALWAYS BENEFIT FROM MASTERY NOW."

However, while PvP combat shows a transmedia shift of agonistic forms of argumentation on the forums, cooperative collaboration is also key to being successful in the game. Players often have to work together to defeat larger monsters that they could not successfully defeat on their own. This collaborative effort is rewarded with increased rewards in the game. In the forums, this collaborative form of argumentation is seen when players work together to solve a problem rather than simply arguing in an effort to be right at all costs. In the "Celestial Blessing" thread, the OP actually modifies his or her original strategy and offers alternate strategies in an effort to help another poster who was struggling with following the original strategy succeed. The OP poster also welcomes other posters' suggestions, even if they diverge from the OP's own strategy.

Unlike both competitive agonistic argumentation and cooperative collaboration, trolling does not mirror acceptable forms of play within *WoW*. Instead, it disrupts and breaks the rules of forum posting. If forum posting is a game, then acts of trolling effectively break the rules of the magic circle as they demonstrate a refusal of the poster to play by the forum's discursive rules by either bringing up topics in posts that are futile, as players can do nothing about them, and/or not being sincere in his or her post. However, acts of trolling still represent a transmedia shift from the *WoW* game space. *WoW* is a social game in which many players often gleefully play by not playing by the rules. For instance, while in groups, players will purposefully not play well in an effort to provoke a reaction from other players, a form of play called griefing. Just like on the forums, players in *WoW* assume that everyone will play earnestly, to the best of their ability. Not playing well, and not taking the game rules seriously in order to provoke a reaction, is thus a form of trolling.

However, these different rhetorical forms also seem to be influenced by a player's sense of agency both in the game and on the forums. As Eyman argues, "agency can be seen in the interactions and interrelationships of any of the components of a given ecosystem" (p. 246). Players in the more collaborative "Celestial Blessing" thread had a high level of agency. The OP simply lays out of a strategy for being successful in the game. Forum participants only had to follow those directions to be successful themselves. With the help of this thread, players, then, had a high level of agency within the game.

In contrast, threads that were more competitive were threads that also exhibited a lower level of player agency. "Deal With It" and "Frost Mage" were both threads largely protesting changes that Blizzard had made to the game. While Blizzard does listen to players' complaints about game changes and has been known to make changes based on suggestions, as Lockpower demonstrates, these changes are never guaranteed. Consequently, while posters do have some rhetorical agency on the forums, this rhetorical agency is never certain as a majority of posts may prove to be unheeded by Blizzard. The changes that Blizzard makes to the game, particularly in how certain classes function within the game, often seem to many players as arbitrary, causing much player frustration. It is not surprising then that this player uncertainty and sense of a lack of agency toward Blizzard creates discursive contention on the forums. For instance, much of the sarcasm within the "Deal With It" post is directed not at specific posters as much as it is directed at Blizzard for making changes that were deemed by many as unfair. For instance, Churchkey (2013) writes, "Progress be damned!!! Deal with it. Lol! Time to go back to maining my hunter. They can shoot and move without an extra key bind if I recall." While Churchkey is appropriating the OP's "deal with it" meme in a sarcastic way, he is also expressing his sense of futility at the recent game changes, and, in this way, aiming his sarcasm more at Blizzard than at the OP.

Trolling actions are also most likely born out of a sense of a lack of agency. In fact, as the whole point of trolling is to bring up a topic that is futile, even if it may seem sincere, trolling might arise because players feel no agency at all. For instance, the whole "deal with it" meme that the OP creates in the "Deal With It" thread is based off of the idea that there was nothing that players could do about Blizzard's changes to a warlock talent. However, if there is nothing that a player can do, if any rhetorical agency at all is just a futile dream, then at least players can provoke interesting reactions from other players, which could at least prove fun to read on the forums—even if it is a nihilistic type of fun. However, while intentional or not, trolling still often creates rhetorical agency just the same. In an effort to provoke a contentious debate, issues still can and do get resolved as Lockpower demonstrated in the "Deal With It" thread when Blizzard made the spell changes he suggested. Furthermore, in reacting to trolling, communities come together and further define themselves, and acts of trolling can force communities to discursively define and then deal with difficult issues they might not otherwise face as Julian Dibbell (1998) demonstrates in "A Rape in Cyberspace." In this way, trolling, whether purposeful or not, might even contribute to a type of civic forum participation that is similar to what Johnson (2008) argues.

The ecological layers here are complex and require further study. Our corpus of 708 posts from a single forum offers a very limited sample of total posts, but they do demonstrate certain patterns in the interactions within the paratext layers comprising gaming ecologies. During our analysis, we noted that the nice/nasty and respect/insult scales did not address the nuance of ethos and pathos as we had hoped. Further research might revise the argument analysis to include more overt connections between a poster's expertise, authority, credibility, and values as a way to further consider rhetorical strategies of these forums. Despite these limitations, we have attempted to show through the lens of participatory culture how certain features of one layer of the ecology might transfer to another—in the case of the shift from game to game forums, we have noted performance, appropriation, collective intelligence, judgment, and networking. We are not arguing that games or game forums own these literacies, just that they appear in our sample. We still contend that what we are seeing here is more a shift of literacies rather than expert navigation. In other words, based on our sample, players seem to treat their interactions with other players in competitive or cooperative ways. Although we noted some negotiation, the posters of our threads seem to attack other players or Blizzard rather than attempt to further understand their position, negotiate compromise, or organize in more thorough ways. If transmedia navigation were occurring, it might take the form of a more organized petition or argument to change a feature of the game the players felt they lost control of. Instead, players seemed to insert their ideas amidst disagreement, and the developers would then have to then read between the lines for these suggestions, indicating more of a transmedia shift.

NOTE

1. Jenkins et al. (2009) invoke the term literacies but more often than not call these "skills," further defining them as "social skills and cultural competencies." For our purposes, we will use the term "literacies" to capture reading, writing, and interacting through semiotic practice and resist oversimplifying these practices as "skills."

REFERENCES

Bkstunt_31. (2013, February 2). The Elder Scroll V: Skyrim FAQ. *GameFAQS*. Retrieved from http://www.gamefaqs.com/ps3/615804-the-elder-scrolls-v-skyrim/faqs/63344

Dahlberg, L. (2001). Computer-mediated communication and the public sphere: A critical analysis. *Journal of Computer-Mediated Communication, 7*. Retrieved from http://jcmc.indiana.edu/vol7/issue1/dahlberg.html

DataGenetics. (2010, December 1). Facebook casual game demographics. DataGenetics. Retrieved from http://www.datagenetics.com/blog/december12010/

Dibbell, J. (1998). A rape in cyberspace. Retrieved from http://www.juliandibbell.com/articles/a-rape-in-cyberspace/

Entertainment Software Association. (2013). Essential facts about the computer and video game industry. Retrieved from http://www.theesa.com/wp-content/uploads/2014/10/ESA_EF_2014.pdf.

Eyman, D. (2008). Computer gaming and technical communication: An ecological framework. *Technical Communication, 55*(3), 242–250.

Gee, J. P. (2005). Semiotic social spaces and affinity spaces: From the age of mythology to today's schools. In D. Barton & K. Tusting (Eds.) *Beyond communities of practice: Language, power and social context* (pp. 214–232). Cambridge: Cambridge UP.

Genette, G. (1987/1997). *Paratexts: Thresholds of interpretation.* (Jane E. Lewin, Trans.). Cambridge: Cambridge UP.

Hardaker, C. (2010). Trolling in asynchronous computer-mediated communication: From user discussions to academic definitions. *Journal of Politeness Research. Language, Behaviour, Culture, 6*(2), 215–242. doi:10.1515/jplr.2010.011

Herring, S., Job-Sluder, K., Scheckler, R., & Barab, S. (2002). Searching for safety online: Managing "trolling" in a feminist forum. *The Information Society, 18*(5), 371–384.

Huizinga, J. (1955). *Homo Ludens: A study of the play element in culture.* Boston: Beacon Press.

Jenkins, H., et al. (2009). *Confronting the challenges of participatory culture: Media education for the 21st century.* Cambridge, MA: The MIT Press.

Johnson, M. S. S. (2008). Public writing in gaming spaces. *Computers and Composition, 25*(3), 270–283.

Lapidot-Lefler, N. & Barak, A. (2012). Effects of anonymity, invisibility, and lack of eye-contact on toxic online disinhibition. *Computers in Human Behavior, 28*(2), 434–443.

Lenhart, A., Jones, S., & Macgill, A. (2008, December 7). Adults and video games. *Pew Internet and American Life Project.* Retrieved from http://www.pewinternet.org/Reports/2008/Adults-and-Video-Games.aspx

Moor, P. J., Heuvelman, A., &Verleur, R. (2010). Flaming on YouTube. .*Computers in Human Behavior, 26*(6), 1536–1546.

Nardi, B. A. (2010). *My life as a night elf priest: An anthropological account of World of Warcraft.* U of Michigan P.

Nyberg, A. K. (n.d.). Comics code history: The seal of approval. Comic Book Legal Defense Fund. Retrieved from http://cbldf.org/comics-code-history-the-seal-of-approval/

Pearce, C. (2009). *Communities of play: Emergent cultures in multiplayer games and virtual worlds.* MIT Press.

Rygarius (2013, June 20). 5.4 PTR Now Live! *World of Warcraft.* Retrieved from http://us.battle.net/wow/en/blog/10158897/

Shin, J. (2008). Morality and Internet behavior: A study of the Internet troll and its relation with morality on the Internet. In K. McFerrin et al. (Eds.), *Proceedings of Society for Information Technology & Teacher Education International Conference 2008* (pp. 2834–2840). Chesapeake, VA: AACE. Retrieved from http://www.editlib.org/p/27652

Swales, J. (1988). Discourse communities, genres and English as an international language. *World Englishes, 7*(2), 211–220.

Taylor, T. L. (2006). Does WoW change everything? How a PvP server, multinational player base, and surveillance mod scene caused me pause. *Games and Culture, 1*(4), 318–337.

Walker, M. A., Anand, P. Tree, J. E., Abbott, R., & King, J. (2012). A corpus for research on deliberation and debate. In *Proceedings of the Eighth International Conference on Language Resources and Evaluation, LREC* (pp. 23–25).

WORLD OF WARCRAFT FORUM REFERENCES

Abracadaver. (2013, June 21). Frost Mage Master 5.4 Not A Nerf. World of Warcraft Battle.net / Mage. Retrieved from http://us.battle.net/wow/en/forum/topic/9344554675

Aesica. (2013, June 15). (•_•) (•_•)>⌐■-■ (⌐■_■) DEAL WITH IT. World of Warcraft Battle.net / Warlock. Retrieved from http://us.battle.net/wow/en/forum/topic/9309260934

Darktide. (2013, March 5). Looks like its the end of wow multiboxing. World of Warcraft Battle.net / General Discussion. Retrieved from http://us.battle.net/wow/en/forum/topic/8087929775

Dazaral. (2013, June 16). (•_•) (•_•)>⌐■-■ (⌐■_■) DEAL WITH IT. World of Warcraft Battle.net / Warlock. Retrieved from http://us.battle.net/wow/en/forum/topic/9309260934

Foomz. (2013, March 5). Looks like its the end of wow multiboxing. World of Warcraft Battle.net / General Discussion. Retrieved from http://us.battle.net/wow/en/forum/topic/8087929775

Grimsock. (2013, June 15). (•_•) (•_•)>⌐■-■ (⌐■_■) DEAL WITH IT. World of Warcraft Battle.net / Warlock. Retrieved from http://us.battle.net/wow/en/forum/topic/9309260934

Hixson. (2013, March 5). Looks like its the end of wow multiboxing. World of Warcraft Battle.net / General Discussion. Retrieved from http://us.battle.net/wow/en/forum/topic/8087929775

Icedlight. (2013, June 16). (•_•) (•_•)>⌐■-■ (⌐■_■) DEAL WITH IT. World of Warcraft Battle.net / Warlock. Retrieved from http://us.battle.net/wow/en/forum/topic/9309260934

Jinza. (2013, June 13). Celestial Blessing for Hunters Strategy! World of Warcraft Battle.net / Gameplay and Guides / Quests. Retrieved from http://us.battle.net/wow/en/forum/topic/9280218947

Lhivera. (2013, June 20). Frost Mage Master 5.4 Not A Nerf. World of Warcraft Battle.net / Mage. Retrieved from http://us.battle.net/wow/en/forum/topic/9344554675

Lockpower. (2013, June 15). (•_•) (•_•)>⌐■-■ (⌐■_■) DEAL WITH IT. World of Warcraft Battle.net / Warlock. Retrieved from http://us.battle.net/wow/en/forum/topic/9309260934

Maebd. (2013, June 15). (•_•) (•_•)>⌐■-■ (⌐■_■) DEAL WITH IT. World of Warcraft Battle.net / Warlock. Retrieved from http://us.battle.net/wow/en/forum/topic/9309260934

Mizar. (2012, July 17). Why TBC and vanilla were better! World of Warcraft Battle.net / General Discussion. Retrieved from http://us.battle.net/wow/en/forum/topic/6079611684

Snarful. (2013, June 20). Frost Mage Master 5.4 Not A Nerf. World of Warcraft Battle.net / Mage. Retrieved from http://us.battle.net/wow/en/forum/topic/9344554675

Uiharu. (2013, June 15). (•_•) (•_•)>⌐■-■ (⌐■_■) DEAL WITH IT. World of Warcraft Battle.net / Warlock. Retrieved from http://us.battle.net/wow/en/forum/topic/9309260934

Wiw. (2013, June 15). (•_•) (•_•)>⌐■-■ (⌐■_■) DEAL WITH IT. World of Warcraft Battle.net / Warlock. Retrieved from http://us.battle.net/wow/en/forum/topic/9309260934

Xanzül. (2013, March 5). Looks like its the end of wow multiboxing. World of Warcraft Battle.net / General Discussion. Retrieved from http://us.battle.net/wow/en/forum/topic/8087929775

7 Data vs. Play: The Digital Rhetorics of Theorycrafting

Lee Sherlock

Achievement and virtuoso displays of skill are among the hallmarks of "hardcore" video gaming culture and gameplay. With the affordances of digital games and the texts surrounding their use, quantifiable, trackable, competitive gameplay goes back to arcade games with high score lists and extends into contemporary online gaming culture. The thrill of competition is one factor, but there is also social and cultural capital attached to racking up achievement points or posting the fastest speed run time through a video game. Competitive, achievement-oriented gaming has become increasingly media-driven, public, and transnational. International professional gaming tournaments are run by a number of organizations, attended by thousands of in-person spectators at a time, and streamed to many more thousands of potential viewers online. Although only a small minority of video game players actually participate as competitors in this kind of environment, the popularity of competitive gaming as a global phenomenon, the increasing availability and diversity of media coverage, and the rhetorical practices that have emerged in and around it signify a much larger public interest. And the desire to engineer play, to experiment with systems and strategies and devise new modes of interaction, is taken up in a variety of spaces. Most of them are not as high-stakes or public, but the rhetorical relationships among human agency, play, and games as procedural systems are still at their core.

In terms of digital rhetoric, the kinds of reading and writing that emerge from this approach to gaming are important because they reflect a deep critical literacy and modes of argumentation that are not only valued academically but are generated from a cognitive position that understands games as designed systems. This chapter examines one form of rhetorical activity in particular, theorycrafting in online writing spaces "around" digital gaming culture (Eyman, 2011). Theorycrafting is an objective-driven, data-rich rhetorical practice, and it foregrounds notions of collective authorship and knowledge as well as what constitutes valid technical argumentation. Ask (2011) positions theorycrafting as a form of "scientific play" in online gaming culture and within the case study of *World of Warcraft* as a "remaking" of the game into one that focuses on numbers and data as the primary mode of discourse. Theorycrafting is typically linked to competitive domains, such as high-end raiding in massively multiplayer online games or the most competitive of real-time strategy games. And indeed, *World of Warcraft* raiders that are dedicated heroic-mode raiders or even part of the race to "world first" (i.e., being the first group of players worldwide to defeat a raid encounter) are more inclined to be active theorycrafters than other types of players. But how theorycrafting is authored, publicly positioned, understood by audiences, and applied by players extends to a much broader set of situations and needs to be accounted for in rhetorical terms. What I am interested in tracing is not so much the content of theorycrafting as its place within a landscape of digital rhetorical practices, particularly in massively multiplayer online gaming. By closely looking at the rhetorical moves being made in online spaces tied to theorycrafting, mediations of data-driven systems and tools in the service of argumentative writing, and values attached to "good" theorycrafting practice, we can situate theorycrafting as not just part and parcel of "hardcore" gaming, but also as an ecology of reading and writing that holds key implications for learning and the experience of collective activity in online gaming.

Theory + Crafting

Part of tracing the digital rhetorical characteristics of theorycrafting involves interpreting its purpose: what exactly are the "theory" and "crafting" the term suggests, how do these processes work, and what are the outcomes of theorycrafting? What does it intend to accomplish? One of the mythologies surrounding theorycrafting is that it tries to achieve a kind of hyper-scientific documentation of the data structures underlying gameplay that, while admirable in thoroughness, is not realistically applicable while anyone is actually in the midst of gameplay. While extensive testing, simulation, and documentation are indeed parts of the theorycrafting process, the most effective theorycrafting authors realize that abstracted data and analyses are of little use if they do not help players accomplish particular gaming objectives. The "theory" of theorycrafting is thus a context-driven one: a theory of how to perform a role or execute a particular strategy the "best" or most efficient way possible given the affordances and limitations of the situation. What "the best way" means is of course up for debate and what keeps theorycrafting lively and interesting. To the greatest extent possible, the "theory" also needs to be reliable and replicable. This is where logging, testing, and digging through numbers help to define a comprehensive understanding of how specific game mechanics work. Theories also need to be aware of context and sensitive to changing factors and conditions. As theorycrafting is applied to particular gaming situations, then, such as playing a specific role (e.g., a Blood Death Knight tank) against a specific raid boss, the objective becomes not just about producing good theories but good *players*. For instance, being among the most "advanced" and successful *World of Warcraft* raiders—in terms of players playing tanks, healers, and DPS roles in the most optimized, efficient way possible and clearing content before anyone else in the world—requires an embodied performance of particular skills with a systematic knowledge of conditions in play. Theorycrafting is a sort of dynamic that happens in conversation with these modes of play; it is not a pre-requisite per se, but a form of discourse that can help players push through challenges that present what can be an extreme degree of difficulty. But this is only one slice of how players use and think about theorycrafting. For many players, it is a much more casual relationship. They might want to understand more about a class or role or how to deal with a certain mechanic, so they read, ask questions, and maybe do a little testing themselves. As theorycrafting has become popularized and more players have become introduced to its associated texts and tools, some interesting rhetorical tensions have emerged that influence the ways theory-building is approached (e.g., forms of argumentation and values attached to "good" theorycrafting) and the production and consumption dynamics of theorycrafting within gaming communities.

As theorycrafting is located in particular gaming communities and contexts—not just in one game or even game genre—players have not only produced and used it but have negotiated its meanings and purposes in relation to what they are playing. For example, on the *World of Warcraft*-community based WoWWiki, theorycrafting is explicitly connected to game theory, which is defined as "the analysis of circumstantial and general factors in order to understand the decision making process of individualized and group players for the purposes of creating generally more favorable predictions, behaviors, and overall outcomes" ("Theorycraft," n.d., para. 1). Theorycrafting also influences the language used within the game as a framing device, as the article points to the construction of DPS (or Damage Per Second) as a theorycrafted concept that now commonly stands in as a player role. The WoWWiki article on theorycraft also recognizes how embodiment needs to be taken into account as a condition of theorycraft's application: "Many of the spreadsheets that analyze rotations, for instance, do not advise the reader that the results may be contingent upon a particular UI placement, or that the players involved used hotkeys, rather than mouse-clicks, both of which can dramatically influence the numbers" ("Theorycraft," n.d., para. 11). Generally, the understanding of theorycrafting documented in this player-community space is not only a descriptive one (i.e., theorycrafting does x and y), but is also accompanied by a nuanced set of implications on what "proper" use of theorycrafting can offer as well as the drawbacks of theorycrafting when "improperly" created, interpreted, or applied. A rhetoric that emphasizes *logos* over *pathos* is also presented as what should be the controlling tone in theorycrafting discussions: "The mathematics involved are a means to explain that data in an efficient and easily understandable way. Don't attack a theorist with words that have strong emotional connotations. Attack the theory by providing strong, logical counter arguments" ("Theorycraft," n.d., para. 19). The use of "attack" in this language lends itself to the kind of (meta-)gaming that theorycrafting is part of, and indeed some players take even more pleasure in theorycrafting as an activity than the gaming spaces it is derived from.

The "crafting" half of theorycrafting is equally complex, and in terms of digital rhetoric it offers an interesting case study if we situate crafting *as* writing, mediated as it is by all sorts of data-driven processes. Both in-game and out-of-game sources of data are mobilized in the "crafting" process. In-game sources include the default combat log and player-created AddOns such as Recount (a damage and healing meter that tracks actions by player and source, even offering pie-chart visualizations that can be sorted by encounter). These are merged with out-of-game sources like raid log websites, simulation programs, Excel spreadsheets, and other computational tools that help theorycrafters filter, test, and make sense of datasets. As a rhetorical practice, one of the key components of theorycrafting to examine is how arguments are made in relation to these sources: in short, how do theorycrafters frame what they are doing and make claims about its merit and validity?

As theorycrafters draw on these computational sources to make arguments about gaming mechanics and scenarios, they do so in a variety of paratextual spaces that have become identified as community resources for theorycrafting. For *World of Warcraft* theorycrafting, Elitist Jerks (http://elitistjerks.com/) has historically functioned as one of the most popular spaces where theorycrafting happens and where players are directed to learn more about specific class mechanics in greater detail. Given its history and self-described ethos of both attitudinal and intellectual superiority, as Paul (2011) notes, Elitist Jerks holds an authoritative status as a theorycrafting arena, but other community spaces such as MMO Champion (http://www.mmo-champion.com) and the official *World of Warcraft* forums (http://us.battle.net/wow/en/forum/) serve as hosts for similar debates and conversations around theorycraft. Given how theorycrafting depends on back-and-forth exchanges between data gathering, experimentation, and online discourse as the form of "crafting" in play, digital rhetoric plays a critical role in accounting for the work theorycrafting does. As Paul (2011) argues in his analysis of *World of Warcraft* theorycrafting, "understanding the connections between process and paratext demonstrates the importance of a broad notion of rhetorical criticism as perspective for analysis of the discourse found in games, especially iterative games" (para. 4). With the analysis that follows, I intend to look closely at theorycrafting discourse to unpack the rhetorical qualities of theorycrafting: what rhetorical moves are being made and what values underpin them? Theorycrafting is also sensitive to the conditions of new and changing content in online gaming—for instance, versions of content iteratively developed over a beta-testing period or launched first on a public test realm (PTR) before moving to the "live" realms. With this in mind, I also want to highlight the implications of theorycrafting more broadly within the cultures of data access and consumption that characterize massively multiplayer online games as well as other contemporary online gaming spaces.

WHAT COUNTS AS CONTENT?

Theorycrafting is a collaborative and dialogic process, but there is also a premium placed on accuracy and relevance of information, especially as new content is released or class changes enter the game. Posters in a theorycrafting thread are often in positions trying to work through a specific mechanic so their raid team can progress further in their next set of attempts. So in an online space like Elitist Jerks, which prides itself on cutting-edge theorycrafting content, members are advised to self-govern their writing in particular ways.

If a post does not directly advance a discussion forward or somehow contribute new knowledge to the topic, it runs the risk of being edited or deleted by moderators or even penalized with a forum infraction. In the Elitist Jerks forums FAQ, the rule covering "new and worthwhile" content states: "Do not bump, quote for truth, cross-post, or post only to say thanks. We don't want to hear your funny story about something that happened in your raid last night, your baseless speculation is unproductive, and your idea for a new ability really isn't that interesting. If you have an idea you'd like to share with the community, support it with analysis, testing, or both that indicates you've put some thought into it" ("FAQ: Rules," n.d.). The set of guidelines put forth by Elitist Jerks places the personal and anecdotal in the middle of a rhetorical tension. Despite the aggressive tone of the FAQ guidelines, the community does value collegiality and even recognizes it in personal ways on occasion.

Another item in the FAQ reminds posters that "all discussion should be both polite and civil" ("FAQ: Rules," n.d.). But the overarching theme is that relevant content will always trump a post that offers nothing "new" to the discussion, however well-intentioned. The anecdotal is also framed as beholden to the demands of "worthwhile" content and rigorous argumentation. It is not that the anecdotal has no place within the community, but if stories are to be told, they need to be used to drive experimentation and frame a specific question or problem.

Where this distinction lies is in a set of literacy practices specific to the Elitist Jerks theorycrafting community. In particular, the meta-level thinking that Gee (2007) associates with gaming environments as *design spaces* is critical in making the connection between anecdotal experience and consensus-driven knowledge production. Gee argues that thinking in terms of design spaces involves viewing a specific semiotic domain (in this case, high-end *World of Warcraft* raiding and the troubleshooting thereof) through two complementary lenses: "internally as a system of interrelated elements making up the possible content of the domain and externally as ways of thinking, acting, interacting, and valuing that constitute the identities of those people who are members of the affinity group associated with the domain" (p. 32). However, part of the challenge in theorycrafting as a literacy practice is not only exercising these forms of meta-level thinking and tacit knowledge, but also making them explicit through targeted, relevant, novel, and timely forms of discourse.

A particular form of personal questioning that is despised by the Elitist Jerks community is what the FAQ identifies as "hand-holding": "In particular, we do not want to take a look at your armory or WWS to tell you what you're doing wrong and we're not interested in making your tough gear or spec decisions for you" ("FAQ: Rules," n.d.). Along similar lines, posters are urged to make a good-faith effort to track down answers independently before posting in a thread. So how is that line negotiated in actual theorycrafting discussion?

CASE 1: TROUBLESHOOTING A TALENT

In the timeline of *World of Warcraft* raiding, Dragon Soul, the last major raid tier of the *Cataclysm* expansion, was released in late November of 2011. As new raiding content going live on the regular servers typically motivates a high level of theorycrafting activity, late November and December of 2011 were critical periods to work out class and boss encounter mechanics and heroic raiding progression tactics. In the Balance druid DPS thread, one member poses a question about a particular talent not triggering its effect (commonly called a "proc" or "proccing") during a boss encounter. The opening statement reads: "I just want someone else to look and tell me if there is something very wrong that I didn't get a single Owlkin Frenzy proc on this Ultrax kill . . .," which is accompanied by a link to a World of Logs raid log ("Balance Cataclysm," 2011). Taken alone, this question might fall into the genre of "hand-holding" that the Elitist Jerks FAQ warns against—in effect, "fix this thing that happened to me." However, the author is quick to qualify the conditions of what happened in that particular boss fight, frame the question as a design problem (a potential bug) rather than a mysterious chance event, and turn the question outward to the community to gather confirmatory data. The author goes on to explain that given the probabilities involved and the length of the fight, it would be unlikely for the talent to not trigger at all: "Is this a bug? I realize that it's a 15% proc chance, but I'd assume a high uptime just because of all the instability damage taken" ("Balance Cataclysm," 2011). Two other authors come in to clarify the nature of how the Owlkin Frenzy talent works with respect to the Ultraxion fight. The first claims that "Owlkin Frenzy doesn't proc from everything, it's quite possible Ultraxion's AOE attack can't trigger it," while the second verifies the experience of the original author by checking another data source, a recorded video from the second author's raid team produced during an earlier kill, and confirming that Owlkin Frenzy did not trigger at all. Meanwhile, the original author replies to explain that Owlkin Frenzy was triggering during the pre-release or "public test" version of the fight according to other sources, but recognizes that a change to this mechanic before release would account for the discrepancy.

As a snapshot of writing that happens around gaming activity, and high-end raiding in *World of Warcraft* specifically, what is interesting in this case is not necessarily the outcome but the modes of framing and argumentation that legitimize this entry into the conversation and enable "theorycrafting" as an activity to move forward. A question put forth without enough evidence or context or one that appears self-explanatory may have been dismissed in this thread, but the original poster mobilizes outside evidence in the form of a raid log and articulates an understanding of both class-based and environmental factors to question how a particular game mechanic operates, which may be at odds with the "official" documentation that can be pieced together. Additionally, in this brief exchange a variety of evidence types (raid logs, in-game technical writing, external websites, and video-recorded game footage) are brought in for the purposes of achieving a certain, final answer.

Hypothesis Testing, Proof, and Scientific Rigor

As theorycrafters map out how game mechanics work and invent the most efficient ways to arrange and execute particular gaming scenarios, they engage rhetorically in what Steinkuehler and Chmiel (2006) identify as "scientific habits of mind" connected to massively multiplayer online gaming. They note that "individuals share their own hypotheses about what strategies work by proposing models for solutions, justifying their 'theories' with evidence (such as tabulated mathematical results aggregated across multiple trials), and debating the merits of conflicting hypotheses" (p. 724). Although there is no level of data or standard of testing that is defined as universally valid, theorycrafting contributors are expected to both account for and build on what has already been done in the community and produce and cross-check evidence derived from appropriate sources. Hypotheses that are supported with sufficient data, verified by other players' research and personal experiences, and articulated in a succinct yet comprehensive way are more likely to be accepted and built on as premises, while breaches of these rhetorical moves are likely to damage the credibility of one's argument.

CASE 2: "THE WAVE THEORY"

On the same boss encounter in the Dragon Soul raid as discussed in Case 1, Ultraxion, a debate emerged in a different section of the Elitist Jerks forums—this time in the Unholy Death Knight thread. The original poster seeks to clarify how a class mechanic works in the fight while offering a strategy tip to ensure its most effective use:

> On Ultraxion what I always do is AMZ + AMS [i.e., activate two class-based damage reduction abilities]. When you pop AMZ make sure you're standing in front of everyone else so that it absorbs for *you*. (HOT is a wave spell so it will not absorb equally for everyone like for e.g. Onslaught). ("Unholy DPS," 2012)

However, two other posters come in to contest the validity of this claim as a working hypothesis. In the first reply, the player cites personal testing performed earlier, claiming the combat log revealed that one of the class abilities is actually overwritten by the other. The nature of the boss ability "Hour of Twilight" is also contested, which throws into question the positioning strategy suggested by the ability working like a "wave" spell. The first respondent writes: "Also, the wave theory hasn't been fully agreed upon, I personally think that it's inaccurate" ("Unholy DPS," 2012). Another respondent goes a step beyond pointing out the uncertain status of the "wave theory" and rejects it outright, claiming that it "has been proven wrong in this very thread. Very easily checked by getting any WoL report with AMZ and using the expression editor. It won't absorb 75% of the hit like on most of other spells (say, Blackhorn big explosion or elementium bolt) but it will be substantial" ("Unholy DPS," 2012). In this case, the original hypothesis, though presented confidently and with a rationale for why it works the way it does, was met with resistance. In fact, the tone was a little *too* confident—rather than framing the claim as a question or a contingent finding with more work to be done, the original author created a raiding tactic derived from an assumption that the boss mechanic would always work a particular way. Both respondents who question the "wave theory" suggest that the original author has not done his or her homework. Both replies mention earlier work done in the thread on the same issue, and one re-quotes a relevant earlier post. Conducting more focused and precise research using raid and combat logs is a strategy used to counter-argue the "wave theory," although the replies differ in approach. In the first case, the respondent suggests that personal testing done contradicts the theory, while the second respondent scolds the original author for *not* taking the time to cross-check the hypothesis with a raid log and filter for that dataset. Another rhetorical tactic deployed, both in the original post and second reply, is a comparison of how the class ability works in other raiding situations (in this case, similar big-hitting raid damage effects in other fights making up the same raid tier) along with a summation of what each case means for the overall effect on the raid group. Even though when many players think of theorycrafting, they conceptualize sheer optimization of one's role within a raiding context, like achieving the highest possible damage output in a fight, this discussion foregrounds that role optimization is counterbalanced by group tactics and an evaluation of overall chances of success in raiding as an activity. In other words, players who theorycraft well and *use* theorycraft well, in normative terms, should never jeopardize an attempt at progressing through a raid encounter for the purposes of looking better on paper.

T.L. Taylor (2008) notes this tension in her discussion of damage meter AddOns as a sociotechnical object. On the use of damage meters as an assessment tool tied to raiding performance and competency, Taylor argues: "While impressions certainly form about who is skilled, particularly powerful, and helpful, they are not visually represented within the system or broken down into numbers. In most situations there is much more breadth to the construction of accomplished play, and people come to be thought of as good players and valuable members to have around because of a variety of factors, actual damage output being only one" (p. 191). Although theorycrafting is already a reflective and metacognitive practice, the objects of theorycrafting—its hypotheses, its data, the advice and tactics it produces—are subject to the social and instrumental goals of particular player groups and must be re-evaluated under those terms to be successful. And this is part of the reason why in a DPS theorycrafting thread, we see entire conversations that are not about maximizing damage output at all, but are about the best use of damage-reduction cooldowns to keep both oneself and as many other raid members alive for as long as possible. Theorycrafting's place in the bigger picture of high-end raiding progression extends to other roles as well, particularly for healers, where an effort to show off one's healing prowess with raw numerical throughput could easily get the entire raid killed after the healer runs out of mana. However, the correlation between "good" theorycrafting and "good" high-level progression raiding cannot be drawn with a simple line. Progression raiders do not always theorycraft (or they may do so in contexts that are private or have more limited public access, especially while the "race" to clear heroic raiding content first is active), the best theorycrafters are not always the most accomplished progression raiders, and application of the objects of theorycrafting may not even improve one's raiding skill or outcomes for a variety of reasons. As theorycrafting has become more distributed across online spaces, popularized, and positioned not only as an exclusive high-end raiding practice but also as something to be consumed to prepare for or be tested by *as* a raiding skill metric, this correlation is increasingly blurred. The tools and technologies used to track and visualize data have also become more complex, and as they continue to evolve, players will need to interpret them with the same critical lenses that they bring to theorycrafting as a literacy practice.

Theorycrafting Texts, Audience, and Consumption

As more players learn about theorycrafting and the texts circulating within the network of theorycrafting are drawn on in more varied online spaces and for different purposes, the status of theorycrafting knowledge as public text plays an important function. In most theorycrafting threads on Elitist Jerks, each class and spec typically has its own thread, the first post (or "lead post") of which takes the genre of a guide intended as an introduction or overview to the spec, explaining key theorycraft findings in an accessible way without overwhelming the reader with technical detail. In some cases it can even offer a compressed set of pointers if one needs to quickly pick up a spec—a Restoration shaman thread includes a section for panicked DPS shamans who are asked to step in and heal for the night ("Resto Raiding," 2011). Authoring and maintaining a class spec guide (also referred to as compendiums, FAQs, or with other terms) is a difficult, time-consuming task, and it happens largely through voluntarism from members of the community. One rhetorical element that makes this genre challenging is attempting to take large sets of discussion and data and not only translate them into generalizable terms but make decisions about what content is important enough to include and what should be omitted. Guide authors write with the awareness that to a certain extent, what they publish will operate as the public status of current theorycrafting for their class. First, it represents arguments and data that have reached a threshold of consensus; if a piece of content is included in the guide, it is something that has typically been verified through research and testing and not pure speculation. Second, when players receive the directive to "go to Elitist Jerks" to read up on how to raid with a certain spec or make sure that their gearing is optimal, guides published in the lead post are often what players encounter first and use as an initial text to familiarize themselves with that spec. Since spec guides are written for a broader range of accessibility and mass consumption, they serve centralizing and organizing purposes that limit the amount of digging players need to do through forum threads. As illustrated already, however, if one wants to put forth questions in theorycrafting threads or contribute original testing, being accountable for fine-grained details contained in threads (which can span dozens of pages and hundreds of posts) becomes more of an obligation.

CASE 3: STAT PRIORITIES?

Class spec guides are intended to be pragmatic: they offer advice on how to select talents and glyphs for a character, which abilities to use (both in a general sequence and in specific situations), what gear to look for and how to enhance it, tips on user interface setup and macros, and other information. Whenever there are important qualifications to make or situational options to discuss, they need to be included in the lead post as well. Some authors try to minimize the level of technical detail—for example, they will point to other places in the thread to find stat priority calculations or recommend that players run simulations for their unique gear setup if they are interested. Some authors decide not to trim down complexity as much and include handfuls of statistical tables and calculation formulas in the guide. After the lead post of a thread is published and the discussion continues on in each thread, the rhetorical decisions made in the opening guide are always subject to revision, and the discussions that play out reflect considerations of the validity, completeness, and relevance of information in relation to audience and purpose. In the Elitist Jerks Discipline priest healing thread for Dragon Soul raiding, a community member enters a few days after the publication of the lead post to question the value of including a set of stat weights: "I don't think including stat weights is a good idea, as all it does is encourage new priests to blindly follow the weights without understanding why they are what they are. I'd suggest a general priority similar to: Int > Spirit > Haste > Mastery > Crit, and leave off the numerical weights. If it's useful, have it around but specify that it's only going to be accurate for one set of gear and will vary wildly depending on comp, gear, strategy, etc." ("4.3 Discipline," 2011). A second respondent quotes this passage and suggests an approach in the guide "based on raid buffs and healing role" that would be sensitive to individual play-style ("4.3 Discipline," 2011). Citing the overarching theme of the discussion—a stat priority list and specifically the value of haste over other stats—a third respondent critiques the methodology of using simulated stat values to generate a priority list for healers to base decisions on and emphasizes the purpose of thinking about stat priorities in the first place, which is to be the most effective raid healer possible. The third respondent notes: "In my experience, haste is always undervalued by sims and theorycrafters because they do not take into account the 'utility' that having extra haste gives. There are times in the game when you need a heal to land quick, or you are waiting for your GCD to end so you can shield someone to save them" ("4.3 Discipline," 2011). In this debate about stat priorities/weights and how to represent them, a number of perspectives emerge about how to "get it right" in the guide. There is an also an explicit concern about audience, especially for players who enter the thread new to raid healing as a discipline priest. Anticipating players who might come in to consume theorycrafting information and apply it without fully understanding its context and rationale, as expressed in the first reply about "blindly following," players negotiate invoked audiences (Ede & Lunsford, 1984) as they discuss the framing of consensus-driven rhetorical work.

Datamining and Cultures of Data Access

The data used to drive theorycrafting and other discussions about class design and balance among player communities is subject to not just iterative change but also a desire to find and leverage it in its earliest form. The aesthetics of new data are appealing, and in player community spaces like MMO Champion, players talk about game mechanics and items that have been data mined and added to third-party databases. What data mining as a technical capacity opens up is a culture of speculation. As players uncover information, they gain glimpses into objects that have an incomplete existence. Data mined information makes transparent traces of things, but the nature of pre-release iterative design means that these things aren't yet final. They may yet go through significant changes or be removed completely from the game. As an article on player community site *WoW Insider* notes, "Stat changes, spell changes, talent changes, set bonuses—none of these things are really *real*. But if they don't suit what people have in mind, people get disappointed, upset, and up in arms—and there's no real reason to be upset or disappointed" (Stickney, 2012, para. 9). The rhetoric of datamining, depending on the case, can be anticipatory and exciting or frustrating and misleading. *WoW Insider* points out that it is the rhetorical situation that matters: "But datamining and datamined material seems to present a host of problems that don't really lie with the information itself so much as what's done with that information and how people respond to it" (Stickney, 2012, para. 4). In the death knight theorycrafting thread discussed earlier, there was a cautionary note about how a boss mechanic may have changed in the shift from the public test realms to the live realms. But not everyone is as cautious when it comes to the finality and certainty of data mined content. In a forum thread on the official *World of Warcraft* forums about an incoming change to a warrior ability that would reduce its statistical effectiveness (a "nerf" in gaming jargon), Blizzard community manager Zarhym steps in to caution against reading data mined material as official documentation: "You can't always trust the automated tools of third-party websites to correctly extract and organize all of the client data being sorted through. This type of misleading information has come out several times now over the course of testing patches 4.0.3 and 4.0.6, so it's a really good idea for players to be suspicious of data-mined material" ("And the roller-coaster continues," 2011).

For the purposes of theorycrafting, data mining is a double-edged sword: it opens up early speculation and planning, but the misuse of data mined information can be confusing if not damaging to its purposes. As of this writing, the newest *World of Warcraft* expansion, *Mists of Pandaria*, is over a month away from release and already there are theorycrafting threads and statistical research being performed on the new class to be released, the monk. In a thread on the monk's Windwalker DPS spec, the lead post author disclaims that it is *not* intended to be a guide although it approximates the form of one. Rather, the lead post will serve as a space to triangulate data sources and tentatively build an understanding of how the spec will work: "It's my understanding that the Windwalker will no [sic] be shipped as we now know it from beta testing, so this is not intended to be a guide; it may serve the purpose to start shaping one out, though. In the meantime I'll be updating this post as we get new beta releases, and with feedback from this thread and others in several discussion boards, datamining sites and live footage" ("Windwalker," 2012). The lead post author also suggests that the speculative nature of writing about a class only existing in a beta state may change how the thread is governed rhetorically: "Please note that, as the monk class is prone to fast changes, it's understandable that the discussion will flow in more speculative ways than usual, and moderation may be a tad more lenient" ("Windwalker," 2012). The wide variety of textual sources mentioned in the lead post as pertinent to the early construction of Windwalker theorycrafting is indicative of the kind of information literacy theorycrafters bring to their work and the diversity of genres and spaces that make up the *World of Warcraft* textual ecology. The relationship between the timing of the thread and the rhetorical qualities of its discussion and moderation is fascinating as well; there is an explicit move to free up the usually strict standards of theorycrafting discourse given the uncertain finality of content while not straying too far off course. In terms of digital gaming culture and writing more broadly, datamining represents another form of interaction of computational literacy with other digital literacy practices in the writing practices around games. It also follows a trend of increasingly complex and blurred producer/consumer and user/designer dynamics in online gaming culture, and the term itself suggests a kind of reconfiguration of access into the designer side of the equation: "mining" or drilling down to pull data out and make it visible.

Theorycrafting as Digital Rhetoric: Implications

Theorycrafting as an activity offers a rich site to examine the set of digital literacy practices that players engage in as they participate in online gaming culture. Selfe, Mareck, and Gardiner (2007), in their case study of a young gamer who plays *Counter-Strike* online alongside clan members, emphasize that online gaming is particularly valuable for exercising multimodal literacies, and that literate activity emerges "not only from the alphabetic exchanges they carry on, but also from their interpersonal interactions; from the images, sounds, gestures, symbols, and movements; from their shared use of specialized knowledge, terms, processes, strategies, and approaches; and from their common set of literacy values" (pp. 28–29). As players draw on data visualizations to make arguments about the games they play, for instance, they are engaging not only with images but sets of data *as* images, so there is a critical interpretive layer required in theorycrafting to know what represents what and *how* it is being represented. Bogost (2007) frames this kind of argumentation via systems-level thinking as procedural literacy, which he defines as "the ability to read and write procedural rhetorics—to craft and understand arguments mounted through unit operations represented in code" (p. 258). The kinds of questions that Bogost identifies as central to the crafting of procedural rhetorics are faced repeatedly by theorycrafters:

> What are the rules of the system?
> What is the significance of these rules (over other rules)?
> What claims about the world to these rules make?
> How do I respond to those claims? (p. 258)

The rhetorical activity of theorycrafting can be explored to view how players view and respond to iterative, massively multiplayer online gaming as a designed system. The tropes of public vs. private access to data, finality and perceived intentionality (i.e., is something *supposed* to be working this way?) of design features, and patterns of designer authority and intervention are just a few perspectives that emerge as metacognitive treatments on massively multiplayer online gaming.

Modes of authorship and audience in theorycrafting are also complex, and rhetorics of citationality and response (Rice, 2009) are central to the effort of cumulative, consensus-driven knowledge production. Response works as a matter of ethos, a context frame, and a way of giving credit for individual contributions to a problem or question. Because theorycrafting relies on thoroughness and precision of argumentation, it is not enough as a contributor to simply walk in to the middle of a conversation. Being accountable for what has already been done is a theme expressed explicitly both in the forum rules FAQ and the death knight theorycrafting thread, and failing to display an awareness of collective knowledge generated in earlier discussions is damaging to one's credibility as a theorycrafter. In terms of authorship, Hunter (2011) describes how a "social interdependent" framework that guides writing and ownership works on WoWWiki, a player community writing space around *World of Warcraft*: "Contributors on WoWWiki need to pool knowledge and resources and negotiate opposing ideas and theories in order for the project to progress. On WoWWiki, talk page discussions suggest that contributors overwhelmingly accept this social interdependent framework that is both cooperative and competitive but always focused on collective effort and aware of the communal nature of the group's writing" (p. 50). Theorycrafting in forum threads does not foreground the notion of collective authorship as much as composing in wiki spaces does, which is due in part to the interfaces and technical affordances of the two environments comparatively, but there are still negotiations of audience and collective authorship happening. For example, the stat priority discussion from the Discipline priest thread refers to the lead post as a collectively authored text representing the consolidated status quo of theorycrafting for Discipline priests. And although the authorship of the guide is attributed to a single, voluntary author, discourse similar to a wiki talk page emerges about what should and should not be represented, how much detail to go into, what content is relevant enough to include, and so on. The genre of the spec guide or compendium is also crafted with audience in mind and to scale with expertise; in its ideal form, it serves as an introduction and offers relevant resources for more complex and exploratory testing to those in search of it without confusing or overwhelming a novice reader.

Given the nature of its content and focus, theorycrafting is particularly interesting as a case of technical writing. Being a theorycrafter involves working with data and computational processes mediated by a variety of tools with the goal of producing clear, detailed, and accurate documentation. We might ask as a parallel question: what forms of procedural or computational rhetoric are at stake in the work of technical and professional writing cases, and how do they align and diverge? The user/designer relationship with respect to the production of documentation is one way to approach this question; we can ask how the set of literacies expressed in theorycrafting contributes to the building of a network (Swarts, 2011) and an organization of the social from globally distributed actors to produce complex documentation.

However, theorycrafting does not stand to produce a "neutral" form of documentation, and this is why its rhetorical processes and forms of interaction are of interest in the study of gaming cultures more broadly. Theorycrafting is tied to a particular way of being in the world, a particular way of doing things. It not only prescribes an approach to gaming that is driven by efficiency and a demanding level of responsiveness to a variety of multimodal factors, but it is used to assess players' social roles and competencies and make decisions about their place within particular collective activities (such as a progression raiding team in *World of Warcraft*). With the popularization of theorycrafting, it is now a rhetorical force in online gaming culture. When players start playing a new massively multiplayer online game, they *expect* to see theorycrafting activity start to happen on the back end once endgame content is reached. Given the cultural shifts in online gaming that theorycrafting is a part of, it is critical to continue tracing how players engage in digital rhetorical practices to drive what happens inside the game—in this case, how do players play with data *to* play the game? Equally as important will be thinking through the implications of that rhetoric: what kinds of power relationships does it set up and whose rhetoric gets privileged?

Theorycrafting undoubtedly holds literate and rhetorical value, but it involves particular positionings of one's identity in relation to broader cultural narratives about achievement and expertise. If we are to account for the digital rhetorical ecologies that constitute gaming culture, then, theorycrafting needs to be put into dialogue with the other realities and potentialities of gaming activity that circulate around it.

References

4.3 Discipline Priest Compendium. (2011). *Elitist Jerks*. Retrieved August 11, 2012 from http://elitistjerks.com/f77/t127522–4_3_discipline_priest_compendium/

And the roller-coaster continues (dps wars). (2011). *World of Warcraft Forums*. Retrieved August 11, 2012 from http://us.battle.net/wow/en/forum/topic/1920713528

Ask, K. (2011, June). *Scientific play? How players remake* World of Warcraft *as a game of numbers*. Paper presented at the Games+Learning+Society Conference, Madison, WI.

Balance Cataclysm 4.3 (Dragon Soul). (2011). *Elitist Jerks*. Retrieved August 11, 2012 from http://elitistjerks.com/f73/t110353-balance_cataclysm_4_3_dragon_soul/

Bogost, I. (2007). *Persuasive games: The expressive power of videogames*. Cambridge, MA: MIT Press.

Ede, L., & Lunsford, A. (1984). Audience addressed/audience invoked: The role of audience in composition theory and pedagogy. *College Composition and Communication, 35*(2), 155–171.

Eyman, D. (2011, April). *Writing and games: Ecologies of praxis and theory-machines*. Paper presented at the Conference on College Composition and Communication, Atlanta, GA.

FAQ: Rules. (n.d.). *Elitist Jerks*. Retrieved August 11, 2012 from http://elitistjerks.com/faq.php?faq=forumrules

Gee, J. P. (2007). *What video games have to teach us about learning and literacy: Revised and updated edition*. New York: Palgrave Macmillan.

Hunter, R. (2011). Erasing "property lines": A collaborative notion of authorship and textual ownership on a fan wiki. *Computers and Composition, 28*(1), 40–56.

Paul, C. A. (2011). Optimizing play: How theorycraft changes gameplay and design. *Game Studies, 11*(2). Retrieved from http://gamestudies.org/1102/articles/paul

Resto raiding 4.1—updating for 4.3. (2011). *Elitist Jerks.* Retrieved August 11, 2012 from http://elitistjerks.com/f79/t121202-resto_raiding_4_1_updating_4_3_a/

Rice, J. (2009). Networked exchanges, identity, writing. *Journal of Business and Technical Communication, 23*(3), 294–317.

Selfe, C. L., Mareck, A. F., & Gardiner, J. (2007). Computer gaming as literacy. In C. L. Selfe & G. E. Hawisher (Eds.), *Gaming lives in the twenty-first century: Literate connections* (pp. 21–35). New York: Palgrave Macmillan.

Steinkuehler, C., & Chmiel, M. (2006). Fostering scientific habits of mind in the context of online play. In S. A. Barab, K. E. Hay, N. B. Songer, & D. T. Hickey (Eds.), *Proceedings of the International Conference of the Learning Sciences* (pp. 723–729). Mahwah, NJ: Erlbaum.

Stickney, A. (2012). The dangers of datamining: A cautionary tale of a not-so-evil magister [Web log post]. *WoW Insider.* Retrieved from http://wow.joystiq.com/2012/04/26/the-dangers-of-datamining-a-cautionary-tale-of-a-not-so-evil-ma/

Swarts, J. (2011). Technological literacy as network building. *Technical Communication Quarterly, 20*(3), 274–302.

Taylor, T. L. (2008). Does *World of Warcraft* change everything? How a pvp server, multinational playerbase, and surveillance mod scene caused me pause. In H. G. Corneliussen & J. W. Rettberg (Eds.), *Digital culture, play, and identity: A* World of Warcraft *reader* (pp. 187–201). Cambridge, MA: MIT Press.

Theorycraft. (n.d.). *WoWWiki.* Retrieved August 11, 2012, from http://www.wowwiki.com/Theorycraft

Unholy DPS: My friend of misery [4.3.0]. (2012). *Elitist Jerks.* Retrieved August 11, 2012 from http://elitistjerks.com/f72/t125292-unholy_dps_my_friend_misery_4_3_0_a/

Windwalker (DPS): A flurry of tender fisting. (2012). *Elitist Jerks.* Retrieved August 11, 2012 from http://elitistjerks.com/f99/t129814-windwalker_dps_flurry_tender_fisting

8 Intellectual Property Pong: Three Classic Matches That Affect Your Play Today

Scott Nelson

While there is some semantic squabbling over what constitutes the very first video game to be invented, legal history has definitively determined the first IP dispute over video games. Ralph Baer, known to many as the "father of video games," may not have been the first to create a video game, but he was certainly the first to invent a home console and protect this intellectual property. Working with Bill Rusch and Bill Harrison, Baer "completed the first television game in June of 1967, which, in 1968, led to the noted United States patent titled 'Television Gaming and Training Apparatus'" (Lipson & Brain, 2009, p. 8). From these same sessions, Bill Rusch developed US Patent RE28, 507, which patented a hit-and-response mechanic (necessary for table tennis games) displayed on television screens. In 1971, Magnavox licensed the invention to produce the Magnavox Odyssey, the first video game console system.

Around the same time that Ralph Baer was developing what would become the Odyssey, a college student named Nolan Bushnell encountered the early game *Spacewar!* on a DEC computer at the University of Utah. A few years later, along with Ted Dabney, Bushnell created a *Spacewar!* clone that played on a television screen mounted inside an arcade video game cabinet (Gross, 2009, p. 246). *Computer Space*, as this new iteration was called, became the first commercial coin-operated video game.

Though *Computer Space* wasn't a smash hit, Bushnell and Dabney founded the Atari Corporation in 1972. In the same year, Bushnell had attended a Magnavox dealership demonstration of the Odyssey. When he returned, he tasked employee Al Alcorn with creating a table tennis game for an arcade machine. The result was *Pong*, an instant hit in bars, where "the video game was literally 'overplayed' as eager customers tried to cram quarters into an already heavily overloaded coin slot" (Lipson & Brain, 2009, p. 9). Video games, both in arcade machines and home consoles, had become profitable, providing the necessary incentive to protect intellectual property.

In the courts over the next fifteen years, Ralph Baer's original patents would stand up against numerous infringers. Judge John F. Grady, in his ruling on the first video game IP case in history, established what was new about these inventions (and thus patentable): "the player-controlled hitting symbol [on-screen paddle], which coincides with a hit symbol [a ball] and causes a distinct change of direction in the motion of the hit symbol" (*Magnavox v Chicago*, 1977, p. 2) and "playing games on a small scale, with the players participating in the game in an environment such as a home or someplace where a large computer would clearly not be available" (p. 3). In other words, Baer and Rusch had patented the mechanics for any game on a television screen where an object was hit and changed direction.

This patent protection extended to nearly any video game invented over the next twenty years. If one object connected on screen with another and changed the second object's direction, then Magnavox owned the rights. Game designers call this "collision detection," and it is a fundamental concept in video games and other physical simulations. Further, the patent was written broadly enough that advances in video game technology were covered. In 1985, developer Activision argued that its games did not infringe because they used newer microprocessor technology, rather than the outdated circuit technology of 1970 (*Magnavox v Activision*, pp. 6–7). The court was not convinced. Rusch and Baer's patents continued to reap royalties and settlements into the 1990s, over a decade after the last Odyssey video game system was built.

It is significant that the first video game IP case was about *Pong*-like games of table tennis. Over the course of video games' brief history, US courts batted the nature of video games back and forth, applying conflicting metaphors to this new form of communication. Much like the original games displayed on CRT screens, the overall picture can flicker and sometimes disappear. Each time the metaphors shift, another layer of IP protection is added, sometimes smothering otherwise lawful innovations in the field. The Baer patent was the initial serve in this game of

"Intellectual Property Pong," but we need to first go back further to see how the game was set up.

SETTING UP THE GAME: THE COPYRIGHT ACT OF 1976 & CONTU

Between the years of 1909 and 1976, the US Congress made no significant revisions to copyright law. In the interim, talking motion pictures, FM and short-wave radio, 3D films, robots, television, stereo records, voice recognition, Polaroid photography, photocopiers, digital computers, software, jukeboxes, video tape recorders, microchips, optic fiber, audio cassettes, CDs, handheld calculators, floppy disks, laser printers, and, of course, video games had been invented. Given changing technologies and the US's desire to join international treaties protecting intellectual property, an update was needed.

Recognizing the limits of politicians' technical knowledge, Congress in 1974 established the Commission on New Technological Uses of Copyrighted Works (CONTU) "to assist the President and Congress in developing a national policy for both protecting the rights of copyright owners and ensuring public access to copyrighted works when they are used in computer and machine duplication systems" (US Congress, CONTU, p. 4). While CONTU conducted its research, Congress moved ahead with legislation, passing the Copyright Act of 1976. The act made significant changes to copyright law: codifying the four factors determining fair use (1§107), enumerating the five (later amended to six) specific copyrights covered (1§106), establishing the term of protection to the life of the author plus 50 years (later extended to life plus 70 years) (3§302), replacing publishing with "fixation in a tangible medium of expression" (3§301) as the requisite act for copyright protection, and defining the six (later seven) categories of "works of authorship" (1§102). CONTU's final report was issued on July 31, 1978, and upon its recommendations, Congress amended the Copyright Act to include protection for computer programs as "literary works." As the CONTU report was careful to note, "The term 'literary works' does not connote any criterion of literary merit or qualitative value" (p. 16), but instead means more broadly those works constituted in the medium of text.

The Copyright Act of 1976 took over twenty years to draft, and since its enactment, has been amended numerous times to catch up to rapidly developing technologies. In the video games industry, this has meant a series of court cases where the nature of this medium and protections for creators have been knocked around as certain clauses are perused, probed, and parsed. For the game of Intellectual Property Pong, the most significant matches play out over Title 17, Chapter 1, Section 102 of the US Code, where the subject matter of copyright is codified. This section contains only two simple paragraphs, but the language therein has been the subject of myriad battles. The first two matches of Intellectual Property Pong deal with the first paragraph of that section:

> Copyright protection subsists, in accordance with this title, in original works of authorship fixed in any tangible medium of expression, now known or later developed, from which they can be perceived, reproduced, or otherwise communicated, either directly or with the aid of a machine or device. [17 U.S.C §102(a)]

Match 1: Fixed vs. Transient

Our first round of Intellectual Property Pong is more of a warm-up, a practice match testing what the law considers "fixed" in a medium. Video games provided a unique legal challenge, as their audiovisual elements change with each play session. Other media covered by the Copyright Act stayed fixed in their original form, arresting a particular configuration of light, sound, or gesture. Paintings did not morph into sculptures, words stayed stationary on a page, and celluloid was sufficient to fix each frame of a moving image. Even pantomime and choreography—new categories of expression covered under the Copyright Act of 1976—needed to be represented in some type of notation to trigger protection. Given the novelty of early video game arcade hardware and software, the courts had to specifically address whether each play session of a video game may be distinct.

Artic International, Inc. was the company to challenge the permanence of this new medium. In the early days of the arcade boom, it was unclear just what aspects of a video game were protectable under the new Copyright Act and its amendments covering computer programs. While the home console market had seen interchangeable video game cartridges since 1976 and eventually interchangeable cassette systems for arcade games would become popular, in 1983, the most common way to change the game in an arcade cabinet was through replacing the circuit board. Though the circuit boards were bulky, arcade owners found swapping circuit boards preferable to swapping entire cabinets. The games themselves were contained on the ROM chips hardwired to the circuit board. In 1982 and 1983, Artic was sued for copyright infringement by two separate companies. In one case, Midway accused Artic of selling a "speed-up kit" for Midway's copyrighted game *Galaxian* along with a clone of *Pac-Man* (*Midway v Artic*). In the other, Artic was accused of selling a circuit board of the game *Defense Command*, "virtually identical to the play of the Williams game, *Defender*" (*Williams v Artic*, p. 872). In fact, Artic's *Defense Command* was so similar, its "high score" screen "contain[ed] the initials of employees of Williams, including its president, who initially achieved the highest scores" (*Williams v Artic*).

Rather than feebly attempting to deny the copying of its competitors' games, Artic took another tack. It argued in both cases that the copyrights claimed by the plaintiffs were invalid for a number of reasons, all of which were rejected. The most significant for the current discussion, however, was that video games could not be copyrighted because the images and sounds emanating from the machine changed each time a new play session was enacted. Under the US Code, a work is considered "fixed" if it "is sufficiently permanent or stable to permit it to be perceived, reproduced, or otherwise communicated for a period of more than transitory duration" (17 USC 1§101). Artic latched onto the "transitory" wording and argued that video games fit this description.

The court disagreed. It ruled that "there is always a repetitive sequence of a substantial portion of the sights and sounds of the game" (*Williams v Artic*, 1982, p. 874), and thus were fixed sufficiently to command copyright protection. This particular aspect of the ruling becomes more significant in light of the procedurally generated game worlds of later titles such as *Diablo*, *Dwarf Fortress*, and *Minecraft*. One of the draws of such video games (and, I would argue, most games in general) is their replayability, the surprise that comes from random elements in the game. To require that every element of a video game permanently be fixed would mistake the medium for some of its components, to limit this new medium to the metaphors of its predecessors. This is like saying that *Pong* is about a moving pixel.

MATCH 2: LITERARY VS. AUDIOVISUAL

As Lev Manovich (2001) has noted, we experience new media through the metaphors of earlier media (pp. 69–93). Just as some grammars of video games are culled from the metaphors of cinema, photography, and the printed word, so too are these metaphors applied when courts are attempting to deal with an alien medium. Video games are described as combinations of previous media or slotted underneath already extant categories such as "literary works" or "audiovisual works," rather than placed in an entirely new category of their own.

Since 1964, the US Copyright Office has allowed registration of computer programs as literary works. Before the 1980 revisions to the Copyright Act (Copyright Amendments) codified this practice, the Office did so under its "rule of doubt," whereby it processes registrations even though there is a reasonable doubt as to their validity in courts. As mentioned above, this designation of "literary" makes no claim as to artistic merit, but instead points to the medium in which the expression is fixed. Since computer programs are expressed (by humans, at least) in alphanumeric characters, they "naturally" fell into the already well-established subject category of "literary works," at least according to CONTU.

In bringing together many forms of media, video games also gather a variety of copyright protections beyond the computer programs upon which they run. Writing during the golden age of arcade video games, attorney Alan Glasser (1986) identified "four elements lodged in a video game" protectable under copyright:

> First, if a video game is based upon a maze, the maze may be copyrightable as a pictorial or graphic work or even as a map. . . . Second, since many video games have various screens which appear during the game as the player advances to the next step of difficulty, the sequence of screens and images may be copyrightable as a compilation or a collective work. Third, if the sounds produced along with the game comprise original music or dialogue, they are copyrightable as musical or dramatic works. . . . Fourth . . . courts have found strong copyright protection for video game characters. (pp. 108–109)

While Glasser's description correctly identifies these elements as copyrightable, what is more significant are the elements he elides. He identifies the audiovisual features, but not the literary ones. This is common among more than a few intellectual property attorneys. For some writing at the time, this mirrors the courts' "unclear indication of whether a video game would be considered entitled to copyright protection" (Blaise, 2004, p. 530). Others, however, continue to argue that computer programs of any type should not be covered by copyright law. This particular match of Intellectual Property Pong is over just what sort of medium video games are.

Glasser's (1986) position is typical of the "games as audiovisual works" player, focusing most on the surface expressions of the medium. Courts in the infancy of the industry tended to skew this way. In the 1982 case *Stern v Kaufmann*, for example, Judge Eugene Nickerson described video games as "computers programmed to create on a television screen cartoons in which some of the action is controlled by the player" (p. 853). This particular case becomes even more significant in light of the infringement found.

Stern Electronics was a licensed manufacturer of the Konami arcade game *Scramble*, a side-scrolling shooter. Omni, one of the defendants in the case, had created a knock-off by supposedly writing its own code that displayed audiovisual elements nearly identical to *Scramble*. In this case, Konami had registered the work as an audiovisual display, and thus Omni argued "Konami was entitled to copyright only the written computer program that determines the sights and sounds of the game's audiovisual display" (*Stern*, 1982, p. 855). Like the Artic cases to come later, Omni also argued that the images and sounds themselves were too transient to warrant fixation. Unlike Artic, however, Omni also argued that these transient images and sounds were not the original work of a human author, but the work of the underlying program.

Nickerson rejected both arguments. Like the courts in *Midway v Artic* (1983) and *Williams v Artic* (1982), he asserted that the images and sounds were fixed within the ROM chips. Comparing video games to music, he noted that "the audiovisual work and the computer program are both embodied in the same components of the game" like when "an audio tape embodies both a musical composition and a sound recording" (*Stern*, 1982, p. 856). Moreover, Nickerson invoked the composition process when he determined what satisfies the "original work" requirement:

> Someone first conceived what the audiovisual display would look like and sound like. Originality occurred at that point. Then the program was written. Finally, the program was imprinted into the memory devices so that, in operation with the components of the game, the sights and sounds could be seen and heard. (pp. 856–57)

Echoing this same sentiment, though for a different argument, Annette Vee (2010) has said that "the compositional contexts for code often resemble those for writing much more closely than those for manufacturing or engineering" (p. 185). For both Vee and Nickerson, coding is a creative process which spawns an original work. In the case of video games, though, it actually generates three original works: the source code in which it is written, the object code that the machine reads, and the audiovisual display as it is rendered by the computer.

In simple terms, source code is in text, written in human-readable programming languages. Using a compiler, this source code is translated into object code, code written in binary, hexadecimal, or octal coding, and readable only by computers or skilled programmers with a lot of time on their hands. One of CONTU's original commissioners, John Hersey, condemned the notion of extending copyright to object code. Hersey—a novelist, journalist, and president of the Author's Guild of America at the time—believed copyright was reserved for communications among humans. Object code, by his reasoning, communicated instructions to machines (Culler, 1983, pp. 539–542). While Hersey's dissent was ultimately ignored, it is significant to note that such a conception of copyright's scope is still contentious among intellectual property scholars today.

Like the *Midway* and *Williams* courts, Nickerson invoked the Copyright Act's requirement that an original work must be able to be "perceived, reproduced, or otherwise communicated, either directly or *with the aid of a machine or device*" [emphasis added, 17 §102(a)]. In placing the originary act before any code itself was written, and allowing object code as a fixation of that underlying expression, Nickerson anticipated the landmark software copyright ruling of *Apple v Franklin* (which held that a computer's operating system could be copyrighted). Currently, the US Copyright Office will take object code for copyright registration, but will do so only under their rule of doubt, as their agents "cannot determine with certainty the presence of copyrightable authorship" (US Copyright Office, *General Copy Requirements* par.2).

Pac-Man was the star of three early copyright cases, as he was a lucrative intellectual property and many wanted to cash in on his fame. Between 1980 and 1982, it is estimated that sales of the arcade version of *Pac-Man* alone totaled $240 million and that it had been played over 2 billion times (*Midway v Strohon*, 1983, p. 743). One of his cases I've already discussed above is *Midway v Artic* (1983), which focused on fixation in a tangible medium. The other two *Pac-Man* cases would center on the dual copyright protection for both the textual program and the audiovisual elements of a video game. In the first of these two cases to be decided, *Atari v North American Philips Consumer Electronics Corp* (1982), Philips was accused of infringing on Atari's port of *Pac-Man* with their own title *K.C. Munchkin*. Like Pac-Man, K.C. Muchkin traveled around a maze, gobbling dots while being pursued by creatures. Also like Pac-Man, K.C. could turn the tides against his adversaries by consuming a special power pellet.

Judge George Leighton presided over the case, and in his ruling, deconstructed all of the audiovisual elements of both *Pac*-Man and *K.C. Munchkin*, carefully comparing each and determining what was copyrightable in the work. Citing an earlier manufacturing case, Judge George Leighton reaffirmed the idea/expression dichotomy, codified in the Copyright Act of 1976. This dichotomy establishes that copyright protects only the expression of an idea, not the underlying idea itself. In this same vein, he stated that "copyright protection does not extend to games as such" (*Atari v N Amer. Philips,* 1982, p. 614). That is, previously, the pictorial representations of game boards, pieces, cards, and the like, along with the specific wording of game rules have been copyrightable, but the rules themselves were not. In this line of reasoning, Leighton was treating video games as audiovisual works, where if two games have a similar look and feel, one most likely has infringed.

However, he also determined what was *not* copyrightable material in *Pac-Man*. For this analysis, Leighton conjured literary works and "scènes à faire"—"stock literary devices . . . not protectable by copyright" (*Atari v N. Amer. Philips,* 1982, p. 614). In this instance, the metaphor of literary works is not only applied to the underlying code, but to the overall concepts found in literary analysis. Using this concept, Leighton wrote

> The maze and scoring table are standard game devices, and the tunnel exits are nothing more than the commonly used "wrap around" concept adapted to a maze-chase game. Similarly, the use of dots provides a means by which a player's performance can be gauged and rewarded with the appropriate number of points, and by which to inform the player of his or her progress. (p. 617)

The "scènes à faire" concept would become central to the video game industry and continues to be a contested legal issue. Later cases would rely upon this concept to defend against claims of copyright infringement. In 1988, the *Data East v Epyx* court found that *International Karate* did not infringe upon the copyright of *Karate Champ*, even though the games shared fifteen characteristics. The court ruled those characteristics— among them a referee, a 30-second timer, and a jumping sidekick—are stereotypical of karate games in general (*Data East v Epyx*, 1988, p. 209). Six years later, Data East would find itself on the other side of that defense when Capcom accused *Fighter's History* of infringing upon *Street Fighter II* (*Capcom v Data East*, 1994). Another, more recent case in 2012 placed a limit on scènes à faire and ruled against a *Tetris* clone (*Tetris v Xio*). Had Judge Leighton not excluded these common elements from copyright protection, it would be possible for developers to secure a monopoly over entire genres of video games.

In the second classic *Pac-Man* case, *Midway v Strohon* (1983), the defendants were accused of selling a modification kit called "Cute-See." This modification kit replaced five ROMs on the Pac-Man circuit board to speed up the game and alter the audiovisual elements. The kit also came with stickers to cover up the *Pac-Man* logos on the game cabinet (*Midway v Strohoni*, p. 744). The modifications made the video game more challenging, and thus more lucrative for arcade owners. If it was more difficult to play, more quarters were needed to continue.

Citing the earlier *Atari v N. Amer. Philips* (1982) ruling, the judge removed any scènes à faire from consideration. Since the modification kit altered the audiovisual display, the judge ruled "[t]he distinctive, copyrightable features of Pac-Man are not present in Cute-See and, therefore, the latter game is not an infringement" (*Midway v Strohon*, p. 747). However, he went further and "agree[d] with *Midway* that the audiovisual display and the computer program are not so 'intertwined' as to preclude their separate consideration. In fact, the computer program is a distinct creation" (p. 749). In so doing, the court validated the separate copyright protections afforded computer programs and audiovisual elements and further affirmed the creative process of programming: "The skill, ingenuity and effort that is required to design the computer program which operates the game is altogether different from the process of conceiving and designing the distinctive Pac-Man characters" (p. 749).

While these early court cases brought some metaphors from cinema and literature to bear upon video games, there are significant aspects that were not immediately transferred. For one, these early courts never took the medium of video games nor its appreciators seriously. In his

Atari v N. Amer. Philips ruling, Judge Leighton made it clear that the audiences of art and video games were separate: "Video games, unlike an artist's painting or even other audiovisual works, appeal to an audience that is fairly undiscriminating insofar as their concern about more subtle differences in artistic expression" (1982, p. 619). Though it was established that video games could be copyrighted, a number of other concurrent cases outright rejected video games' right to be protected as speech. In *America's Best Family Showplace Corp. v City of New York* (1982), an arcade owner challenged the constitutionality of a New York zoning ordinance. In the ruling, the court cited a Supreme Court case where a coin-operated peep show was found to be protected speech, but went on to say it was "not persuaded" that "video games, unlike the nude dancing . . . are a form of speech protected by the First Amendment" because video games do not communicate an idea (p. 173). It would not be until 2011 in *Brown v Entertainment Merchants Assn.* that the Supreme Court would uphold First Amendment protections for video games.

Match 3: Copyright v. Patent

The previous two matches dealt with Section 102(a) of the USC regarding copyright. For our final match of Intellectual Property Pong, we'll need to revisit Section 102 of the US Code on copyright, this time focusing on the second paragraph:

> In no case does copyright protection for an original work of authorship extend to any idea, procedure, process, system, method of operation, concept, principle, or discovery, regardless of the form in which it is described, explained, illustrated, or embodied in such work. [17 U.S.C §102(b)]

It would seem that this section neatly delimits the scope of copyright while reserving some room for patent protection. As I mentioned above, the original Baer invention was not the first type of media that could be considered a "video game," but instead, it was the first to file a patent for games that would be played on television screens. At the time, it leveraged the ubiquity of televisions across America to reach a broader audience than personal computers could, and thus hinged upon its marketability as much as its ingenuity. Though the courts consistently ruled in favor of the Baer and Rusch patents, the fight about where video games fit in the current intellectual property scheme continues today.

There are three classifications of patents: plant, design, and utility. Until video games integrate asexual reproduction of flora, we'll put the first category by the wayside. That leaves design and utility patents. Kyle Gross, in his "Game On: The Rising Prevalence of Patent-Related Issues in the Video Game Industry" (2009) notes that "[o]f the few patents in effect during the early years of the video game industry, most focused on gaming hardware—the actual machines used to play the game" (p. 247). The Baer and Rusch patents fell into this category because the games they played were inextricable from the hardware on which they ran. The video games industry is rife with utility patents on hardware and peripherals and design patents covering the ornamental, nonfunctional aspects of those devices. As examples, in 2012, Nintendo won utility patent litigation over its Wii remote (Hilliard, 2012), and Microsoft recently applied for a utility patent on a "Holodeck-style immersive display" (Orland, 2012). Design patents cover both gaming systems' outer cases, and like a trademark, prevent consumer confusion. Since the most controversy in the video games industry is actually around the use of utility patents for video game mechanics, we'll stick to that match-up.

In order to obtain a patent, an inventor must create or discover "a new and useful process, machine, manufacture, or composition of matter, or any new and useful improvement thereof" (35 USC §101). According to intellectual property lawyers Stanford Warren and Steve Chang, "Video games and virtual worlds are useful inventions, and are therefore patentable, provided they are new, nonobvious, and meet the requirement that patentable subject matter be tied to a particular machine or transform data into a different state or thing" (2010, p. 114). A number of court cases since the 1960s have volleyed the concept of what qualifies for utility patents. For our purposes, it's significant to look at two aspects of video games under patent law: the patentability of games and the patentability of software.

With regard to toys and traditional games, it would seem that patent and copyright laws have struck a balance. As both Pamela Samuelson (2007) and Shubba Ghosh (2008) have asserted, the exclusion of any "idea, procedure, process, system, method of operation, concept, principle, or discovery" [17 USC §102(b)] from copyright protection can be traced back to an 1880 case, *Baker v Selden*. Selden owned a copyright on a book about accounting procedures. In a book of his own, Baker reproduced the ledgers and blank forms of Selden's work. While lower courts found copyright infringement, the Supreme Court reversed these rulings, indicating that copyrighting the processes in the book would be the same as granting a monopoly on one form of knowledge. As the Court put it, "[t]he very object of publishing a book on science or the useful arts is to communicate to the world the useful knowledge which it contains. But this object would be frustrated if the knowledge could not be used without incurring the guilt of piracy of the book" (qtd. in Samuelson, p. 1933). Applied to traditional games, "patents typically cover the gaming apparatus itself—the board, the dice, and other items that facilitate the game play—as well as the rules of the game" (Ghosh, p. 876), while copyright covers the expression of those rules in text or pictorial form. But video games present an interesting hybrid—computational processes are necessary to express the pictorial (along with all other) aspects of the game. The fact that video games are software complicates the matter.

Around the same time that the Copyright Office began accepting computer software under its rule of doubt, the US Patent and Trade Office began rejecting the same "for reasons of impracticality" (Brody, 1982, p. 487). In reality, the Patent Office in the 1960s lacked the necessary infrastructure and expertise to deal with computer programs. The patent process is rigorous and expensive, while (since the Copyright Act of 1976, at least) copyright is automatic and free (though works must be registered to sue for statutory damages). Faced with a new technology that needed a higher-than-average expertise to understand, the Patent Office knocked the ball out of its own court, sending it back to the Copyright Office's side. Moreover, "[t]wo Supreme Court Rulings in the 1970s affirmed the idea that computer programs were unpatentable; decisions in *Gottschalk v Benson* (1972) and *Parker v Flook* (1978) both indicated that the algorithms under review were not far enough removed from pure math to make them patentable" (Vee, 2010, p. 184). It seemed like copyright would be the only protection for any type of software, video games included.

Naturally, another legal deflection was on the way. The earlier rulings of *Benson* and *Flook* left the door open for computer programs when the court stated in *Parker v Flook* (1978) that the presence of an algorithm didn't automatically rule out patentability (*Parker v Flook,* p. 591). In 1981, the Supreme Court ruled in *Diamond v Diehr* that "an *application* of a law of nature or mathematical formula [a computer program] to a known structure [a computer] or process may well be deserving of patent protection" (original emphasis, p. 1056). Software patent applications then began connecting software to "a general purpose computer," "essentially changing software patents from patents on process to patents on machines" and eventually the ruling in "*State Street Bank and Trust v Signature Financial Group* [in] 1998 unambiguously confirmed that . . . software . . . was patentable, as long as it was useful" (Vee, 2010, p. 184).

A final move by the Supreme Court still left the issue up for debate. In *Bilski v Kappos*, the Court upheld a "machine or transformation" test for whether a process can be patented. In order for a process (such as a computer program) to be patented, it must be "tied to a particular machine or apparatus or . . . [transform] a particular article to a different state or thing" (Warren and Chang, 2010, p. 123). As Warren and Chang have observed, "The [lower Federal Court] *Bilski* decision expressly noted that the transformation of certain electronic data into a visual depiction may be sufficient" (p. 123). However, the Supreme Court's affirmation of that ruling continued to leave doubts as to what can be patented. The Court ruled that while valid, the "machine or transformation" test is "not the sole test for patent eligibility" (*Bilski v Kappos* 2010, p. 3220) and rejected that a process would need to be tied to a machine to be patentable. In other words, the eligibility of software patents is yet to be decided. In the meantime, though, they are still being granted. For the video games industry, that means utility patents on not only the hardware innovations above, but for game mechanics as well.

Annette Vee, in her article "Carving Up the Commons: How Software Patents are Impacting Our Digital Composition Environments" (2010), has delineated some of the problems plaguing the US patent system: "The conditions of novelty and nonobviousness have been poorly applied to software patents in particular, in part because the patent examiner's manual does not suggest a review of prior art located in software" (p. 183). She additionally states that the growth in patents over the past thirty years, coupled with vague applications, have contributed to the Patent Office's backlog (p. 183). In such a situation, patent agents have much shorter periods of time to review prior art to see if the applications are overreaching. Kyle Gross (2009) agrees, and further contends that the video game industry, especially, is subject to overly broad patents because "video games have a number of elements that could be patented within any of the different steps involving hardware, software, algorithms, and data structures of a single game" (p. 254). From his perspective, "[t]he problem is that the courts have validated patents on subject matter that those in the business of video games consider to be obvious and common sense" (p. 255).

In 2004, Swedish researcher Ola Davidsson published a thesis on video game patents. Although the major purpose of her study was to organize patents more efficiently to benefit game developers, her research revealed quite a few approved patents that could be considered either "common sense" or at the very least, standard conventions for certain video game genres, what under copyright law would be classified as "scènes à faire." As Davidsson puts it, some of these patents "almost touch the copyright realm of 'look and feel.' They protect the 'effect' that is produced in the video game" (p. 33).

One, titled "Multi-player, Multi-character Cooperative Play Video Game with Independent Entry and Departure," was filed by Atari and entails, "A multi-player, multi-character video game where the games rules force the players to cooperate in negotiating the maze at least until the characters reach a portion of the maze where a specific objective is located" (Davidsson, 2004, p. 127). As described, this could be the mechanics of any multiple-player co-op video game. Another, filed by Sega, is titled "Videogame System for Creating a Simulated Comic Book Game," and is "an audiovisual presentation designed to simulate the episodic nature of a comic book page" (Davidsson, p. 130). While this one is unquestionably an awesome idea, patenting it precludes anyone from developing an entire genre of games. As a final example, there's "Drug Abuse Prevention Computer Game," a role-playing game whose patent will prevent anyone else in the Serious Games community from "realistically portraying the consequences of drug abuse" until 2023 (Davidsson, p. 167). Davidsson outlines over fifty patents in her study, most with similarly broad descriptions.

Patent reform has proven difficult because two very large sectors of the economy often find themselves on opposite sides of litigation. According to Kyle Gross (2009), technology companies are often defendants protecting themselves from patent trolls, and thus support reform. Large pharmaceutical companies, on the other hand, are most often plaintiffs protecting their patents against smaller companies and generic manufacturers, and thus favor the status quo (p. 269). In 2011, however, President Obama signed the America Invents Act into law, signaling some upcoming changes to the US patent system. Among those changes are some that make it more difficult for patent trolls to acquire large portfolios of patents not being developed and sue for large settlements.

While this match often vacillates between copyright and patent protection, there is one place where the law provides overlapping protection, the "center line" in a game of Intellectual Property Pong. For most of the history of US intellectual property, the subject matter of patent and copyright law was "initially divided along physical and abstract lines," respectively, and according to some commentators, "covered the entire breadth of intended subject matter with no intervening 'gap'" (Brody, 1982, pp. 486–487). Even though copyright was thought of as the "abstract" side of the equation, this did not mean that ideas were copyrightable. On the contrary, ideas always were in the public domain, with "[p]atent . . . emphasiz[ing] protection of processes embodying ideas while copyright . . . stressed protection of expression of ideas" (Brody, p. 487). Early cases tended to keep these two forms of law separate, and in some instances, courts outright denied double registration under both copyright and patent. Marilyn Brody (1982) points to one case in 1927 where a court of appeals denied dual registration of a hosiery sales ticket under both copyright and design patent (p. 489). However, in a ruling over whether a lamp base in the form of a copyrighted statue also could be registered as a design patent, the 1954 *Mazer v Stein* court stated that "[n]either the Copyright Statute nor any other says that because a thing is patentable it may not be copyrighted" (Brody, p. 217). In an official policy change in 1995, the Copyright Office began accepting registrations on pictorial, graphical, and sculptural works even if they had already been granted a design patent (US Copyright Office, Registrability 15606).

Winners and Losers

When Magnavox enforced the Baer and Rusch patents in the early 1980s, everyone accused of infringement ended up either buying a license or paying in court. While video games were lucrative at the time, the industry was not diverse. The video game industry today is made up of varied strains of developers, from AAA studios to the truly independent game development company with an employee of one. Distribution channels are no longer limited to national arcade chains and home consoles. The Internet means the independent developer can find her audience more easily; it also means corporate IP lawyers can find her more easily as well.

An industry that relies more on patents presents a barrier to entry for smaller companies and autonomous developers. Though patents last approximately one-fifth of the duration of copyrights, they are exclusionary to any form of competition, even independent discovery. Accordingly, they are exponentially harder and more expensive to obtain than copyrights. Beyond the first few cases at the beginning of the industry, there have been relatively few game design patent infringement lawsuits brought before a court, and anecdotal evidence from both Vee (2010) and Davidsson (2004) indicate that game designers take a negative view to patents. These negative views, however, do not always preclude patents from being filed. Patents become bargaining chips when developing a new game: if one studio wants to use a feature that another has patented, it helps to have something to trade.

A video game industry that turns more to copyright protections, however, presents a different set of challenges. While copyright is free or relatively inexpensive ($35 for a basic registration at the time of this writing), it provides somewhat weaker protections for intellectual property. To further complicate matters, copyright adds layers of protection to a single video game, and each must be negotiated for full protection. The system default is to copyright new creations; developers must actively seek to put an expression in the public domain. And unfortunately, "free" doesn't back many paychecks.

Finally, neither intellectual property is cheaper to defend. As Vee (2010) has observed, "the trend in patentability follows roughly the same arc as copyright, favoring individual creators (or 'inventors') over the public domain" (p. 184). As these commons are closed off by increasing numbers of patent and copyright claims, any intellectual property is only as strong as the lawyers you can hire to litigate for it. While growth of the Internet has been fueled by commerce, it has also allowed for gift economies of writers, filmmakers, photographers, illustrators, animators, and musicians working outside the bounds of capitalistic markets. Video games have already become part of that gift economy, albeit on a smaller scale.

In *Pong*, there is always a clear winner and loser; there cannot be a tie. Fortunately, video games have progressed beyond the initial mechanics of objects hitting other objects, and creativity has escaped the original rectangle of play. Perhaps intellectual property law can take a similar route and find new ways of dealing with media that balances the interests of commerce and culture.

References

America's Best Family Showplace Corp. v City of New York Dept. of Buildings. 536 F. Supp. 170–75. (US E.D.N.Y., 1982).

Apple v Franklin. 714 F.2d 1240–55. (3d Cir. 1983).

Atari, Inc. v N. Amer. Philips Consumer Electronics Corp. 672 F. 2d 607. (7th Cir. 1982).

Baer, R. (1973). Television gaming and training apparatus. U.S. Patent 3,728,480. *USPTO.*

Bilski v Kappos. 130 S. Ct. 3218–59. (US S. Ct., 2010).

Blaise, F. (2004). Game over: Issues arising when copyrighted work is licensed to video game manufacturers. *Albany Law Journal of Science & Technology 15,* 517–543.

Brody, M. A. (1982). Copyright protection for video games, computer programs, and other cybernetic works. *Comm/Ent: A Journal of Communications & Entertainment Law, 5,* 477–515.

Brown, et al. v Entertainment Merchants Assn., et al. 131 (US S. Ct. 2729, 2011).

Capcom v. Data East. U.S. Dist. LEXIS 5306. (US N.D. Cal., 1994).

Copyright Act of 1976. Pub. L. 94–553, 90 Stat. 2541. 19 Oct. 1976.

Copyright Amendments. Pub. L. 96–517, 94 Stat. 3028. 12 Dec. 1980. *NIH.*

Culler, M. P. (1983). Copyright protection for video games: The courts in the Pac-Man maze. *Cleveland State Law Review, 32,* 531–567. 2012.

Data East v. Epyx. 862 F.2d 204–10. (US 9th Cir. 1988).

Davidsson, O. (2004). *Game design patents: Protecting the Internal Mechanisms of Video Games?* (Unpublished thesis). IT University of Göteborg, Göteborg, Sweden.

Diamond v Diehr. 101 S. Ct. 1048–72. (US S. Ct., 1981).

Ghosh, S. (2008). Patenting games: *Baker v. Selden* revisited. *Vanderbilt Journal of Entertainment & Technology Law, 11,* 871–898.

Glasser, A. R. (1986). Video voodoo: Copyright in video game computer programs. *Federal Communications Law Journal, 38,* 103–134.

Gross, K. (2009). Game on: The rising prevalence of patent-related issues in the video game industry." *SMU Science & Technology Law Review, 12,* 243–274.

Hilliard, K. (2012). Nintendo claims victory against Wii patent lawsuit. *Game Informer.* Retrieved from http://www.gameinformer.com/b/news/archive/2012/08/01/nintendo-claims-victory-against-wii-patent-lawsuit.aspx

Lipson, A. S., & Brain, R. (2009). *Computer and video game law: Cases, statutes, forms, problems, and materials.* Durham, NC: Carolina Academic Press.

Magnavox Co. v Activision, Inc. 848 F. 2d 1244. US (ND Cal. 1986).

Magnavox Co. v Chicago Dynamic Industries, et al. 201 U.S.P.Q. (BNA) 25. (US ND Ill., ED. 1977).

Manovich, L. (2001). *The language of new media.* Cambridge, MA: MIT Press.

Mazer v. Stein. 347 U.S. 201–21. (US S. Ct., 1954).

Midway Manufacturing Co. v Artic International, Inc. 704 F.2d 1009–14. (7th Cir. 1983).

Midway Manufacturing Co. v Strohon. 564 F. Supp. 741–54. (US N.D. Ill., ED. 1983).

Orland, K. (2012). Microsoft patent application shows holodeck-style 'immersive display.' *Ars Technica.* Retrieved from http://arstechnica.com/gaming/2012/09/microsoft-patent-shows-holodeck-style-full-room-immersive-display/

Parker v Flook. 437 U.S. 584–600. (US S. Ct. 1978).

Robinson, E. (2011). New patent reform law could reduce lawsuits by non-practicing entities. *Opensource.com.* Retrieved from http://opensource.com/law/11/9/new-patent-reform-law-could-reduce-lawsuits-non-practicing-entity

Rusch, W. T. (1997). Television gaming apparatus." US Patent RE28, 507. *USPTO.*

Samuelson, P. (2007). Why copyright law excludes systems and processes from the scope of its protection. *Texas Law Review, 85*(7), 1921–1977.

Stern Electronics, Inc. v Kaufman, et al. 669 F.2d 852–57. (US 2d Cir. 1982).

Tetris Holding v Xio Interactive. LEXIS 74463. (US D.N.J. 2012).

17 USC Sec. 102. *Legal Information Institute.* Cornell U Law School.

35 USC Sec. 101. *Inventions Patentable.* Cornell U Law School.

United States Congressional Commission on New Technological Uses of Copyrighted Works. (1979). *Final report of the national commission on new technology uses of copyrighted works.* 93rd Cong., 2nd Sess. Washington: LoC, 1979. *Digital Law Online.* Retrieved from http://digital-law-online.info/CONTU/

United States Copyright Office. (2006). *General copy requirements.*

United States Copyright Office. (1995). Registrability of pictorial, graphic, or sculptural works where a design patent has been issued. *Federal Register Online, 60*(57), 15605–15606. Retrieved from: http://www.copyright.gov/fedreg/1995/60fr15605.html

Vee, A. (2010). Carving up the commons: How software patents are impacting our digital composition environments. *Computers & Composition, 27,* 179–192.

Warren, S., & Chang, S. (2010). Real-world patent issues for a virtual world. In Ross A. Dannenberg, Steve Mortinger, Roxanne Christ, Chrissie Scelsi, & Farnaz Alemi, (Eds.), *Computer Games & Virtual Worlds: A New Frontier in Intellectual Property Law* (pp. 111–144). New York: American Bar Association.

Williams Electronics Inc. v Artic International Inc. 685 F. 2d 870–78. (3d Cir. 1982).

PART III: GAMES AND/AS RHETORICAL PRODUCTION

(OR, WRITING IN OR THROUGH GAMES)

9 "Leeroy Jenkins!" What Computer Gamers Can Teach Us about Visual Arguments

Andréa Davis

INTRODUCTION

In January of 2008, Blizzard Entertainment® announced that it reached a milestone of 10 million subscribers worldwide to its Massively-Multiplayer Online Role Playing Game (MMORPG), *World of Warcraft*. According to their press release, "*World of Warcraft* now hosts more than 2 million subscribers in Europe, more than 2.5 million in North America, and approximately 5.5 million in Asia" (Blizzard Entertainment®, 2008). Such a pervasive base of customers is just one example of the many digital gaming and social environments rapidly gaining recognition as legitimate sites of cultural production and learning. No longer are video or computer games merely seen as scapegoats for violence and adolescent angst; rather, digital games and MMORPG environments are rich sites for understanding economics, identity formation, cultural production, socio-cultural learning theories, rhetorical strategies, and even economies of cultural capital.

An example of the kinds of cultural production that stems from MMORPGs like *World of Warcraft* can be seen in the machinima[1] video "Leeroy Jenkins!" Through appropriation and adaptation of game play, a group of players, mostly in their 20s, stage their characters in a particular moment of gameplay in order to humorously promote their in-game guild. In the process of doing so, the video creators show a keen sense of the different components of their rhetorical situation such as audience, purpose, and rhetorical appeals. Although the video was released on the World Wide Web in 2005, it remains a popular cultural reference in the parlance of business people and gamers alike—even appearing on the game show *Jeopardy!*; it is not just an inside joke for game players, but, in fact, is a very sophisticated, rhetorically savvy, and multi-layered argument.

In this chapter, I offer first a description of the multilayered and multimodal environment of *World of Warcraft* as a site of production and composition. I follow this with a discussion of the pedagogical relevance of such composing environments, noting the importance of the social aspect of composing in these spaces and the relationship to multitasking that such a composing environment engages. Once this framework is established, I discuss the "Leeroy Jenkins!" video in more detail, performing an analysis of its arguments and rhetorical moves. I conclude with a set of implications for incorporating student arguments outside of the classroom in writing instruction.

THE COMPOSING/GAME ENVIRONMENT

In order to understand what digital gamers/composers can teach us through visual arguments like the "Leeroy Jenkins!" video, it might first be useful to understand something about the environment in which they compose. Today's digital landscape of composing is one of intensely social interaction and multitasking, and one that moves in and across genres and modes. This complex and highly social composing environment is significantly different from the romanticized notion of the lone composer/writer that has become an outdated and outmoded icon of the past. For those not familiar with *World of Warcraft* (*WoW*), it is an online role-playing adventure set in a rich, 3D graphical interface designed to resemble the world of computer game series *Warcraft*, which preceded the online *WoW*. According to the *WoW* website, "Players assume the roles of *Warcraft* heroes as they explore, adventure, and quest across a vast world" (Blizzard Entertainment®, 2008). Through their game play, questing, and exploring, players interact with thousands of others simultaneously in an environment designed to foster teamwork and group participation. While offering a vast and rich resource for social networking and entertainment through interactive gameplay, the *WoW* environment is also a multifaceted one requiring communication skills, multitasking, and the ability to understand visual interfaces.

The default *WoW* interface is a complex of visual and textual information that the game player must negotiate to participate in the game and in the socializing amongst other players. To begin this negotiation process, players must first make a series of decisions.

Briefly, the character creation screen (figure 1) allows players to select either Horde (supposedly the "bad guys") or Alliance faction; select from among five races within those factions; select an available character class such as warrior or warlock; and then personalize their character by choosing gender, hairstyles and colors, other physical features, and a name.

Figure 1. *World of Warcraft* character creation screen. Blizzard, 2007.

Once the character is established, players are ushered into a visually rich environment through a mini-movie introducing them to the game storyline and environment for the character they have created. This storyline forms the basis for faction and character-race interaction, game quests, and often guild formation.

Figure 2 illustrates a default interface through which players interact with the game environment and each other. Depending on their character type and particular training specification, players have a variety of actions, tools, spells, and other abilities and talents available through this interface.

Figure 2. *World of Warcraft* default interface. Blizzard, 2007.

Upper Right—Mini Map

In the upper right corner, a mini map indicates the player's location, along with "buttons" around the map indicating local time, in-game mail notifications, and options for tracking specific things on the map such as a particular type of computer-controlled character (NPC) or a special resource such as various plants for the alchemy and herbalism skills.

Bottom—Action Bars

Along the bottom of the screen is the action bar. This interface shows character abilities such as spells or talents, information for quests, help, ability information, character details, and other such information. Also along the bottom, players have a brief view of their inventory and means by which to interact with it.

Bottom—Chat Windows

Slightly above the action bar, players interact with each other through a series of chat windows. At any given time, players interact with copious exchanges that may include the local, guild, group, general area, trade chat, and more, with nothing more than color-coding to differentiate between them. All of these actions, decisions, and attention to both visual and textual elements occur simultaneously while at the same time players may be speaking to one another through a voice program such as Ventrillo or Team Speak designed for MMORPGs. It is often the case in *WoW* that guilds host an in-game voice support server so that members of the guild can communicate verbally while involved in instances requiring instant decisions and complex coordinated actions.

Upper Left—Character/Party View

In the upper left- hand corner, players can view their own character showing things like health and mana or energy with which they perform their character's special abilities. If the player is in a group, the other members will also show in the upper left.

More advanced players may choose to customize this interface either through the features built into the game options, or by adding third-party applications called "mods" or "add-ons." Within this, players work to negotiate interactions in this space where the social interaction, narrative game structures, and player interface converge. Such a multifaceted environment may seem overwhelming at first glance, but the kinds of social networking and multitasking necessary to negotiate these complex systems is second nature to players of all ages, perhaps especially so with our students. Perhaps because these processes are second nature, they are also same the processes much recent scholarship identifies as the composing processes of the "digital generation" (Urbanski, 2010).

PEDAGOGICAL RELEVANCE

So how, you might ask, is this complex social/game environment and concomitant multitasking relevant to the writing classroom (or any classroom for that matter)? How do these new composing processes translate to the classroom? With the recent buzz about Web 2.0 and social networking, it is clear that changes are afoot that educators are trying to understand and address. Whether or not we like the changes in our students' thinking brought about by their social and collaborative environments, multitasking, and high levels of technological input, they are here to stay and we must learn to address our students' ways of thinking. As writing instructors, we are often concerned with teaching our students how to think critically, consider the rhetorical situation, and establish authority and voice in their writing. We further aim to find ways of making the writing process relevant to our students' other fields of interest and their personal interests in hopes of getting them to engage in the composing process more deeply and thoroughly with the multiple tools and multiple media available for us as writers to use (DeVoss, 2005). Our goals as instructors are to make writing classes more relevant, to meet students at their own level of interest and technological preparedness, and to engage them in different literacies. Citing his earlier work with Resnick (1999), Shaffer argues that the social and multifaceted game environments provide a "thickly authentic" experience where activities are "simultaneously aligned with the interests of learners, the structure of the domain of knowledge, valued practices in the [real] world, and the modes of assessment used" (Shaffer, 2005). Tapping into these "thickly authentic" resources, which are available through digital games and social environments, is one way to address our students' new ways of thinking.

Much recent research in social environments, the sociology of technology, and digital games for pedagogical purposes suggest that connections between multitasking abilities and media-rich, social interactions are of great benefit. For example, in his contribution to *Science, Technology & Human Values*, Whalley (1991) wrote of the "deep social embeddedness of the invention and innovation process." He further describes the intense negotiation processes required for inventors to flourish, which involve social support for resources as well as for validation and feedback (Whalley, 1991). Similarly, Lindquist and Smith (2008) posit that invention is an activity deeply imbricated in cultural practices and social interactions as evidenced by their respective research. Smith notes in her discussion the invention of an extremely productive and uplifting movement to develop a local old town that was once destitute and is now a thriving art community. This community invention came about through the social and civic interactions of a community of people. Likewise, Lindquist notes her ethnographic and linguistic research of argumentation at a working-class bar in Chicago. In her work, group identity and invention practices for argument come from the social interaction of the bar's regular patrons (Lindquist & Smith, 2008). So while the multifaceted and deeply social interface of MMORPGs may appear overwhelming at first glance, it is precisely the kind of social interaction necessary for invention practices we hope to foster in student writing.

In addition to understanding the deeply social aspects of invention and composing practices, it is also helpful to understand the role of multitasking or toggling between and across multiple applications, resources, and interfaces. While I do not wish to offer a comprehensive discussion here of the current debate regarding what some have termed the "digital generation" and the issues of multitasking, I do wish, briefly, to summarize some of the main concerns. Some recent research suggests that the multitasking activities of our students may have the potential to be detrimental, reducing their overall ability to engage sustained thinking on a single topic. The research also suggests that habits of the mind formed in multitasking may prohibit effective use of "down time" to reflect and think. Citing a neurological study of brain waves, Wallis (2006) suggests that we do not multitask simultaneously as some may think, but that we toggle between activities. Wallis summarizes the research stating, "Habitual multitasking may condition their brain to an overexcited state, making it difficult to focus even when [students] want to" (Wallis, 2006). This neurological research follows on earlier reports in education trends noting, "Today's average college grads have spent less than 5,000 hours of their lives reading, but over 10,000 hours playing video games (not to mention 20,000 hours watching TV)" (Prensky, 2001). The result of such increases in technology-enhanced input overwhelmingly suggests that our students' thinking has changed. However, it is unfair and premature to declare these changes as either negative or positive, as additional research is needed. As the other contributors to this volume suggest, there are facets of multitasking and complex systems of social and technological interfaces that are useful and need further theorizing and researching. Perhaps most poignant, however, is the fact that these changes in our students' thinking and composing have already occurred and we must now learn to address our students at their levels of interest and technological preparedness.

Does that mean we have to play digital games in the classroom? No. One way to accomplish these ends may be to examine the arguments students, and those like our students, have made outside of academia and encourage similar approaches. Examining this media provides insight into the ways in which we might encourage our students to move beyond the typical paper essay to construct persuasive arguments; tapping into "thickly authentic" environments and activities as both models and motivation may bridge the gap in our classroom making writing practices relevant and vital to our students. It helps if we can understand the complex social/game environment and concomitant multitasking as a composing space. It is what game researcher Shaffer (2005) terms an "epistemic game" (Shaffer, 2005). In other words, Shaffer notes that epistemic games provide a rich apprentice-like context for students to gain experience with the demands of a fast-paced work world where multitasking talents and high levels of productivity along with the ability to work in team environments are deeply valued. Therefore, not only do multiplayer game environments provide students with motivation through "thickly authentic" contexts, but they also reinforce the social and multitasking practices necessary for invention and creativity.

VIDEO INTRODUCTION

The "Leeroy Jenkins!" video was created in 2005 by guild members of *PALS for Life* (P4L), including Ben Schulz (aka Leeroy), then aged twenty-four and a recent college graduate. As mentioned in the introduction, when the video was first released on the World Wide Web, it immediately turned "viral," becoming an extremely popular video and sparking some controversy over whether the video was staged or spontaneous. In a 2006 interview in *Played to Death* Schulz claimed, "We want people to make that decision [whether the video was staged] themselves. It seems more fun that way" (Hufford, 2006). However, whether the video was created as promotion for the guild, or simply for fun, it is clear that the video has traveled far and wide.[2]

In the opening scenes of the video, we see the guild *PALS for Life* (P4L) hard at work in the high-level instance of Upper Black Rock Spire. An instance in *World of Warcraft* is a special team project requiring anywhere between 5 and 25 members (with each subgroup containing up to 5 players) to coordinate their activities to successfully complete a series of missions. When the team enters the instance, the game design enables them to have their own instance of this particular dungeon so that no other players are competing for these missions. According to the WoWWiki, "Instance dungeons tend to feature the most difficult and rewarding content, both in terms of enemies and items, but also in terms of level design. Getting through an instance requires a well-trained and well-balanced group of players who are of an appropriate level for the challenge" (WoWWiki contributors, 2008).

In the video, the players are about to begin the segment of the Upper Black Rock Spire instance known as "the Rookery," famous for its masses of dragon whelp eggs, which hatch if anyone steps near enough. The eggs reappear very quickly, so trying to clear the room is pointless or exceedingly difficult at best (WoWWiki contributors, 2008).

Rhetorical Analysis

As the video begins (figure 3), the thirteen-man raid team is gathered and all using voice-chat through *Team Speak* or some other similar voice support system and taking cues from the raid leader.

Figure 3. opening scene

Just as in a "traditional" paper, the author creates an introduction for the audience, setting up several arguments presented through the video. The composers of this video also pull from multiple genres such as drama and satire. Within this media argument, the authors use analysis, exposition, description, personal experience, satire, and they employ rhetorical archetypes and appeals. The transcript of the video excerpt will allow for further analysis:

Jamaal: Okay guys, these eggs have given us a lot of trouble in the past
. . . does anybody need anything off this guy or can we bypass him?

Ritter: Uh I think Leeroy needs something from this guy.

Jamaal: Oh, he needs those Devout shoulders? Doesn't . . . isn't he a
paladin?

Ritter: Yeah, but that'll help him heal better; he'll have more mana.

Jamaal: [sighs] Christ . . . okay.

Spaulders of Valor	Devout Mantle
Binds when picked up	Binds when picked up
Shoulder Plate	Shoulder Cloth
470 Armor	64 Armor
+11 Strength	+21 Intellect
+9 Agility	+9 Spirit
+17 Stamina	+4 Stamina

Figure 4. Armor comparison chart

Just as in a traditional essay, within this introduction, the author(s) make
the rhetorical move to hook their audience with intrigue and humor.
In the first few lines of the transcript, we learn that Leeroy, a paladin
character, wants an item dropped by the Rookery boss. Leeroy wants
the Devout Mantle (cloth armor for shoulders) instead of his current
plate armor, the Spaulders of Valor. An item comparison chart (figure 4)
shows the difference between the item benefits. The Devout armor set
it typically worn only by character classes that wield magic (casters) and
do damage from a range. Whereas paladins (like Leeroy) and warriors
are expected to meet the foe with brute force and engage in hand-to-
hand melee combat requiring additional protection (the armor value)
and health (stamina). Thus, when it is determined that Leeroy wants the
Devout Mantle, and yet hardly anyone questions why a paladin would
want this cloth armor instead of the plate set which he already has, the
scene is rendered extremely humorous. To achieve such ironic humor
requires a sophisticated audience analysis, which this group of authors
does very well.

In the longer segment that follows, the guild builds suspense and interest (as well as expressing humor and satire) through the long speech

preparing for the boss. It should be noted that the main character, Leeroy, is away from the keyboard (AFK) while the raid leader explains their plan of action.

Jamaal: Uh . . . well what we'll do; I'll run in first and gather up all the eggs so we can kinda blast them all down with AOE. Um, I will use Intimidating Shout to kinda scatter them, so we don't have to fight a whole bunch of them at once. Uh . . . when my shout is done, uh I'll need Anfrony to come in and drop his shout, too. Uh, so we can keep them scattered and not to fight too many. Um, when his is done, Bas, of course, will need to run in and do the same thing. Uh . . . we're gonna need Divine Intervention on our mages, uh . . . so they can uh AE uh so we can, of course, get them down fast 'cause we're bringing all these guys; we'll be in trouble if we don't take 'em down quick. Uh . . . I think it's a pretty good plan; we should be able to pull it off this time. Uh . . . what do you think Abduhl? Can you give me a number crunch real quick?

Abduhl: Uh . . . yeah . . . gimme a sec. I'm coming up with 32.33 uh repeating, of course, percentage of survival.

Jamaal: Uhm . . . that's a lot better than we usually do. Ready guys . . . [interrupted]

The raid leader describes the plan of attack to his patient team members, explaining how each should use their respective skills and talents. However, lest the video audience grow bored with this discussion, there is intense humor for the audience of this video in the "number crunching" at the end of the segment. This humor is made more pronounced by the long drawn-out directions beforehand. Not only have the authors done some extensive and accurate audience analysis for this video, but they also employ a rhetorical archetype of the pre-battle speech. This may be likened to Shakespeare's famous St. Crispin's Day speech given before the Battle of Agincourt by the eponymous king in Henry V (Shakespeare, 1599).

In the next sequence, the video's authors bring the drama to a climax with the unexpected actions of the character Leeroy as he returns to the game. Here the composers continue to draw on satire as well as employ expert timing (kairos) in the sequence of events.

Leeroy: [Interrupting Jamaal] Alright. Guns up! Let's do this! Leeeeroooy Jenkins!

[Runs into the Rookery]

[short pause]

Forekin: [incredulous] Oh my god, he just ran in!

Ritter: Save him!

Jamaal: Oh jeez, stick to the plan.

In the remaining moments of the video, absolute chaos ensues as lag (the time delay between the player's computer and the game server) and various spell failures prevent the team from "saving" Leeroy.

Forekin: Oh jeez, let's go, let's go! [follows]

Abduhl: [laughing] Stick to the plan!

Jamaal: Stick to the plan!

Forekin: Oh jeez, oh _____.

Therien: Gimme a Divine Intervention, hurry up.

Jamaal: Shouting!

Therien: It's saying I can't cast! I can't move, am I lagging, guys?

Spiffy: I can't move!

[Chaotic action continues until at last all team members' characters are dead]

In the final scene, the team expresses its deep frustration and disappointment in Leeroy who counters with, "At least I have chicken."

Perhaps after watching the video, one wonders what are the arguments presented in this video about MMORPG game play? There are, in fact, several arguments that this video serves to make:

- *PALS for Life* is a fun and exciting guild who appreciate humor and sarcasm along with commitment and teamwork.
- *PALS for Life* is also a highly organized and well-run guild.
- *World of Warcraft* can be a lot of fun to play and/but requires teamwork.
- The plan they try to execute is a good example of how *not* to succeed in killing the Rookery boss.
- Don't be a Leeroy!

All together, the short (2:51 minute) video packs in a rich visual argument employing humor, satire, and rhetorical appeals and archetypes. The video creators also employ all the elements of a good written argument: an introduction that hooks the audience, an issue or problem for discussion or argument, evidence to support the various assertions, and a satisfying conclusion that leaves the audience with a call to action. The video composers clearly know their audience—other players of approximately the same age range as themselves. The composers take full advantage of the ethos provided through oratory and the timing of the event. Additionally, the purpose (to have fun and/or to promote the guild) is accomplished through the example of teamwork and humor. Furthermore, the content and the form fit the media, which allows the group to appeal to ethos, pathos, logos and kairos all at once.

CONCLUSION

So how do we use something like "Leeroy Jenkins!" in the classroom? This video serves as an example of two different ways we might take advantage of this kairotic moment. This video serves as an example of what students can accomplish as authors of multimodal texts—and also encouraging such production (or even analysis of them) can help students make connections between their academic activities and their real life contexts. What this phenomenon can teach us about writing in the classroom is simple and yet profound. If we expand our notions of what "writing" is, we find that various technologies allow for our students to create persuasive arguments with tools and knowledge they already possess. As instructors, we can take advantage of "thickly authentic" sites that connect real world contexts and student interests in order to make the connections between what they already do and the rhetorical moves made in writing for academic purposes.

Furthermore, noting and encouraging expression through "popular media" forms will help us as instructors to build a repertoire of relevant and useful models both to inspire and guide our students and to help us see the connections between practices of everyday life and in-class assignments. Alternately, engaging in rhetorical analysis of existing popular media, as I have done here, provides opportunities for students to make connections with the activities they participate in outside of the classroom with those inside.

Cultural phenomena such as the "Leeroy Jenkins!" video generated by players should be examined more closely for what digital games and gamers may teach writing instructors about constructing complex and sophisticated visual arguments in today's multimedia writing environments.

NOTES

1. The term machinima is a portmanteau of machine cinema. Perhaps the most comprehensive explanation is found at Wikipedia (Wikipedia contributors, 2008).

2. The concept or term "Leeroy Jenkins" has traveled across Urban Dictionary; has spawned a number of fan resources for other games besides WoW; was picked up by researchers looking at how viruses spread; and became a topic on the game show *Jeopardy!*. The video was even a discussion for research scientists in Human-Computer Interactions (HCI) for the government of Canada working on projects concerning collaborative work and virtual reality. Additionally, several online and print magazines such as PC Gamer, Played To Death, and Spike featured articles about the video and interviews with the creator. Perhaps the greatest testament to the video's popular culture status is the Toyota Tacoma commercial, which spoofed World of Warcraft and included Leeroy.

REFERENCES

Blizzard Entertainment. (2008, Jan.). *Blizzard Entertainment—press release.* Retrieved March 8, 2008 from World of Warcraft® reaches new milestone: 10 million subscribers: http://www.blizzard.com/us/press/080122.html

Blizzard Entertainment. (2008). Retrieved March 8, 2008 from World of Warcraft Guide: http://www.worldofwarcraft.com/info/basics/guide.html

DeVoss, D. N. (2005, Aug.). Class lecture. *Michigan State University* .

Hufford, P. (2006, Jan.). *PTD interviews—leroy jenkins. Played To Death Magazine.* Retrieved November 20, 2015 from https://web.archive.org/web/20070308021528/http://ptdmagazine.com/2006/features/ptd-interviews-leeroy-jenkins/

Lindquist, J., & Smith, L. (2008). Finding time responsibly: narrative as emergent rhetoric. *13th Biennial Conference of the Rhetoric Society of America.* Seattle, WA.

PALS For Life. (n.d.). *PALS For Life.* Retrieved November 20, 2015 from http://thepalsforlife.com.

PALS For Life. (n.d.). *Leeroy Jenkins!. YouTube.* Retrieved November 20, 2015 from http://youtube.com/watch?v=Zll_jAKvarw

Prensky, M. (2001, Oct.). On the horizon. *Digital Natives, Digital Immigrants, 9*(5).

Shaffer, D. W. (2005). Epistemic games. *Innovate, 1*(6): http://nsuworks.nova.edu/cgi/viewcontent.cgi?article=1165&context=innovate

Shaffer, D. W., & Resnick, M. (1999). Thick authenticity: New media and authentic learning. *Journal of Interactive Learning Research, 10*(2): 195-215.

Shakespeare, W. (1599). *Henry V. Barbara Mowat & Paul Werstine, (Eds.).Washington Square Press, New Folger Edition, 2004.*

The Urban Dictionary. (n.d.). *Leeroy Jenkins.* Retrieved November 12, 2015 from http://www.urbandictionary.com/define.php?term=leeroy&r-f

Wallis, C. (2006, Mar.). genM: The multitasking generation. *Time Magazine, 167*(13).

Whalley, P. (1991). The social practice of independent inventing. *Science, Technology & Human Values , 16*(2), 208–232.

Wikipedia contributors. (2008). *Machinima.* Retrieved November 12, 2015 from http://en.wikipedia.org/w/index.php?title=Machinima&oldid=215954140

WoWWiki contributors. (2008). *Instance.* WoWWiki. Retrieved November 12, 2015 from http://www.wowwiki.com/Instance

WoWWiki contributors. (2008). *The rookery.* WoW Wiki. Retrieved November 12, 2015 http://www.wowwiki.com/Rookery

10 Playing with Play: Machinima in the Classroom

Wendi Sierra

PLAYING WITH PLAY: INTRODUCING MACHINIMA

"So, machinima is really a genre, and not a medium?"

The students in my Digital Media and Rhetoric course are grappling with both how to define machinima and how to evaluate whether one is "good" or not. I frustrate them by refusing to provide a definitive answer to this and other similar questions they have asked about the form. This intentional frustration continues as, after watching a few examples they ask me what grade I would give those machinima, if they were turned in for this assignment. Rather than providing a simple answer I redirect, asking them what criteria they would use to evaluate machinima and how the examples we've seen in class stand up to this scrutiny. At the beginning of this particular unit, when I announced that we wouldn't be writing another research paper, they were exuberant. Now, however, the complexity of the task before them is slowly unveiling itself. While a majority of these students are gamers, few of them have experience in video production. None of them have previously looked at fan culture as a source of meaning and knowledge production. We are in unfamiliar territory, and they are getting restless.

Eric Klopfer, Scot Osterweil, and Katie Salen (2009) in "Moving Games Learning Forward" identify twelve possible means of incorporating games into classroom situations. Of these twelve, scholars of composition and rhetoric most often focus on just a few, typically those means that see games as content systems. In this article, I argue for another use of games, and one that more closely aligns with existing research on multimodal learning and pedagogy: the use of games as authoring systems. However, before discussing how games can become authoring systems and vehicles for the creation of multimodal assignments, I first examine how composition and rhetoric scholars have typically seen the value of games in pedagogy: as content systems.

Klopfer, Osterweil, and Salen describe the use of games as content systems as when educators use games to "deliver understanding about a particular subject or content area . . . reflection on and discussion of the content in spaces external to the game in order to allow students to see the game as part of a larger body of knowledge on that subject" (2009, p. 21). Rebekah Shultz Colby and Richard Colby's (2008) use of *World of Warcraft (WoW)* in their first year writing classroom, described in "A Pedagogy of Play: Integrating Computer Games into the Writing Classroom" is an excellent demonstration of the productive uses games can have when seen as content systems. Colby and Colby sent students into the game "looking for rhetorical exigencies that create opportunities for emergent learning" (p. 309). They describe two different student projects, a quantitative study on in-game economics and an official proposal to game designers (p. 309). They explain that their use of *World of Warcraft* "highlights play as an important part of the writing process, intertwining work and play in ways that more productively highlight areas of the rhetorical canon that have often been underutilized within composition" (p. 309). In examples of student projects, *World of Warcraft* served as a content system, providing students with information on a particular subject (economics, for example) and offering spaces for connection with larger issues and structures.

Similarly, Ian Bogost's work, which has been particularly influential for its focus on procedural rhetoric, focuses primarily on games as content systems for persuasion and learning. Games, he argues, "offer meanings and experiences of *particular* worlds and *particular* relationships . . . they remain coupled to a specific topic" (Bogost, 2007, p. 241). Thus, games present players/learners with the opportunity to learn (and be persuaded) through doing—precisely the characterization Klopfer, Osterweil, and Salen (2009) give of games as content systems. An example of this principle can be found in one of Bogost's own games, *Arcade Wire: Airport Security*. In this game, players take on the role of an Airport Security Officer. At beginning of the game, players need only flag

NPCs (non-playable characters) whose luggage includes a gun or knife. However, as the game progresses players are asked to search for more and more difficult to see items of contraband. Some of these items mimic current TSA regulations (bottles and liquid containers) and others that poke fun at seemingly arbitrary restrictions (red shirts only, etc.). The game continues to increase in difficulty until it is impossible for players to do anything but allow security risks to pass through their checkpoint. In this example, the content is the purpose of the game. *Airport Security* has been thoughtfully designed to gradually reveal a critique of post 9–11 airport security measures and their effectiveness.

The above examples are just two of many that show how pedagogical and educational studies traditionally approach games. I do not wish to critique these innovative uses of games, but rather to suggest an additional potential, a perspective Klopfer, Osterweil, and Salen identify as the use of games as authoring systems. Unlike the previous examples, which see games as systems that can teach students through gameplay experiences, using games as authoring system has "students use games to produce an artifact, be it a game (Spore), a mod (Starcraft), a video (machinima in WoW, the Sims, Second Life, etc.), a visual text (Sims Family Album), an avatar (Miis), a written text (MiLK, an sms-based game platform), or a body of code (Alice, Scratch)" (Klopfer, Osterweil & Salen, 2009, p. 22). This use of games in the classroom is not focused on traditional game play (playing a game as it was designed to be played). Instead, this approach might be called playing with play. Using games as authoring systems means asking students to create a new text out of game materials. Having students work, through games, to create new narratives and texts builds upon research both about games in the classroom and on the discussion of multimodality in composition classrooms, a discussion that has been taking place for quite some time. Prior to explaining how those conversations support the use of machinima, however, it would perhaps be best to briefly define machinima and present some examples.

As its name implies, machinima is very much a mixed media form. The word is a portmanteau of the two key aspects of the form: machine-animation (through a game) and cinema. Strange Company, a group that declares themselves the "world's oldest pro machinima company," expresses the definition and value of machinima as "making films in 3D virtual worlds to tell stories that couldn't be told any other way" (2007, "About Us"). The self-accredited Academy of Machinima Arts and Sciences offers a similar, but more expanded, definition: "the convergence of film-making, animation and game development. Machinima is real-world film-making techniques applied within an interactive virtual space where characters and events can be either controlled by humans, scripts or artificial intelligence" (2005, "The Machinima FAQ"). As the still image taken from "World of Workcraft" illustrates, machinima is a hybrid art that uses a game (in this case *World of Warcraft*) to create films. Machinima is, therefore, a hybrid media that sits on the border of film and gaming It is also an almost entirely user-created form of media.

Figure 1. *World of Workcraft.*

Less than ten years ago few people would recognize the term machinima, much less have seen one. However, it is now an emerging video form that allows authors the ability to work within pre-existing environments. Indeed, machinima as a young art form may be hitting an adolescent phase, in which scholars and practitioners are pushing the boundaries of what the form can express. While some advocate for the emergence of machinima as a more serious and socially engaged form. Kate Fosk (2011) and Henry Lowood (2006, 2008) each argue for the importance of highly political uses of machinima. Fosk explains how new virtual worlds, spaces that are only quasi-games, offer creators the potential to develop machinima that are less solidly tied to specific game systems than the examples I will present below. Because these spaces are not explicitly (visually) marked by their connection to gaming, they enable greater interaction and connection with more traditional media outlets (p. 29). Lowood (2008) demonstrates Fosk's claims by providing the example of "French Democracy," a thirteen-minute movie made only two weeks after a series of riots in France (p. 167). The availability of machinima, and the relative ease with which the author was able to learn the tools needed to create one, allowed "French Democracy" to be produced in record time and provide local commentary on events that had only just occurred.

Whatever purposes one is working toward, creating machinima requires authors to consider how their work is both constrained by the virtual environment that they use: setting, character models, costuming, and camera work must all be provided by the game engine they work in. Lowood (2006) explains how machinima helps viewers and creators to re-conceptualize both gaming and film: "like the cellphone camera craze, we also learn from machinima how the dissemination of accessible tools—even if they are not necessarily easy-to-use—creates opportunities for the emergence of unexpected content in a postmodern environment that places playful experiments and throwaway pieces alongside startling and original instances of creative expression" (p. 26). Creating machinima involves utilizing a variety of software programs in ways that they may not have initially been intended, what Lowood describes as the "emergence of unexpected content," to create surprising new content, thus encouraging play *with* technology as opposed to simply *through* technology. Obviously, the most effective way to truly understand the potential of machinima would be to watch several different machinima and get a general sense of how gamers and creators are using this tool to critique, explore, and narrate. A variety of different genres or styles of machinima exist, and, as Lowood suggested, these range from fascinating and powerful to mundane and crude. For the purposes of this argument, I will briefly summarize three different types of machinima and offer a quick example for each.

One of the more interesting applications of machinima for those interested in new media studies is the use of machinima to explore how game systems forward and normalize certain actions. The process of creating a machinima, when used to interrogate game systems, becomes a mode of critical, emergent play. As Irene Chien (2007) observes, this allows players to participate in the game in a unique mode, "instead of simply playing the game to win, players started to test the boundaries of the simulation itself, using the game as a playground, laboratory, or stage" (p. 25). The short mock commercial "Counter-Strike for Kids" offers one example of how creators can use machinima to creatively rethink the rules a game system imposes on players. In this clip authors have used the standard actions available to them through the first-person shooter game *Counter-Strike*, but they have re-skinned (a term for applying different visual attributes to something) many of the textures.

Figure 2: Counter Strike for Kids

"Counter-Strike for Kids" is a mock commercial for an imaginary game that promises to offer an alternative to the overly violent games currently on the market. The title frame, featuring a solider wearing a clown wig and holding a toy gun, displays how this machinima re-contextualizes the brutal fighting game as a game for young children. In this imaginary version of the game grenades are presented as Pokéballs (a reference to the popular children's game and cartoon series Pokémon), knives are re-skinned as pillows, and a character's death is explained as taking a nap. The video employs elements of crude gallows humor, but it also forces viewers familiar with the *Counter-Strike* gameworld to reconsider actions that may have become second nature. By de-familiarizing actions that, for players, have become ordinary, the machinima highlights the senselessness and violence of the game. As the "Counter-Strike for Kids" example demonstrates, machinima opens up new modes of critical play. Player/creators have the opportunity to question both the actions the game allows and the context the game provides (including not only the narrative but also the visuals, audio, and other thematic elements). In playing with these elements machinima creators destabilize traditional game systems.

If we might consider the "Counter-Strike for Kids" machinima to be a sort of game-based parody (one that inspires both creators and audiences to think about a specific game in different terms), another common type of machinima is parody that does not refer directly to the game system. This style of parody commonly involves taking game characters and placing them in real-world situations, blurring the line between on-screen avatar and player. "World of WorkCraft" is one example of a machinima that derives humor from placing heroic game characters in mundane situations, but also offers an interesting perspective on gaming culture and the real lives of gamers. The narrative opens with a group of *World of Warcraft* characters valiantly slaying a vicious dragon before it can destroy a small village. The townspeople cheer, but as the heroes leave the scene they complain about the tedium of having to fight yet another dragon. Eagerly, the group rushes home to load up their favorite online game, *World of WorkCraft*. We then see the dragonslayers in their gameworld, completing epic tasks that include making copies, changing memos, and equipping their casual Friday gear. "World of WorkCraft," like "Counter-Strike for Kids," repurposes common game mechanics, presenting them in a new light that comments on the game system and the world outside the game. Meetings are presented as "quests" and paychecks and vacation time are the rewards for successfully completing tasks in the parody game. Through a careful consideration of in-game mechanics and real life analogs the video inverts the stereotypical image of an MMO player, someone who works a dull office job during the day and relishes the excitement of slaying dragons online at night.

While the majority of popular machinima use humor to comment on game systems, a small but significant number of creators use machinima to dramatize a previously existing text. The examples I give here refer specifically to literature; however, machinima relating to all aspects of popular culture have found popularity on video-sharing websites. The Strange Company (2008) has made two excellent examples of this type of text, one an interpretation of Lord Byron's "When We Two Parted" and the other a dramatization of Shelley's "Ozymandias."

Strange Company's interpretation of "When We Two Parted" includes a reading of the poem and a number of scenes that loosely depict what is being described in the poem, although the scenes are re-imagined for a game setting. The short uses a variety of visual effects, including mixing black and white and color artistically, and appears quite stylized and ornamented. In contrast, "Ozymandias" has no audio track other than a whistling wind. The less than three minutes of the clip primarily depict a lone character walking in the desert. The character approaches the broken statue of Ozymandias, reads the inscription, and departs. The piece concludes with a black screen and the text from the poem. Both of these pieces use the elements game spaces allow to dramatize their sources and create new texts based on both the source material and the game engine. "When We Two Parted" presents viewers with a dramatization that pulls out the emotion from the poem, but re-imagines the action to fit a modern context. "Ozymandias," a much more stark and bleak clip, presents a very literal scene of what the "traveler from a foreign land" claims to have seen. They intensify the emotion of their short film by placing only the sound of wind over the game images. This clip attempts to capture the emotion the poem itself hopes to convey, the desolation and emptiness implicit in the imagery.

As Fosk and Lowood's examples demonstrate, these are not the only types of machinima that exist. However, the four machinima discussed above illustrate how players take on the role of content creators in a way that is highly critical and demonstrates rhetorical awareness. Most machinima are small productions made by fans and gamers with limited commercial potential or value; however, it should be noted that machinima are gaining prominence and the limits of this technology have yet to be reached. Many pioneers, including The Strange Company, have already made full-length films using machinima that are available for streaming from a number of websites. Rooster Teeth Productions began a small machinima web series in 2003, which expanded to become an Internet sensation and many gamers' first exposure to machinima. Their series, *Red Vs. Blue*, is made using *Halo* and its sequels, and is now sponsored by Microsoft (the makers of *Halo*).

MACHINIMA AS DESIGN-BASED CULTURAL PRACTICE

> *For homework my students have read the first chapter of Henry Jenkins's (2006)* Convergence Culture. *The chapter does not once mention machinima, and only in passing does it mention gaming. Now, in class, I ask them a question I imagine they already are wondering: why did I have you read this? They have a good grasp on the chapter. They talk about narratives moving across different media types and they particularly enjoyed Jenkins's description of trying to buy a phone that only made calls. They get that media technologies are increasingly converging. Despite their solid understanding of the chapter, they're still not really sure why I've assigned it. I pull out my copy of the book and read a section out loud: "this book is about the work—and play—spectators perform in the new media system . . . Rather than talking about media producers and consumers as occupying separate roles, we might now see them as participants who interact with each other . . ." (Jenkins, 2006, p. 3). After reading about two paragraphs, I ask them again: why, in a unit on machinima, have I had you read this particular piece? After a moment one student speaks up. He references a different text we read earlier in the semester about interactivity, Eric Zimmerman's (2004) "Four Naughty Terms in Need of Discipline." Games, my student recalls, take us up to what Zimmerman identifies as a third level of interactivity, interaction with a system that responds to you. Machinima, he suggests, based on the Jenkins reading, has the possibility to take us to Zimmerman's fourth level, interaction with culture and the social world. Now, I think to myself, we're getting somewhere interesting.*

There are a variety of compelling reasons to introduce students to machinima as a tool. Fosk (2011) and Lowood (2006, 2008) present examples that demonstrate how many creators turn to machinima for political and activist purposes, in part for the speed with which they can create content that responds to current events. Kenneth Morton, in his article "Machinima-to-Learn: From Salvation to Intervention," (2010) describes an assignment in which his students used the virtual world *Second Life* to make videos that offered a critique of their own campus culture. Morton's project demonstrates a local application of machinima as social critique. While I recognize the value of other approaches, in this chapter I wish to propose machinima as a tool through which students can be invited to engage in participatory culture and think more critically about issues related to composition and design practices.

Engaging in participatory culture introduces students to new methods of thinking about authorship/ownership of texts and knowledge production, important skills in postindustrial society. Many authors have already provided anecdotal evidence that suggests the skills and opportunities students gain through interacting in a participatory culture. Henry Jenkins's (2006) description of the student-run, imaginary newspaper *The Daily Prophet* in *Convergence Culture* and Jonathan Alexander's (2006) presentation of the youth-created website *Hyperreal* in *Digital Youth* both present positive examples of young people using technologies available to them in productive ways. However, while these anecdotal cases are encouraging, statistical evidence suggests that the majority of American students have rarely explored their ability to create media content. Requiring students to engage directly with media culture through machinima creates a context in which new models of creation, knowledge production, and participatory culture can be considered.

Despite the importance of this work, statistical evidence suggests that students are not doing this kind of work in their day-to-day lives. Jenkins, citing a 2005 Pew study, claims that just over half of teens can be considered content creators. This particular Pew study defined content creation in alarmingly loose terms, including both posting one's own content and commenting on another's work. While this percentage seems encouraging, José van Dijck (2009) cites a similar survey from 2007 with drastically different results. Differentiating between active participants (those producing content) and passive users (who might comment in addition to simply viewing, but do not produce content themselves), the Organization for Economic Co-operation and Development (OCED) report she cites identifies only twenty percent of users as active participants. A similar survey, also conducted in 2007, also found that while many students and young adults knew about and visited content-sharing sites like YouTube, MySpace, and Flikr, only a fraction of those who visited these sites contributed their own material (White, 2007). Most users (roughly 80%) fall into a category termed lurkers—those who exist on the periphery of content-creation communities but neither comment nor submit any of their own material. Finally, a more recent Pew study provides additional evidence suggesting that the participatory approach to media implied in the 2005 survey might not be so common. Taken in September 2009, this survey found that only 28% of teens maintained an online blog or journal, and only 26% create remix projects using music, text, or images. The largest percentage of content creators, those who share their own artwork, photos, stories, or videos, accounts for just under two-fifths of all users (39%). However, even this number may not reflect as much participation as some optimists suggest. Xavier Ochoa and Erik Duval's (2008) quantitative survey of several popular user-generated content websites suggests that sustained engagement is substantially lower. Their study, which surveyed the content uploaded at document sharing sites, fan-fiction sites, and video sharing sites, found that participation on these sites is vastly unequal. The largest group of content creators, 90% across all sites, tended to produce only a few items. In contrast, single users could sometimes be responsible for as much as 10% of a site's total content individually. The combination of these more recent studies presents a less optimistic picture of the interactions young people have with media culture, suggesting that occupy a relatively passive stance.

However, if our students are not currently engaging with media culture, they should be. Doing so not only helps students develop a more nuanced understanding of the composing process and their own choices, but also invites critical reflection on contemporary media culture and disrupts the traditional separation between content producer and consumer. Such a disruption is a crucial part of media literacy. Jenkins (2006) identifies the following five characteristics as being markers that define participatory culture as distinct from traditional consumer culture: "relatively low barriers to artistic expression . . . strong support for creating and sharing . . . informal mentorship . . . members who believe their contributions matter . . . members who feel some degree of social connection" (pp. 5–6). He goes on to add that while not all members of a culture need to engage for it to be participatory, all members should *believe* that engagement is possible.

Some of these criteria are, I argue, essentially non-issues at this point in time. Low barrier, non-professional programs, both proprietary and open source (many of which are free), exist to allow users to become creators. While access to hardware is, of course, a perpetual concern in any production work, the resources needed are often little more than what one would use for a standard word processing assignment. Scores of websites and YouTube videos, as well as active online communities, exist to provide informal mentorship to those wishing to get started as creators. But while these tools and resources exist and are easily accessible, the mindset of a participatory culture—the sense of engagement that Jenkins argues is essential—seems to be less prevalent. As the evidence presented previously suggests, students are by and large not content creators. Most fall into the category both White (2007) and van Dijck (2009) identify as lurkers, moving at the borders of content sharing communities but never truly entering the conversation. They have found themselves, Jenkins suggests, on the wrong side of the new cultural divide.

Inviting students into participatory often requires them to reconsider authorship. Lawrence Lessig's (2005) model, which he describes as a rip-mix-burn process, provides a useful model to consider how media content is continually shared, rewritten, and redistributed. This process is not unique to contemporary digital culture and has been available to mass media for decades. Lessig uses Walt Disney's legacy to demonstrate the process in a professional context: "Disney (or Disney, Inc.) ripped creativity from the culture around him, mixed that creativity with his own extraordinary talent, and then burned that mix into the soul of his culture" (2005, p. 24). The distinction in a participatory culture, then, is in how this model is available not only to traditional mass media producers and major corporations, but also to media consumers. The rip-mix-burn model provides a new metaphor that presents cultural artifacts as open to play and critique, indeed, as the source materials for thoughtful reflection and commentary.

The goals I have identified, reconsideration as authorship/ownership of texts and knowledge production, are especially important in the new information age. As educational theorists such as John Seely Brown (2012), and Cathy Davidson and David Theo Goldberg (2009) discuss, contemporary educational systems are not preparing students to succeed in a knowledge culture that is highly collaborative and participatory. Davidson and Goldberg argue that students are increasingly turning to informal learning institutions, those that are self chosen and exist outside standardized education, to gain skills and knowledge that conventional institutions fail to teach them. Indeed, Brown recently proclaimed to a popular webzine "I would rather hire a high level *World of Warcraft* play-

er than an MBA from Harvard" (2012, "How *World of Warcraft Could .
. .*"). He reasons that these high level players are better at brainstorming,
finding and appropriating strategies, and sharing knowledge. Brown's
description of players and the valuable skills they develop through their
gameplay echoes Johndan Johnson-Eilola's (2005) description of symbolic-analytic work. This new model of labor is distinct from previous
situations because Johnson-Eilola explains "in a postindustrial age, the
most valued workers no longer produce concrete objects, but conceptual objects" (p. 28). For these workers, traditional understandings of
authorship, productivity and creation are outdated and no longer useful.
He writes "notions of authorship that prioritize the creation of original
content and subordinate work that seems derivative and functional" (p.
30) fail to address the level of abstraction that contemporary workplaces
value, abstraction that helps them to function in complex information
systems. Symbolic-analytic workers spend much of their time sifting
through information, relying on technologies and each other. In such
an environment boundaries between authorship and ownership become
unclear. Ultimately, in this model of postindustrial work, "creativity is
no longer the production of original texts, but the ability to gather, filter,
arrange, and construct new texts" (p. 134).

If, as I have argued, the importance participatory culture and symbolic-analytic work provides the motivation for incorporating machinima
into curriculum, the scholarship on multimodal composition provides a
theoretical framework that demonstrates precisely how elements of machinima can approach these issues. Multimodal composition has been a
rich topic of scholarly discussion in the field of Rhetoric and Composition, and multimodal composing practices are perhaps one of the most
discussed issues related to technology and composition. Of course, identifying multimodal composition as either only mediated through technology or as a predominantly recent phenomena are both problematic
assumptions, as Jody Shipka (2011) and Jason Palmeri (2012) respectively demonstrate. Given the breadth and depth of literature on multimodal
composition, this brief discussion focuses specifically on that element
which ties multimodality most strongly to the symbolic-analytic work
and participatory culture: design.

Gunther Kress and Theo Van Leeuwen (2001) create a four-tiered
heuristic for both creating and analyzing multimodal artifacts, which
includes discourse, design, production, and distribution. It is important
to note here that Kress and Van Leeuwen identify design as a mode

of creation distinct from production. They argue that in an era of "monomodality" design issues are elided—"representation was treated as monomodal: discrete, bounded, autonomous, with its own practices, traditions, professions, habits" (p. 45). Thus, in a monomodal knowledge culture, such as what students traditionally experience in their education, design concerns and practices are unquestioned assumptions. Composing often moves directly to the production stage. Multimodality forces us back from the teleological process-in-service-of-product aspect of production to the more abstract design phase. Anne Frances Wysocki (2004), in her introduction to one of the foundational works on multimodal composition in the field, *Writing New Media,* emphasizes the importance of digital media for scholars and writers as "encourag[ing] us to consider not only the potentialities of material choices for digital texts but for *any* text we make" (p. 10). From Wysocki, and Kress and van Leeuwen, we have the argument that critical engagement with and production of multimodal text strengthens one's understanding of the composition project as a whole. However, if multimodal composing has the potential to deepen rhetorical awareness, it is not something that is innate. As Mary Sheridan-Rabideau and Jennifer Rowsell (2010) demonstrate, even digital natives (those who have grown up with technology and are comfortable creating with it) often lack a "meta-awareness" to describe their rhetorical choices and process in creating (p. 32). Thus, as Cynthia Selfe (2004) argues, "teachers of composition should not only be interested in new media texts but using them *systematically* in their classrooms to teach about new literacies" (p. 44, emphasis added). Approaching new media systematically requires both conversations about the materiality and affordance that specific design choices entail and theoretical backing in participatory culture that situates the importance of these composing practices.

Jody Shipka (2005) argues that multimodal remix assignments, a heading machinima would certainly fall under, place many students in unfamiliar territory and encourage more thoughtful reflection not simply on an assignment prompt, but on "systems of delivery, reception and circulation" in the contemporary knowledge culture (p. 278). Some examples of projects her students have turned in include games, websites, organized gift boxes, and puzzle tests. These types of projects require an attention to the material aspects of composing not traditionally attended to with written composition. Shipka's remix assignments are not by necessity digital, but she emphasizes that they require students to "draw upon multiple semiotic resources as they compose work" (p. 300); the importance, Shipka argues, is "that students are doing something that is at once more and other than writing" (p. 300). The 'more and other' that Shipka's students are doing involves interacting with multiple media, and learning to recognize the affordances and limitations of each. When coupled with reflective assessments of the composition process, these assignments teach students both about new media authoring and about written composition, as they explore how each enables and constrains different arguments, assumptions, and modes of persuasion. In addition to constructing greater knowledge both about the written media and about other media forms, introducing students to remix compositions, to new media authoring, requires students to directly tangle with and attempt to sort out concepts which are still in flux: copyright issues, design issues, questions of authorship. Of course, students could simply read about how new media is distinct or different. Asking students to create a machinima contextualizes these theories by giving them the opportunity to literally play with these concepts. Doing so invites a deeper exploration of their meaning, as Shipka suggests, and opens up a space for thoughtful reflection on the creation process involved in new media texts.

PRACTICAL CONCERNS

The final projects for these units are often the most interesting and nuanced pieces of student writing I receive the entire semester, and yet this course unit is the most stressful to plan. How do I balance the theoretical material that situates the unit as rhetorical practice with technical instruction into the process of creating a video project? Will any of my students have production experience that I can draw on to assist total novices? The first time I assigned a machinima project I gave students the option to write a rhetorical analysis instead—not a single student choose to do the paper. They were anxious about the process of multimodal composing, but they were also eager to create.

Creators of machinima begin, of course, with a game. The most commonly used games among popular creators are *World of Warcraft, Counter-Strike,* and *Halo.* Each of these games has a distinct theme and game system, inviting strikingly different opportunities for critique and customization. However, each of these games requires a paid retail copy, and some require monthly subscription fees for multi-player use. While students may have copies of these games available, there are a number of other options for creating machinima. Any game or virtual world that allows multi-player interaction and can be played on a computer can potentially be used to make machinima. Morton's (2010) students use *Second Life,* a virtual world with a free basic version that many universities have institutional access to, and Lowood (2006) provides examples of how activists in France have used *The Movies,* a game designed solely for the purpose of creating machinima. The game a creator chooses immediately limits the options she has available to her in terms of setting, character design, and background. Thus, when multiple options exist, this decision is highly rhetorical and one that students should reflect upon carefully.

While a game is the most necessary and obvious tool a potential machinima creator will need, a few more programs must be acquired for the technical production of the project to move forward. These tools, like the games a student might choose to work with, range from paid and complex to free and fairly simple. Students will need:

- a screen capture tool
- a video editor
- an audio recorder
- (optionally) an audio editor

Screen capture software is used to record the video portion of the machinima. These programs will begin recording whatever is being displayed on the screen of a computer at the push of a button, and stop recording at the push of the button, turning a student's computer screen into the set for their machinima. As students "play" their game, moving their characters to motions that they have scripted, they record their footage using screen capture programs as the machinima equivalent of a camera. Most students will not already have these programs, but they can easily download free tools from the Internet.

While a screen capture tool will almost certainly have to be downloaded, students that own a desktop or laptop computer should already have access to basic video and sound editors, though it is quite likely that most students will not have used them. Both Windows and Mac machines come with a video editor, either Windows Movie Maker or iMovie. These programs are both perfectly serviceable. Neither program easily allows for some of the complex content editing that Adobe and Sony video editing software might make possible for students, but what they lack in functionality they gain in usability. Students simply need to be able to import clips, shorten them as needed, put them in proper order and layer an audio track on with the video.

Similarly, most computers come with some program that will enable voice recording. Windows PCs are equipped with the basic program Sound Recorder and Macs have an equivalent program called Simple Sound. For a basic machinima, students simply need to record their voice acting and integrate it with their video. Sounds effects can be used, and many of these programs have stock sounds included. If students wish to do complex sound editing, or if instructors wish to encourage it, Audacity is freely available as a trial version. Students can play with mixing their audio if they wish, to add effects or change the sound of their voices, but like complex video editing this is solely at the students' discretion and not required for a successful machinima project.

Having discussed several examples of machinima in popular culture in the first section, I conclude this section with an example of a student-created machinima. As I've already discussed, assigning the creation of a machinima can be an excellent way to teach students about new media, both from a theoretical perspective and a technical perspective. In the class focused on narrative, I tasked my students with using machinima to dramatize on aspect of Joseph Campbell's (1949) explanation of the hero's journey. This project thus required students to synthesize a number of important concepts. First, they had to understand the hero's journey well enough to depict some aspect of it in a scene. Second, they had to think critically to construct a scene that logically emerged from the limitations and availabilities of a game system. Finally, they had to develop the technical skill to capture video, edit footage, record music and voice tracks, and mix them appropriately. One of the better projects followed "Sir Epicus the Epic, the Chosen One, Future Master of the Four Corners of the World." Having read *Hero with a Thousand Faces,* this group chose to dramatize several elements of the first stage of the hero's journey. In their narrative Sir Epicus meets his mentor, a harbinger of fate who presents to him a portal that represents his call to adventure. However, Sir Epicus doubts the caliber of his portal (thus refusing the call) and demands that he be shown a more heroic call. After being rebuffed in her initial attempt to lead the hero to his path, the Harbinger takes Sir Epicus to a several different portals until he finally accepts one.

Sadly for our "hero," this call to adventure is not his, and he is quickly dispatched by a dragon.

In this project my students integrated a several elements from stage one of the hero's journey. They not only demonstrated their knowledge of this specific portion of the content I asked them to learn, but also incorporated jokes and allusions to other elements of the book. While standing in front of a portal imbedded in a tree, Sir Epicus asks the Harbinger "Has not this book already had a chapter on the world tree?" Both characters pause for a moment, startled by the meta-awareness, and then continue their argument about Sir Epicus' destiny. This project not only identifies and plays with concepts from the hero's journey, but also pokes fun at the relatively commonplace occurrence of being a hero in an online role-playing game, in other words, a game in which every player takes the role of hero. The original assignment sheet called for a three-to five-minute video, but this group's project (which includes edited video, voice acting, several sound effects, and a number of musical numbers) is just over seven minutes long.

Despite these benefits, there are a few cautions those interested in assigning machinima should be prepared to address. First, as with any digital media creation project, students can easily get frustrated by the technology. Many students, particularly those in a first year composition course, will have little to no experience in working with video and sound editing software. While this represents one of the main reasons to incorporate a unit like this, it is also a clear stumbling block for many students. There are a variety of ways that this concern can be dealt with. The primary way to help students overcome this obstacle is to place them in groups. Each time I have assigned a machinima project it has been as a group project. Working as a team, students can more easily and quickly overcome technological difficulties and can, with proper instruction, rely on each other rather than their teacher to work through a project. As Jenkins (2009) points out, one of the key features of a participatory culture is the ease of access to tools and informal mentorship on the use of those tools. I instruct my students in production basics, but I also teach them to search for and identify the resources that will help them teach themselves. Any program or strategy I can teach them will likely become outdated in a relatively short amount of time, but the ability to locate and utilize informal learning tools will help them succeed in a postindustrial work environment. This strategy has been overwhelmingly successful, as I have yet to see any insurmountable technical difficulties. However, even with students collaborating and learning together, teachers must be prepared for the occasional emergency. In these cases, it is best that teachers are able to direct students to useful resources. A number of guides exist online, both for creating machinima and for using each of the different software applications required to complete a machinima project. Being prepared to direct students to online technical resources, troubleshooting, and FAQ guides can stave off a number of problems.

Another potentially more problematic issue is student resistance to the project. In my experience this has been minor, and students are generally more excited by the idea that they can make a video than concerned with the gaming aspect. Still, contrary to popular media depictions, many students do not play video games, and approaching this as a project specifically for or about games may lead to student resistance. One way to combat this concern is to provide students a number of platforms with which to create machinima. An engine like *Second Life*, or even *The Sims*, has a less identifiable style and often provides many more customization options to allow students to create something less game-like and more film-like. Another possibility that allows students the ability to integrate a variety of digital source material without involving games, would be suggesting the creation of videos that still use screen capture software but do not require games. An excellent example of this style of film is Michael Wesch's (2007) "The Machine is Us/ing Us." This video uses screen capture software to record webpages, editing, and Microsoft Word; and to make a persuasive argument about the nature of web 2.0 technologies. Many of the same principles of creating a machinima apply directly to the creation of this style of video and do not require the use of gaming technologies.

CONCLUSION

As one of the final daily activities for this unit I have asked my students to get into pairs and create rubrics. While I intend to keep the purpose of this activity a surprise, my students jokingly accuse me of using their labor to create a rubric I will then grade them on. "Not so!" I gleefully exclaim. You are making a rubric that you will grade yourselves on. This twist shocks them into a momentary silence. Seizing the opportunity, I continue: fifty percent of their grade on the video project will be in their hands, but they must defend the grade they assign themselves in a reflection paper that explains how their video meets each criterion. The other fifty percent of their grade will be my assessment of the project's strengths. And, as if this information is not shocking enough, one final twist. While they will produce rubrics in pairs, they will vote as a class to decide which rubric best assesses a well-designed machinima project. I worry that their rubrics will be largely arbitrary, including superfluous categories like "meets the time limit requirement," but I am impressed by the results. Categories like "Cultural Context" (which counts for 30% in their rubric) and "Thematic Development" (which counts for 20% and refers to the thoughtful incorporation of game elements) suggest that they have developed an awareness of the issues I have tried to put forward in this unit.

Using machinima in the classroom offers teachers and students a chance to look behind the screen, so to speak, and explore the theories and assertions that many contemporary theorists make about new media. While we can certainly lecture students about current copyright laws and the restrictions they place on creativity, situating students in a space where they can actually experience these issues firsthand provides a much more compelling learning environment. We cannot expect students to come to us ready to create exciting and challenging multimedia projects without significant scaffolding, and yet it nonetheless seems crucial that, for students to be savvy media users and consumers, knowledge about multimedia and multi-modal composition is imperative. Whether students intend to make another machinima ever again or not, creating one provides a valuable experience that can, hopefully, make other forays into the creation of new media projects more appealing and less intimidating. Perhaps more importantly, even if students never intend to make another machinima, we might hope that creating one will engender a new and more nuanced relationship with all media objects. After creating machinima projects, concepts like the modularity and remix-ability of new media are more evident and relevant to students, who have now experienced them. As Olli Sotoma (2007) writes "if we assume that the consumption of film allows a certain amount of play through interpretation, then the making of fan fiction becomes an act of transformative play" (p. 386). Inviting students to play in machinima invites them to play in media, to push against the boundaries in technology and forms, to find out what is and isn't possible, to question, to challenge.

References

Alexander, J. (2006). *Digital youth: Emerging literacies on the World Wide Web.* Cresskill, NJ: Hampton Press.

Bogost, I. (2007). *Persuasive games: The expressive power of videogames.* Cambridge, MA: MIT Press.

Brown, J. S. (2012). How *World of Warcraft* could save your business. [video]. Retrieved November 12, 2015 from https://www.youtube.com/watch?v=BhuOzBS_O-M

Campbell, J. (1949). The hero with a thousand faces. Princeton: Princeton University Press.

Chien, I. (2007). Deviation / Red vs. Blue: The blood gulch chronicles. *Film Quarterly, 60*(4), 24–29.

Counter-Strike for Kids. (2008). Dir. Xanatos and the Janus Syndicate. [Video file]. Retrieved November 12, 2015 from https://www.youtube.com/watch?v=mB6fq9Aadwk.

Davidson, C. N., & Goldberg, D. (2009). *The future of learning institutions in a digital age.* Cambridge, MA: MIT Press. .

Epicus: Crossing the First Threshold. (2009). Dir. MizHeald. [Video file]. Retrieved November 12, 2015 from https://www.youtube.com/watch?v=qQFpjyCJnY4.

Fosk, K. (2011). Machinima is growing up. *Journal of Visual Culture, 10*(1), 25–30.

Jenkins, H. (2009). *Confronting the challenges of participatory culture: Media education for the 21st century.* Cambridge, MA: MIT Press.

Jenkins, H. (2006). *Convergence culture: Where old and new media collide.* New York: New York UP.

Johnson-Eilola, J. (2005). *Datacloud: Toward a new theory of online work.* Cresskill, NJ: Hampton Press.

Klopfer, E., Osterweil, S. & Salen, K. (2009). *Moving learning games forward: Obstacles, opportunities, and openness.* Cambridge, MA: Education Arcade.

Kress, G., & van Leeuwen, T. (2001). *Multimodal discourse: The modes and media of contemporary communication.* London: Arnold Press.

Lessig, L. (2005). *Free culture: The nature and future of creativity.* New York: Penguin.

Lowood, H. (2006). High-performance play: The making of machinima. *Journal of Media Practice, 7*(1), 25–42.

Lowood, H. (2008). Found technology: Players as innovators in the making of machinima. In Tara McPherson, (Ed.), *Digital youth, innovation, and the unexpected* (pp. 165–196). Cambridge, MA: MIT Press.

The Academy of Machinima Arts and Sciences. (2005). The Machinima FAQ. *Machinima.org.* Retrieved October 13, 2005from https://web.archive.org/web/20051013055635/http://www.machinima.org/machinima-faq.html.

Morton, K. (2010). Machinima to learn: From salvation to intervention. *Currents in Electronic Literacy.* Retrieved November 12, 2015 from http://currents.dwrl.utexas.edu/2010/morton_machinima-to-learn

Ochoa, X., & Duval, E. (2008, April). Quantitative analysis of user-generated content on the web. In *Proceedings of webevolve2008: web science workshop at WWW2008* (pp. 1–8).

Ozymandias. (2008). Dir. Strange Company. [Video file]. Retrieved November 12, 2015 from https://www.youtube.com/watch?v=30DsJ8eOmKA.

Palmeri, J. (2012). *Remixing composition: A history of multimodal writing pedagogy.* Carbondale: Southern Illinois UP.

Selfe, C. (2004). Students who teach us: A case study of the new media designer. In Anne Frances Wysocki, (Ed.), *Writing new media: Theory and applications for expanding the teaching of composition* (pp. 43–66). Logan: Utah State UP.

Sheridan-Rabideau, M. P., & Rowsell, J. (2010). *Design literacies: Learning and innovation in the digital age.* London: Routledge.

Shipka, J. (2005). A multimodal task-based framework for composing. *College Composition and Communication, 57*(2), 277–306.

Shipka, J. (2011). *Toward a composition made whole.* Pittsburgh, PA: U of Pittsburgh P.

Shultz Colby, R., & Colby, R. (2008). A pedagogy of play: Integrating computer games into the writing classroom. *Computers and Composition, 25*(3), 300–312.

Sotomma, O. (2007). Let me take you to the movies: Productive players, commodification and transformative play. *The International Journal of Research into New Media Technologies, 13*(4), 383–401.

Strange Company. (2007). About Hugh Hancock and Strange Company. Retrieved November 12, 2015 from http://www.strangecompany.org/about/

van Dijck, J. (2009). Users like you? Theorizing agency in user-generated content. *Media, Culture & Society, 31*(1), 41–58.

Wesch, M. (2007). Web 2.0 . . . The machine is us/ing us. [Video file]. Retrieved November 12, 2015 from https://www.youtube.com/watch?v=6gmP4nk0EOE

White, D. (2007). Results of the 'Online Tool Use Survey' undertaken by the JISC funded SPIRE project. Retrieved from http://www.oei.es/tic/survey-summary.pdf.

World of Workcraft. (2008). Dir. Lagspikefilms. [Video file]. Retrieved November 12, 2015 from https://www.youtube.com/watch?v=msmRwlg23Qc.

Wysocki, A. F., (Ed.). (2004). *Writing new media: Theory and applications for expanding the teaching of composition.* Logan: Utah State UP.

Zimmerman, E. (2004). Narrative, interactivity, play, and games: Four naughty concepts in need of discipline. In Noah Wardrip-Fruin & Pat Harrigan, (Eds.), *First person: new media as story, performance, and game* (pp. 154–164). Cambridge: The MIT Press.

11 VoIP, Composition, and Membership: Constructing Working Identities through Collaborative Play

Emily Stuemke

The widespread addition of VoIP (Voice over Internet Protocol) communication systems to multiplayer digital gaming communities has created a new site of meaningful composition and collaborative play. Players enact hybrid communicative strategies involving digitized speech, text, nonverbal visual cues, and interface commands in order to enhance their participation in a variety of online games. These communication strategies are not easily separated into a simple binary posed between speech and writing. The multimodal methods used by online gamers are deeply embedded within one another, and the isolation of any single communicative mode would violate player expectations and introduce a risk of negatively impacting player engagement and performance. Among the results of implementing hybrid communication techniques are a shift in how players experience their social relation to the game and significant changes in how they perceive their fellow players. Research on communication, interpretation, and response in gaming communities can be productively applied to other digital composition communities in order to examine how digitally mediated language use can be understood and taught.

A player's construction and management of ethos within their community operates on a model that was not available before digital self-presentation. Players construct a coherent virtual identity around a visual representation of a body, or avatar, their textual participation in the many chat channels within the game, and, increasingly often, use of their physical voice over a VoIP client (usually Ventrilo, Mumble, or Teamspeak). This amalgamation of expressive forms may or may not affect how players see themselves, but it is deeply influential in determining how teammates perceive one another. Players synthesize data from many sources to form an image of their fellow gamers, and they respond to and reinforce that fabricated identity in turn. Vocal interaction has become an expected part of the social toolbox available to gamers. This chapter considers what this addition does for players within and around their play space, keeping carefully in mind that voice chat operates as a supplement rather than a substitution for textual composition.

Voice chat access is frequently required for entry into competitive or "endgame" content where its inclusion dramatically transforms cooperative interaction. The communication technologies I will discuss are relevant to a wide range of digital games, including the popular multiplayer PC games many players know from the cross-genre work of Blizzard Entertainment: *World of Warcraft*, *Starcraft II*, and *Diablo III*. Similar structures can be found in other online multiplayer PC games such as *Rift*, *TERA*, *Guild Wars*, *Lord of the Rings Online*, *Star Wars: The Old Republic* and *Everquest II*. Voice chat is also commonly used in console gaming, where games such as the best-selling *Call of Duty* series are frequently bundled with headsets to encourage vocal communication between players who want to optimize game experience. PC gaming provides a richer space for rhetorical analysis because of the increased range of options available to each player, individually or as a member of a team, to modify the technologies they bring to their play.

My discussion will take as its case study the use of VoIP chat as an identity-building tool for players who incorporate gaming into their strategy for disability management or rehabilitation from injury or illness. The specific rhetorical affordances of communal voice chat positioned within a larger visual and textual ecology enables new communication strategies and points of relation among players in a variety of real-world situations (Williams, Kaplan, & Xiong, 2007). An increased range of approaches to communication and self-presentation bring the material and embodied nature of gaming back to the forefront. Games continue to provide resistance to the common impulse to separate a digital identity from the human actor behind it. The frequency with which persons struggling with disability or illness find coping methods or access to wider expression in gameworlds stresses this linkage between material body and digital identity. While the gaming community is a particularly

rich site for the study of multimodal composition, theoretical understanding of communication that happens around games can enhance
our research on a wide range of related Internet services and activities.

There are a few theoretical minefields to tread carefully while exploring speech and identity in virtual communities, including discussions
of what constitutes a self and formulations of the troubled relationship
between speech and writing. These two issues are closely linked by the
contentious struggle over the concept of "voice" in rhetoric, which experienced a high level of popularity in the early 1990s and is returning
to prominence in rhetoric and composition journals and conferences.
Efforts to disassociate voice from potentially harmful conceptions of nature or essence may risk carrying composition studies too far from issues
of materiality, embodiment, and access. Gaming theory frequently calls
into question the relation between the body of the player and its representation as a speaking avatar on the screen, refocusing our attention on
the materiality of the speaker or writer (Hayes, 2005; Bates, 2009). Any
time we take action in a digital world, we put on a carefully and contextually constructed working identity through which we can best interact
with other teammates, systems, or objects. In order to increase trust and
respect in a digital community, we develop personae appropriate to the
situation. While games present an ideal arena for identity play and experimentation (Alexander, 2009), most team-based play is based on the
assumption that the players can come to know each other as familiar
community members and that these members will present similar traits
and behaviors over time.

Voice as an expression of identity presents a number of issues that
have been taken up by theorists of linguistics, rhetoric, and philosophy.
The primary tension lies in using voice as a metaphor for certain kinds
of expression found in written texts. We have inherited a long tradition
of logocentrism in which the spoken word is imbued with additional
validity and authority over the written word, which is, by contrast, removed from the speaker's identity, open to incorrect interpretation and
distortion of meaning, and only a weak representation of speech. Claims
that writing is improved by the addition of "voice," or the related recom-
mendation that a writer must "find their voice" rely on this hierarchy
of speech as a more authentic form of language than text. According to
this popular view, if a text can express a speaker's voice, it will be more
present, sincere, and closer to truth. In response to poststructuralist re-
jections of the metaphysics of presence, particularly as articulated by

Jacques Derrida in *Of Grammatology* (1967), language theorists fought to establish a separate place for writing as a unique technology for making meaning and therefore opposed the conflation of speech and writing within a single discipline (Harris, 1989; Moxley, 1990; Kravchenko, 2009). Theorists including Harris and Moxley promote this separation by arguing that writing fills a separate role, independent of speech, and by problematizing the idea of speech itself as a transparent tool for conveying truth. If all language is mediated, is text any further removed from the ideas that prompt its creation?

Reed Dasenbrock (1988) provides a clear theorization of the state of the debate on voice that lead to its prominence in the early 1990s. His position on writing as a formulation of language distinct from rather than supplemental to speech gives a precise view of the situation as it stood *before digital composition became widespread.* Dasenbrock claims that in our position as rhetoricians and teachers of writing, we have given undue weight to the similarities between speech and writing, treating writing as an unproblematic transcription of the spoken word. We are, in fact, reenacting the logocentrism described by Derrida insofar as we want our writing and our students' writing to feel more present and aware of its audience by exhibiting this feature we call "voice." In this situation, we assume that writing and speech belong to the same model of language, which is itself based upon speech. Dasenbrock reminds us that writing cannot be present and unmediated, and suggests that it is unlikely that speech would ever be able to meet these conditions either. The differences between speech and writing, Dasenbrock contends, are easily seen in texts where the writing fails to convey its message clearly because it attempts to operate too similarly to speech (e.g., by inclusion of colloquialisms and speech markers that are difficult to represent in writing).

Dasenbrock notes that "new technologies help shatter or deconstruct any simplistic speech/writing model and help blur the overly neat speaking/writing distinction . . . that most research in this field assumes" (p. 8). Recent discussions that take such technology into account often approach voice as an infusion of authority and individuality into the text of a specific author, while carefully reconsidering what this might imply about essentialism, agency, and identity (Elbow, 2007; Danielewicz, 2008; Stewart, 2010). Peter Elbow's contribution to this movement urges us to consider a compromise, allowing both voice and text to act as "lenses" through which to consider the other, even if doing so creates potential contradictions (2007, p. 174). Following this system, a text-based lens shows us "words as interchangeable and not attached to persons; the voice lens highlights how language issues from individual persons and physical bodies and how the same words differ, depending on who says them and how" (p.175). Elbow believes that voice is a useful metaphor for attending to the concepts of "sincerity" and "resonance" that may otherwise be difficult to discuss, while remaining important to textual meaning. We must still be mindful of how our discussions of voice influence our imposition of meaning onto the texts of others.

With the introduction of digital communication technologies, speech becomes more overtly mediated and separated from the body of the speaker. Can we refer to our technological skill sets as acquired technological *literacy*? When we use literacy as a metaphor for modes of speech, we may again be conflating the traits of these expressions of language. Where does VoIP use fall within a contested set of relations between writing and speech? The multimodal world of digital multiplayer gaming cannot unproblematically privilege voice or text as representative of truth or presence, and all relevant communicative strategies are deeply embedded in hybrid constructions as composition is enacted in a virtual world. I am presenting VoIP communication as an addition to (not a replacement for) the textual and visual literacies required for mastery in gaming worlds.

VoIP does not supply the authorial "presence" implied in most analyses of speech. Its use requires rapid manipulation of multiple modalities inside and outside of the game client. VoIP connections are usually mediated through text-based interfaces that allow users to individually manipulate incoming audio, adjust volume, noise, pitch, or even mute undesired voices in the conversation. This highly manipulable vocal-aural interaction requires specific technological proficiencies, constrains posture and motion in predictable ways, and is often accompanied by text comments, URLs, and chat channels to make up for unexpected audio distortion or to voluntarily avoid "talking over" other players. No standard theory of speech as part of or separate from writing can incorporate the complexity of integrating VoIP use.

In order to clarify how these technologies are commonly used, I'd like to describe the typical setting for speech incorporation in multiplayer video gaming. When a player has gained a desired level of mastery or proficiency within a game, often corresponding to character level or rank, they are able to play at a level frequently described as the "endgame." Endgame play presents challenges that require advanced understanding of game mechanics, team collaboration, and access to knowledge that exists in distribution among group members (i.e., different members will know and have mastery of different sections of the information required to complete the challenge.) This situation may be illustrated by using a simple example from the game *World of Warcraft*: Ten players whose characters have reached the maximum level and have appropriate armor and weapons want something engaging and exciting to do. Naturally, they decide that the appropriate course of action is to kill a dragon. On the screen, players who best meet the needs of the group must locate one another, join forces, distribute assignments, travel to the correct virtual location, and perform their roles accurately without standing in any fire. Physically, each player must also undertake a set of actions, including adjusting computer settings, taking into account the other activities they must limit or place on hold, and, in many situations, logging onto a separate voice chat program and putting on a headset with a microphone.

Our players are now seated comfortably, headsets on, monitor brightness set, beverage at hand, and they must navigate the rhetorical complexities of the game before them. They need to verify that everyone is present, has made it into the correct VoIP channel, is familiar with the task, and knows what role they will be performing. If they are playing with a familiar team or with members of a guild in which they all share membership, the process may be quick and simple. If the players have just met, there may be varying degrees of chaos, but this is navigable because there are rules, both explicit and implied. Who is going to lead this battle? Who will be distracting the dragon from eating the healers? Who will be watching to make sure nothing else sneaks through the side door? How will the various players establish their authority among all those who are speaking? There are many available means of communication, each with its own means of persuasion. Players may use commands to make their virtual bodies on the screen wave their arms frantically for attention, or they may use an interface marker to place a large star over their head that makes them easy to see and follow. For exchange of more detailed or complicated information, they will probably choose to type or to speak through the VoIP client. Most will do both, often simultaneously, as the situation changes over the duration of the in-game encounter.

Sometimes shifting between communicative modes is a simple choice: I type "I only see nine people in voice chat. Who are we missing?" because the missing person obviously cannot hear me. If my character is on fire, I may instead shout "turn the dragon around!" because if I take the time to type this request, my avatar may experience serious discomfort. (This necessity for speed and economical typing leads to many of the unusual mechanics and spellings common in *gamespeak*. Gamespeak demonstrates group membership and serves as an identity marker, but also meets a very practical need where correct comma placement is of comparatively lower importance than addressing the condition of being on fire.) A player's choice to shift among text and speech communication methods can be influenced by a number of more complex factors.

Two driving desires behind communication choices are establishing authority and maintaining clarity. For example, multiple players often try to explain the same set of rules before a battle. In the process, they may speak over one another, refuse to clearly pass lead, and end up contradicting each other, leaving out different parts of the fight that are crucial to roles they have not personally performed and creating much more confusion than existed before the encounter began. I may choose to use text as a kind of override procedure in this situation by typing out a simple explanation of the encounter, possibly using the command "/ rw" to post it in huge red letters across the top of the screen, and trying both to establish a clearer sense of purpose and to wrest some authority back by sounding more concise, organized, and useful to the group. This is both an organizational move and a power move. The speakers may choose to ignore my text, to stop their own vocal explanations to read it and respond in some way similar to "yeah, what she said," or any of the possible responses in between. In this case, the speakers are simultaneously addressing each other, me, and the other players, who all have different needs and are situated in different places relative to the conversation. I stress these moments of text/voice integration and overlap to emphasize my point that neither proficiency is able to replace the other. I do not believe that we are moving toward a technological future free of text, but instead toward one that includes text as one of many situationally appropriate tools.

In a confusing VoIP-mediated explanation, I may also attempt an approach that is more confrontational and has a higher chance of failure, but that also offers an opportunity for gaining authority for my own voice. I can attempt to interrupt the speakers vocally, explaining "do you mind if I step in and clear up this part of it?" which they may allow or ignore. If they ignore me, I will probably revert to text, which is usually considered more subtle but cannot be "talked over." If they let me speak,

I will be faced with the choice of how to make myself into a speaker who will be trusted and listened to or even obeyed for the remainder of the task. It has been pointed out to me, for example, that when I speak to a group over a VoIP server, I pitch my voice a bit lower than it would naturally sound. In such a situation, I am speaking from the position of a female gamer in a community with a male majority, and I am (perhaps unconsciously) trying to distinguish myself from an untrue but common stereotype of female gamers being uncertain, too excitable, and more easily upset than male gamers. Firmly worded, precise, and calm instruction on VoIP chat has a great deal of significance to the working identity I take on as a gamer, both when attempting to establish what I am and when trying to stress what I am not.

A number of curious things happen when I speak from this embodied position rather than using text. In some settings, there is an immediate reaction of surprise to my voice as it is marked female. Sometimes, and especially in player-versus-player competitive events, this is accompanied by crude remarks, questioning of my ability, and creative offers of the more undesirable sort. In most cases, the group simply synthesizes the new information into the body of knowledge they already had about who I am to them in game. Even in the case of a positive response (e.g., I frequently receive well-intended private messages informing me that it's nice to meet a competent woman for once), the dynamic between a female player and the rest of the group often changes after this information is disclosed. As a result, many female players indicate an unwillingness to speak over VoIP because they prefer to retain the anonymity of text that will continue to allow them to be recognized as a good or bad player, not a good or bad female player. Suddenly, my materiality has come crashing back into my game persona. For players who highly value their anonymity, VoIP can be a massive obstacle to maintaining distance between their material lives and their gaming identity.

A player who declines to speak on VoIP chat may lose authority and potential for personal connections and trust (often giving the explanation that their microphone is missing or broken as a common way to avoid saying, "I'd prefer not to be heard"). In 2007, a team of Human Communications researchers conducted a quantitative study on gaming communities and voice that addressed issues of VoIP and trust (Williams, Caplan & Xiong). While their study focused on theorizations of social behavior rather than language use, Williams et al. drew rhetorically applicable connections between the introduction of a VoIP client

(Teamspeak) and increased communication volume, trust, and relationship maintenance. They attempted to discover whether VoIP use might cause balkanization between different groups of people, or whether cross-border bonding might be enhanced. While they found no correlation between VoIP use and either hypothesis, they discovered that the differences between text-only and voice-plus-text communication become more significant with study duration, and that there were "significantly higher levels of happiness and lower levels of loneliness among voice users over time" (p. 439). Perhaps most relevant to my discussion was their finding that additional "media richness" in communication reduced levels of uncertainty that group members felt toward one another, allowing stronger grouping. They conclude that, whereas "communities found across the internet are consistently plagued and blessed with quasi-anonymous media," the conditions in their study revealed "[w]hen that anonymity is removed—even by simply reintroducing voice—it is apparently enough to improve relationships and insulate members from losses that might occur without intervention" (p. 441). Williams et al. are careful to point out that this study did not contrast text to voice, but a "richer *mix* of media versus a poorer one" (p. 441). A player's access to richer media has a profound influence in how they are perceived within the game community and how they can be involved in group play.

The players who choose not to use these additional types of media are limiting their own possibilities for interaction, but may be practicing important self-defense routines and communicating their desires to keep themselves removed from the game community. The importance of gaming identity varies highly from player to player, with some players coming to the game to attempt to take on an identity very different from the one they enact in their daily lives. Gender-swapping within games is a popular activity (Alexander, 2009), and one that could be limited by use of voice-based technologies. Similarly, players who fear that they may be discriminated against based upon their gender, accent, speech-related disability, or other physical situation potentially revealed by VoIP use may opt to remain silent and construct a gaming identity in alternate ways.

As suggested by Williams et al., the richness of the available mixed media is pivotal to the ability of the player to interact with the game and maintain group memberships within a gameworld. A quantitative anthropological study conducted in 2010 by Keating and Sunakawa provides valuable insights into gameplay and richness of communication media. Keating and Sunakawa focus specifically on "participation cues" observed among gamers at LAN parties. While the study mentions the possibility of achieving similar results over VoIP connections, the researchers observed gamers that were physically present in the same room and had additional means of relating to one another. Even in this semi-mediated gameplay situation, Keating and Sunakawa find that a new meaning of "space" had become relevant as gamers "adapt by reorganizing the distribution of meaning across modalities, making changes in the coordinated production of gesture, gaze, and language" (p. 333) as the players' bodies were enhanced by the multiple communication options made available by the game. Strikingly, "new possibilities for how to participate include magical properties that reconfigure boundaries of the individual body and its capabilities, which make it possible for bodies to behave differently in space" while playing computer games (p. 338). The environments created by games do not yet have corollaries in non-virtual worlds. Keating and Sunakawa found a moment where different spatial worlds had to be conflated by players in order to "generate coherence across simultaneous, multifaceted fields of participation" (p. 352). By synthesizing the work of Keating and Sunakwa and Williams et al., we are able to see that the physical body of the player is able to relate differently to this new space because of the rich assemblage of media that enhance communicative possibilities.

In each of these studies, it is not the presence or absence of voice that changes the participatory landscape, but the amalgamation of multiple modes of communication. We have arrived at a time and place, both in gameworlds and in other online communities, when a binary division of speech and writing is dangerously over simplistic, and the assimilation of either mode under the rubric of the other cannot be accomplished without ignoring how that mode participates in ecologies of virtual exchange. Both of these modalities are combined with additional literacies in visual rhetoric and interface manipulation to create an expansive communicative toolkit. The resulting combination reorients online gaming as a deeply embodied practice and opens up that activity to a large number of possible rhetorical applications. A powerful example of the use of multimodal communication is the construction of a player's ethos and working identity within the gaming community. To illustrate the usefulness of richly multimodal game-based communication, I will spend the remainder of my discussion showing how voice-enhanced gameplay can especially help ill, injured, or disabled players (re)construct themselves as active and speaking identities within gaming communities.

> *My avatar is just so damn magical, not because she can cast spells even, but because she works. She never has to stop to go to physical therapy, or wonder if she'll be able to hold her arm steady enough to finish a spell cast. When I turn off the game, when I separate myself from her, well . . . I'm nothing but a broken body again.*
>
> —Pennyroyal, *Everquest II* player, 2010

Over the past three years, I have been collecting stories and conducting interviews with gamers who have used their gaming avatars as therapeutic healing or coping tools. The frequency with which players referred to VoIP chat as a necessary part of how they related to others and were consequently able to feel like their community and relationships were "real" lead me to my current project on voice and gaming identity. I preface my rhetorical explorations of these responses with a clarification that none of the gamers I have worked with would normally be defined as casual, occasional, or typical players. In her best-selling 2011 edition of *Reality is Broken*, Jane McGonigal suggests a guideline that gaming ceases to be beneficial and should be limited at the threshold of twenty-one hours of playtime per week. The gamers I have included in my own studies all exceed this mark, with most claiming roughly thirty to forty hours of gameplay per week, and some passing seventy-five weekly play hours. These players do not participate in gaming as a recreational activity that supplements their lives, but as a major life activity that acts as a vital support for rehabilitation or as a coping strategy for prolonged illness. I do not make any claims regarding the healthfulness of this more intense, but far from uncommon, play style. I am examining a specific rhetorical situation in which a person whose physical body and ability to communicate and interact has been limited uses VoIP-enhanced gaming as means of acquiring social support and meeting their communicative needs.

The above quotation from Pennyroyal, a devoted *Everquest II* player, emphasizes the intensity with which some gamers are able to relate to their avatar as an extension of themselves. When explaining gaming avatars at academic lectures and conferences, I frequently present my own nine-year-old *World of Warcraft* avatar as a prosthesis that I have acted through in order to accomplish tasks that my physical condition prevented me from completing. In a more literal sense, virtual reality and role-playing games have been used for several years by medical and military establishments to help patients come to feel a connection to a prosthetic device (Resnik, Etter, Klinger & Kambe, 2011). Resnik et al. have shown that the avatar-based "structured learning environments" that immerse players in virtual worlds also allow them to develop a sense of connection between body and machine. Could a similar rehabilitative practice be used to shape a player's perception of their body (or embodied self) as expressed in their gaming identity in a richly multimodal gaming world?

The ability of a game to act as a learning environment that supports active exploration, embodied experience, and situated acquisition and synthesis of knowledge is at the foundation of game-based pedagogies, most notably those based on the work of James Paul Gee (Gee, 2007). Active, situated, embodied learning allows the player to more clearly see herself as a member of a community and to derive support from that membership (Taylor, 2003; Longman, O'Connor & Obst, 2009). Highly immersed gamers who interact with a well-connected community are able to derive substantial benefits from their gameplay, in addition to the increased happiness levels noted by Williams et al. In the case of players whose social mobility is limited outside of the game, the game environment becomes a productive site of compositional practice when a rich mixture of media, including voice interaction, is available to them. *World of Warcraft* player Saif explains "I had purpose and meaning in the game. I was there because things mattered to my character personally, and so they mattered to me. Her voice began to speak to me, and we became friends" (2012). Once connected to a character with a sense of reality and relatability, players extend their gaming identity by communicating with fellow gamers.

A few commonly held perceptions regarding voice chat come through in most conversations about gaming identity. Saif argues that VoIP "humanizes, and personalizes the experience. It bridges gaps and puts faces (voices) to anonymous names and green or white text." This response highlights the relation many players make between voice as a marker of identity that operates similarly to seeing a face, the perceived anonymity of text in contrast, and the necessity of voice to bring humanity to an experience. The relation of physical voice to individuality can be demonstrated by the use of voice recognition in modern security technology; the ubiquity of the opinion that voices give essential identifying information is easy to understand. Another person who has obtained a player's login information can impersonate that player in text, but certainly not over VoIP. The sense that a player needs to hear someone before they really know them is more complicated, but seems equally widespread. Speaking in-game is an action of trust that is often required for entry into group membership. Once the group recognizes a voice and relates it to a virtual character, an individual and humanized identity is granted to that character by its audience.

The identity reflected and recognized by the group is given the power to participate and to create stories both within the game and about the player behind it. The player joins in the game world as a participant who composes his or her own story, whether that is a detailed role play characterization, as described by Saif, or a more casually fabricated persona that reflects the skill set, aptitudes, and mannerisms of the player. The extent of characterization frequently depends on the importance that the player assigns to gaming in their life. *World of Warcraft* player Jennifer describes gaming as a survival strategy she relied upon after experiencing extensive physical injuries and corrective surgeries: "*WoW* was something of a lifeline for me. After the accident I could barely move, but I was able to *go* to and *do* things in-game. I could see and talk with friends. I had something to stimulate my mind and a way to feel accomplished while otherwise immobile" (2012). Over time, Jennifer used her involvement in the game as a way to get back into painting and writing, which additionally influenced her gameplay. Her many characters represent different parts of her personality, allowing her a fuller range of expression. She notes that "Gaming most assuredly plays an important role in my life. Being a 'gamer' is part of my identity and having a regular guild schedule where I can meet and chat with friends is comfortable and helpful in my day-to-day life." The ability of the game to help a gamer build a persona from which they can speak, write, or compose "in real life" is one of the most powerful examples of gaming as rhetorical practice.

Stories like this are not uncommon. Players frequently connect descriptions of their acquisition of communication skills to their ability to speak and write within the game. While Jennifer finds the game itself an important tool for organizing daily life, Saif finds that the speech skills he acquired while gaming have improved his experience of daily life in significant ways. He equates his rise from a new player to an authority figure in his gaming group to his rise from a new employee to senior lead at work, and asks, "Did raid-leading have something to do with it? I don't know. I like to think so." Similarly, *Diablo III* player Nettle describes these games as essential to his communication strategies for managing mutism arising from autism, claiming that "[i]t's the community surrounding games that has motivated me to get better and be a better person overall" (2012). Part of gaming identity involves how players see themselves as members of a group, which is a factor that has made gaming an important object of study for group management and social interaction research (Järvelä et al., 2012; Longman, O'Connor & Obst, 2009). *Rift* and *TERA* player Helmos describes multiplayer role-playing games as crucial tools in his battle for addiction recovery: "as I matured, game chat turned into something more: support, friendship, imaginative simulation, a way to connect to people on a higher level" (2011). Before the addition of voice to the game, it was easier for Helmos to view gaming as a personal activity without consequence. Voice chat clarified to him, as it has for many players I have encountered, that games are social tools "full of real people."

The persistence of the success obtained by using an avatar, voice, and writing as rehabilitative tools is surprisingly high (Bates, 2009). *World of Warcraft* player Ves, who feels that games played a central role in his process of learning to read, also credits them with aiding in career success: "Being introduced to [VoIP] community through *WoW* brought me to a greater understanding of the gaming culture and helped me take the first step in a career path by becoming employed at a gaming store where I was promoted all the way up the ladder to store management" (2012). To add a personal example, I feel that I developed the crucial speaking skills that I needed to succeed as a teacher by developing my voice as a guild leader in the online RPG *Guild Wars* during a time when I was struggling with recovery from multiple bone fractures. My interest in the connection between gaming, voice, and rehabilitation is closely linked with the practice of sharing narratives over VoIP while engaged in the embodied work of endgame problem solving. Access to deeply interlinked communicative media creates a multitude of opportunities for identity construction and development of ethos within online gaming communities.

It is my hope that the enhanced communication abilities that have allowed many players to construct rehabilitative gaming identities will persist in a media-rich digital world. I want this amalgamation of embedded compositional modes to remain available to players like Pennyroyal, who struggle with the translation of in-game success into coping strategies and real life skills. I also want them to be made available to writers, speakers, and students who have not yet had the experience of constructing a working identity in a deeply embodied, situated, and engaging learning environment. A future where visual and aural rhetorics are kept apart or simply replace rather than inform and augment reading and writing skills will be infinitely less rich and less able to serve those whose ability to connect and communicate has been negatively impacted by illness or injury (Perrachoine, Del Tufo & Gabrieli, 2011). By engaging the maximum available methods of communication, making spaces for different modes of compositional play, and defending those spaces as sites of meaningful work in our communities, we will allow writers, speakers, and multimodal composers to continue to find new ways to participate in each world they encounter.

REFERENCES

Alexander, P. (2009) He's the kind of girl who wants matching daggers. In L. Cuddy & J. Nordlinger (Eds.), *World of Warcraft and Philosophy* (pp. 153–164). Chicago, IL: Open Court Press.

Bates, M. (2009). Persistent rhetoric for persistent worlds: The mutability of the self in massively multiplayer online role-playing games. *Quarterly Review of Film and Video, 26*(2), 102–117.

Danielewicz, J. (2008). Personal genres, public voices. *College Composition and Communication, 59*(3), 420–450.

Dasenbrock, R. W. (1988). Becoming aware of the myth of presence. *JAC: A Journal of Composition Theory, 8*(1–2), 1–11.

Elbow, P. (2007). Voice in writing again: Embracing contraries. *College English, 70*(2), 168–188.

Keating, E., & Sunakawa, C. (2010). Participation cues: Coordinating activity and collaboration in complex online gaming worlds. *Language in Society, 39*(3), 331–356.

Harris, R. (1989). How does writing restructure thought? *Language and Communication, 9*(2), 99–106.

Hayes, E. (2005). Women, video gaming and learning: Beyond stereotypes. *TechTrends, 49*(5), 23–28.

Järvelä, S., Chanel, G., Ekman, I., Ravaja, N., Kivikangas, J. M., & Salminen, M. (2012). Social interaction in games: Measuring physiological linkage and social presence. *Simulation & Gaming, 43*(3), 321–338.

Kravchenko, A. (2009). The experiential basis of speech and writing as different cognitive domains. *Pragmatics & Cognition, 17*(3), 527–548.

Longman, H., O'Connor, E., & Obst, P. (2009). The effect of social support derived from World of Warcraft on negative psychological symptoms. *CyberPsychology & Behavior, 12*(5), 563–566.

McGonigal, J. (2011). *Reality is broken : Why games make us better and how they can change the world*. New York: Penguin Press.

Moxley, R. A. (1990). On the relationship between speech and writing with implications for behavioral approaches to teaching literacy. *The Analysis of Verbal Behavior, 8*, 127–140.

Ong, W. J. (2002). *Orality and literacy : The technologizing of the word*. New York: Routledge.

Perrachione, T. K., Del Tufo, S. N., & Gabrieli, J. D. E. (2011). Human voice recognition depends on language ability. *Science, 333*(6042), 595–595.

Resnik, R., Etter, K., Klinger, S.L., & Kambe, C. (2011). Using virtual reality environment to facilitate training with advanced upper-limb prosthesis. *Journal of Rehabilitation Research and Development, 48*(6), 707–718.

Stewart, M. A. (2010). Writing with power, sharing their immigrant stories: Adult ESOL students find their voices through writing. *TESOL Journal, 1*(2), 269–283.

Taylor, T. L. (2003). Multiple pleasures: Women and online gaming. *Convergence: The International Journal of Research into New Media Technologies, 9*(1), 21–46.

Vygotsky, L. S. (1962). *Thought and language*. Cambridge, Mass.: M. I. T. Press.

Williams, D., Caplan, S., & Xiong, L. (2007). Can you hear me now? the impact of voice in an online gaming community. *Human Communication Research, 33*(4), 427–449.

INTERVIEWS

Helmos (personal interview, August 2011). *Rift,* Trion Worlds.

Jennifer (personal interview, July 2012). *World of Warcraft,* Blizzard Entertainment.

Nettle (personal interview, December 2011). *Diablo 3,* Blizzard Entertainment.

Pennyroyal (personal interview, January, 2010). *Everquest II,* Sony Online Entertainment.

Saif (personal interview, July 2012). *World of Warcraft,* Blizzard Entertainment.

Ves (personal interview, July 2012). *World of Warcraft,* Blizzard Entertainment.

12 Gaming Between Civic Knowledge and Civic Know-How: Direct Engagement and the Simulated City

Sean Conrey

Between Knowledge and Know-How

Anyone who has played any of the *SimCity* games, particularly the more recent editions, has probably had an experience something like this: after playing the game for a couple hours, you head outside for a walk (needing some fresh air after all those pixilated hours spent building and destroying your virtual city). Walking down the street, you notice a few things you hadn't before. The fire hydrants, you know now, are plugged into a water main that runs down one side of the street. You never noticed before that the electrical lines are buried behind the houses. The street itself seems a bit too wide. *How big did they expect the cars to get when they made this street?* There's a tinge of cut grass in the air mixed with exhaust from a lawn mower. *Their yard was getting a bit long,* you think, *long enough they were in violation of the neighborhood ordinance.* All these things, you think, didn't happen by accident, and yet before now you hadn't really considered them. You'd just spent a few hours putting in water mains, running electrical lines, and signing off on local ordinances in the game, and these things now take on new meaning.

In the inordinate amount of time I've spent playing various incarnations of *SimCity*, I have had experiences like this often, and with varying degrees of profundity. Sometimes, it's a simple thing like a small city park with its single park bench, and I think about who had come together to make that place possible. Other times, I'll be in the car, driving through the malaise of parking lots, strip malls, and fry pits that ring the town I live in, and the strong-armed politics of Big Box companies are all the more obvious; I can more readily imagine how their unilateral vision has scraped and piled our commerce into an ugly, largely uninhabitable landscape of corporate profits. I have noticed these things to a lesser degree since I was a kid, but it wasn't until I began playing *SimCity* in earnest, becoming the "mayor" of my own virtual city (and thereafter following up by reading urban design and placemaking theories), that the pieces began to gel. For years I was frustrated and put off by the dreary exurban fringe of the various places I'd lived, but the frustration began to abate when I finally had a lexicon to describe what I was looking at and began to recognize what, in fact, may have been the causes of it.

The game, while fun in its own right, requires a large amount of theorizing and reflection in order to play it well, and I was simply dissatisfied with letting the machinations of the game dictate what theories and reflections were available while playing it. I also got interested, the more I played the game, in what the biases of the game designers were. Surely there would be particular political predilections attached to the game that would punish certain kinds of thinking and action and reward others. An interrogation was in order, and I thought it best not to go it alone.

Being a writing teacher, it seemed fair to bring the game into the classroom where students could engage it directly through their writing and consider their civic environment while doing so. But more than that, I wanted the game to be a springboard for recognition, reflection, and theorizing of actual civic and environmental systems, so that the knowledge and know-how the students acquired by playing the game could be brought into real, lived fruition in their daily lives. This is in part an answer to Andrew Feenberg's (2002) call to democratize technology, but it is also an attempt to use technology to teach democratic principles. Because of its nature as a contemporary "world-building" game, *SimCity* seemed to provide an ample middle ground where a dialog could be opened about the various civic and environmental systems that are already in place, and students could take their knowledge (and know-how) from the game and begin to apply it directly in their everyday lives. Through a variety of related assignments, the game itself is deliberately considered (in an attempt to steer students away from passive technology consumption), and the principles discussed and learned through game play are applied analogously into students' real, civic lives.

It was something I was already attempting: getting students to engage with their everyday lives as citizens through writing. I was trying to break down the notion that "civic learning" is largely volunteerism and helping students choose which political candidate to jockey for come October. These things are, of course, part of the program, but I wanted to extend the notion of civic learning and civic duty to include the everyday concerns and day-to-day practices we are involved in through work, home, and social life. I wanted to see civic life as everyday life, as a daily practice and concern that permeates every choice we make, that extends into the smallest nooks and crannies of our environment.

Most writing pedagogies have a go at some level of engagement, but too few require (or even ask) students to go beyond the classroom, or the page, through their writing. Those that do very often place themselves in a reactive position, where there is something that must be struggled against, some injustice that must be corrected, or some remote or distant concern that must be brought closer to home. Ethically, two primary things mattered to me in this regard: one was that I wanted students to consider civic engagement, especially as it relates to writing, to be an everyday, moment-to-moment concern and practice that (perhaps included, but) goes beyond volunteerism; and secondly, I wanted a pedagogy that focused on a knowledge and know-how of civic engagement that is primarily proactive and deliberative rather than reactive and judgmental.

To do this, I needed to adopt a model of the civic environment that students can readily comprehend and that is sufficient to describe the complexities of their actual civic lives. With most students having had minimal training in civics and government at the high school level, they often arrive in our writing classes with only a rough comprehension of the civic environment that they inhabit. Before diving into extensive studies of ethics and politics, students often need a primer, by way of a model, that simplifies yet still details a more comprehensive version of their civic environment than they probably received in secondary school. Oftentimes readings are not enough, and tend to focus exclusively on one aspect of the civic environment or another. This exclusion, while perhaps inevitable when assigning readings, can come across as too diffuse, and without some model to draw them together students are often left hanging; they are prepared to engage aspects of their civic lives but don't see the relations between the various aspects clearly enough.

Phenomenologically, I believe there may be two general steps in getting students to recognize the various aspects of their civic environment: first, a variety of phenomena within that environment would have to be made conspicuous; and second, those phenomena would thereafter have to be glued back together somehow into some kind of whole. A primary risk of the first is, similar to what has been said of assigned readings, that some aspects of the environment will be made more conspicuous and/or more important than others. This can easily be softened by taking care that a space is made for the students to choose their own primary concerns amongst the various aspects brought forward in the class. In other words, while the teacher brings attention to many different aspects of the students' environment, the students are encouraged to pursue those that are of their greatest concern (rather than those that are the greatest concern of the instructor, or some writer who has been read for class). Bringing various phenomena of the civic environment to the fore, the teacher enables students to work with these phenomena, and this recognition, I believe, is the beginning of civic responsibility and deliberate engagement. I believe that playing a game like *SimCity* provides a vehicle to bring various aspects of our civic environment to the fore, and, as will be discussed shortly, I believe the game is open enough to allow students to pursue those aspects that interest them most, thus allaying the risk of imposition.

The risk of the second (gluing the various aspects back together into some kind of whole), is perhaps more profound. Offering an inclusive worldview, one that glues the various parts of our world together into a comprehensive whole, is tricky.[1]

Without personally offering a viable, comprehensive worldview that provides a just and ethical solution to the dilemma, I instead propose that we allow the game itself to largely do that work for us, using the shortcomings of the game (its very American way of arranging its streets, for example), as a chance to talk about the issues while still giving students a chance to bring the various aspects of their environment, having recognized them, into some kind of comprehensive world that works for them. The assumptions that the designers of *SimCity* make about the world of the game already encompasses a particular worldview, and bringing students into dialog about that is one way that they can begin to integrate and reconsider the world they personally inhabit (which is, in varying degrees, both similar and different from the game).

In integrating and reconsidering the world they inhabit as some kind of analog to the game, students are given a program that encourages recognizing, theorizing, and reflecting on civic principles and political, economic, and ecological systems. While this is imperative to promote deliberate engagement, it is not enough. A model that allows for an experience-based approach to student writing is needed that integrates the acquisition of textual, language-based civic knowledge with a comprehensive know-how that works with students' everyday lives and concerns.

By using the simplified civic space of the game *SimCity*, students may directly (if only virtually), apply and adapt their civic concerns and principles, which they have explored through their writing prior to playing the game, in an environment much like the one they inhabit in their everyday lives. Interacting with the game's simulated environment makes many previously unseen or ignored civic and ecological systems conspicuous in a way that gives students a rough knowledge of these sites in real life and glues them together in a comprehensible (albeit simplified), and thereby useful, whole. This knowledge is also, through game play, translated into a semblance of civic know-how. Transferring this semblance into a real, lived experience is possible by directing writing assignments to both consider the game itself, and also how the things revealed by playing the game may play themselves out in our actual lives. If a theoretical model can be elucidated that demonstrates how the game provides an active space between theoretical knowledge and applied knowledge, then a variety of civic-based writing assignments and pedagogical approaches can be constructed that take advantage of that epistemological middle ground.

By using the game as a site where civic concepts can be applied and the dynamic and systemic aspects of the civic environment can be learned, students experience a place where they may recognize, theorize about, and reflect upon their own principles while simultaneously getting used to various governmental, ecological, and communicative structures.

RECOGNITION AND KNOWLEDGE

I'll begin theorizing, then, by stating a few biases and assumptions. The first would be that I assume students live in a lifeworld, much like those discussed by Husserl, particularly in the *Crisis of the Western Sciences* (1970), by Heidegger in *Being and Time* (1962), and later in a well said, easier to digest version by David Seamon (2005). Seamon, discussing

Husserl particularly, calls the lifeworld the "taken-for-granted pattern and context of everyday living through which the person conducts his or her day-to-day life without having to make it an object of conscious attention." I assume that students, in various ways, show up living in a particular lifeworld where some aspects of their world have either fallen from their purview and are no longer conscious concerns, or have never come before them to begin with. Of course, we can't make any assumptions out of context as to what the students are currently explicitly considering or not when they arrive, but I'll assume, for this theory, that there are some things in their civic environment that they have either never consciously considered or have considered and disengaged with.[2]

Secondly, I'll assume that Heidegger's famous theory of tool use (where he talks about how things come and go from our view by way of breaking down and getting fixed again), is valuable pedagogically, though with a few caveats. One caveat is that I believe it is possible for something to be made conspicuous without "breaking down" in Heidegger's sense. I believe something may be brought into view while still in good, operating order by way of a teacher who compassionately and purposefully demonstrates it somehow.

For Heidegger, this continuum between something being hidden and something being present moves between two poles of being "ready-to-hand" (largely hidden, fallen into the lifeworld where it just works for you, without you necessarily taking note), and "present-at-hand" (where a thing kind of jumps out of the soup of the lifeworld and shows itself, typically because it has somehow broken down). An example of this for Heidegger might be:

You are walking down the street and suddenly you step in a puddle and realize you have a hole in your shoe. At that moment, the wide world you'd been walking through (where the shoe is ready-to-hand, or ready-to-foot, as it were) narrows to the problem on your foot—the broken shoe (thus becoming "present-at-hand," when you notice it). You stumble home, wet-footed, and must contend with the obstinacy of the shoe until it's either fixed or you change it with another pair. Until then, you are, to some degree, focused on the shoe.

Examples of a less "broken down" conspicuity might be:

A teacher has her students consider the importance of the tennis shoes in the movie *The Children of Heaven*; or walks into class without shoes on (which would seem out of place but hardly an obstinate breakdown in Heidegger's sense); or has the students try on each others' shoes (with socks on, of course); or perhaps simply holds up a shoe and says "have you ever seen such a thing?"[3] This brings about a need to reconsider the place of shoes in our lives, but the struggle (Heidegger was fond of the term "strife") is less strident (and perhaps, if not done well, less visceral) for the students.[4]

These kinds of assumptions, about lifeworlds and phenomenological conspicuity, are useful in terms of the kind of civic engagement I'm talking about. They are useful if for no other reason than that they give a way of describing how students will see something (sometimes, as if for the first time), in class, and the "lightbulb" that teachers are always talking about is not just the students' recognition that it is there in front of them, but the students' recognition that they may interact and participate in the life of the thing thereafter in a way that they couldn't before. In other words, they may, if demonstrated well, deliberately involve themselves with it, having recognized it.

How this plays out in a writing class that is struggling to find ways to engage students with a "civic life" or "civic duty" is that the aspects of civic life may be brought to the fore, evaluated for ethical content and cultural value, and then shuffled back into the deck of the student's experience. Again, this is often done through readings that focus on political concerns (paper topic for Monday: how is the current administration failing or helping America?), or through ethical debate (abortion: right, or wrong?), or by way of research ("find ten library sources," whatever those are) and write an annotated bibliography that summarizes and evaluates their content). There is, obviously, value in a lot of this.

But, again, the danger is in focusing too closely on a few key issues and not elaborating or encouraging the wider rhetorical tools that bring all such debates into a common fold, and allowing students to place the sundry aspects of them into some kind of relationship, one with the other, and the other with the others, etc. Grand theorizing and comprehensive world-modeling is not the solution for most of us, but how, then, do we get the students to shuffle their knowledge back into the deck without it becoming some kind of imposed tyranny, some "It works like this, kid," pedagogy? To overcome these tyrannies, I believe it is possible to place the students in a position where they personally discover those "conspicuities" in their civic environment on their own terms as much as possible, and they are then encouraged to recognize, theorize, and reflect upon those things which surface by being taught techniques for pursuing those ends.

This, of course, is one way of thinking about what happens when we sit students down in front of a video game: they have a learning curve where the rules and possibilities are laid out for them and they begin to negotiate the terrain of the game (note that this curve is pretty steep when playing *SimCity*), and they then, having developed a somewhat graceful relationship with the grammar of the game, begin to explore those things that trip their neurological and physiological triggers. Pretty quickly, students take note of the various systems that the game models ("what's the difference between a residential and an industrial zone?") and begin arranging their cities into less accidental and more deliberate patterns that support the kind of "life" that they would want to have. The key is to try to keep them in an interrogative and exploratory mode, where they are really questioning and concerning themselves with the various systems, for as long as possible. This can be done by breaking the assignment into chunks and having them concern themselves at different times with different aspects of the game and the writing they are doing in relation to the game. If this interrogative mode can't be maintained somehow, you end up with students who become so infatuated with, say, planting trees, that they spend most of their time and money in the game on that one thing. Some diversity of interest is required for the "civic learning" aspect of the game to really work well, particularly the second "gluing the world together" part of learning.

Recognition and subsequent interest in the various systems and structures of the game sparks a kind of phenomenological domino effect that ripples through the various systems of the game, and there is often an overwhelming "this is way too complex" moment where students suddenly realize that the there-for-you-when-you-need-it civic environment they inhabit, with all of its electricity, water, streets, tax cuts, corporations, and ecologies, is a much more robust place than they ever expected. In playing the game with this explicitly as an agenda, they experience the tripping of a multitude of physiological triggers (sometimes tripping over their physiology), and it therefore takes time, and a lot of reflection, before the knowledge gained in those moments is brought into valuable fruition both in the game and in their everyday lives.

As this is the case, the relationship between knowledge and know-how must be worked out so that what happens between the students' recognition of these systems and their ability to utilize them in their everyday lives is adequately theorized and pedagogically accessible. For this to truly happen, we should ask: how can we theorize knowledge and know-how in such a way that the game is both useful and ethically viable beyond its digital walls? An epistemology should be developed that considers these differences (as well as what's been said regarding how we take note of things in our environment) as a starting point.

THEORIZING DELIBERATIVE KNOW-HOW

So let's call the recognition of something (being "present-at-hand") a kind of awareness-knowledge, and we'll say that as something slips from our concern (becoming "ready-to-hand" either because we are distracted from it, forget about it, or are convinced, somehow, that we've worked it out well enough to let it go for a while), it becomes a kind of corporeal knowledge, a kind of muscle memory, if you will. Merleau-Ponty alludes to this condition, what he calls "motility," where something has been repeated enough times, regardless of whether through conscious practice or ignorant repetition, that it escapes the grasp of the conscious mind (if ever done by choice) and commits itself to the flesh. This is perhaps most easily seen in the way that we may practice etudes on the piano so that we may play a concerto, some day, without a thought getting between us and the music. Or, for purposes here, we may take note of a civic system through the game, practice putting it to use in the game itself (thus gaining a game-motility), and thereafter work to enact it in our everyday lives.

This is obviously a move from knowledge to know-how if we take something we've learned and reified it (to use the cog-sci term) over time and repetition, to the point that it "becomes a part of us." Writing, in general, I believe, like any other art, takes on, through practice, this eventual commission to the flesh. For evidence of that, consider the fact that if you think about where to put your hands when you type, you become clumsy; if you stop to consider a particular word's spelling, it often seems more and more strange the longer you look at it; if you question your grammar too deeply as you type, you find there is little that is not pliable about any grammar and are crippled by the proliferation of choices that arise. Keep writing as you've practiced in the past and it's a much more fluid affair. But try to integrate something new in your writing, and you are back in the domain of the practitioner, probably dancing fairly well through most of what you're doing, but stumbling your way through the new technique.

Engaging the everyday civic life of students wouldn't be so different. Put a game that roughly models their civic environment in front of them and they pick up certain things: water pipes need water towers or pumps to do their job; trees lessen air pollution; wider roads create more traffic; give industry a tax break and they build like there's no tomorrow, tax them a lot and they run off to Sim China. Students learn these things playing the game. They pick up a tremendous amount of knowledge about basic services and systems. After a while they even learn how to operate these systems, to some degree, within the closed economy and ecology of the game. They take their knowledge and transfer it into game know-how, sometimes even gaining a proficiency where they enjoy the game and can fluidly deal with the concerns of their respective cities in a responsible, thoughtful, and consistent way without constantly pausing the game to make these decisions.

But acknowledging the systems and services within the game, and gaining the know-how to operate them well, is a kind of know-how that I believe more closely resembles the enacting of "thought experiments" in philosophy, or the operative know-how that it takes to plug and chug within the limited-by-design theories of mathematical modeling in the sciences. In this way, the know-how that gets committed to "muscle memory" through game play transfers more by way of analog out to the physical world of the player than through some kind of deep-learned and visceral response gotten by playing the game. Students can experiment with various ethical problems and make decisions that effect thousands of virtual citizens, but if asked to do the same in their everyday lives, they are forced to consider analogous situations within the game and learn how to deliberatively act, given the analog. The difference being that now the consequences are that much more real (and that much more precarious, being more real).

This has proven a valuable tool in the writing classroom because the act of writing is the perfect opportunity to allow students to draw those analogies and work out ethical dilemmas, considering their real-world implications. As long as assignments account for this, drawing from the game and pointing out from it analogously, then the students' writing, in relation to playing the game, becomes a kind of epistemological event horizon. The game, then, coupled with the writing that bridges the two environments (virtual and real) is a solid middle ground between civic knowledge, on the one hand, and civic know-how on the other. It is not an end unto itself, but provides a kind of knowledge that can be drawn analogously into student's everyday lives.

The key issue is that assignments that intend to operate in this liminal space must find a way of pointing students both to the game as a place where deliberative action (and conscious ethical choice) can be enacted, and where their reflective writing about playing the game (both during game play and after the fact), points them out of the game and into their daily lives.

REFLECTION: A CASE STUDY

On a very practical level, there are some initial considerations when attempting to use *SimCity* (or any game, really) in the classroom. Namely, questions of student access and whether or not it is possible for students to load and play games on campus computers. For the last couple years, nearly one hundred percent of my students have had access to computers at home (be they laptops or desktops), and as such I have been able to use the game in such a way that they play the game at home. In the rare event that I had a student who didn't have access to a computer at home, I gave them a choice: they may either borrow a friend's computer to play the game for class, or they may play the far simpler, free abandonware version of the original version of the game online (which limits their experience dramatically, as discussed below). There are also many free, online city simulators available, but most of them are motivated, as so many similar online games, to market in-app purchases (which gets in the way of a common experience and frankly switches the focus of the gaming experience to the acquisition of bought in-game commodities rather than on city building). There is also the fact that in-app purchases could change the common gaming experience among a group of students.

An exception has been when I tried using the game at a local community college, where access was severely limited comparatively, and other courses of action were necessary. Because of the access problem, we were forced to use the *SimCity Classic* game, which is available for free.[5] This version is the original version of the game that was released in 1989. As could be imagined, this version of the game is extremely simplified compared to later editions of the game, having only basic zoning and services available for game play. As recognition of civic systems played a major role in what I was attempting to do in playing the game, playing the simplified version of the game allowed there to be far fewer things to recognize through game play, and the fairly abstract interface did not allow for the analogs (that were to be drawn out through student reflection) to be easily accessed and developed. A later version of the game (*SimCity 4*), proved itself a worthier exponent of civic systems than did the earlier version of the game, and its age now makes it a reasonable used purchase for most students. The newest version of the game, titled simply *SimCity* and released in 2013, offers online, multi-player gameplay but has not received favorable views from the community due largely to the fact that the game must be played and saved with a persistent internet connection. SimCity Societies, released in 2007, largely reviled amongst SimCity fans, is not recommended for the kind of civic-focused work discussed here.

THE ASSIGNMENT

Regardless of which version of the game I used in class, my syllabus followed a common trajectory, and I got good results from both. The arc of the assignments were roughly as follows:

1.   Prepare students to play the game deliberatively by having them read some urban design and city planning websites and theories.[6] They then reflect on these theories, through brief writing assignments, and consider what aspects of them are most relevant to themselves and what parts they believe fit and don't fit well with their personal beliefs (and, of course, why or why not).

2.   Students then fill out what I call a "building code worksheet" that details what kind of city they would like to build if they had complete say.[7] This code is a grid that outlines many of the various civic systems from their everyday lives, many of which are not represented (or not represented very well) in the game. Very basic concerns are dealt with (tax levels, importance of education, police, etc.) as well as some that are more aesthetic (placement of parks, trees on the streets, terrain) and philosophical ("who is your model as a leader?" "As a politician, how popular do you want to be?"). The code is expressly set up to be a template for a real city, however, not one within the game.[8] As a building code, it is to be very concise, though not mathematically concise in the way that real city plans are.[9] The level of concision, they are told, is established by having them "imagine you were to give this

document to a fellow student. It must be concise enough that they could build a comparable place to the one you imagine."

3. We then have a brief, one class introduction to the *SimCity* game. I prefer to give them a basic rundown of the game and encourage them to do the game's tutorials rather than elaborately, over several classes, "show them the ropes." This allows them to develop their own gameplay style and allows them to more freely explore the various civic systems that are of interest to them, rather than imposing my preferences and interests on them by extensive instruction.

4. Once introduced, they are given a couple days to practice playing the game on their own. I assign amounts of time they should spend playing the game ("play *SimCity* for at least 2 hours between now and Wednesday"), and encourage them to slowly begin attempting to implement their building codes when they reach a level of proficiency with aspects of the game that correspond to some aspects of their building code.

5. They then take their building code and have a go at trying to deliberatively build the city of their dreams (or nightmares, for some students). After a practice run of 50 game years (which can take anywhere from 1 hour or 5 hours, depending on game speed), they are then told to play 50 consecutive years fully according to code. They may restart as often as they like, but must start from scratch when they do, and must play 50 consecutive years of the same city in order to fulfill the assignment. As they play, students take notes of various events and problems that arise as they attempt to build to code. This is typically done by hand, as the game makes it difficult to toggle to a word processing program while in play.

6. Once completed, students must write a follow-up assignment that reflects on the successes and difficulties of trying to build their city according to their code. They are also encouraged to reflect upon the shortcomings of the game ("I wanted to have curvy, winding roads, the game only allows straight roads;" "I wanted to build mixed-use neighborhoods, but the game doesn't allow that . . . I had to instead make do with putting zones adjacent to each other;" "I'm from India and nothing in the game

looked like home"). This document then becomes a springboard for a later assignment where they involve themselves with their immediate civic environment directly, considering what they've learned through game play.[10] The assignment has a direct and explicit call for students to reflect and then deliberate on how their knowledge and know-how of the civic systems in the game can be made analogous to actual civic systems in their everyday lives.

Where the assignment has been most successful, students have begun to see the arrangement of systems in the game as what they really are: simplified versions of their real-world counterparts. The interaction of the various systems (say, waterworks and electricity) is oftentimes something students have never explicitly confronted. The fact that factories pollute the air and town dumps pollute the water is something they typically arrive to class implicitly knowing, but they very often have not considered how, why, and where these kinds of places get built.

WEAKNESSES AND STRENGTHS OF THE GAME

One of the more interesting things to have come out of the game is that students, after having played it, seem critical of the game itself. As a follow-up to playing the game (after their reflections have been written), we discuss how the biases of the game push the students to do things they wouldn't otherwise do. This goes beyond the expected ethical compromises and deliberations anticipated through the assignment. There are many things unnatural and downright inaccurate in the game, and discussion following the game tends to bring those things into focus. Discussion of these inaccuracies and biases lends itself to helping students more accurately gauge their actual civic environment and leads to better and more accurate analogs between the game and those environments. [11]

In the classes where we played *SimCity Classic*, this follow-up conversation centered largely on how simple and abstract the game is and how the systems in the game are only vaguely analogous to their real-world counterparts. The *Classic* game, as mentioned before, *can* be used for the assignment, but the results are far less compelling and the game itself is far less difficult (thus far less frustrating) for students to play. While the conversations about the vague interface of the game and the super simplified civic environment it models can be useful, and students certainly seem to grasp the game more easily in the older version, I have found the frustrations of playing the later versions of the game are actually a boon to the project, and that in the frustration of learning how the systems in the game work, students are both humbled and impressed by the complexity of the real-world counterparts. The *Classic* game does not bring about these conversations on the same level, and, really, is recommended only when accessibility and/or finances disallow using the more advanced versions.

Through discussions, of course, the biases of the game designers are brought out, and we can see them more explicitly by discussing how students' philosophies and ideas played out through the game. One such bias that often surfaces is that students who believe deeply in a "free market economy," for example, find that the free market in the game tends to bring about a wasteland of exurban fringe and dirty industry. This seems on par for what typically happens in the real world, but it is certainly a choice that the game designers have made: the free-market capitalists in *SimCity 4* are not particularly interested in ecological neighborliness and "business ethics." Said another way, businesses in the game never take the incentive to be good citizens on their own, it is always a matter of compliance with the law. And, as I said, while this may seem like the norm to many of us, it is a choice the game designers made. There are no corporate social responsibility or sustainability programs in the Big Businesses of *SimCity 4*. There is no game equivalent to Ben and Jerry's, Costco or Timberland.

A similar issue that I typically bring up is that there are no real lobbyists in *SimCity 4*. I bring it up because I have found that students normally don't know much, if anything, about lobbyists, and as they play such an important role in our government today, I believe the imposition on my part is worth the risk. In the game there is a vague "business is being strangled by high taxes" kind of message that appears periodically in your news ticker, but it is more reportage than lobby. The closest students come to actual lobbying practices are when they go broke (a common occurrence to new players of the game) and are approached by a variety of nefarious businesses and governmental organizations who will pay good money to plop their toxic waste dump, federal prison, or missile range within city limits. Nowhere in the game is the mayor (the player), given a personal monetary advantage by "becoming more green," or "loosening the belt on industrial ordinances." This may be because there are never any elections in *SimCity*, therefore no campaign promises and no campaign contributions. As I said, most students only have a rough sense of what political lobbyists do to begin with, and the game does little to promote the recognition of this particular aspect of our civic environment.

There is also another major issue that surfaces related to the power of the mayor in the game: the mayor in *SimCity* pretty much has complete dictatorial control over what happens in the city. I trust that this is a choice on the part of the game's designers to make the game more fun, based on the obvious algebra of a certain kind of gaming that says "more power = more fun." The player-mayor in *SimCity* can obliterate an entire neighborhood of poor, hard-working folks and replace their homes with a super-highway and receive nothing but praise for having done so. The lack of accountability and lack of actual deliberative negotiation with anything other than the player's own conscience is something that must be contended with after the game's been played if a goal of having students play the game is to get them to consider the real-life implications of how these systems work. As mentioned previously, this comes, I believe, from a complete disconnect between real human empathy involved in actual human affairs and there being no equivalent for empathy within the game.[12]

The closest the *SimCity 4* game comes to actually helping or hindering the mayor in his or her deliberations is the "advisory board," granted by the game to help the mayor make better decisions. The board complains when things are going poorly (although they do recommend how to fix it), and praises the mayor when things are going well (or "well" in the eyes of the designers who made the game). There is never a time when the city planning advisor, Neil Fairbanks, for example, tells you that the lack of sidewalks in the exurban edge of your city is hindering pedestrian use. The advice is always general and somewhat out of context (perhaps just because of the difficulty in developing an AI that could do otherwise). This sets the grounds for there being less of a local, situated rhetorical negotiation and more of a general sense that something is wrong somewhere and you should perhaps figure out what.

Part and parcel to the advisory board, the game also encourages urban expansion (again, probably so the game is more fun to play) rather than continual maintenance of a smaller town over time. Various organizations and advisors in the game will constantly recommend expansion of the city limits and of various kinds of zones, as desirability rises. Never do the citizens of your city complain that the suburbs have gotten out of hand or that crucial local farmland has been paved over. The closest the game comes to that is when a group of hippies or other activists asks you to plant more trees or fund more parks.

On a similar note, students who come from farming communities and small towns find it difficult to build realistic representations of such places in the game because there are almost no game features that deal with rural issues (you can't, for example, build grain silos, pass organic farming legislation, or decide what kind of farms or ranches to build). Consequently, small towns, by nature of the game, want to always expand. A small town is never just right, and is certainly never quaint and well-run in *SimCity*.

Regardless of their background, a feature of the game that students seem to really enjoy, and that gives an angle on what is happening "on the street," is the "My Sim" mode, where players are allowed to place a range of individual "sims" (what the game calls its inhabitants) into various neighborhoods around town. (this is expanded in the 2013 edition, where every individual sim can be tracked.) Depending on where the sims live, and where they work and play, they will report back to the mayor about the conditions that they are currently living amongst. They do not speak in English or any actual, real-world language, but instead communicate through a collection of symbols that appear as thought balloons when a player clicks on the sim. This "man/woman on the street" opinion provides a more contextual and local critique that the player can then use to make local choices based on where the sim lives.

Of the game's strengths, the most obvious is that it gives a space for students to practice applying their personal ethics (if framed similar to how the prior assignment is, which assumes the students have an explicit, deliberative project in mind when they play). One compelling aspect of this is that students typically come to the game with a very strict code and, over time, the code becomes not so much softened but realistic. As students work to apply their beliefs in the world of the game, they are forced to compromise, not just practically ("I couldn't put in the big city park because I ran out of money"), and not just ethically ("I wanted a waste-free city, but realized it is impossible for people to live together without there being some waste"), but also reflectively in terms of the game's shortcomings ("I wanted there to be cattle ranches, but had to settle for generic farms").

All of these negotiations lead, I believe, to student's applying knowledge gained through the game to similar negotiations in their everyday lives. Once aware of some of the civic systems around them, and once they are given some basic tools for theorizing such systems, students can begin to work from civic knowledge to civic know-how in a way that integrates their personal concerns and ethics with minimal imposition on the part of the teacher. While there are obvious biases in the game, those biases provide a good springboard for discussion, and on a very basic level, students are afforded a chance to see how basic civic systems relate to each other, and, more importantly, how they relate to the students themselves. Writing assignments that consider the game in this light can use the game as a strong and viable middle ground for ethical experimentation, theorization and reflection that leads, subsequently, to better informed, more civically-engaged students.

Notes

1. I point to Christopher Alexander's *The Nature of Order,* for one approach to this problem. He, like Husserl before him, roots the current malaise in the sciences, and by extension, architecture, to a particular trajectory from Descartes to the present.

2. There is interesting work to be done with more recent theories of object-oriented ontology (Harmon, Bogost, and Bryant, particularly) in this regard, as well.

3. I'm reminded of a story I read years ago involving two Buddhist masters, one the younger Korean Zen master Seung Sahn, and the other an older Tibetan, Kalu Rinpoche. The point of bringing the two men together was for an instructive "dharma combat," wherein they would debate some deep problem and those watching would find in it a lesson. The younger monk started by reaching into his robes, pulling out an orange and thrusting it into rinpoche's face, saying "What is this? What is this? What is this?" Rinpoche sat for several minutes and finally, between provocations, turned to the interpreter and said "What's wrong with him? Don't they have oranges where he comes from?" Check. Mate.

4. And, to be fair, Heidegger did allude to this kind of conspicuity in his work, as well. Especially in his later work when he became so interested in the nature of a work of art and how it may bring about a recognition of a thing in this way.

5. The URL is: https://archive.org/details/msdos_SimCity_1989

6. I use the websites for the Congress for the New Urbanism (cnu.org), the Project for Public Spaces (pps.org), and Smart Growth America (www.smartgrowthamerica.org).

7. I will gladly email a copy of this "building code" to anyone interested in trying the project for themselves.

8. In the past I have also had students attempt to write a building code for their hometowns, and use that as the place they later attempt to model in the game.

9. Students do not, for example, have to state how far the setbacks of houses will be from the sidewalk, nor state some measured width for how wide streets will be, nor how deeply pipes must be buried, etc.

10. For my class, this later assignment is either a letter to someone who can help solve a local problem that they research, or a poster that has an explicit call to action to involve other people in their problem (which then post around town). Considering various analogous systems and structures from the game, students therefore begin to operate in their actual civic environment as described earlier in this essay.

11. In *SimCity,* for example, the "sims" are not stratified in any way beyond income. Richer sims can afford to live in more affluent neighborhoods, creating a kind of simulated gentrification. But sims do not (presumably because of the tensions it would cause in the gaming community, hindering sales) stratify according to race or gender. Female sims, presumably, are paid an equal wage and sims of a particular race and/or ethnicity do not seem to subject to any pressure to live near each other.

12. Though, to be sure, in some games that involve other real world people (the online aspect of the 2013 release of *SimCity,* MMORPGs, etc.) there may be an actual emotional response when making such decisions (although I am skeptical that it is typically as strong as those dealing with a real, embodied and standing-in-front-of-you person).

REFERENCES

Feenberg, A. (2002). *Transforming technology.* New York: Oxford UP.

Habermas, J. (1987). *Theory of communicative action volume two: Lifeworld and system.* (Thomas McCarthy, Trans.). Boston: Beacon P., 1987. (Original work published 1981).

Heidegger, M. (1962). *Being and time.* (John MacQuarrie & Edward Robinson, Trans). New York: Harper and Row. (Original work published 1927).

Husserl, E. (1999). *The essential Husserl.* (Donn Welton, Ed.). Bloomington: Indiana UP.

Merleau-Ponty, M. (1958). *Phenomenology of perception.* (Colin Smith, Trans.). New York: Routledge. (Original work published 1945).

Seamon, D. (2005). Phenomenologies of environment and place. *Phenomenology + Pedagogy, 2*(2), 130–135. Retrieved from http://www.phenomenologyonline.com/articles/seamon.html.

PART IV: COMPOSING GAMES IN INDUSTRY AND

CLASSROOM CONTEXTS (OR, WRITING GAMES)

13 Narrative Realities and Alternate Zombies: A Student-Centered Alternate Reality Game

Jill Morris

INTRODUCTION

Narratology and ludology have been at odds in gaming studies for some time. Games don't have to tell a story in order to be playable and replayable. The theoretical difficulty of narrative in games is actually fairly simple: traditional, non-digital narratives are nearly always telling stories about the past or at least from the point of view of a narrator reflecting on past events (Juul, 1998). Games, on the other hand, are always played in the present. When you press a button on the controller or keyboard, something happens on the screen in the present, even though the story is occurring in the past. Jesper Juul originally theorized that flashbacks and flashforwards would be impossible in games, though this has largely been proven untrue (*Braid*, for example, has you play the game both in the "present" and with time reversed, and other interesting chronological elements are appearing in increasingly advanced games). However, even if flashbacks and forwards are possible, the story already has a more or less set plot. If you play a dungeon in *World of Warcraft* that is set in the past, your winning or losing does not change the overall narrative of the game, even though you are given the chance to "be there." Interactivity, therefore, keeps most games from being true narratives.

So when two colleagues—Mary Karcher and Wendi Sierra—returned from viewing a panel at Computers & Writing 2010 very excited about planning an Alternate Reality Game (ARG) that could be played between the campuses they taught at via the Internet, I did not think that eventually teaching a course based around a game would make me rethink the place of narrative in both games and composition. At the time, they were throwing around ideas about zombies and apocalypses, and somewhere on the way to the Purdue parking garage I said that I wanted my dog to play an evil cyborg Pomeranian in the game. The game that was played by my students in Spring 2012 did not look much like our original plan, but instead created an opportunity to re-examine the ways that gaming and narrative could interact in a classroom and between universities.

The ARG—eventually titled "Glen is Dead?"—was developed by Mary Karcher, Sheryl Ruszkiewicz, Wendi Sierra, Doug Eyman, Scott Reed, Anthony Harrison, and myself and was played by students enrolled in Sheryl Ruszkiewicz's Composition 1 course at Baker College of Allen Park. Students enrolled in my two sections of Business Writing at Frostburg State University did not "play" strictly as players, but instead were tasked with creating NPCs (non-player characters), writing letters from the evil corporation that created the zombie virus, and responding to player students on our ARG message boards.

What started as an ARG completed the term as an encompassing narrative written by students for students about zombies, corporations, and the fallout of national disasters. My students were originally intended to create puzzles modeled after earlier successful ARGs—clues of which would be worked into the letters, websites, and reports they wrote as the normal process of the business writing class. Students at Baker would then decipher, analyze, and re-articulate those clues and the game in their own writing. The composition students would also have the opportunity to interact with the evil zombie-producing company about their own projects via a "Service Learning Initiative." My students, however, were more interested in the opportunity to create convincing characters, play roles, and even create businesses outside of the corporation that added to the story than they were dropping hints and creating puzzles and games. As my students became involved in the narrative that was emerging in real-time (with only a few set dates by the instructors—such as the first zombie "death"), they became more invested in the class, the outcome, and their own work. On the other hand, students at the second institution wanted to know "what happened" but were less involved in the game even though they were the intended "players."

As my students began interacting with one another and creating characters, videos, and documents, I realized that what we were doing didn't really look like an ARG, but it didn't look like a traditional role-playing game either. As Pat Harrigan and Noah Wardrip-Fruin note in their introduction to *Second Person* (2010), "[n]ew forms of media not only require new approaches to story, but may even force us to re-examine our assumptions about how stories are told in more traditional forms" (p. xiv). What emerged, primarily because the instructors involved chose not to force the students into an ARG format, wasn't a traditional game or a narrative. However, the emergent form was one that had characteristics of both game and narrative *and* worked with the class structure very well. A fully traditional role-playing game or ARG might not have engaged students, but by adapting the game to their needs during the semester, the finished product was additive to the course, improved student engagement, and produced interesting and thoughtful student projects.

Many composition courses have "themes" that are related to the readings the instructor chooses or are about writing in general. The only underlying story behind composition courses seems to be the learning outcomes—that set of skills that must be learned in 10–15 weeks. Unfortunately, these skills are not always valued by students nor are they intrinsically interesting to them either. Despite being very useful to students and important to their success in college and after, critical thinking, research, revising, development, and organization of writing are not usually topics that students would study in depth or write about on their own. While narrative has been focused on too heavily in game studies, we have not focused on it as a way of organizing composition courses. Instead of students writing papers because they have to practice specific writing skills or genres, they *could* be writing papers and other documents because they add to the story or the discourse the story is creating. This is what happened in my course, and what I will argue should happen more often in composition courses.

NARRATIVES AND GAMES

Prior to the 1970s, the idea that games can or should have a story was rarely considered (Costikyan, 2010). However, in that decade text-based games for computers were developed that put the user into a story like *Adventure* or even *Hitchhiker's Guide to the Galaxy* (asking them to make decisions, move around, and figure out puzzles in order to advance through the story) and the first *Dungeons and Dragons* game book was released. Within a few years, games with stories (or that allowed you to play through stories) not only existed but became very popular.

But just because games had been made with stories did not mean that there was now a simple relation between them. Stories are linear—many games are not. Stories are told by an author in one very specific way in order to maximize their impact. Games require some flexibility and agency on the part of the player in order to be fun and interesting. Stories end up being constrained by games and vice versa, and it is for this reason that many people who study games (ludologists) to this day do not believe that games and narratives are a good match (Costikyan, 2010).

Ludologists have argued that narratives address "what has happened" and require external observers; games must have active players engaged with the story who care about what will happen (Frasca, 2003). What I witnessed in my class was that fully immersed game creators/writers telling a real-time narrative to others, creating materials only briefly before they were distributed (a necessity in the course schedule), looked a lot more like these ludologists' players who were fully immersed in the situational domain than external observers.

Raph Koster, author of *Theory of Fun for Game Design*, argues that narrative in games often functions as a form of feedback in game design (2012). We enjoy finishing the board on *Pac Man* not only because it means we get to advance, but also because we get to watch a brief cartoon featuring Pac-Man and the ghosts. Koster states that our brains love feedback and that games have built-in reward systems that keep us playing and keep making us think we have achieved something when we really have not. Narrative in such early games was an afterthought stuck in as a reward for finishing a level.

Good games exist that have no narrative at all. Think of *Tetris*: there are certainly those of us who might imagine ourselves either building or breaking down walls around the now-defunct Soviet Union, but this narrative is neither suggested by the game nor required for its enjoyment. Games instead contain puzzles that must be solved by certain procedures—traveling to a certain location, collecting items, unlocking a door, defeating enemies, or matching up blocks—and when we do these things properly we receive rewards or feedback.

However, some forms of entertainment that are today recognized as games could not exist without stories. Will Hindmarch (2010) refers to these as "storytelling games." Tabletop role-playing games have expanded from "simple" games of exploring dungeons and finding treasure to players designing complex characters they may play and develop over many years. In general, like normal tabletop games, the player is in charge of his or her character's development and decisions, but the story is told and given to them by one dungeon master. Good dungeon masters have to give the players freedom, however, in order for the game to be enjoyable for everyone. They must give up their expectations for what is going to occur if the players come up with something better (Hindmarch, 2010). While the ARG hybrid that we developed for our classes ended in many students developing and playing characters, they could all also affect the plot—so it was not a true role-playing game either. However, like a good dungeon master, I had to give up my own expectations for what would occur and grant the students greater agency in order to engage them in the ARG. The stories that they told through their characters and the plotlines they developed were much more interesting and convoluted than what was originally planned, and also better received by their audience.

ALTERNATE REALITY GAMES—GLEN IS DEAD?

Alternate Reality Games are a relatively new form of gaming; Dave Szulborski (2005) notes that they are also often called immersive fiction, or even viral marketing because corporations often produce them. These games take place mainly via the Internet, but they may point players to other media, physical locations, and even commercial products with hidden messages in them during play. Unlike stereotypical games that feature a standard interface like a game board or a GUI, ARGs instead try to pass themselves off as being real, as not being a game at all. Hence, ARGs are governed by the notion that "This is not a game"—sometimes abbreviated as "TINAG"—and the most important principle in creating one is to immerse the players in an environment that will make them forget they are playing at all. For this reason, ARGs often ask people to use deductive and analytical skills to find clues strewn across websites, call phone numbers to access information, appear in person at certain locations and certain times, and exchange information with one another in a community in order to solve the final puzzle. In some ARGs this means rescuing a person who is being held captive or helping them rescue themselves (as is the case with the "Mime Academy," http://www.internationalmimeacademy.com/) or the end of the game might feature an advance copy of a popular video game being given to winners.

For example, *I Love Bees* (2004) was an ARG created as a marketing campaign for the release of *Halo 2* (Halo Nation, 2012). A strange message that only said "I love bees" was inserted into the theatrical trailer for the game, and was spotted by viewers who would be lead to what seemed to be a beekeeper's website. Of course, since this was a game, it wasn't a real beekeeper and a countdown on the page eventually pointed to dates when strange messages like "network throttling will erode" would appear (Halo Nation, 2012). These strange phrases directed players to a blog and eventually to real world pay phones on specific dates and times when they could receive a phone call and hear a message. Players began sharing these messages online with one another, and they discovered that the messages they heard could be pieced together to tell a story. Winners who played through to the end were able to play *Halo 2* multi-player before the game's actual release date (Halo Nation, 2012).

ARGs have successfully been used in classrooms in the past, though not across several different universities. For example, at the University of Southern California, PhD Candidate Jeff Watson used an ARG to help incoming freshmen to the college's School of Cinematic Arts collaborate with one another (Maton & Thomas, 2011). Three hundred cards that could be used in collaborative story-telling projects were hidden across the USC campus. Students used the cards to tell stories, but also to gain access to the game's secret campus headquarters and to make posts to the game's website. Their projects were also posted to the website so that other participants could rate and review them. Watson wanted the game to be optional so that students would choose to play rather than feel forced to participate. Like many ARGs, the beginning of play was a mysterious message asking other players to meet. Students that played noted that this made the semester a lot more interesting and eventually rival teams were created during its play (Maton & Thomas, 2011).

My own interest in using ARGs in the classroom grew from wanting to find a direct application of James Paul Gee's (2003) video game and literacy work to teaching composition. I understood personally why games were addictive and fun, and wanted a way to sink my students into the semiotic domain of writing in the same way that video games sunk Gee and his son into *Pikmin*. Although in 2003 I had no immediate answer to this problem, as most of my students don't feel like writers at the beginning of their college career, ARGs have slowly become one possible solution to creating a space within which students can do *meaningful* and *empowering* writing. In order to not feel like a game, ARGs by their very nature must be immersive. They ask players to call upon existing skills and knowledge and pool those skills to reach the end of the story.

Early in the development of "Glen is Dead?" I suggested that my students, rather than being players, could be co-authors of the game. Working singly or in small groups, one of their assignments would be to create part of the ARG. This would allow us to create timely and meaningful responses to student questions, papers, and discoveries without overburdening ourselves.

I created an assignment that gave students a list of potential ideas that they could create for the ARG. My students were enrolled in Business Writing (ENGL330) at Frostburg State University, and I had approximately twenty students in each of two sections of the course. I always have students form fake companies and corporations from which to write their course materials for this class, both for added "reality" and fun. This time they also had the option to be a subsidiary, competitor, or even grass-roots organization against Rove, Lacier, and Piton (RLP)— the manufacturer of the zombie virus (that company name is an anagram of "Evil Incorporated"). Additionally, each student got to decide whether they would play a character (via Facebook, Twitter, and other social networking sites), make a brief movie that would later be shared with students at our sister school, do peer review on essays submitted to the RLP website, make puzzles, or even create a website for their own company that would then need to be added to the storyline of the ARG. From the very beginning, many more students than I expected chose to play characters, even though I warned them it was easily the most time-consuming project as characters had to post every day or so throughout the entire semester in order to be believable.

In designing a game for a course, I did not want my students to be earning false achievements. Instead, I wanted their sense of having accomplished something (their feedback) to not only be to receive a passing grade, but also to see their work used by others, published online, analyzed, and ultimately used to solve the game as we had written it. It would be easy enough to gamify a course—giving students quest lines and achievements to complete by the end of course or to move to higher levels—but since our goal at the outset was to create an ARG, I felt that these rewards were too basic.

In "Composition and the Circulation of Writing," John Trimbur (2000) argued that the isolation of writing from production and delivery is a problem. He stated that it would be ethical for us to devise delivery systems that circulate our students' ideas, opinions, and knowledge beyond the classroom. In doing so, we would also expand the public forums through which people can discuss the issues of the day (including doom and gloom predictions of the future *a la* the Zombie Apocalypse). Rather than just writing for the teacher, students writing for a larger audience with the intent to deliver content outside the school would likely spend more time and care on those writing tasks. However, Trimbur also noted that what circulates tends to be cultural products, media messages, and commodities—not usually essays. The easiest thing to exchange, then, might not be stereotypical essays. Our students exchanged essays, yes, but more successful was the exchange of letters, graphics, and videos. Essays can only be successfully used as part of the ARG if they are part of the story itself. Increasingly standardized curriculums make this difficult, but not impossible.

While some students did work on the message boards, exclusively reviewing student essays for credit, they were not as much a part of the story as those who created characters or starred in videos. If the student essays they were reviewing had an impact on the story (instead of just being those assigned by the standard curriculum), those student reviewers also had the added experience of helping create the narrative of the course.

The ARG was based around a company we created—Rove, Lacier, and Piton (RLP)—and its employees. Via a website (http://www.rovelacierandpiton.org), students could learn that RLP was a research organization that supported public and private medical, scientific, and media-based projects around the globe, including an implant that returned the sense of smell to people who had lost it and a new pain-killer for dogs. RLP also had a new initiative to reach out to college students and to help them with their research through a Service Learning Initiative, headed by one Glen Wheatley (nearly all characters in the game had names influenced by Science Fiction and Fantasy media—in this case Wheatley is a character from *Portal 2*). Student players were invited to share their research and drafts with RLP staff via a forum while employees (played by my students as well as the other instructors involved) would give them recommendations about the development of their research projects, sources they might use, and publication venues. As papers were uploaded, I would instruct my students to share sources that might not be available on the player-students' campus, recommend how their papers could be further developed even if they had already been graded, and show them how their topics could relate to potential majors, jobs, and other real-world events outside of the classroom. The students playing the ARG were introduced to the SLI project through a video of Glen Wheatley played during class and invited to explore the website. Hidden frames and errors in the video suggested that all was not what it seemed.

Unfortunately, the student "players" were largely resistant to participation, which could not be required as per the rules of that institution (not to mention good practice amongst ARG developers). They were afraid RLP would steal their research, and so, like my students, they were shown that it was a game, that there was a plot, and that their participation would help drive that plot. After they were told that the company was not "real" and introduced to the students who were running the game, more of them signed up and became interested. At the same time, my students began to communicate with them personally, letting them know that Glen was ill and writing to the participants about their topics.

In the planned plot of the ARG, a love triangle between three upper-level executives at RLP (including Glen Wheatley) led to executive Belladonna's dog Riddle (played by my dog—also named Riddle) being injected with the recently developed zombie virus in hopes that he would bite Belladonna and infect her. At the time, no one knew the zombie virus's effect on dogs. Instead of biting Belladonna, Riddle bit Glen. In the series of the videos that Glen made for the SLI participants, he looks progressively worse and becomes more disconnected—all symptoms of zombification. Furthermore, Glen reportedly visited several campuses during this time, infecting students at each one. Student participants were to be instructed to analyze an area of their campus or town rhetorically and also consider contagion as one factor in their analysis—supposedly to help out RLP. Early in the course Glen was to die, only to be discovered later in a lab at RLP being experimented on in order to discover the cure for the zombie virus. The player students then would have to make the major decisions about the end of the game. Would they choose to be whistleblowers that expose the experimentation at RLP? What would happen to RLP's employees? What has stereotypically happened to whistleblowers in the past? How could the cure be disseminated? How long would it take the FDA to approve it? Who would be eligible? How much would it cost? And if everyone could not be cured, what would happen to the zombies?

When my students became involved, one immediately wanted to play Riddle (the dog) in the game. I agreed, but said that this student would have to come up with a believable plotline and way to represent himself as a dog. During class discussion, he said that he wanted the zombie virus to have the opposite effect on dogs as it does on humans—instead of becoming dumb and craving brains and biting people, infected dogs would become increasingly smarter and less dog-like. He created a Twitter account for Riddle, and on that account throughout the term showed the dog's increasing intelligence, starting with barks and peaking midterm with increasingly intellectual observations about current events and politics. In the end, he decided to have Riddle take the zombie cure and become a dog again, as he was happier that way. In this *Flowers for Algernon*-esque style, the dog's story was actually quite sad.

Other students who wanted to play characters did so through Facebook, Twitter, and personal webpages and blogs. The Facebook profiles were particularly well crafted, as another student went so far as to play games on this fake account. The woman he was playing in the game was approximately his mom's age, and so he played games that his mom and aunts enjoyed on Facebook instead of ones that he liked, in order to make the account more believable. "You can always spot a fake Facebook account because they don't play games or post pictures," he said.

Our in-class discussions immediately showed to me that students were more engaged at the beginning of the term by silliness and whimsy than by the serious issues that the game presented. However, once engaged by whimsy, serious discussion arose about corporations, power, non-profits, and medicine in America. For example, early in the term students created a subsidiary of RLP that produced a non-fattening version of high fructose corn syrup from unicorns (that RLP had attained through a blood-contract with the Fae). Later in the term, not only were they discussing whether or not PETA should attempt to release the unicorns, but they were also researching articles about what happens to animals released by PETA (many are put to sleep) and whether PETA was or should be considered a domestic terrorism agency.

By the end of the term, one student decided to play a zombie himself as part of his project and "break in" to the end of Glen's last transmission. In his brief role, he suggested that, once given the cure, Glen was mostly able to contribute to society and communicate once more. However, most zombies were not being given the cure because it was expensive and as yet unapproved by the FDA. Throughout the video he made grunts and other noises that were then interpreted through captions. He argued that the cure should be given to all zombies and that zombies should not be killed and announced the formation of the New Zombie Alliance—an organization that called for human rights for all zombies. In class writings, other students analyzed historical movements for rights for AIDs patients, children with autism, and other groups historically marginalized because of medical conditions to draw up what would *probably* happen to zombies in this situation.

In the first few weeks of the class, I realized that the whimsical materials my students were presenting gained far more attention from the "player" students at the other institution than the serious materials that we had created in order to obey the "This is Not a Game" mandate. Because the pedagogy we were using was highly experimental, I was willing to allow my students more control over the plot as their materials "worked" in ways that those created by the instructors had not. In so doing, they gained greater agency over a part of the class and became more conscientious about the materials that the other students would be reading. During the fifth week, I stood by about ten minutes after class ended as one student continually held up a finger and said to me, "It's not ready yet. Let me proofread one more time. This has to represent the company." If only they were so excited about the writing that had to represent themselves!

They had gained Trimbur's real audience in a way that our more traditional methods of publishing student materials (like blogs) often fail at. By writing for other students who wanted to listen to them (because the story they were telling was about zombies and unicorns and dogs), they practiced the skills that I wanted them to learn about revision, voice, and professionalism—all necessary in a Business Writing class.

This could have been more effective if the second class had been more engaged at the very beginning and if the two terms of the participating schools were not offset by several weeks. Although an outside-the-university audience was a boon in some respects (my students reported being more excited by meeting students at another school and also less afraid of being judged by someone they knew due to the distance separating the schools), if the student players' classes had been at the same institution, it would have been easier to choose similar course times (to allow for interaction), play for more of the term, and assure that all puzzles were found and solved.

Despite the fact that all of their materials weren't found or sent (the players' class ended several weeks before our term ended, so assignments completed in the latter part of the term could not be used for this iteration of the game), the students did not drop their quality on those last few projects that pertained to the New Zombie Alliance. Rather than the realism coming from the audience, as I had originally assumed, they wanted the materials to be good because, as one student noted, "This has got to have a good ending!" My students viewed each other as part of their audience, wanting to tell the best story to their classmates as they possibly could.

While we had originally set out to create an ARG and parts of the game looked like one (hidden messages in videos, for example), in the end what occurred in my class seemed to be more like a tabletop role-playing game with forty dungeon masters and no rule book. The sort of chaos that could have occurred did not because of the careful framing provided by the instructors at the outset, but also because the students wanted to tell a cohesive story.

Even when required to form companies and design materials and products for them, students often choose to change their topic, products, and company on a whim in this type of course, or to come up with companies that could not possibly exist (one of my favorites was a "car-burning" company that would help people commit insurance fraud). Having an overarching narrative to the course seemed to keep the students focused and also helped them see where their projects needed revision if they were going to be included in that narrative.

CONCLUSION

I'm not particularly concerned with whether what we did in our classes in Spring 2012 was an ARG or not. Perhaps another term like *interactive fiction* or even *massive interactive fiction* would be better, but ARG is still less contentious to both ludologists and those parts of the public convinced that Massive Multiplayer Online Role-Playing Games (MMOR-PGs) are just as likely to produce serial killers as first person shooters (or any game at all). In short, what was created was engaging to my students as they wove their own character stories or videos into the larger plot, class was more fun than usual, and so I'm not very worried about whether someone else could argue, "That's not an ARG." I might even agree with them.

However, by introducing an element into the class (originally conceived of as an ARG) and allowing my students to develop it, I was aware of pedagogical elements that were immediately reusable. I will not be team-teaching this course with teachers and students from other universities every semester, but that won't stop me from keeping the interactive elements in the course that were most effective.

First, I believe that narrative has not been examined enough as a way of engaging students in writing classes. Over the past ten years, I have heard from administrators, conference presentations, and publications about "today's student" not being engaged by lecturing or traditional-style delivery formats in the classroom. Generalizing broadly, the "answer" to "today's student" often falls to increased technology use. If you use PowerPoint, if you introduce clickers, if you have them make a personal website, this will somehow make class relevant for them. Narrative is not considered as a technological solution to student engagement, though I believe in this case it was employed as one.

As mentioned earlier, classes don't often come with a story attached, even in cases where stories (movies, poetry, books) are the objects of study. This is, no doubt, in part because participating in role-play seems childish when compared to the serious tasks of grammar instruction and genre awareness. However, introducing a narrative such as a zombie apocalypse, oil shortage, or other fake or real world disaster can give students a position from which to frame their writing. Instead of asking them to write about these topics themselves, we can instead make them part of the narrative of the class. I would like to ask students in their writing: If the zombie apocalypse started tomorrow, how would that change your research? How would it change the business practices of the hair salon that you have created as a mock company for the class? How do you think various politicians would react?

In coming terms, my Business Writing classes will be so affected. Minus the setting of the ARG, I will plan 4–5 dates during the term when I will give the class a news announcement (in my case it will likely be fake, but other teachers could use real world events as well)—it might be that zombies have been seen in Zambia, or a nuclear plant meltdown in Japan, or any number of other stories. From this, they will have to decide how their company will react, how they will personally react, what their employees will think, what they will want their employees to think, and so on. Future assignments will have to take this new part of the story of the class into consideration, and based upon their reactions (or non-reactions) I will then write the next press-release for the next planned update. As happened during the ARG, I will adjust my plans based upon what is most effective with them and take into consideration the most thoughtful and exciting student responses when working on the next part of the story.

In this way, a jointly-told story can become the framing technology for a course, even one that does not meet in a computer lab or take place online. Students' willingness to engage with whatever story is being presented will affect the outcome of the story and the course and give them some agency over the *story* if not what they have to learn.

While the website, videos, and other techniques that we used to present the ARG made it more believable, believability (This is Not a Game) was not ultimately necessary for the success of a classroom-based ARG. The strange sort of interactive fiction that emerged, on the other hand, was a success. Teachers struggling to engage students should consider narrative as a technology to improve student interest, especially if they are willing to give up some of the control over the story to the students themselves.

References

4orty2wo Entertainment. (2004). *I love bees.* [Game.]

Costikyan, G. (2010). Games, storytelling, and breaking the string. In Pat Harrigan & Noah Wardrip-Fruin (Eds.), *Second person: Role-playing and story in games and playable media* (5–13). Cambridge, MA: MIT Press.

Gee, J. P. (2003). *What video games have to teach us about learning and literacy.* New York: Palgrave MacMillan.

Halo Nation. (2012). I love bees. *Halo Nation.* Retrieved from http://halo. wikia.com/wiki/I_love_bees?cb=8588

Harrigan, P., & Wardrip-Fruin, N. (2010). Introduction. In Pat Harrigan & Noah Wardrip-Fruin (Eds.), *Second person: Role-playing and story in games and playable media* (xiii-xv). Cambridge: MIT Press.

Hindmarch, W. (2010). Storytelling games as a creative medium. In Pat Harrigan & Noah Wardrip-Fruin (Eds.), *Second person: Role-playing and story in games and playable media* (47–55). Cambridge: MIT Press.

Koster, R. (2012, January 20). Narrative is not a game mechanic. *Raph's Website.* Retrieved from http://www.raphkoster.com/2012/01/20/narrative-is-not-a-game-mechanic/

Juul, J. (2005). *Half-real: Video games between real rules and fictional worlds.* Cambridge, MA: MIT Press.

Maton, N. & Thomas, R. (2011, December 30). USC film students practice artistic craft through games. *Wired.* Retrieved from http://www.wired.

com/magazine/2011/12/usc-film-students-practice-artistic-craft-through-games/

Szulborski, D. (2005). *This is not a game: A guide to alternate reality gaming.* Macungie, PA: New-Fiction Publishing.

Trimbur, J. (2000). Composition and the circulation of writing. *College Composition and Communication, 52*(2), 188–219.

14 Procedural Rhetoric, *Proairesis,* Game Design, and the Revaluing of Invention

James J. Brown, Jr. and Eric Alexander

In 2012, we taught a course called "Digital Rhetorics" at the University of Wisconsin-Madison, during which students studied rhetorical theory in various digital environments. One portion of the course was focused on videogames, and students both played and designed games with an eye toward what Ian Bogost (2007) calls procedural rhetoric. In *Persuasive Games,* Bogost argues that games use computational procedures to make arguments. Rather than explaining procedures with language, "procedural representation explains processes with other processes" (p. 9). By building a model and then asking players to interact with that model, video games simulate processes and use them to mount arguments. Students in our class played the game *Braid* and studied its various procedural arguments. They also used the programming language Scratch to *create* games in an attempt to craft procedural arguments about Wisconsin politics. In addition to building a broad theoretical framework for understanding the rhetoric of games, Bogost argues that political videogames have often neglected to engage the procedurality of the medium. Instead of modeling and critiquing political processes, political games have often merely put new skins on old games or used games as delivery systems for textual arguments. Students in our class were tasked with answering this challenge by creating (that is, *writing*) games that used computational procedures to make arguments about Wisconsin politics.

The games intervened in ongoing political arguments by using procedurality as a rhetorical tool. This type of intervention is in keeping with Rhetoric and Composition's concern for linking classroom writing to broader social and political problems. Games can accomplish this in a unique way by making arguments with procedures and by making arguments about how the world works (or how it *should* work). However, games also offer another set of resources for scholars, students, and teachers in Rhetoric and Composition. In addition to presenting a unique way of intervening in a controversy, games also present complex *inventional spaces* for both designers and players. For the rhetorician, invention is concerned with determining what to argue, and games engage with invention in complex and often contradictory ways. In teaching procedural rhetoric and game design, we (as well as our students) found that games can often make more than one procedural argument and that they can also serve as spaces in which players invent various arguments, some of which have nothing to do with what the designers intended. Games are complex rhetorical devices for both designers and players, and modeling political processes with computation can make for open-ended inventional spaces.

While any argument (textual, visual, aural, procedural) exceeds an author's intention, the procedurality and participation inherent to games amplifies these complications. In this chapter, we discuss how we used game design in the writing classroom, and we discuss the implications of this approach for rhetorical theory. Video games allow the rhetor to count computational procedures amongst the available means of persuasion as they intervene in controversies and make arguments, but games also complicate our notions of invention. When designing a videogame, invention cuts across the entire process, from design to gameplay. Arguments reveal themselves throughout the process, even long after the designer has released his or her creation into the world, and this is because procedural expression values what Collin Brooke (2009) calls *proairetic* invention, an open-ended mode of invention that resists closure. These revelations call for a rethinking of how the canon of invention plays out in the writing of games. In the pages that follow, we describe the course we taught, explain our video game design assignment, and show how game design revalues the canon of invention.

GAMES AS RHETORICAL INTERVENTIONS

Our course asked students to both theorize and practice digital rhetoric. The textbook for the course was Sharon Crowley and Debra Hawhee's (2011) *Ancient Rhetorics for Contemporary Students*, and we built the class around two major projects. The first project asked students to take a chapter of Crowley and Hawhee's text and transform it into a comic book. In this project, the students' primary rhetorical constraint was *ComicLife* software, and we asked them to carefully consider the available means of persuasion in both *ComicLife* and the genre of sequential art. We read Scott McCloud's (2006) *Making Comics* in order to provide students with a vocabulary for the various ways of composing and arranging image and text when creating comics. In *Understanding Comics* (1994) and *Making Comics* (2006), McCloud offers a set of observations that are useful both for readers and writers of comics, and he presents these observations in comic form. In fact, Ben McCorkle (2010) argues that McCloud's *Making Comics* can be seen as a rhetoric of comics since "it not only offers readers practical and theoretical advice for producing aesthetically effective and engaging comics of their own [but] . . . also demonstrates its own argument in a sophisticated yet visually appealing manner" (n.p.). Students used McCloud's rhetoric of comics as they learned *ComicLife* and created their own comics. Our hope in this first unit was that students would get an opportunity to explore the available means of persuasion in a particular software platform. But while this first project asked students to explore rhetorical theory and practice by *using* software, the second project asked them to explore and theorize rhetoric in the *composition* of software. It is this second project that we will focus on in this chapter.

Before any discussion of computer programming or game design, we first asked students to read excerpts of Ian Bogost's (2007) book *Persuasive Games* and to play Jonathan Blow's (2008) videogame *Braid*. Bogost's text presents a theory of procedural rhetoric that connects game design to the long history of rhetorical theory, and it presented students with a critical vocabulary for our discussions of *Braid*. Bogost argues that video games use computational procedures to make arguments. Those procedures build a system and then ask a player to move through that system. The rules that dictate what can or cannot happen in the system make arguments about how the world works (or how it should work). By situating his theory of procedural rhetoric within the rhetorical tradition, Bogost presents rhetoricians interested in digital media and students with a valuable tool for conducting rhetorical analysis. Students carried out such analysis by playing and analyzing *Braid*, a game that weaves together its story and its computational procedures in a particularly intriguing way.[1] However, our primary use of procedural rhetoric was as an inventional tool. While Bogost's theory presents a useful way for players of games to think (and play) critically, its most powerful application is in the creation of procedural arguments.

To this end, we asked students to create a video game that mounted a procedural argument about a political issue in Wisconsin. We designed the project in this way for two reasons. First, we wanted students to see their games as intervening in a rhetorical situation. In this case, students were actually creating games as a response to two different rhetorical situations. The first situation was the Wisconsin political issue they chose to address, but the second situation was more directly linked to our classroom discussions. In *Persuasive Games*, Bogost argues that political videogames have largely failed to make use of the procedurality of videogames. For instance, he argues, most political campaigns using games have focused on the participatory nature of the Internet while failing to take "significant advantage of the procedural affordances of the medium" (2007, p. 124). For Bogost, this ignores a powerful mode of persuasion and representation:

> Procedural rhetoric is particularly devoted to representing, communicating, or persuading the player toward a particular biased point of view. Playing such games can have a political impact because they allow players to embody political positions and engage in political actions that many will never have previously experienced, and because they make it possible for eplayers to deepen their understanding of the multiple causal forces that affect any given, always unique, set of historical circumstances. Procedural rhetoric is precisely what is missing from current uses of technology for political and civic engagement. (p. 135)

Bogost extends this argument in *How To Do Things With Videogames* (2011), arguing that most political games are more concerned with politicking (campaigning) than with questions of politics (the policy actions of elected officials): "reskinning classic arcade games and placing billboards in virtual racetracks doesn't take advantage of the potential games have to offer to political speech" (p. 60). As Bogost sees it, the procedurality of games makes them well suited for political argument since they are able to model complex systems and pose difficult questions: "*What should be the rules by which we live?* Such questions are rarely posed or answered seriously in elections" (p. 61, emphasis in original). Though politicians have rarely used games to make serious political arguments,

a video game's model can in fact forward arguments about existing policies that are poorly constructed and can propose new policies that better address political problems. We tasked students with filling the void
noted by Bogost. We should also note here that we chose the context of
Wisconsin state politics so that students would engage them with local
political issues and so that we could prevent student projects from getting mired in broad, sprawling problems like "taxes" or "abortion."

While games do not always have to make a political argument and
while they do not need to mount a procedural argument that intervenes
in a controversy, we would argue that overtly political games do offer a
particularly useful way of linking the concerns of rhetorical theory and
game design. We would never want to confine the concerns of rhetoric (or of games) to any one realm, and we can imagine a wide array of
games that would help students see how video games can serve as rhetorical interventions. However, we designed this assignment as a way to link
student games to particular rhetorical situations. More important than
a game design assignment that is overtly political is an assignment that
allows students to see their game as responding to a rhetorical exigence
and engaging with existing arguments. In such a situation, students are
not creating games in a vacuum or within the confines of the classroom
but are rather able to see computer programming and video game design
as a type of public writing—as a rhetorical practice that can travel outside of the classroom.[2]

GAMES AS INVENTIONAL SPACES

While our assignment was built around the idea that games and computational procedures should be counted among the available means of persuasion, it also presented both us and our students with an opportunity
to consider how computation allows us to reconsider the basic terms and
concepts of rhetorical theory. In particular, games present both designers
and players with inventional spaces—possibility spaces that encourage
exploration and invention. While a political videogame is an attempt to
make a particular argument (or set of arguments), the procedural and
participatory aspects of games mean that arguments continue to reveal
themselves well beyond the time when designers release their games.
While any rhetorical text opens itself up to various interpretations, we
believe that games revalue rhetorical invention by resisting closure and
coherence. Designers compose procedures that create a model of the

world, but players move through that world in unpredictable ways. A print essay or a visual argument can perform this same type of resistance to closure, but procedural rhetoric's call for participation pushes this resistance to the surface. The following discussion of two games—one that we designed and another that our students designed—will step through how games present inventional spaces and how those spaces distribute the process of invention across the entire process of game design and gameplay.

For the video game design project, we restricted the scope of the students' games to state and local politics. Our main goal was to keep them from having to tackle broad and polarizing social issues like abortion at the same time that they were learning to program and developing a game—all in four weeks. They still had plenty of topics to work with, as Madison had been a hotbed of political action in recent years. In February of 2011, Governor Scott Walker proposed a budget repair bill that included drastic budget cuts and rescinded almost all collective bargaining rights for public employees. In the ensuing backlash, upwards of 100,000 protestors descended upon the state capitol, Democratic state senators literally fled the state to avoid a vote, and Walker was eventually forced into a recall election (which he won).

We created a small game to use as an example both of good code and a procedural argument about politics. We sought to examine part of Walker's influence, specifically how it affected the way protests are organized and run in Madison's Capitol square. In the aftermath of the 100,000-person protest, Walker enacted a new law called the Wisconsin State Facilities Access Policy. This policy requires anyone wishing to hold an event in a public area to apply and pay for a permit:

> "All members of the general public wishing to hold an event or to display an exhibit shall apply for a permit, unless the event is a spontaneous event . . . Exhibits displayed without permits will be removed; exhibits removed may or may not be returned to the owner. Events occurring without permits will be terminated if the use conflicts with a previously permitted event." (*Wisconsin State Facilities Access Policy* p. 4)

The policy defines spontaneous events as events "where four (4) or more persons gather to exercise their First Amendment rights in response to a triggering event that has occurred within the preceding calendar week, or is currently occurring," and defines regularly scheduled events as "events that are advertised by any means (including, but not limited to, via electronic social media) seven (7) or more calendar days prior to the starting date of the event" (*Wisconsin State Facilities Access Policy,* p. 5). Scheduled events require permits from the State Capitol Police, and organizers may be charged "reasonable fees and charges" for the use of equipment and facilities. While the policy states that normal staffing levels at the Capitol allow for security and monitoring of events and that "the vast majority of events will not be subject to any excess law enforcement or maintenance costs" it also states that events exceeding the abilities of the normal staffing level will require that organizers provide either "sufficient trained event marshals or private security for crowd management" or must request (and pay for) "additional police services" (*Wisconsin State Facilities Access Policy,* p. 8). While the governor claimed these sorts of restrictions were necessary to relieve costs, this struck many as an attempt to censor the public debate by effectively putting a price on free speech. One attorney suggested that the policy seeks to protect the governor from public protests: "It's very hard to avoid the conclusion that, essentially what Scott Walker is trying to do is wall himself off completely from the people of Wisconsin" (2011, "Update"). The ACLU also expressed numerous concerns.

Laws and government policies like the WSFAP are, of course, procedures. We sought to simulate this procedure in order to explore its implications. In our game, titled *Pay to Play* (*P2P*), the player is a vocal citizen trying to change government policy.[3] He or she starts the game on the steps of the state capitol and must harangue the multitudes through a series of keystrokes until garnering enough support to change the policy in question. However, players cannot devote their entire attention to this simulated speechmaking. They also start with a variable amount of money in their pocket. They must hire police officers as the crowd grows. If the crowd gets larger than can be handled by the security force, or if the player runs out of money, the game ends in defeat. As a player performs keystrokes in the proper order, her on-screen counterpart delivers speeches that draw more protestors to their simulated rally. However, this oral rhetoric acts as a double-edged sword. In the mechanics of the game, more protestors allow players to build support for the cause. However, the increase in protestors also requires more police officers, causing players to run out of money more quickly. Players must balance these conflicting forces in a way that makes the best use of their budget. If their starting budget (randomly assigned in the beginning of the game) is too low, it may be impossible for them to win.

One obvious take-away is that the game becomes much easier if you happen to have a lot of money in your pocket. Players without enough money are unable to affect any sort of change; even the extra hassle of applying for a permit and hiring police officers is distracting enough in the game to feel suppressive to free speech. These were the arguments we started with when we began designing the game. However, the process of invention extended into the process of design. While we invented a set of arguments in conceiving of the game, those arguments changed as we began to build the game. In addition, other arguments revealed themselves. Creating this type of game is a balancing act, where the developer must weigh simplicity of gameplay with realism of the procedures being shown. To make a fair argument, the procedures ought to be close simulations to those existing in the real world. However, the real world is both noisy and complex. In order to pare down irrelevant procedures and create something we might actually be capable of programming, we must make assumptions and simplifications. We found that by examining these assumptions closely, further arguments arose from our game that we had not anticipated.

For example, during development, we needed to come up with a way for players to attract followers. Initially, new protestors would simply arrive at a constant rate the longer the player's protest remained active. Apart from being simply boring, this did not give the player enough agency in the situation. If they were to feel that they had a stake in the success of this on-screen sprite, we had to make them work for it. However, it was not feasible to have the player input their own political rhetoric and test it against the whims of our simulated crowd. At the cross-section of these desires for both realism and simplicity, we decided upon a mechanic incorporating timed keystrokes. A letter would flash on the screen, and the player would have to press the corresponding key. If they pressed the correct key in time, their argument would ring true to the crowd and more people would join up. If they pressed the wrong key, the flow of people would decrease. A decrease in supporters meant that the player would lose the game—they would fail to garner enough support for their cause.

This was a helpful mechanic from a gaming perspective. It effectively achieves the balance we wanted, on top of making the game more engaging to play. However, this design choice has further reaching implications for the game's procedural rhetoric. By reducing the rabble-rousing to merely hitting the proper key at the proper time, we have removed all rhetorical content from the player character's speeches—and yet in the procedural world of our game, he or she is still able to gain followers. Based on the rules we created, gaining political support is not about the content or validity of one's arguments but rather about money, and about pushing people's hot buttons at the right times. An interesting implication, and not one we intended to make when we authored this set of procedures.

Another example of invention in design comes from another mundane, real-world constraint. In the game, it is impossible for the players to get more money than they start with. While one could imagine expanding the game to include some sort of fundraising mechanic, we were limited by time and decided such features were outside the scope of the arguments we intended to make. Again, we sacrificed realism for simplicity. This choice ultimately reinforces the power of chance within the game. Though a talented player might be able to win in some marginal cases where others would lose, players must make the most of the hand they are dealt, which sometimes simply is not enough. This fatalistic procedure seems to argue that not only does money control political speech but that the dispersal of money is arbitrary. In real-world situations, money can be earned through the hard work of fundraising campaigns or other means that involve power and persuasion, but our game does not simulate these processes. Thus, the game ends up arguing that the allocation of resources is entirely random. This procedural argument actually runs directly counter to how we think the world works.

The process of game design is one of constant invention. For every rule with an intentional argument, there are many rules created out of necessity that have implications the developer never intended. If these "hidden arguments" are recognized during design, they can shape and refocus the designers' intended arguments. At some point, however, the game must leave the hands of the designer and be taken up by players. As we discovered, gameplay is part of a game's inventional space as well. When we finally had our students play *P2P*, they realized a procedural argument we had not thought of by playing the game in an unexpected way. With limited computers in the room, and wanting to foster discussion, we had the students play the game in pairs. We assumed this would result in students taking turns, but some students found a way of dividing the work. If one person controlled the dispersion of funds (pushing buttons to hire police, etc.) and another person focused on recruiting followers (by hitting the correct letter keys), they were much more successful than if a single person tried to juggle both tasks at once. This sort of divide and conquer strategy is employed by basically every political organization. Two players collaborating on *P2P* opens up a range of new arguments about the division of labor in any political movement, something that our game design process missed entirely by assuming that players would act individually and would be forced to choose how their attention was allocated.

There were also countless examples of invention in gameplay when it came to student-designed games. One of these, called *Walker, Wisconsin Ranger* (*WWR*), sought to make a sympathetic (or rather, empathetic) argument for Governor Walker's budget slashes by making the player play *as* Walker. This is a very powerful rhetorical technique that is particularly well suited to games, which can sometimes immerse a player in a world in ways that print media cannot. Games ask players to embody certain positions as they navigate procedures. When a player is put into an unfamiliar position, they will often find they are forced to confront decisions that they would never otherwise face and take actions they might have condemned in other situations. Reconciling this cognitive dissonance must come through a more nuanced understanding of the situation. The designers of *WWR* attempted to foster this type of broader understanding by forcing the player to make budget cuts (as Walker) and then try to deal with the political fallout.

The game effectively has the player walk a mile in Walker's shoes. The player starts in rural Wisconsin and walks to work at the Capitol building, passing through cornfields, suburbs, and city streets. The player must balance the budget before reaching the Capitol. Along the way, the player is presented with expenses and given the choice of cutting them or not. As budgets are cut, angry badgers representing voters gather at the Capitol building (the badger is both Wisconsin's state animal and the university's mascot). However, the player does not see this growing group of badgers until the game's final screen. If the player accumulates enough angry badgers before reaching the Capitol, the game ends in a loss with the player being recalled. If the player isn't able to balance the budget before reaching the capitol, the game ends in a loss with the player unable to make good on his campaign promises. The parameters of the game are tailored to make it exceedingly difficult (though not impossible) to win.

The main procedural argument being mounted by this game is that a balanced budget and voter approval are mutually exclusive. Playing as Walker, it is easy for the player to conclude that being the governor of Wisconsin is a thankless job. To that extent, the game successfully delivered a clear and concise argument, and it did so by designing procedures that constrain the player and force that player to embody another worldview. As the designers argue, the game makes a three-fold argument about balancing budgets and political capital:

> "The game reflects budget cuts in three aspects: First, it tracks the amount of money left needed to balance the budget. Second, Walker's approval rating fluctuates in proportion to his cuts. Third, the cuts affect the population of badgers protesting Walker in the final scene of the game. At the end of the game, if the player has both balanced the budget and kept a good approval rating, he wins. However, achieving both is incredibly difficult, [this is] meant to illustrate Walker's dire plight of both balancing the deficit whilst appeasing his myriad constituents." (Cartegena et al., 2012)

Thus, the designers hope that the player learns how difficult it is to balance the budget and gain (or retain) voter approval.

Other arguments emerge as one plays the game and reflects on its procedures. For instance, the game's procedures argue that any budget cut results in a net loss in voter approval. While this may in fact be the case for a number of budget cuts, one could certainly imagine that cuts to education could result in a net gain in approval numbers. Certain constituents will support such cuts even if others disapprove. In addition, every cut made is coupled with a textual description of the results of that cut, and those results are always negative. For instance, one cut to the public works portion of the budget results in the following text bubble: "City Sanitation Department Cut: Voters Hospitalized with Disease." This is indicative of various other cuts made in the course of gameplay. Regardless of the type of cut made, the results are always negative for both Walker's approval ratings and from the citizens themselves. So while the game aims to place the player in Walker's shoes and to empathize with him, it also tends to portray the results of the player's actions in a negative light. One could read this game as both an attempt to expose the complexity and difficulty of Walker's plight, and one could also read it as a critique of Walker's determination to balance the budget regardless of the effects on infrastructure. Neither of these readings would be wrong, given the game's procedures, and while these kinds of contradictory arguments could be considered a design flaw when it comes to presenting a coherent and consistent argument with words, images, video, or sound, they are seemingly unavoidable when presenting a procedural argument. As we have argued, certain design decisions made in the interest of feasibility will always mean that games contain various procedural arguments, some of which contradict one another. As we will see in the closing section of this essay, we argue that such complexities are built in to many new media objects and that they allow us to recon sider and revalue the canon of invention.

REVALUING INVENTION

In *Electronic Literature: New Horizons for the Literary* (2008), Katherine Hayles argues that electronic literature revalues computational practice. Electronic literature uses computation to create literary meaning, and this pushes computation beyond its typical role as a technical practice carried about by expert programmers:

> In electronic literature, computation evolves into something more than a technical practice, though of course it is also that. It becomes a powerful way to reveal to us the implications of our contemporary situation, creating revelations that work both within and beneath conscious thought . . . Thus understood, computation ceases to be a technical practice best left to software engineers and computer scientists and instead becomes a partner in the coevolving dynamics through which artists and programmers, users and players, continue to explore and experience the intermediating dynamics that let us understand who we have been, who we are, and who we might become. (p. 157)

Hayles argument becomes clearer if we consider a specific example. *Regime Change* (2006) by Noah Wardrip-Fruin, David Durand, Brion Moss, and Elaine Froehlich is a work of electronic literature (the authors call it a "textual instrument") that uses n-grams, a statistical model used to find patterns in a particular corpus of texts (Wardrip-Fruin et al.). In this case, n-grams are used to mash up news stories about various assassinations. Interaction with *Regime Change* comes by way of clicking on text and watching how text from one story is placed into another. A user "plays" *Regime Change* by exploring, clicking, and cutting up these various stories. Given that *Regime Change* mixes these stories (including accounts of the killing of Saddam Hussein and pieces of the Warren Commission's report on the assassination of John F. Kennedy), we could read the piece as a statement about the forces that conspire to assassinate political figures. We might also consider the title of the piece to be a remark on the shifting informational regimes at work in the world of journalism. Perhaps this textual instrument is commenting on how journalism is changing in a digital world. Given that *Regime Change* uses a computational machine to manipulate news stories, we might also consider the piece as a commentary on how technology actively shapes how information is delivered and manipulated.

But in addition to these possible readings, the piece has a pedagogical goal. As Wardrip-Fruin (2009) explains in *Expressive Processing*, the piece was designed to teach users how n-grams work and to give a user "a kind of feeling for the algorithm, for the processes at work, for potentials and limits" (p. 395). While Wardrip-Fruin grants that *Regime Change* mostly fails in this enterprise and that it is too opaque in its demonstration of n-grams, he still believes that playable digital media have the potential to develop "deeper understandings of the 'software society' in which we live today" (p. 396). This latter goal is what Hayles has in mind when she argues that works of electronic literature can "revalue computational practice." A work like *Regime Change* is not a tool designed to streamline our work or to automate some task (this is often how we view software) but is rather an attempt to use computation to express an idea. Thus computation becomes something much more than a way to increase efficiency.

While Hayles (2008) argues that electronic literature revalues computational practice, the reverse relationship can work as well: computer programming can revalue rhetorical and literary practice. Using computational procedures to make arguments allows us to *revalue* certain portions of rhetorical theory. That revaluation happens in various ways, and we could discuss how programming revalues each of the canons: invention, arrangement, style, memory, delivery. For instance, we might think of programming style—the use of white space, compact code, effective use of recursion—to rethink the rhetorical canon of style. A computer program is written for both a human and machinie audience, and this complicates our notion of rhetorical style. But our focus in this discussion of games is on the canon of invention and how the procedural rhetoric of a videogame forces the rhetorician to assume a complex, distributed notion of invention. The games created in our class demonstrate how invention is distributed across various phases of design (drafting, design, testing, game play) and is distributed amongst designers and players.

Collin Brooke (2009) has argued that the field of Rhetoric and Composition has often considered invention as an approach to prewriting or planning, and this is mostly because of the field's ties to the formal essay: "When that formal essay serves as the basis for evaluation, the process leading up to it is likely to acquire secondary status, regardless of teachers' theoretical adherence to process pedagogy" (p. 62). By this way of thinking, invention is a first step in the crafting of an argument. The author determines what to argue and then begins composing. Brooke shows that while there have been some corrections to this approach, the discipline has mostly remained tied to a textual orientation. This textual bias has also meant valuing texts and objects that guide a reader toward a particular argument or endpoint. Drawing on the work of Roland Barthes, Brooke suggests that this is only one way of thinking about invention.

Typically, we would describe the writer's task in terms of managing complexity and guiding the reader to some conclusion. While certain narratives and styles might thrive on a reader's frustration, these are exceptions to the rule, and this is especially true in the Rhetoric and Composition classroom. Composition classes value clarity and closure. Brooke reminds us that the "closing of alternatives" and the "reduction of a text's plurality," is indicative of what Barthes called the "hermeneutic" code (p. 76). But the hermeneutic code is always in tension with what Barthes' calls the "proairetic":

> The hermeneutic marks the goal(s) toward which the reader (and the plot and characters) are headed. The proairetic works in concert with the hermeneutic, but from the other end of things. Barthes uses the proairetic to indicate actions or events . . . Within the context of a murder mystery, for example, the discovery of a corpse might serve as an example of each code. On the one hand, it establishes an enigma (who did it? how did this happen?) that such a story will eventually resolve. On the other hand, it is an irreversible action that precludes some actions and predisposes the character(s) to others (who could have done it? what will we do next?) (p. 75)

These two codes work together to create what Brooke calls "textual momentum," the hermeneutic establishing mysteries and the proairetic laying out of pieces of information that enable or constrain the characters. However, the hermeneutic code almost always "overwhelms the proairetic" since the print paradigm assumes that the story is moving toward resolution: "Actions or events that fail to move the reader toward the resolution of the hermeneutic enigma are quite literally extravagant: They are off-track and may even be resented as wasteful or distracting" (p. 76). When our rhetorical theories are tied to the world of print, we are much more likely to teach a mode of invention that leans toward the hermeneutic end of the spectrum.

But Brooke asks whether the proairetic might be considered something more than a nuisance, and so he leans on this term in his new media remix of rhetorical invention. Instead of focusing on the individual writer and her product, "new media encourages us to consider a more radical distribution of individual intention" (p. 80). Invention is distributed in various ways as a new media object invites interaction and iterates over time. When it comes to the games we've described in this essay, this becomes especially clear. Invention happens continuously, as an audience, computational machines, authors, and other entities contribute to a new media object. Closure and resolution are not necessarily the primary goal or value of many new media objects, and video games are perhaps a perfect example of this. Game designers may have certain procedural arguments in mind as they create a game, but those arguments are mediated by various collaborators, not the least of which are computers, computer languages, and the players that will interact with the game. At every stage of a game's development and release, invention is unfolding in a proairetic fashion. Arguments are revealing themselves and opening up while other arguments are closed off. A videogame is not only a tool for making an argument; it is also a possibility space in which rhetorical invention is continually taking place.

Any argument is open to interpretation, and Brooke does not argue that proairesis is unique to new media. When writing an essay, an author may start with an argument, but that argument could very well change as he does research, organizes his thoughts, and articulates his claims. Further, people may interpret what he writes in ways the author didn't anticipate. However, the print essay (and our approaches to evaluating it) does lend itself to a hermeneutic mode of invention. Valuing the closure of hermeneutics is a product of our ties to print as a medium. As we move to other media, other forces in the inventional matrix reveal themselves. The intended arguments of authors and designers are still important, but they are also only one part of a complex rhetorical ecology. As Brooke suggests, "Closure is no less important now than it has ever been, but with the advent of new media and interfaces that resist closure, proairesis provides an important corrective to the hermeneutically oriented inventional theory that has prevailed in our field to date" (p. 86). Video games are a perfect example of this, and they value Brooke's proairesis in interesting ways. This is what we mean when we say that computation (and video games in particular) revalue rhetorical invention. A video game's resistance to closure is only a negative if we think of invention in terms of the hermeneutic.

The value of theoretical tools like procedural rhetoric and proairetic invention is that they attune us to the affordances of computation and new media. Procedural rhetorics use computational processes to make particular arguments, but they are more committed to simulating processes than they are to the intended arguments of the designer or author. This latter commitment can often mean that the intended argument is only one possible vector and that invention is an ongoing process that extends across time and space. The designer builds certain arguments into those processes, and the procedures themselves make arguments about how the world works. But those procedures establish an inventional space that then invites interaction and play. Regardless of what a game designer hopes she has communicated with her procedures, a player's movement through that inventional space will be an opportunity for more arguments to reveal themselves.

Video game design does not line up perfectly with the traditional concerns of rhetoric (writing and speech). While contemporary theories of rhetoric, digital and otherwise, have expanded what we think of as "fair game" for rhetorical theory and writing studies, it is important to remember that writing prose and writing code are in fact different. This is why Bogost's (2007) theory of procedural rhetoric and Brooke's (2009) reimagining of the canon of invention are so important for the rhetorician delving into the world of new media—they link the long history of rhetorical theory with the concerns of new media without allowing either to swallow the other. These concepts allow us to apply the theories of Aristotle and Cicero while also granting that computer programming raises new and interesting questions for rhetoricians. Games can serve as arguments, enacting procedures and reshaping our orientations to a particular set of arguments, and they can serve as inventional spaces in which all parties to the situation—designers, players, critics—can take an opportunity to explore a messy and chaotic set of possible arguments without worrying too much about closing down alternatives.

Game design allows for a unique mode of rhetorical intervention. Procedural arguments can participate in rhetorical situations in ways that other types of arguments cannot. In addition to adding to the available means of persuasion, procedural authorship also revalues invention. Procedural rhetoric does not necessarily fundamentally change writing, invention, or argument, but it does force us to reconsider what modes of writing and invention we most value.

NOTES

1. We are currently working on a separate forthcoming essay that details how Braid offers a particularly useful way of teaching computational thinking.

2. In another paper, we have argued that game design can serve as one way to introduce computer programming into higher education general education curricula. See: "Game Design and Computer Programming in the General Education Classroom." Proceedings of the Games, Learning, and Society Conference 8.0. 2012.

3. Both games discussed in this essay along with other student-created games are available at: http://courses.jamesjbrownjr.net/political_procedures

REFERENCES

Blow, J. (2008). Braid. [videogame]. Number None, Inc.

Bogost, I. (2011). *How to do things with videogames*. St. Paul, MN: University of Minnesota P Press.

Bogost, I. (2007). *Persuasive games: The expressive power of videogames*. Cambridge, MA: MIT Press.

Brooke, C. G. (2009). *Lingua fracta: Toward a rhetoric of new media*. Cresskill, NJ: Hampton Press.

Cartegena, A. Metcalf, C., Paese, A., Schneider, E., & Zhang, S. (2012) Walker, Wisconsin Ranger. [video game]. Retrieved Novmeber 12, 2015 from http://courses.jamesjbrownjr.net/walker_wisconsin_ranger

Crowley, S., & Hawhee, D. (2011). *Ancient rhetorics for contemporary students*. Fifth ed. Boston: Longman.

Hayles, N. K. (2008). *Electronic literature: New horizons for the literary*. Notre Dame, IN: University of Notre Dame Press

McCloud, S. (1994). *Understanding comics*. New York: William Morrow.

McCloud, S. (2006). *Making comics*. New York: William Morrow.

McCorkle, B. (2010). A rhetoric of sequential art: A review of *Making Comics: Storytelling Secrets of Comics, Manga and Graphic Novels* by Scott McCloud. *Enculturation, 7:* http://enculturation.net/a-rhetoric-of-sequential-art

"New Capitol access policy enacted." (2011). Retrieved November 12, 2015 from http://www.weau.com/home/headlines/New_Capitol_access_policy_enacted_134846413.html?site=mobile.

State of Wisconsin. *Wisconsin State Facilities Access Policy*. Retrieved from 104.236.214.136/wi-administrative-code-wisconsin-state-capitol.pdf

Wardrip-Fruin, N. (2009). *Expressive processing: Digital fictions, computer games, and software studies*. Cambridge, MA: MIT Press.

Wardrip-Fruin, N. Durand, D., Moss, B., & Froehlich, E. (2006). Regime change. In N. Katherine Hayles, Nick Montfort, Scott Rettberg, & Stephanie Strickland, (Eds.), *Electronic literature collection 1*. Retrieved Novemer 12, 2015 from http://collection.eliterature.org/1/works/wardrip-fruin_durand_moss_froehlich__regime_change.html

15 Games and the Search for "Contextually Valid Settings" in the Writing Classroom

David M. Sheridan and Kym Buchanan

> *It is tempting to reproduce the workplace within the classroom in order to have students learn to write professional discourse. If discourse is embedded in social situations, do simulations provide sufficient contextually valid settings?*
>
> —Patrick Dias, Aviva Freedman, Peter Medway, & Anthony Paré

If you had to design a game to teach writing, what kind of game would it be? A board game? A video game? A first-person shooter? What would gameplay look like? What rules would you devise? What would count as winning? What mechanics in the game would motivate players to write? How would it be determined that this writing was successful or not? How would you move the focus of gameplay beyond more easily quantifiable issues of grammatical correctness or T-units to sophisticated rhetorical practices like analysis, argument, and deliberation?

At Michigan State University, a group of teacher-researchers have been confronting questions like these while working together to develop a game called *Ink*.[1] Currently in beta testing, *Ink* is an online multiplayer game designed to create a playing/learning environment within which players can practice (in the Brittonian sense of the word)[2] rhetoric as an integral part of personal, public, and professional life in an information age. In order to create this environment, however, we first needed to grapple with some fundamental questions: What in our personal, professional, and public lives motivates us to write? What are the most salient characteristics of the contexts within which we write? How do we know, after any given rhetorical intervention, that we have been successful?

These questions are not new of course, but have been central to rhetorical theory from the beginning. But the implications of these questions and their answers for classroom practice is far from clear. A persistent criticism of the current-traditional writing classroom is that in it, as Lester Faigley (1992) observes, "the writer and potential readers are removed from any specific setting and are represented as living outside history" (p. 15). In this de-contextualized approach, students are asked to generate what James Britton et al. (1975) call "dummy runs" (p. 10405)—writing that is produced for its own sake rather than to achieve a particular goal with a particular audience within a particular cultural and material context. But creating for students what Dias et al. call "contextually valid settings" is no easy trick; it is fraught with ethical, practical, and pedagogical problems. This chapter will explore the way an emergent kind of online game can potentially address some of those problems. Using *Ink* as our central example, we will demonstrate that the affordances of a particular kind of online game—which we call Persistent Alternate World (PAW)—can provide contexts that allow for several fundamental rhetorical practices that are notoriously difficult to capture in the writing classroom. Within PAWs, players use rhetoric in order to bring about change—to solve problems, to address exigencies. They make decisions about the specific material form of their rhetorical interventions (choosing between, for instance, a web document or a postcard, a digital animation or a white paper), based on contextual factors. Additionally, they confront complex processes of textual circulation, planning for patterns of distribution and consumption that will be conducive to accomplishing their goals. They learn that rhetorical practice does not end with the completion of a given composition, but requires that a composition be distributed to and received by particular audience, and moreover requires that the effects of this reception be assessed.

IN SEARCH OF A COMPLEX SOCIAL ECOLOGY

A number of educational theorists have pointed to the promise of games to provide effective contexts for learning because of their ability to situate learners in socially, culturally, and sensorially complex systems or "ecologies" (Dede, 1996; Gee, 2003; Young, 2004; Young, Schrader, and Zheng, 2006). Fundamental to this affordance of games is their *immersiveness*. Immersion is the semi-voluntary experience of being transported into a new context—a narrower or alternate context—for an extended duration. The experience of being transported is psychological: the individual may or may not physically travel. Immersion is not unique to playing video games; an individual can become immersed in many kinds of activities, including recreation, learning, and work. For many immersion experiences, imagination is the vehicle—especially games.[3]

Immersion is potentially valuable in teaching for two main reasons. First, immersion and even the promise of immersion are often highly *motivating*—immersion elicits attention and effort. By transporting a player to an alternate context for an extended duration, an immersive game can be very stimulating and enjoyable. A player who desires this stimulation and enjoyment will be motivated to start playing and keep playing, and will be more receptive to the experience of being immersed.

The second reason immersion is potentially valuable in teaching is that immersion is *semi-voluntary*. An individual chooses whether to be transported, but once immersed, an individual no longer has complete control over his/her thoughts and emotions. Immersion makes the individual highly sensitive to the content and tone of the experience: he/she perceives the peculiarities of the new context with *palpable immediacy*. This immediacy of perception is one of the goals of more "authentic" teaching strategies: students will be better prepared to deal with the peculiarities of "real" contexts if they vividly experience those peculiarities during the learning process. For example, students will be better prepared to write for a variety of purposes and audiences if they experience such purposes and audiences with palpable immediacy—not as hypothetical constructs but as vivid pressures and opportunities.

Immersion is not a new idea among motivation researchers. For example, Csikszentmihalyi (1990) describes *flow* as a state of intense concentration and pleasure-in-doing. An individual in flow becomes very focused on the present experience; he/she perceives the peculiarities with palpable immediacy. The individual is effectively transported into a narrower context, is immersed. Schraw, Flowerday, and Lehman describe *situational interest* as "temporary interest that arises spontaneously due to environmental factors such as task instructions or an engaging text" (2001, p. 211) (see also: Schraw & Lehman, 2001; Bergin, 1999). Mitchell (1993) and others emphasize that teachers can design experiences to increase students' situational interest, and thus their motivation and learning. High situational interest can produce immersion.

As teachers, we want our students to bring considerable attention and effort to learning to write. Recreational video games often excel at eliciting motivation via immersion. Moreover, games like *Ink* can have rich social ecologies, making such games particularly useful for teaching writing.

We place *Ink* in a category of games we call "Persistent Alternate Worlds" (PAWs). This category includes Massively Multiplayer Online Role-Playing Games (MMORPGs) like *World of Warcraft*, and Multi-player User Dimensions, Object-Oriented (MOOs) like *LinguaMOO*. As Haynes and Holmevik (2001) and others have persuasively argued, Persistent Alternate Worlds have great potential utility in teaching because they can be immersive. They have some of the general immersive properties of games, like intriguing, compelling alternate worlds (contexts). However, many single-player games have similar properties. What distinguishes PAWs is their persistence and their social ecologies.

A PAW like *Ink* is persistent, which means that players are immersed in a single, shared world with a continuous flow of time. Even when an individual player isn't playing, the world "keeps spinning:" other players come and go, and any in-game systems continue functioning. This can make one player feel insignificant among many. However, it also means that one player's actions can have long- and far-reaching consequences. A player can "act on the world": his or her actions can affect into the experiences of other or all players. Persistence means all players are in a single "pond," so every action creates "ripples" that every other player experiences (a "butterfly effect"). Of course, in a large PAW, it usually takes many players creating the same ripple for most people to feel a "wave," just as political or cultural movements usually require many adherents to affect the mainstream.

The metaphor of ripples in a pond also illustrates the social ecology of a PAW like *Ink*. The social ecology of a game is partly determined by the metaphysical ecology. In a PAW, the persistence of the game means that the social ecology can become vast and sophisticated. There are usually challenges to best in the game itself (e.g., slaying a dragon, earning a new level), but on the way, or afterwards, or instead, there are plenty of challenges and enjoyments to be found by interacting with other players. Friendships, romantic relationships, groups, factions, businesses, commerce, and even nation-states can arise, thrive, and fracture in a PAW.

These social structures are inevitably accompanied by reputations, rivalries, shifting loyalties, miscommunication, feuds, and open conflict. In short, the social ecology of a PAW usually develops most of the social ties, lubricants, and frictions that we all encounter in the "real" world. In fact, navigating the social ecology can become a game unto itself, and many players enjoy PAWs because of their social ecologies (e.g., being a member of an in-game guild). The owners of some PAWs even empower the players to partly govern themselves, making a game of government and civilization (cf. *A Tale in the Desert, Second Life*).[4]

The social ecology of a PAW can become very sophisticated, as evidenced by the extensive in-game and out-of-game online textual communities that form around many games. Social activity in these communities focuses on gameplay, but often spills over into more general social matters.

In short, as a general design, a Persistent Alternate World like *Ink* has great potential to motivate an individual to try playing, to immerse a player and make him/her sensitive to its peculiarities, and to offer the opportunities and challenges of a sophisticated social ecology. Many educators are already experimenting with re-purposing recreational PAWs (cf. *Second Life*). Kym calls it Playful Interest Bridging: re-purposing a motivating media or technology (like PAWs) for teaching and learning. Many adolescents and young adults play MMORPGs (a kind of PAW), so we set out to re-purpose the basic game structure to support teaching writing.

THE DESIGN OF INK

Imagine this scenario. Tonight you're surfing the Web and you discover a site called *Ink*. You click ENTER, and your browser loads a chat window and the image of a cityscape. A caption informs you that you are in the City Center. Almost immediately, someone notices that you've arrived and begins talking with you in the chat window. "Welcome to *Ink*," the stranger says. "This is a great place. I think you're going to find *Ink* a compelling and imaginative space. There's something new and surprising around every corner. But we have a problem right now, and I'm hoping you can help. Our neighborhood isn't doing well. We need to get a group of people together to address this problem. We need to design a flyer that will motivate people to attend a meeting where we can talk about this problem. We need to draft a resolution that we can circulate to those who show up. We also need a brochure that explains why other citizens should vote for our proposal. And we're going to need a white paper to explain to City Council the principles that inform our proposal. We've got a lot of work to do. Can you help us?"

Ink is a Persistent Alternate World game played through a web browser. Adopting the central metaphor of a city, the world of *Ink* includes a city government, a currency (ink), and public spaces such as libraries and municipal buildings. As a PAW, *Ink* is designed to facilitate online social interaction. Players interact by chatting in shared game space and by circulating compositions, including documents and other "objects" like baubles, toys, and food. Optimal gameplay should be reached with a critical mass of about a hundred players. A much larger community is also possible.

One way that players advance in Ink is through Paths. A Path is a series of activities that are thematically linked. For instance, the Path of Government might include activities related to submitting a proposal to City Council, such as going to the meetings of action groups, helping to create supporting documents, and drafting the proposal itself. Artifacts related to these activities are incorporated into a journal, and players are asked to critically reflect on each artifact. For instance, if a player includes a proposal submitted to City Council, s/he might explain why the proposal was or was not successfully passed. Once complete, journals are reviewed by other players who have already completed a particular Path or by staff players who have been specially trained to facilitate the activities of the game. Journals function similarly to writing portfolios, asking players to document and reflect on a set of learning activities.

To sum up, then, *Ink* is

- persistent: the world of the game is continuous, allowing for both shorter and longer arcs of gameplay; the game never ends or resets, but is a continuously unfolding narrative.
- immersive: players feel they are "in" a world, not looking at an object; they are surrounded by the reality of the game.
- a complex social space or world: game mechanics and structures are designed to facilitate complex social interaction situated in space; players can travel from place to place, talk to other players, buy and sell things, call meetings, organize groups, engage in fund-raising, build and operate community centers, parks, zoos, coffeehouses, clothing stores, and establish publications such as magazines, literary journals, and fanzines

As an immersive, socially complex environment, *Ink* is precisely the kind of context that demands rhetoric. In the following sections, we map the game space in terms of rhetorical theory, detailing how the world of *Ink* functions as a site of rhetorical practice.

EXIGENCY: WHAT MOTIVATES US TO WRITE?

In his famous discussion of the "rhetorical situation," Lloyd Bitzer (1968) asks us to "regard rhetorical situation as a natural context of persons, events, objects, relations, and an exigence which strongly invites utterance; this invited utterance participates naturally in the situation, is in many instances necessary to the completion of situational activity, and by means of its participation with situation obtains its meaning and its rhetorical character" (p. 5). Essential to any rhetorical situation is an "imperfection" or "exigence"—something that we wish to change, some problem we wish to solve: "a work of rhetoric is pragmatic; it comes into existence for the sake of something beyond itself; it functions ultimately to produce action or change in the world; it performs some task. In short, rhetoric is a mode of altering reality [. . .]" (pp. 3–4). Rhetorical theorists who have responded to Bitzer point out that an exigence is not a simple matter of an external reality that exists independently of the rhetor (see, for instance, Vatz, 1973; Biesecker, 1989). Rhetors create exigencies through rhetorical interventions. Carolyn Miller (1992), following Scott Consigny (1974), writes that "As an art, rhetoric engages the phenomena of concrete experience and itself is engaged by the force of human motivation; it is thus the site of interaction between situation and rhetor" (p. 313). We see this "interaction" or (as she later calls it) "struggle" between situation and rhetor as one of the chief dynamics of any rhetorical intervention (p. 313).

Based on their study of workplace writing, Dias et al. (1999) echo Bitzer's emphasis on the pragmatic nature of rhetoric. Indeed, for some of the professionals they studied, writing was invisible as a daily routine; their attention was on the ends (what the writing was meant to accomplish) not on the means (the writing itself), and so they did not identify themselves as "writers" even if writing was an important part of their work (p. 27). Dias et al. conclude that the pragmatic and situational nature of rhetoric should occasion a shift in writing pedagogy: "If as we argue, writing is a by-product of other activities, a means for getting something else done, we ought to consider how we might engage students in activities that commit them to write as necessary means—but only as a means not an end" (p. 235).

This is no easy task. In the world outside the classroom, as part of professional and public life, we are immersed in complex social ecologies that can be variously understood as "activity systems" (Dias et al., 1999), "ecosystems" (Porter 1997; Dobrin and Weisser 2002), and "semiotic domains" (Gee, 2003). Within these systems of practice, we are charged with solving problems and we turn to rhetoric (sometimes without being aware of it) as a means to solving those problems. The traditional writing classroom is an impoverished context by comparison to these social ecologies. Students don't turn to rhetoric because they need it in order to solve a problem; they turn to rhetoric because they are placed within an institutional system that demands the production of rhetoric-like compositions as part of credentialing and sometimes gatekeeping practices. Students are required to take writing courses and within those courses instructors demand that they produce certain kinds of documents. Students are motivated primarily by the need to fulfill a curricular requirement set by the school and to achieve a certain grade while doing so.

Immersive multiplayer games, by situating writers within complex social ecologies, can recover the productive motivating force of exigence, of writing to get something done as opposed to writing to fulfill the requirements of an assignment or to get a grade. We see this as one of the chief pedagogical affordances of games for facilitating literacy learning.

We introduced a moment ago an example of a rhetorical situation that might emerge in the social ecology of *Ink*: a neighborhood is not thriving. In terms of the game mechanics of *Ink*, this might mean that there is insufficient social activity within the neighborhood: players are not visiting the spaces, and they are not interacting with each other in those spaces. Social activity in *Ink* generally translates into a movement of capital: when a players visit a coffeehouse (for instance), they pay a small amount of ink to the owner of the coffee house to enter and to remain. They might pay additional ink to buy items (such as a foamy cappuccino) or documents (such as a newspaper). Spaces within *Ink* require a periodic maintenance fee—the game mechanic that corresponds to utility bills, replacing worn-out infrastructure, etc. When there is insufficient social activity within a given space, the owner of that space has to maintain it with ink earned from some other source (such as ink earned from other spaces, from reviewing drafts of documents, from selling documents, etc.). When space is not maintained, it generates "entropy." When entropy accumulates to a certain level, it discharges, causing the space that generated it to "fade"; its text will become unreadable, a garbled experience for other players.

In the world outside *Ink*, when a space is not maintained—whether it's a factory, a house, a store, or a park—it often affects other spaces around it. An abandoned factory hurts surrounding neighborhoods because it is an eyesore and is potentially unsafe. It becomes a NIMBY[5] that reduces the quality of life for those who experience it on a day-to-day basis and lowers the property value of nearby homes. Likewise, in *Ink*, when a space is not maintained and an entropy discharge occurs, it affects the surrounding spaces as well, causing some of them to fade too. Thus there is an incentive for players to work together, especially players whose game spaces are proximal to each other.

In our example of the neighborhood that fails to thrive, then, residents and local business owners would have a strong motivation to collaborate on a solution to their problem. Importantly, while this motivation is supplied in part by the game mechanics of ink, maintenance, and entropy, those mechanics are only a part of the motivation. Players in multiplayer games, as in the world outside those games, are socially motivated; they get a strong satisfaction, a sense of success, by having players visit and appreciate spaces they have created, just as in the world outside the game we might take pride in living in a thriving neighborhood with interesting, enjoyable things to see and do. We might be especially proud when our friends visit and admire the interesting, enjoyable things. Managing entropy can be a pragmatic imperative, but players often bring their own aspirations into a PAW and set their own goals. For example, one player might want to increase the diversity of the residents in a neighborhood. Such a player could derive pleasure from helping achieve that self-set goal and view the entropy issue as happy happenstance.

In order to address the exigency of the neighborhood that fails to thrive, players will need to engage in various rhetorical practices. At the very least, they will need to communicate in real-time, text-based chats to brainstorm possible courses of action. Spaces within the game are themselves textual: each is composed of alphabetic text describing the space for other players, possibly coupled with images and other media elements. To improve spaces within *Ink* means recomposing them (e.g., improving the description for a more vivid, immersive player/reader experience). More importantly, however, players will have the opportunity to address an exigence like a failing neighborhood through a set of coordinated rhetorical interventions. If they decide to have a planning meeting, they will need to distribute a flyer or email message to promote attendance. If a group of players agrees upon a course of action, they will need to elicit the investment of other residents, an exigence requiring documents such as brochures or websites that can represent the proposal in a rhetorically effective way.

The fundamental point here is that this turn to rhetoric is motivated by a desire to accomplish something, to get work done. It is not motivated by a grade or class requirement. As such, writing in the game more closely parallels the writing we are asked to do in personal, professional, and public settings. If asked to write an essay for a class, I immediately begin to ask questions like: What are the formal requirements such as page length? What is my teacher looking for? What's the minimum necessary to get a 4.0? But when I write in the world outside the classroom, I ask questions like: What is this piece of writing meant to accomplish? What work is it supposed to perform? Who is my audience? What do I need from my audience? What attitudes and beliefs define my audience? What genres, modes, and rhetorical strategies will be effective with this audience? These are the kinds of questions that writers in *Ink* will need to ask in order to succeed in the game.

Again, exigence in *Ink*, as in the world outside of *Ink*, is not a purely external matter; it's a social construct, formed by a rhetor that is located within material, discursive, and cultural contexts. For instance, a neighborhood might be thriving within *Ink* as measured purely by the amount of ink that it generates; but that wouldn't preclude a player or group of players from deciding that the neighborhood needs substantial improvements. Perhaps the neighborhood is a popular destination within *Ink*, but does not facilitate the richness of social interaction that residents are hoping for. One rhetor might be content with such a case, while another might be motivated by such a situation to advocate for change.

Planning meetings, securing funding, recommending and motivating courses of action—these practical concerns are defining characteristics of *Ink* and are precisely the kind of activity that is difficult to facilitate in classroom settings. Theorists who emphasize exigence and situation often advocate that writing be taken out of the classroom and placed in the world beyond it, whether in the guise of the standard letter to the editor or richer service-learning opportunities in which students are producing important documents aimed at helping community partners fulfill their missions. In his discussion of kairos, for instance, James

Kinneavy (1986) concludes that "Real publication of the students' papers, in any local or state or national medium, directed to real audiences for specific purposes, is ideal for any composition program" (p. 103). But a host of ethical and practical considerations limit the level of intensity with which students can become immersed in environments outside the classroom. Publication is not an unproblematic or innocuous activity; to publish is to expose oneself to public scrutiny on many levels, often resulting in unforeseen consequences. Additionally, rhetorical practices in many public and professional contexts are inextricably linked to high-stakes decisions about people, money, and other resources. If, for instance, David's annual report about the Language and Media Center is rhetorically ineffective, funding might be cut and employees of the Center might lose their jobs. Asking students to make executive decisions about people, money, and other resources; about when to make a given document public; when to call a public meeting; when to revise an organization or municipal policy; or when to hire or fire an employee—these activities are fraught with risks and practical problems. In an immersive PAW like *Ink*, however, these things are possible because, as games, PAWs mitigate risks (e.g., no one will go to prison for illegal accounting practices) and because the limitations of time and space have been solved to some degree by the dynamics of an online virtual environment. For example, players can travel through the spaces of *Ink*, visiting neighborhoods, community centers, and the headquarters of organizations, without leaving their dorm rooms.

By recovering situated exigencies as the motivation of rhetorical intervention, *Ink* and other PAWs can help create the conditions in which learners will practice rhetoric in ways that echo the rhetorical practices associated with personal, professional, and public life. At the same time, if they are designed effectively, such games can elicit a higher level of engagement from students, creating the conditions within which students will become highly invested in the success of their rhetorical interventions. Players are motivated from the "bottom up" ("I am challenged by this problem and wish to solve it") rather than the top down ("I have been forced by an authority/teacher to perform some task").

RHETORIC AS A MATERIAL PRACTICE, PART I: MODE AND MEDIUM

Another set of characteristics that define public and professional settings for rhetorical practices is that they demand attention to materiality. Rhetoric is a material as well as a socio-symbolic practice. Ideas do not flow from mind to mind directly; their flow is always accomplished through a medium of some kind, and that medium always has a material form. But, as Carole Blair (1999) has observed, "materiality . . . has rarely been a starting point or basis for theorizing rhetoric" (p. 18). Classroom practice has largely ignored rhetoric's materiality as well. We wish to focus on two important dimensions of rhetoric's materiality: in this section we explore rhetorical choices related to mode and medium of production; in the next, we examine the way rhetorical compositions circulate.

One reason the materiality of rhetoric has remained invisible in writing classrooms is that in the traditional writing classroom rhetoric has largely adhered to a single semiotic mode (written words) and a single medium (8 1/2" X 11" paper) (see Wysocki, 2004, p. 10). At a moment of such uniformity, it is easy to forget materiality altogether. Materiality is dispensed with a few perfunctory instructions (e.g., use one-inch margins and Times New Roman).

The elision of rhetoric's materiality in rhetorical theory and pedagogy has, in recent years, been thoroughly critiqued, particularly from those interested in the way emergent technologies are changing rhetorical practices (see Faigley, 1999; Kress and Van Leeuwen 2001, pp. 66–72; Trimbur, 2000). Rhetoric is being reconfigured as a multimodal activity in which words do not stand alone, but "cooperate"—to use Barthes' (1988) word—with images, sounds, and other media elements. It is commonplace today to speak of "visual rhetoric" and "multimodal rhetoric," and increasingly these rhetorics are taught in the "writing" classroom.

In other words, there is an increased awareness among students, teachers, and theorists that rhetoric's material form is not a given, but the result, in part, of contextualized rhetorical choices. In public and professional life, we are increasingly asked to make decisions about modes and about production media as new technologies make a wider variety of semiotic options available to us. The historical focus on ink and paper (and, before that, on speech) was to some extent imposed by the kinds of material resources that were and were not available. Twenty years ago, it might not have occurred to us to use video in response to a particular exigence, but in the age of smartphones and free editing software, video is often a readily available option. Likewise, inexpensive desktop publishing applications allow us to produce layouts—including type-set words, images, and graphical elements—at a level of sophistication that was unachievable for most non-specialists twenty years ago (see Sheridan, Ridolfo & Michel, 2005).

Choices about mode and medium are kairotic—based on the opportunities latent within a particular context (see Sheridan, Ridolfo & Michel, 2005; Shipka, 2006). An email might work in certain circumstances, while a hardcopy printed on letterhead might be more appropriate for others. A colorful brochure with lots of photographs might be a more appropriate way of promoting initial interest in a non-profit organization, while a lengthy written document might be a more effective way of explaining its mission and philosophy. Each of these material forms implies a host of considerations, from rhetorical strategy to use of production technologies. Emerging technologies can empower rhetors as never before, yet come with their own considerations (e.g., whether to blog, post, tweet, pin, share, all of the above, etc.). We best learn how to navigate all these affordances and constraints through repeated opportunities to experiment.

PAWs like *Ink* ask players to make contextual decisions about mode and medium, echoing the rhetorical practices that increasingly characterize professional and public life. Players are not given assignments ("write a paper") but are asked to craft responses to exigencies within complex social situations. In our example scenario, players would not automatically compose academic essays in response to the problem of a neighborhood that is not thriving. There would be no assumption that a monomodal word-based approach was appropriate. Instead, they would need to critically evaluate the diversity of semiotic options available, choosing a visually rich brochure distributed as a PDF, a flyer, a video clip, or a white paper in accordance with their understanding of the entire rhetorical situation, including exigence, audience, and available resources. For example, there will be a variety of publishers in *Ink*, with various institutional structures and degrees of gravitas. To muster a plurality of political support for a neighborhood revitalization policy, players may want to experiment with seemingly-radical formats and venues—just like in the "real world" (e.g., MoveOn.org).

In this sense *Ink*, as a pedagogical approach, is consistent with the models like those proposed by Jody Shipka (2006) and Sheridan, Ridolfo, and Michel (2005) in which the instructor does not specify mode and medium but asks students to make rhetorical choices about the material form of their intervention based on a critical assessment of the rhetorical situation. Confronting materiality in this way necessitates attention to resources like people, time, money, and technologies. A full-color brochure might be technically possible but too expensive or might be affordable but too time-consuming to produce, etc.

DeVoss, Cushman, and Grabill (2005) argue the need to address rhetoric's materiality in their exploration of "infrastructure," which includes, among other things, "computer networks," "network configurations," "operating systems, computer programs, interfaces, and their interrelatedness," "network, server, and storage access rights and privileges" (pp. 21–22). DeVoss et al. argue that "infrastructures are absolutely necessary for writing teachers and their students to understand if we hope to enact the possibilities offered by new-media composing" (p. 16). Players in *Ink* will need to negotiate the challenges and affordances of infrastructure as they use rhetoric to accomplish their goals.

RHETORIC AS A MATERIAL PRACTICE, PART II: RHETORICAL CIRCULATION

In addition to enabling contextualized choices about mode and production media, contextually valid settings for professional and public rhetorical practices need to allow for the ability of rhetorical compositions to *circulate*. John Trimbur (2000) has argued that a shortcoming in the traditional writing classroom is the reductive way that processes of circulation are modeled. The classroom tends to focus on processes of composing, eliding the essential processes that continue once composing has ceased. Circulation is often limited to the reductive clichés "trade papers with a partner" or "hand in your paper" (p. 195). In professional and public contexts, however, the circulation of texts is not an afterthought but a central concern. Again, this grows out of rhetoric's essentially pragmatic role: a text cannot address its exigency unless it circulates in appropriate ways (see Rude, 2004).

Following Trimbur (2000), we use the term *circulation* to refer to the total circuit a text makes within a complex social ecology, including production, reproduction, distribution, and consumption. In professional and public life, rhetors need to critically reflect on and proactively facilitate processes of circulation. In fact, all decisions made by a composer are made in anticipation of processes of circulation. Salient in this awareness are writers' internal representations of the encounters their intended audiences will have with their compositions. But this is only one moment in a larger process. Decisions about length, for instance, are related to processes of reproduction and delivery. A twenty-page printed essay only makes sense if the writer has the means to copy those pages and deliver them to the intended audience. If the intention is to reach ten thousand geographically dispersed people, copy and postage costs for longer documents might not be affordable in some cases. A full-color glossy brochure might best suit a particular exigency, but if there's no budget for printing (i.e., the chosen process of reproduction), a brochure is not a good option.

Because they provide immersive social environments, *Ink* and other PAWs create opportunities for rhetors to participate in and reflect on processes of textual circulation. In order to address exigencies through rhetorical interventions, players will think beyond processes of composing to strategize about processes of distribution and reception. They will assess the affordances and limitations associated with distributing emails, HTML documents, PDFs, and animated GIFs. They will elicit the help of other players, seeking volunteers to distribute copies of documents within the public spaces of the game world (e.g., on street corners and in coffeehouses). They will seek out existing publication venues like in-game newspapers and magazines, and will establish new publication venues.

As Rude (2004) points out, however, publication itself is not the end, but merely a means to an end. Players cannot afford to limit their rhetorical intervention to successful publication of compositions. They will need to monitor and understand reception practices—the way members of a target audience did or did not read and respond to a given composition. If a flyer is aimed at motivating people to attend a meeting, players will be able to observe whether or not people actually show up for the meeting. If they don't, players can assess where the process broke down. Was the flyer poorly designed? Did it leave out important information? Did it fail to convey a sense of urgency? Why didn't readers respond to it in the intended way?

INTERTEXTUALITY: MOVING BEYOND THE ISOLATED COMPOSITION

Circulation in professional and public life is not a matter of single readers encountering single texts in isolation. Rhetors need to understand rhetorical interventions as the act of entering into a complex web of textuality. For instance, when author David Sheridan writes the annual report for the Language and Media Center that he directs, he often begins by copying language and other semiotic elements (graphs, photographs) from existing documents, some of which he might have written himself, but many of which he has not: from previous reports, from the mission statement posted on the web, from grant proposals, from spreadsheets, and so on. The organization of his report might be suggested by university policy documents or vision statements. Further, the report might refer the reader to still other documents that the audience can be reasonably expected to access: documents posted on the web or previously published by the LMC. Finally, the report itself is written in such a way as to encourage its own propagation. The report is structured in a way that will hopefully encourage the dean to quote from it in his or her annual report to the provost. Jim Ridolfo has called this ability of rhetorical compositions to become embedded in subsequent compositions "rhetorical velocity" (see Ridolfo and DeVoss, 2009). He uses the example of a press advisory, whose purpose is to provide language and information that reporters can easily copy and paste into their articles.

There is a growing awareness of the need for rhetorical theory to confront intertextual dynamics and for a composition pedagogy that helps students understand and (to the extent possible) exploit intertextual processes. Dias et al. (1999) "hypothesize that workplace writing, by contrast with students' writing in universities, is marked by complexity and density of intertextual connection . . ." (p. 225). In architecture, for instance, writers are "involved in a vast symbolic web that encompasses technical, legal, professional, and financial spheres and embraces large numbers of players and a great variety of communicative means. It is because of this depth of intertextual allusion and this range of association with other communicative processes that the sparsest-looking workplace texts may" provide more meaning than "the most densely-referenced student paper" (p. 226).

Several theorists have observed that our models of public rhetoric need to move beyond the single text to explore how social change can be accomplished through the orchestration of multiple rhetorical interventions (see Rude, 2004; Welch, 2005). Carolyn Rude (2004), for instance, in her exploration of the intersection between civic rhetoric and technical communication, notes that traditional writing pedagogies tend to "focus on short-term projects that have stopping points and fairly predictable consequences. But social change is a long-term process that may span years" (p. 272). She goes on to propose that "the concept of rhetoric itself may expand beyond the usual classroom focus on individual instances (the document, the speech) to accommodate persuasion over time: delivering a message repeatedly and in different media, actively seeking out audiences, and promoting action in response to the message. The publication is not an end in itself but a means to an end of change in policy and behavior" (p. 272).

In the complex social ecologies that PAWs like *Ink* make possible, rhetors will need to confront intertextual dynamics. They will need to strategize about the ways in which a particular composition on which they are working relates to other texts that are more or less proximate or that might be composed simultaneously by them or by others. A brochure might list the URL for a website which might contain the PDF of a white paper. A single rhetorical intervention might not accomplish what it was supposed to; further interventions might be necessary. It will be clear in certain circumstances that a particular exigence will require several players to collaborate to produce several related documents. This is one of the most exciting lessons *Ink* can teach: the potential influence of a dedicated *group* of people with determination, organization, and complementary skills.

CONCLUSION: (A) REAL WORLD

Some readers might be struck by an apparent irony in our argument: that we critique the artificiality of the traditional writing classroom only to advocate for an even more artificial context: a gameworld, a simulation, a fiction. We have tried to avoid binaries that valorize the "real world" in relation to some allegedly less real space, such as the classroom. Instead, we have focused on what we take to be fundamental characteristics of contexts in which we are asked to write and have asked how those characteristics are or are not operationalized within different learning environments. In PAWs, real people interact with other real people, engaging in activities meant to accomplish real work and achieve real goals. Within the frame of the activity, writers are interested in solving problems and see rhetoric as part of the solution. In the long-term, participants in a PAW often develop a sense of citizenship and community: real psychological connections to the PAW and each other.

By allowing players to become immersed in complex social ecologies, PAWs provide opportunities for players to participate in rhetorical interventions in ways that parallel, in certain fundamental respects, the kinds of rhetorical practices that characterize personal, professional, and public life. Within the playspace of PAWs exigencies emerge, inviting players to fashion a rhetorical response. Because rhetoric functions as a problem-solving technology, players need to confront dimensions of rhetorical practice that the traditional writing classroom has often elided but that are nevertheless important in the world outside the classroom. Players need to grapple with the material nature of rhetoric, to reflect on the affordances and constraints of available modes and media within particular contexts. They cannot be content with merely composing texts, but will need to address the challenges of reproducing and distributing them. They cannot be content with producing single isolated compositions, but will need to plan rhetorical interventions comprised of multiple related compositions.

We are not arguing that games are the only way to achieve contextually valid settings. We see games as a set of options that exist alongside opportunities for service learning, internships, and other approaches that ask students to become immersed in complex social ecologies. The classroom itself might become such an ecology. Thinking about these options in relation to each other helps to expose the affordances and constraints of each one, ultimately strengthening our pedagogical models.

NOTES

1. *Ink* is a collaborative project of the MSU Writing Center and the Writing in Digital Environments (WIDE) Research Center. The Ink development team includes Kym Buchanan (Lead Designer), David Sheridan (Project Manager), Janet Swenson (Producer), Andy Koelewyn (System Designer and Programmer), Andrew Detskas (Artistic Designer), and WIDE Co-Directors Jeffrey T. Grabill and William Hart-Davidson.

2. "What children use language for in school must be 'operations' and not dummy runs. They must continue to use it to make sense of the world: they must PRACTISE language in the sense in which a doctor 'practises' medicine and a lawyer 'practises' law, and NOT in the sense in which a juggler 'practises' a new trick before he performs it" (Britton, 1970, p. 130; qtd. in Gere, 1980).

3. There is a happy synergy between the role of imagination in both playing a game and creatively choosing rhetorical strategies. See "Rhetoric as Material Practice," especially the need to imaginatively overcome constraints. If we design Ink correctly, players/writers won't need to change "mental modes:" playing and writing will be a convergent imaginative activity.

4. Some PAWs like *Second Life* continue to grow as real economies, with in-world currencies and goods being exchanged for out-of-world currency. The

entrepreneurs in such worlds view issues like in-world zoning and policing as far more than "just a game."

5. Not In My BackYard: an informal term used in politics and city planning to refer to our collective tendency to wish that unpleasant things were far away from our homes and neighborhoods (e.g., power plants, low-income housing). Of course, these things usually have to be in somebody's backyard.

References

Barthes, R. (1988). Rhetoric of the Image (S. Heath, Trans.). In *Image, music, text* (Noonday Press ed., pp. 220 p.). New York: Hill and Wang.

Bergin, D. A. (1999). Influences on Classroom Interest. *Educational Psychologist, 34*(2), 87–98.

Biesecker, B. A. (1989). Rethinking the rhetorical situation from within the thematic of *différance. Philosophy and Rhetoric, 22*(2), 110–130.

Bitzer, L. (1968). The Rhetorical Situation. *Philosophy and Rhetoric, 1*(1), 1–14.

Blair, C. (1999). Contemporary U.S. memorial sites as exemplars of rhetoric's materiality. In J. Selzer & S. Crowley (Eds.), *Rhetorical bodies* (pp. 16–57). Madison, Wis.: U of Wisconsin P.

Britton, J. N., Burgess, T., Martin, N., McLeod, A., & Rosen, H. (1975). *The Development of Writing Abilities (11–18).* London: Macmillan Education.

Britton, J. (1970). *Language and learning.* Middlesex, England: Penguin.

Buchanan, K. (2006). *Beyond attention getters: Designing for deep engagement* (Unpublished doctoral dissertation). Michigan State University.

Consigny, S. (1974). Rhetoric and its situations. *Philosophy and Rhetoric, 7,* 175–86.

Csikszentmihalyi, M. (1990). Happiness Revisited. In *Flow: The Psychology of Optimal Experience.* New York: HarperPerennial.

Dede, C. (1996). The evolution of constructivist learning environments: Immersion in distributed, virtual worlds. In B. G. Wilson (Ed.), *Constructivist learning environments: Case studies in instructional design* (pp. 165–175). Edgewood Cliffs: Educational Technology Publications.

DeVoss, D., Cushman, E., & Grabill, J. (2005). Infrastructure and composing: The when of new-media writing. *College Composition and Communication, 57*(1), 14–44.

Dias, P., Freedman, A., Medway, P., & Paré, A. (1999). *Worlds apart : acting and writing in academic and workplace contexts.* Mahwah, N.J.: L. Erlbaum Associates.

Dobrin, S. I., & Weisser, C. R. (2002). *Natural discourse: Toward ecocomposition.* Albany: State U of New York P.

Faigley, L. (1992). Fragments of rationality: Postmodernity and the subject of composition. Pittsburgh: U of Pittsburgh P.

Faigley, L. (1999). Material literacy and visual design. In J. Selzer & S. Crowley (Eds.), *Rhetorical bodies* (pp. 16–57). Madison, Wis.: University of Wisconsin Press.

Gee, J. P. (2003). What video games have to teach us about learning and literacy. New York: Palgrave Macmillan.

Gere, A. (1980). Practice into theory. *The English Journal, 69*(1), 92–94.

Haynes, C., & Holmevik, J. R. (Eds.). (2001). *High Wired: On the Design, Use, and Theory of Educational MOOs (2nd Ed.).* Ann Arbor, Michigan: University of Michigan Press.

Kinneavy, J. L. (1986). Kairos: A neglected concept in classical rhetoric. In J. D. Moss (Ed.), *Rhetoric and praxis: The contribution of classical rhetoric to practical reasoning* (pp. 79–105). Washington, DC: Catholic U of America P.

Kress, G. R., & van Leeuwen, T. (2001). *Multimodal discourse: The modes and media of contemporary communication.* London: Oxford University Press.

Miller, C. R. (1992). Kairos in the rhetoric of science. In N. N. Stephen P. Witte, Roger D. Cherry (Ed.), *A Rhetoric of doing: Essays on written discourse in honor of James L. Kinneavy* (pp. 310–327). Carbondale: Southern Illinois University Press.

Mitchell, M. (1993). Situational Interest: Its Multifaceted Structure in the Secondary School Mathematics Classroom. *Journal of Educational Psychology, 85,* 424–436.

Ridolfo, J. & DeVoss, D. N. (2009). Composing for recomposition: Rhetorical velocity and delivery. *Kairos 13*(2), http://technorhetoric.net/13.2/topoi/ridolfo_devoss/index.html

Rude, C. D. (2004). Toward an expanded concept of rhetorical delivery: The uses of reports in public policy debates. *Technical Communication Quarterly, 13*(3), 271–288.

Schraw, G., Flowerday, T., & Lehman, S. (2001). Increasing Situational Interest in the Classroom. *Educational Psychology Review, 13*(3), 211–224.

Schraw, G., & Lehman, S. (2001). Situational Interest: A Review of the Literature and Directions for Future Research. *Educational Psychology Review, 13*(1), 23–52.

Selber, S. A. (2004). *Multiliteracies for a digital age.* Carbondale: Southern Illinois University Press.

Sheridan, D., Ridolfo, J., & Michel, A. (2005). "The available means of persuasion: Mapping a theory and pedagogy of public rhetoric." *JAC, 25*(4), 801–844.

Shipka, J. (2005). A multimodal task-based framework for composing. *College Composition and Communication, 57*(2), 277–306.

Trimbur, J. (2000). Composition and the circulation of writing. *College Composition and Communication, 52*(2), 188–219.

Trimbur, J. (2004). Delivering the Message: Typography and the Materiality of Writing. In C. Handa (Ed.), *Visual Rhetoric in a Digital World: A Critical Sourcebook.* Boston: Bedford.

Vatz, R. E. (1973). The myth of the rhetorical situation. *Philosophy and Rhetoric, 6,* 154–161.

Welch, K. E. (1999). Electric rhetoric: classical rhetoric, oralism, and a new literacy. Cambridge, Mass.: MIT Press.

Welch, N. (2005). Living room: Teaching public writing in a post-publicity era. *College Composition and Communication, 56*(3), 470–492.

Wysocki, A. F. (2004). Opening new media to writing: openings and justifications. In A. F. Wysocki, J. Johnson-Eilola, C. L. Selfe & G. Sirc (Eds.), *Writing new media : theory and applications for expanding the teaching of composition* (pp. 1–41). Logan: Utah State University Press.

Young, M. (2004). An ecological description of video games in education. Proceedings of the International Conference on Education and Information Systems Technologies and Applications (EISTA).

Young, M., Schrader, P., & Zheng, D. (2006). MMOGs as learning environments: An ecological journey into Quest Atlantis and the Sims Online. *Innovate, 2*(4).

16 Programming, Pedagogy, Play

Brian Ladd

PEDAGOGY OF DESIGN

This chapter takes a slightly tilted view of pedagogy, play, and the pen. Rather than discussing games that are assigned by teachers and *played* by learners, it focuses on games that are *built* by the learners. Pedagogical game design emerged for me from the use of games purely as motivational hooks. The similarity of the design problem of writing a game and the design problem of writing a computer program crystallized when I explored the text-adventure game genre. Text-adventure games have *locations* with direct *paths* to other locations; text adventures can be considered branching or *multicursal* stories (Aarseth, 1997, p. 6). A computer program has *methods* with direct *calls* to and *returns* from other methods; computer programs are also branching, multicursal texts normally followed by a machine rather than a human.

Modern technology instruction, including much computer science instruction, focuses on *design* (Burghardt & Hacker, 2004). The Accreditation Board for Engineering and Technology (ABET) defines design in the Criteria for Accrediting Engineering Programs as "the process of devising a system, component, or process to meet desired needs. It is a decision-making process (often iterative), in which the basic sciences, mathematics and engineering sciences are applied to convert resources optimally to meet these stated needs" (ABET, 2013). Compare this description with the process of writing: goals and audience are defined, decisions are made as to what research to apply to optimally meet the stated goals. Text adventure games (and other game design and implementation assignments) combine both technological design problems (software design) with the design of a multicursal story (narrative design). These two different design tasks reinforce one another, helping students reflect on their own learning in two separate but similar spheres.

INTRODUCTION, OR *IT'S ALL WRITING*

Proper software development requires preparation, appropriate use of established design patterns, and the ability to recognize and rewrite problem code; these requirements parallel those of good composition.

—Andy Hunt and Dave Thomas

In this simple opening statement lies the seeds of many modern trends in software development: *extreme programming* is continuous editing through the use of pair programming, one programmer typing source code whilst the other monitors the work looking for problems; *agile development* focuses on incremental creation of the source program, moving forward one quantum of usable code at a time; and *refactoring*, a methodology for identifying and rewriting problem code in a structured way. These software engineering techniques parallel similar methods for prose composition.

The opening statement is the kernel of my belief that it *is* all writing (thanks again to Andrew Hunt and David Thomas for the phrase [2000, p. 248]). For a decade I have leveraged students' familiarity with writing to teach them how to program. Writing across the curriculum brought composition assignments to my attention and I have actively modeled programming assignments on prose composition so as to leverage students' familiarity with other forms of writing in computer science education (CSE).

Lately, my research interests have turned to "digital games" in the broad sense used by Aphra Kerr (2006, p. 13). I have been able to bring digital game studies, digital game design, and digital game implementation into the CSE classroom. The link between writing and programming has led to the successful use of digital game *design* assignments to teach students how to approach general design problems and, in particular, the design of computer programs.

HISTORY

This work traces my growth in understanding of how digital (and other) games can fit into CSE as well as the growing strength of my belief that it's all writing. It discusses my introduction to writing across the curriculum and how I brought the ideas of guided rewrites and portfolios into the classroom. My introduction to using digital game programming to motivate students led to teaching game design and implementation courses with a strong digital game studies component. Finally, the two threads came together in an introductory project course where students develop both a text-adventure game *and* a program to play any text adventure game. The separation of the two tasks is necessary to teach programmers about the separation of data and algorithm; it also supports mutual reinforcement in learning about design tasks.

My university is a small, liberal-arts university. With a 150-year history of excellence in teaching, close to 20 years of experience teaching computer programming and computer science as part of the mathematics department, and 6 years experience with a separate computer science major.

There is also almost a quarter century of experience with a First Year Program (FYP), a required course fostering college-level writing and research in some discipline. Drawing faculty from across the campus, the FYP drives campus support for *writing across the curriculum* (WAC). Most FYP instructors fulfill the requirement of learning how to teach writing in an annual FYP writing seminar. Some follow this up with additional research into teaching writing in their own discipline; this has led to upper-level writing intensive courses being offered in many departments.

Several years ago my wife, a professor of mathematics, was preparing to teach in the FYP for the first time. By the transitive property of married couples, her attendance at the FYP writing seminar introduced me to the idea, as espoused by Art Young, that "students [should] use written language to develop and communicate knowledge in every discipline and across disciplines." (1999, p. 3)

During graduate school, I had worked as a consultant to some large organizations in both the private and public sectors (e.g., IBM Research and the US Naval Postgraduate School). I had seen firsthand the need for college graduates to learn and practice effective spoken and written communications. With this experience, I quickly embraced the ideas of WAC and sought to apply them in the introductory computer science classroom.

Writing in the Computer Classroom

All introductory computer science courses on our campus are taught in a smart computer lab. The lab would look familiar to Stephen Bernhardt (1989, p. 93) or anyone else who has taught in a computer writing classroom designed in the late 1980s: the instructor's workstation is projected onto a screen visible to all students while they are seated before their own networked computers. All computers in the room have access to on-campus shared storage and the Internet, and all machines in the room run some variant of the Windows operating system.

The computer programming lab has an integrated development environment (IDE) installed; an IDE combines a text editor with compiling and debugging tools so that students can edit, compile, and run their programs from within a single application. It provides a computer programmer with support tools similar to those provided to a writer by a word processor. The exact IDE, compiler, and programming language has changed over the years as the mathematics department moved to support an accredited computer science major.

Introductory Computer Programming (CS1) serves both as a starting point for potential majors and as a mathematics distribution for other students. Many students are in the same boat computer composition students were in two decades ago: they have no experience with the software *or* the way of thinking required to write a computer program. John Dinan and his coauthors discussed how to introduce students to the technology in the computer writing classroom thirty years ago (Dinan, Gagnon, & Taylor, 1985, p. 33). Though students today are not as frightened of the machines themselves, many of the same guidelines apply on the first day of CS1.

In CS1, the computer classroom supports "type along with teacher" sessions. These sessions are useful when teaching the IDE. Beyond that point, the classroom supports the use of hypertext course slides and display, modification, compilation, and execution of sample code used in the course. It also supports class-wide collaboration: students work out loud, taking turns typing on the instructor's computer, and completing in-class programming assignments.

Given this environment and an introduction to the literature of WAC, I was able to hijack three different kinds of writing assignments for use in CS1: one-minute essays, multiple drafts, and portfolios. The one-minute essay (Young, 1999, pp. 14–16) is turned into the one-minute *design*. Rather than write an essay responding to a question in one minute, students are presented with a problem and are given only one minute to design a software solution to the problem. As with one-minute essays, some are collected and some are not. This permits the instructor a glimpse of how students are using their minute (and how their design skills are coming along) and makes sure students focus on the assignment. Afterwards, the class takes a few minutes to discuss the various proposed solutions. The comparison of different designs is an integral part of design-based instruction such as *Informed Design* (Burnhardt & Hacker, 2004).

When the scale of the problem is properly selected, this type of assignment is very successful. Poor students may not get very far by the end of the minute, but they have begun to see the shape of the solution space and that increases their engagement in subsequent discussion about that solution space. Better students get further and engage some of the subtleties in the problem. Subsequent project designs benefit from both the one-minute design and the discussion.

Software design, as mentioned in the ABET definition above (ABET, 2000), is "often iterative." This means that rewriting code to correct bugs or meet new requirements is standard practice in the software industry. Unfortunately it is *not* standard practice in CSE. As I have previously written (Ladd, 2003), I introduced voluntary rewrites into CS1. Students write an out-of-class programming project and turn it in online (so that I can compile and run it). Each program is then graded and considerable comments on correctness and style is provided. Students have two weeks to rewrite the program, guided by the comments, and turn it in again for up to half of the credit they had lost.

Student comments on the voluntary rewrites indicated that struggling students greatly appreciated the chance to improve their grade. Student retention of material was improved (as seen on midterm and final exam performance) but few realized how much rewriting even a correct program improved it. That led, in turn, to an attempt to really use "multiple drafts" of a program, requiring *all* students to rewrite a quarter of their exercises throughout the semester. This was a failure in CS1.

CS1, as an introduction to the field of computer science, is full of domain knowledge that students *must* know to go on to CS1.5 and CS2. This means that the class moves very quickly and there are a large number of out-of-class exercises (typically ten assignments in a fourteen-week semester). This meant that rather than rewriting being seen as a chance to improve a program, it was seen as a waste of students' already limited time.

Though a failure in CS1, multiple drafts or phases, of a single, semester-long project has proven useful in upper-level courses. A single project is designed and then implemented in a series of assignments, each building on those that came before. Students are motivated to rewrite earlier phases to correct shortcomings that either were found by the instructor's testing or that impinge on later phases. Directed rewriting is recognized as part of the process of creating a large software project.

Finally, looking at the results from one-minute designs and program rewrites, I realized that students needed to reflect on what they were learning. The missing piece in applying rewrites was the *student's* understanding of what they were learning. Looking at WAC, one place where self-reflection is emphasized is in the preparation of a writing portfolio. For more than six years I used a *programming portfolio*, a collection of all graded programs, in CS1.

Initially, students were directed to write a reflective essay on the entire portfolio; this matched the assignment used at the end of the first semester of the FYP. Upon reviewing what students had to say, this was modified so that students were required to pick out three programs from their portfolio and use examples from those three to highlight their self-reflection. This worked much better as students were given guidance to select three programs that best exemplified what and how they had learned programming that semester. This made the students justify why the three programs were selected which, in turn, greatly improved the amount of self-reflection found in the portfolio essay.

I was not the first computer science educator to use portfolios. John Estell reported on interactive, Web-based portfolios (Estell, 2000; Estell, 2001). The real novelty in Estell's student portfolios is their online, always visible nature and the use of them by students to comment on each other's work. Other CSE and software engineering uses of portfolios can be found in the references of (Ladd, 2003, p. 64).

GAMING IN THE COMPUTER CLASSROOM

David Moeller's negative observations concerning teaching students to write in a computer classroom (2002, p. 15) apply to teaching students to program in such classrooms as well: student dependency on the environment, difficulty in tearing students' eyes away from their own computer screen, and limited amounts of prewriting.

Dependency on the environment is an inability to translate what they learn in the computer classroom to another location. Transfer is easier for computer programming students than for traditional writing students: while prewriting and design can be done longhand, in the end, programming *requires* a computer. Students can usually set up a suitable environment on any computer they have access to so long as it uses the same operating system as that in the computer classroom.

Student distraction by their own computer is endemic to the computer classroom. Each student can check e-mail, surf the Web, or even play their own digital games. The best answer to these distractions are engaging, in-class assignments and the use of multi-phase programming assignments that build student buy-in across a semester. Engaging assignments mean students *want* to learn how to do them and multi-phase assignments help insure that students *own* their solution across multiple drafts. Structuring assignments this way helps keep students focused while at the same time helping the instructor gauge how well they stay on task.

Multi-phase assignments use the multiple drafts to encourage sufficient design (prewriting) in the computer classroom and out. Immediate access to the IDE pulls students to write code before considering the shape of the solution space; required comments or design documents are only an afterthought.

Beginning students tend to write some code and then use the compiler to find their errors. This is similar to students starting a paper and then expecting the spelling and grammar checking of their word processor to correct their work. Requiring one-minute designs and complete design documents before finished programs are due motivate students to actually do the design work. This is not unlike requiring students to submit an outline before the first draft of a paper. One challenge in requiring early design is finding properly scoped assignments, assignments that beginners can complete but that are sufficiently complex that they require prior design work. Computer games easily fit this niche.

As Diana and James Oblinger remind us, the current cohort of college students grew up with computer games and are immersed in digital technology (2005, p. 2.12ff.). These sophisticated consumers of digital entertainment must be engaged before they can learn to program, and the traditional "Hello, World!" program is not enough.[1] Many students' interest in computer programming followed their immersion in digital games in the home or K-12 classroom.

The impact of computer games on computer science students has been discussed for more than a decade. Elliot Soloway talked about it at the beginning of the Nineties and, with Mark Guzdial, revisited the topic a decade later; these two suggest that since the "Nintendo generation" is bored by simple text-based programs, introductory courses should rely on visual programming environments and sophisticated, pre-programmed widgets that students can link together to make interesting programs (Solloway, 1991; Guzdial & Solloway, 2002).

I initially brought digital games into my CS1 classroom because one of my colleagues, Scott McElfresh, had done it. He designed a capstone project for CS1 that addressed the need for engagement while avoiding the instructor's need to supply preprogrammed widgets. Scott's original assignment required students to make something move on screen, permit the player some sort of interaction, to score the interaction, and then keep a running score. The breadth of solutions received, from simple laser/missile games to bumble bees in search of nectar, attests to the openness and success of the assignment.

◇◇

This assignment will give you a chance to exercise your knowledge of Turing graphics and your creativity. You will be using procedures, loops, graphics, animation. This program will bring together **everything** we have learned to date.

This is a *long* and *involved* assignment. Start early. You will note that you have twice as long as usual to write the program; this assignment is worth **twice** as much as a normal programming assignment.

1. Design a target game of some sort. The definition of the game is very open—you have great flexibility within the following requirements:
2. Prompt user for their name near the beginning of the game. Refer to the user by name from then on.
3. There should be some sort of graphical target.
4. The user must be prompted for some input to determine their "shot."
5. The user should be provided with some guidance in choosing their shot (say a range of legal numbers).

6. The user's input must be validated: If the input is out of range you must inform the user and permit them to enter another shot value. All input must be validated.

7. There should be an animation for each shot (an object moving on the screen with the target).

8. For each shot, the program must evaluate it (did it hit? how close did it come?). The evaluation can be a verbal description of how the shot did, it can be a numerical point score, or it could be some sort of graphic display of success or failure.

9. The user must be able to make more than one shot. Within this requirement, you may chose how the game is played:

10. Give the player a fixed number of shots and keep a running total score.

11. Permit the player to keep shooting until they hit the target.

12. Prompt the user after each shot if they want to take another shot.
    a. Be creative! As Scott McElfresh says, "There are many possible ways to follow these guidelines in a 'game' of a non-violent nature." If that doesn't appeal to you, *I* say there are many possible ways to follow theses guidelines in a game of aggression and wanton violence. Your imagination is your only limitation.

13. Grading

14. You have a great deal of freedom in how you write this program. A portion (30%) of your grade will be based on your documentation. I need a design document describing the problem you set out to solve (describing the game you are programming) and how you broke the problem up into smaller subproblems; note above when this is due.

◇◇◇

Figure 1. Capstone Game Programming Assignment, CS1

Later I extended the assignment, maintaining the openness but adding a few more requirements and assigning a graded *design document* that was due before the finished program. The design document, written *about* the game (program) that was to be written, serves as prewriting; it is a chance for students to consider what they want the game to do, how the task can be decomposed into simpler tasks, and how the various components interact. Figure 1 is the modified assignment from the last time it was used for a CS1 capstone.

This assignment is an example of what Sindre, Line, & Valåg call an "open assignment" (2003, p. 608), an assignment where each student defines a significant portion of the work for themselves. This type of assignment improves student engagement, enhances student outcomes, and limits chances for plagiarism (Sindre, Line, & Valåg, 2003). Students take ownership of a project that they designed and they are able to discuss solutions without copying one another's code. I will return to the power of open assignments later.

Computer games in CSE are sometimes questioned because of gender differences in video game players. As Sara Kiesler and her coauthors report, adolescent boys were much more likely to play computer games than their female counterparts (Kiesler, Sproull, & Eccles, 2002, p. 164). Marc Natale discusses the impact this has on female programmers in the industry, observing that males tend toward "war" games and females to "other" games (though genre definition in game studies is still contentious, these abstract labels, from early studies, seem to stand up fairly well [Kiesler, Sproull, & Eccles, 2002, p. 164]) and that the predominance of war games in the market explains why females might be turned off by digital gaming assignments (Natale, 2002). This computer game assignment side-steps this problem by having each student design and define their own game, a game that they would like to play.

To demonstrate the breadth of games that can fulfill this assignment I make it a point to tell students about various William Tell-style games that have been turned in. I also talk about the bumble bee that players had to steer to each budding flower, racing to gather nectar before the flower wilted and the equestrian leap game where the object was for the horse to *miss* the bar to make full points. Then, to avoid inappropriate stereotyping (the last two games were designed by female students), I discuss "Mathematician Invasion," a shooter where orbiting physicists must protect Earth from the scourge of space mathematicians from another galaxy, a fun and furious game designed by another high-achieving female student.

Success with the digital game capstone assignment in CS1 led directly to the use of a game engine in CS1.5 as well as the offering of an independent game development course. The next section discusses the upper-level game development course and how game studies, student presentations, and version control all supported an active connection between composition skills and game design and programming skills.

◇◇◇

GAME EVALUATION PRESENTATION ASSIGNMENT

Class Evaluations

- *Knights of the Old Republic*
- *Super Collapse!*

Description

You are to select a computer/video game and do a formal evaluation of the game. While the visual and audio effects are part of the game remember that you are evaluating the game as a whole.

You will need to be familiar with a game to be able to evaluate it; select your game accordingly. You will not be able to evaluate games that are evaluated in class; each student will evaluate a different game and games will be claimed on a first-come basis.

You will write a 3–5 page evaluation of the game and prepare a 5–8 minute presentation for class. You may show a short demonstration of the game if you feel it drives home your evaluation but your demo cannot be more than half of your presentation.

You need to address the points raised below; you will probably want to consider the design dimensions we discussed in the first lecture, too. The organization of your paper (and presentation) is up to you but you should have an introduction that presents a *thesis,* a body that supports your thesis, and a conclusion. And, one more time, remember that you are evaluating the game as a whole, not just the number of pretty polygons that it pushes.

Basic Information	Game Summary
• Title	• Overview
• Publisher	• Storyline (narrative components)
• Developer	• Point of view (player character)
• Designer (lead)	• Installation
• Genre	• User interface
• Price	• Gameplay (ludic components)
• Minimum hardware requirements	• Scoring/powerups
• Actual hardware requirements	• Game length
	• Art design
	• Sound design (including voice work)
	• Manual
	• Bugs/patches
	• Special features ("box points")

◇◇◇

Figure 2. Computer Game Review Assignment, Computer Games and Simulation.

Computer Games and Simulation

The Nintendo generation wants more in their upper-level courses as well as in their introductory courses. To satisfy this desire I have designed and offered a 300-level course: *Computer Games and Simulation*. Students in this course focus on an introduction to game studies, developing an open assignment for the semester project, in-class oral presentations, and the use of modern software engineering tools.

When I started using computer games in the CSE classroom, I taught very pragmatic game design. Students were guided to games that were easy to implement with the technology and knowledge they had available. When I turned to games as a research topic, I augmented my own limited experience in game design with readings by capable game designers such as Chris Crawford (1982) and Richard Rouse III (2002). These led, directly, to readings in the field of game studies (such as Bogost's *Unit Operations* [2008], Newman's *Videogames* [2004], and Salen and Zimmerman's *Rules of Play* [2003]) which I have also added to students' reading lists.

Game studies, the study of games as artistic, cultural products, is a young field. Many students have never heard of it, but a digital games course is greatly enhanced if students begin to think of games in a broad context. The first assignment that gets them thinking in this way is a game review, like the assignment shown in Figure 2 above (based on Laird, 2007).

Students are, at this point, focusing on what makes a game fun or frustrating. Fun is difficult to define or to quantify but students need to begin to reflect on their experience with digital games if they are to understand the task of designing one. Reviewing a game in a game design course is similar to reading essays in a composition course: absorbing examples, good and bad, gives the student models on which they can base their own work. This assignment is also a direct response to the WAC literature: students write and make oral presentations inside the computer science discipline.

In order for students to mature in their oral communication skills, they review and present at least two games, they design and present their own, personal, game and then, as part of a programming group, they design and present a group game design and three revisions of the game. Each presentation is accompanied by a short (~5 page) paper or, in the case of the game revisions, a complete copy of their source code and design documents.

Students in *Computer Games and Simulation* also give a presentation on one software design pattern. Design patterns are high-level descriptions of solutions to common programming problems; they form a meta-programming language that lets programmers talk about problems and solutions while abstracting away many details. Using a mix of both open and closed presentation assignments provides students with invaluable experience before they select, complete, and present their senior project.

Software engineering is the discipline of efficient, correct software implementation. Its literature provides best practices and tools computer scientists should know. Three such tools are automated build tools, automated regression testing tools, and version control. The first and third of these tools can also be useful when writing compositions.

Automated build tools include Feldman's *make* (1979) and its modern descendants (*ant, maven, gradle*); *make* uses a description of how various executable programs depend on various source files and how to create the executables when a source file changes. This system permits executable programs to be rebuilt *only* when something on which they depend changes. This reuses output from previous runs of *make* to accelerate updating a projects output files. Complex typesetting operations (such as running the TeX typesetter on a book, generating an index, or generating a table of contents) are resource intensive for the same reasons program compilation is; authors of large compositions or books can benefit from the use of *make*. It is a tool students are not always exposed to in computer science education, but software engineering best practices require student familiarity with it.

Regression testing, in computer development, means testing that new or fixed code does not break functionality that was in the program before code was added. Automating this type of testing is very important so that programmers *always* integrate their code into the project and *always* make sure that all the tests run correctly. In group projects, individual programmers change the code in different ways. Just as it is necessary to make sure that collaborative writing holds together with a single voice, so, too, must *each* programmer's changes pass *every* programmer's tests before they can be considered complete.

Software supported version control is familiar to many writers and writing instructors through their use of wiki software (Leuf & Cunningham, 2001). When a page in a wiki is changed, one can see a summary of what changed and, with appropriate permissions, instantly revert the page to some previous version. This same type of software has been in use with software source code since Marc Rochkind presented the first paper on the Source Code Control System more than forty years ago (1975). The use of a code repository, shared by all members of a coding team, is the current software engineering ideal.

Students in the *Games* class are surprised at how well such a system supports collaborative development. The typical project is divided into a collection of source files. Each student "checks out" all the files from the repository, modifies them to add whatever features they are responsible for, and then builds and tests the project using *make*, assuring their changes pass the regression testing. Then, when all the tests pass, the programmer "checks in" their changes. As long as student changes do not directly overlap, most modern source control systems automatically resolve file-level conflicts (so changes at the beginning of a file and separate, parallel changes near the end of the same file are automatically *both* applied because there is enough context for the program to avoid confusion).

Versions tied to dates or software releases permit programmers to "reset the clock" to match the version that a user reports a bug in. Version control also supports "branches" or parallel development; branches can be used to try out more experimental changes while permitting the rest of the team to continue working. Version control is a great help when writing, either collaboratively or on one's own, since editors sometimes change their mind and want some portion returned to a previous state. It frees an author to try different things because there is always a large-grained "undo" operation available.

Computer Games and Simulation is an example of a discipline-centric course that makes use of writing across the curriculum as Young suggest it should be used (1999). The course has standard writing to learn and writing to communicate assignments in game studies, game design, and programming practices. It also introduces software engineering best practices to students. These practices include automated building of the system, something that hypertext and multimedia authors can make use of; automated regression testing, another practice that multimedia authors can make good use of (did a link or reference break when I added my new titles to the composition?); and automated version control, a practice that has saved this author unimaginable amounts of work as both composition backup and protection from waffling editors.

AN INTRODUCTION TO COMPUTER SCIENCE
WITH A TEXT-ADVENTURE GAME

The palest ink is better than the best memory.

—Ancient Chinese Proverb

The Association for Computing Machinery, the professional organization for computer scientists, has a model curriculum for liberal arts colleges offering two one-semester introductory courses, known as CS1 and CS2 (Joint Task Force on Computing Curricula, 2013). Students at our college found the learning curve too steep with only two courses so almost twenty years ago a third course, CS1.5, was introduced *between* the other two course. CS1.5's purpose is to practice the material from CS1 and introduce software engineering topics through a semester-long project. This section discusses the background on how this class was taught and how success with open videogame assignments in CS1 led to a successful conversion to a game-based project. Further, because the game is text-based, writing techniques apply to both the game design and the game engine programming and design.

Educational Context

Traditionally, CS1 introduces students to programming in some computer language and problem solving using sequence, selection, iteration, and delegation. CS2 teaches students how data can be structured to solve different kinds of problems efficiently. This sequence, taught in two semesters, is very demanding, too demanding for students in our university. Instead, the introductory sequence is stretched across three semesters with CS1 matching most of the traditional course, CS1.5 serving as a "baby" software engineering course that introduces how to compare the efficiency of two different programs and some of the first data structures while students write a semester-long project, and CS2 finishing the material traditionally taught in that course.

CS1.5 begins with a refresher of CS1, a series of review programs, and then the design and implementation of a large, multi-phase, individual programming project. Working on a single project for close to two months through multiple phases, students learn to design for change, why their code must be readable and maintainable, and how important guided rewriting of their code can be.

CS1.5 has survived almost twenty years, several programming language changes, changes of instructor, and even a complete overhaul of the curriculum for instituting a new computer science major. Every time it has come up, instructors always find students benefit from the shallower learning curve that CS1.5 permits and that they really benefit from the project.

Projects were changed almost every term to avoid cross-term plagiarism. The effort involved in defining all the phases of an appropriately scaled project made this course difficult to staff. Some instructors had students build operating system simulators while others had them build polynomial calculators. The great variety meant that student workload and learning outcomes often suffered. These projects were seldom clearly remembered by students a semester or a year later.

After the success with open computer game assignments in CS1, I looked at applying that approach in CS1.5. I sought a single, standard, reusable project that met five goals: works in the standard C++ programming language; provides a context for the introduction of a wide range of software engineering topics; includes opportunities for student oral and written communication in the discipline; requires creative, student-designed content; and engages our students. Additionally, I sought a strong connection between the required content design and the required program design expected of students; having settled on using a game-based project, I also sought to include game studies and game design elements to the greatest extent possible.

Upper-level courses use C++ and CS1 uses a different programming language (Java, at present); CS1.5 is where students are introduced to the new language. Standard C++ and, by definition, a simple, text-based interface, keeps the students' focus on computer science fundamentals (functions, containers, and classes) rather than on loading different animated images on each of their buttons. A similar problem is faced teaching composition with multimedia: students become enamored of the "shiny" and stop paying attention to the content they are creating.

Graphical user interface (GUI) programming is an important skill for some jobs; rather than being driven by current openings in the classified ads, however, we recognized that student success in CS2 depends on the mastery of problem solving with a standard programming language. Standard C++ is also platform independent. While the university provides only Microsoft-based workstations, learning to program text-based interfaces with standard C++ permits students in the course to use almost any development platform they desire.

One fear in a project-based course, especially one where a standard project is used multiple times, is that the lectures become narrow and workman-like. The project should be abstract enough that instructors can customize it for each class they teach. Further, the project should reflect many subdisciplines of computer science so that project discussions can range across the breadth of computer science.

CS1.5 is most student's introduction to the computer science major. This means that expectations set here have a tendency to remain in effect for the rest of their academic career. A project with many opportunities for oral presentations and written (natural language) phases was important as our students need to develop their ability to communicate about their programs before they graduate. Having written design phases and multiple in-class presentations help them improve and give the computer science faculty a chance to begin to shape their writing and presenting skills to match those in the discipline.

The strong, creative, student-designed component of the project serves dual purposes: it limits opportunities for plagiarism and it increases student engagement. Our department's experience just before adopting this project was that student plagiarism, either from others in the course, others who had previously taken the course, or off of the Web, was on the rise. The use of open assignments in CS1 had decreased the instance of copying because the assignment is customized *by each student* with guidance from the instructor. This lowers the likelihood that code from other sources fits the student's needs, making it less likely that they can plagiarize. It also makes detection of plagiarizing much simpler for the instructor as copied code is unlikely to be in line with the student's customized assignment.

Students "buy in" to a project that they have helped design. Sindre's work in computer science education indicates that the more creative their input, the deeper their investment in the project (Sindre, 2003). Increasing their interest tends to also increase their effort, their success, and their engagement with the project.

Engaging our students was the most important goal in the search for a standard project. We sought to improve student retention from CS1 to CS1.5 and, more importantly, from CS1.5 to CS2. The workload in a project-based course, particularly one where students are learning a foreign language (C++ *is* a foreign language), is high. We wanted to make sure that students' emotional payoff was proportional to the amount of work they did. To date, the choice of a text-adventure game has been very successful in meeting these five goals and bringing out the best in our students.

Standard Review Assignments

CS1.5 has always begun with a series of review assignments. These short lab programs are assigned during one class and collected during the next. They review basic programming concepts of sequence, selection, iteration, and delegation as well as present the syntax of a new programming language. Prior to settling on the text-adventure game project, review assignments were *ad hoc* affairs, designed by the instructor but seldom tied to the course project. Student evaluations indicated that they were not happy with the lack of connection. With a consistent, well-defined project, these assignments have been redesigned to support the creation of a text adventure game system.

Thinking about a text-adventure game, one feature of the game is that objects within the game have attributes that, in turn, have values. That is, the lamp (an object) has an on state (an attribute) which is either true or false (a value). Or the oven has a temperature setting which is "off," "low," "medium," or "high." Now review assignments emphasize string and file processing in the context of working with attribute/value pairs. These pairs are the basis of game configuration files. The review assignments culminate in the creation of a **dictionary** class that maps the attributes to values. The first use of the dictionary is to translate abbreviated commands to their full names. For example, input of "**n**," "**no**," or "**north**" should all result in the system receiving the "**north**" command. This is done by associating the value "**north**" with each of the appropriate abbreviated attributes. Knowing that their review program is part of their game's user interface keeps students motivated through the rapid review of concepts.

Let the Adventure Begin

The CS1.5 project is about designing and building both a *game* and a *game engine* in parallel. The separation of the engine, a program built to play any text-adventure game, and the game, the specific data for the game the student authors, is known as *data driven* programming. Many students have been exposed to this idea without even being aware of it. Music and chat programs that can have different themes and different themes for on-line community pages are two examples. Many computer science students have also played game "mods" or modifications. The modifications are made by changing the data files provided to a commercial video game engine. Students are typically amazed that they, too, can write games that can be modded. It also permits each type of writing to support and reinforce the other.

Phase 1: Introduction to Interactive Fiction

The first day of class begins with an overview of the text adventure game project and a brief history of Will Crowther's *Adventure* (Crowther, Woods, and Black). Current students were born after the golden era of the text adventure game so they are sometimes surprised to find out how much game play there is in such games (see Figure 3 below for a screenshot of *Adventure*).

A *text-adventure game* is a simulated world in which players use text commands to control their character's actions. Espen Aarseth identifies text-adventure games as a *cybertext,* a form of *ergodic literature* in his volume of the same name (Aarseth, 1997). Text input and output fit well the capabilities of mainframe computers in the early 1970s when Crowthers developed the *Colossal Cave Adventure* and bequeathed it to the world by permitting free download across the ARPAnet (Crowther, 1976). The first lecture includes playing through the first puzzle in *Adventure* in front of the class, giving them a feeling for the genre.

Text-based input and output also fit well with the capabilities of early home computers in the 1980s. Companies such such as Infocom, Level 9, Magnetic Scrolls, and Adventure International enjoyed financial success with games like *Zork, The Hitchhiker's Guide to the Galaxy,* and *Amnesia.* The lecture continues with some of the history of these games, following Nick Monfort's history (Monfort, 2003, pp. 65–169) as well as introducing his book, *Twisty Little Passages,* to the class.

As the power of home computers grew, consumers and producers of computer entertainment began to move from text-based interactive stories to more and more graphically intensive games; as the commercial viability of text-adventure games declined, a crop of community-produced *interactive fiction* rose. Free interactive fiction authoring kits were developed and deployed, including *Inform* and *TADS.* Over the past decade, the quality of interactive fiction produced by the online community has surpassed even the best commercial games, and the Interactive Fiction Archive (Interactive Fiction Archive [IFA], 2006) hosts the winners of the Interactive Fiction Awards (for winners of *the Comp,* an annual competition for short works) and the XYZZY Awards (for longer works of interactive fiction).

After the lecture, students are assigned a short presentation on an interactive fiction of their choosing with the stipulation that everyone must review a unique title and titles are first-come, first-served. Students are guided to the IFA and, in particular to *Comp* winners; *Comp* entries are designed to be completed by experienced text-adventure gamers in less than two hours so these titles offer a reasonable-length game experience to novice gamers. The author also has many commercial titles from the golden era for loan and there are Websites hosting reviews of a large number of community offerings. Going off and playing a game, particularly one that has won awards, helps students learn about the expectations of the genre. It also gives them a good read on which to model their own writing of a game.

One difference between composition in a natural language and programming in an artificial language is the lack of "good" writing for beginners to read; Diomidis Spinellis addressed the need to read code with his book of that title but his work assumes the reader (of the book and the code) is fluent in the programming language (2003). Learning a new programming language *is* learning a foreign language, so the instructor is left coming up with model programs using the students' limited vocabulary. Short, engaging text-adventure games give the students something to read that they can understand and build upon.

Student presentations focus on the narrative, the interface, and the gameplay. Because most students are playing their first text adventure game, few recognize the interface conventions of the genre. Having multiple students present different games, many conventions (such as the use of abbreviations described above) become apparent. Students get a much broader view of the genre than they could gain on their own in an equivalent amount of time.

Phase 2: Game Design

After playing one game and hearing about several others, students are tasked with designing their own game. While designing their games, students get inside the head of an author of great interactive fiction and a great interactive fiction *system* by reading Graham Nelson. His *Craft of Adventure* (1995) contains five short essays on what makes good interactive fiction and is a classic in the IF community.

◇◇◇

Phase 3: Design a Game

- Audience: Game Producer
- Deliverables: (in a 3-ring binder)
- Game design document: ~4 double spaced pages
- Rough-draft map diagram: ~1 page

A computer game does not begin with writing code. It does not even begin with writing a design for writing code. A computer game begins with a design for a *game*. This phase of the project is your chance to design an adventure game.

The game you design is constrained to be a text-based adventure game. This means text descriptions of places, items, monsters, and actions are all the player sees and simple declarative "senteces" are the only input to the game. While this may seem like a burden, constraints like this are no barrier to creating interesting or even great games. Play Adventure or, if that seems too old-fashioned for you, head on over to the Interactive Fiction Archive for some really cutting-edge adventure games; many IFA games are based on an old text adventure engine from Infocom known as zCode; zCode interpreters are available for most modern computing platforms.

This design document is being written for the manager charged with overseeing your game's production. That means you can mention the things that will make your game most cool but you want to make sure that you address all aspects of the game. At a minimum, *you* should consider the following questions when designing your game:

- What is the player's goal? How do they win?
- What is the scale of the game? How far are locations, one from another?

◇◇◇

Figure 3. Game Design Instructions

The design assignment takes a page from the CS1 capstone by specifying as little as possible. Students make their own creative contribution at this stage. As can be seen in the assignment (see Figure 4) the student decides the *who, what, where,* and *how* of the text adventure game: *who* the player's avatar in the game is; *what* their goal in the game is; *where* the game takes place; and *how* the avatar interacts with the gameworld, its contents, and its inhabitants. Students decide whether their game contains combat, conversations, or some other form of interaction with the world. This is crucial; as noted before, Kiesler, Sproull, & Eccles (2002) found that violent games turned some women off of computer science; an open design assignment lets each student match their own level of comfort.

Experience bears out the difference in desire for violent games. In a recent semester, during game presentations, a young woman reported on an educational text-adventure game where the player navigates the countries of South East Asia, learning about their cultures to solve the game's primary puzzle. She finished with the comment that she has appreciated that the game was not like most she had seen (she was *not* a gamer) and had not required her to interact violently with anyone.

The next student, a young man who loved video games, began his presentation by listing the number of different verbs his game supported for killing gang members and how each one produced a different gruesome description of the death. Anecdotes are not data, but it would have been hard to pay the students to act out the research any more clearly.

Thinking about the similarities between essays and programs also led to considerations about how designing a text-adventure game and a program are similar. The game and the game engine are, in many ways, the same.

Consider the execution of a single-threaded program. The point of control begins in a **main()** function and "visits" lines sequentially unless directed otherwise. Thus an executing program can be compared directly to a single player moving into and through the world of a text-adventure game. So designing a program is akin to designing a game; designing a method is akin to designing a room; the calling stack is akin to the history of the path from where the avatar is back to the beginning of the game. These similarities are explained as each portion of the game project unfolds. This permits students to see that groups of nodes can provide a useful abstraction (so that they can talk about "the mansion" without having to specify exactly which nodes are in it) just as defining classes can provide abstraction for groups of methods.

In the classroom (and on-line discussions with students) the author has seen the light come on for some struggling students when the explanation from the "other" strand of writing is given to them.

Phase 3: The Location Class

After students design their game, it is time to begin working on the game engine. A text-adventure game engine consists of about four different types of objects: the **Game** itself that contains a collection of interconnected **Locations** that can contain **Items** or **Critters**. In object oriented programming, each of these is represented by a data class. **Location** is the most obvious type in the game so students make a detailed design and code the **Location** class next. They also build a very simple program, one that reads a data file of **Locations** and displays all information about any **Location**; this is what is known as a "programmer's interface" and does not yet follow the conventions of a text adventure game of moving only from one **Location** to one of its neighbors. Along with the **Location** class students must put 10% of their game locations into a data file for the program to read.

The data file format is left up to the student though it must support internal comments and be self-describing in Jon Bentley's sense of the term (Bentley 37–44). A simple format, based on attribute/value pairs is encouraged.

This is the first coding phase, the first trip from design to running code and back again on their own project. Students begin to learn that program design, just like writing, is an iterative process. As they decide to change how the game plays, they find they must change how the Location class is defined, loaded from a file, and displayed for the user. Seeing multiple levels of abstraction simultaneously is an invaluable skill to a programmer; it is one that writing a game and game engine together encourages almost from the start.

Phase 4: Detailed Game Design

No game design survives contact with the code.

Guided by feedback on their initial design and their experience with the Location class, students now fill in the blanks in their design. Gameplay is specified by listing all the verbs their game accepts and all the command forms it parses. Natural language processing is a large, open field of study on its own so text-adventure games typically support only limited command phrases and forms. Students must now determine the complete lexicon their game understands (though synonyms can be added through the Dictionary class discussed above). This also determines what avenues are open to the player to complete the game. Students also determine the attributes needed for Critters and Items.

While working on this design, students are introduced to different views of games. Lectures and readings from Katie Salen and Eric Zimmerman's *Rules of Play* (2003) present games as simulations, entertainment, and stories. Monfort's analysis of text adventure games in terms of the riddle is also presented at this point (Monfort, 2003, chap. 2).

Phase 5: The Game Class

As students begin their next phase, the implementation of the Game class, they are presented with a high-level architecture or design of the relationship between the four major types identified above. Suggesting a particular architecture means the programs have similar structure and runs counter to the idea of open assignments. While this admittedly compromises some of our goal, this is a necessary evil: CS1.5 students lack the design maturity to create a moderately complex multi-class solution on their own and on schedule.

The **Game** class is a special type, a *singleton*. Singleton is a design pattern used when there should only be one object of a given type. There is only one **Game** and it is responsible for loading all the data files, keeping track of all **Locations**, **Items**, and **Critters**, and the player. Note that the player's avatar can usually be represented as one of the **Critters**. The **Game** object also runs the primary *game loop*. The game loop is at the heart of every computer game (Figure 4).

```
while (!gameOver()) {
showGameState();
getUserInput();
updateGameState();
}
```

Figure 4. The Main Game Loop

Here each step in the loop is implemented as a function call (this explains the () after each name) and the functions are named with internal capitalization so they are easy read. The loop, identified by the **while**, runs forever, or, rather, until the game is over ("!" should be read as "not"). The body of the loop, the three core functions, are to show the user their view of the diegesis, project user actions (if there are any) into diegetic actions, and then determine (calculate) the diegetic response. Students must again think at two levels of abstraction, understanding how the presentation of state and user actions are mediated by the hardware used.

Surprisingly, to many students, this loop resides at the core of almost all interactive programs. Students are now using the design they wrote in the last phase to flesh out what user input is acceptable; this is the verb and command list they put together. They also use the design to code the semantics of each command. They are building a small artificial language and implementing the meaning in the get and update functions.

Phase 6–8: Critter, Item, and Playable Game

At the end of the Game phase, students have a navigable map of a quarter of their game world without any interaction. It is possible to see how going from this to a playable game could be considered a single, five-week-long, step. CS1.5 students are not yet mature enough, as programmers, to go five weeks without feedback. The insertion of two internal milestones when they have to have Critter and Item working serve to focus students' attention.

For pedagogical reasons related to the three-course introductory sequence, the Inventory class is the one container class constructed during the class. Students learn about the linked list data structure in this course. Few programmers really understand a data structure until they have implemented it for themselves. Students practice using pointers, reading different kinds of configuration files, and implement all additional commands designed in previous phases.

Phase 9: Extended Game

The playable game phase ends two weeks before the end of the semester. Using a grading method described by Katrin Becker, this represents a threshold of the project. Students who have done one hundred percent of everything on the project up to this point can expect a 2.5/4.0 grade. Note that the timing of completion is actually the end of the semester. This means that students who do not complete through Phase 8 of the project on-time have an additional two weeks to earn a 2.5.

The final phase of the project, due at the end of the semester, is to extend the game using some techniques presented in class but not already in the game. C++ topics such as inheritance or template metaprogramming and game ideas such as conversation or combat (if the game already had only one of them) or saving and restoring games are all valid extensions.

We also present MS Windows specific graphical user interface (GUI) programming at this point and offer students the chance to extend their project by adding a GUI to it. The change from having control of the game loop to an event-driven program is a real challenge, but many students want to have a "pretty" program (Figure 5) when they are done. Student feedback on this led us to bend our rule to use only standard C++.

During the final exam period, all of the students return to the classroom for one last time, each having prepared a slightly longer presentation on their completed game. They highlight the extensions they completed and lament the extensions they could not get working. These presentations are well received by everyone in the class. They are the capstone on the course, showing students just how far they have all come.

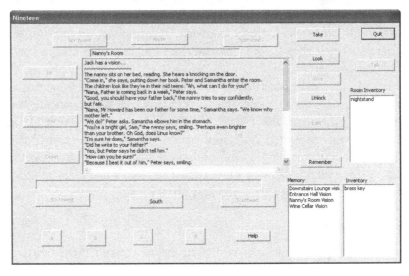

Figure 5. GUI for Nineteen, a student text adventure

EVALUATION

Creating a text-adventure game is a lot of work; creating a text-adventure game *assignment* is even more work. Creating a text-adventure game, a text-adventure game engine, and doing it all in one semester is a whole lot of work for everyone involved. Is it worth it?

One measure of success is the number of students in CS1.5 who go on to CS2. To date, only one student (in six semesters) who completed

CS1.5 chose not to go on to CS2. Another sign of success is how well students do in CS2. Prior to the text-adventure game project, CS2 success varied from ninety percent of students passing down to as low as sixty-five percent passing, depending on what instructor and what project they completed in CS1.5. Again, with six semesters of data, we have seen more than ninety percent success with only one student withdrawing and one student failing CS2.

An alternative measure of success is the anonymous course evaluations students fill out. Comparing the last three semesters taught by the author *before* the text-adventure game and the most recent three semesters teaching CS1.5, every measure of student satisfaction has improved. The only measure that gives pause is the self-reported workload of the course. Students perceive that they are working much harder with the new project than they did with any of the *ad hoc* projects in previous semesters.

It is possible that this perception is real since the project is very big. Students work very hard to use the high-level architecture and useful code from class in their game engine. They work just as hard to weave an interesting text-adventure game, designing compelling locations, items, and critters. One problem we have found is that both parts of the assignment require outside-class contact time and this puts a considerable load on teaching assistants and professors. We are working on integrating the use of a classroom management system or a Wiki into the class so that students could answer one another's questions when possible, speeding up turn around time on their simpler questions. This would permit students to use the time they do allocate to the project and make more progress in that time. Of course the efficacy of such a system is purely speculative at this time.

Integrating program design, oral presentation, coding, and technical and adventure game writing makes the new CS1.5 a fantastic introduction to software engineering as well as writing in the discipline of computer science. The multiple strands seem to provide a disproportional boost to middle-of-the-road students. Anecdotally, several students that would have been considered at risk in previous semesters have become very engaged and have succeeded in both the main program and in designing and implementing very interesting extensions.

Student engagement, our primary goal, has certainly improved. Seniors who completed the class three years ago still talk about their text-adventure games among themselves and with more junior students.

Several seniors have commented that every program they wrote after CS1.5 contained pieces of their text-adventure game engine design.

The project is a great deal of work but it has met the goals we set for the class, for the instructor, and, most especially, for the students. The use of writing in support of coding has improved student outcomes in CS1.5 and follow-on courses.

CONCLUSION

The use of digital games in CSE is successful when students find them motivating. That motivation is best captured using open assignments where students design the content and goal of the game; this permits students to tailor the amount of violence and other potentially offensive content to please themselves (though they need to be careful not to offend the instructor, either).

Student motivation improves their engagement with the material. Digital gaming assignments in CSE need to be designed so that the material students engage is fundamental rather than superficial. It appears that students work on the "shiny" in preference to the "deep" whenever they are given a choice. This is not surprising but it should be taken into account when designing digital game assignments.

The success of these three examples of combining the design of a game, writing in the discipline, and program design confirm my belief that it *is* all writing. Students benefit when multiple strands of writing and oral communication mutually support one another. In computer science, it is important that all of the strands show that preparation, a good command of tools, and an iterative approach to writing that includes editing, testing, and rewriting, work regardless of whether the intended audience is a person or a computer.

NOTE

1. "Hello, World!" (or, more historically, "hello, world") is the output of a standard first test program for many new programming languages. It is found in many introductory programming texts and was based on a sample program in Kerrnighan and Ritchie's influential *The C Programming Language* (1974, p. 14).

REFERENCES

Aarseth, E. J. (1997) *Cybertext: Perspectives on Ergodic Literature.* Baltimore: The Johns Hopkins UP.

Accreditation Board for Engineering and Technology. (2013). Criteria for Accrediting Engineering Programs: Effective for Evaluations During the 2013–2014 Accreditation Cycle. ABET. Baltimore, MD.

Becker, K. (2001). Teaching with games: The Minesweeper and Asteroids experience. *Journal of Computing in Small Colleges, 17*, 23–33.

Bentley, J. (1988). *More programming pearls*. Reading, MA: Addison-Wesley Publishing.

Bernhardt, S. (1989). Designing a Microcomputer Classroom for Teaching Composition. *Computers and Composition, 7*, 93–110.

Bogost, I. (2008). *Unit operations: An approach to videogame criticism*. Cambridge, MA: MIT Press.

Burghardt, M. D., & Hacker, M. (2004). Informed design: a contemporary approach to design pedagogy as the core process in technology. *The Technology Teacher, 64*, 1.

Crawford, C. (1982). *The art of computer game design*. Boston: Osborne-McGraw Hill. Retrieved from http://www.vancouver.wsu.edu/fac/peabody/game-book/Coverpage.html.

Crowther, W., Woods, D., & Black, K. (1976). *Colossal Cave Adventure*. [Video game]. Retrieved from ftp://ftp.gmd.de/if-archive/games/pc/adv350kb.zip.

Derrick, T. (1985). DOSEQUIS: An Interactive Game for Composition Students. *Computers and Composition, 3*, 40–51.

Dinan, J., Gagnon, R., & Taylor, J. (1985). Integrating computers into the writing classroom: Some guidelines. *Computers and Composition, 3*, 33.

Estell, J. (2000). Programming portfolios on the web: An interactive approach. *Journal of Computing in Small Colleges, 16*, 55–67.

Estell, J. (2001). IPP: A web-based interactive programming portfolio. *SIGCSE,* 149–153.

Feldman, S. I. (1979). Make—a computer program for maintaining computer programs." *Software Practice and Experience, 9*, 255–265.

Gee, J. P. (2003). *What videogames have to teach us about learning and literacy*. New York: Palgrave Macmillan.

Guzdial, M., & Soloway, E. (2002). Teaching the Nintendo generation to program. *Communications of the ACM, 45*, 17–21.

Hunt, A., & Thomas, D. (2000). *The pragmatic programmer: From journeyman to master*. Boston: Addison-Wesley Pearson Education.

Interactive Fiction Archive. (2006). Retrieved from http://ifarchive.org/.

Joint Task Force on Computing Curricula, Association for Computing Machinery (ACM) and IEEE Computer Society. (2013). *Computer Science Curricula 2013: Curriculum Guidelines for Undergraduate Degree Programs in Computer Science*. New York, NY: ACM.

Kernighan, B., & Ritchie, D. (1974). *The C programming language*. Upper Saddle River, NJ: Prentice Hall.

Kerr, A. (2006). *The business and culture of digital games: gamework/gameplay.* London: Sage Publications.

Kiesler, S., Sproull, L., & Eccles, J. (2002) Pool halls, chips, and war games: Women in the culture of computing. *SIGCSE Bulletin, 34,* 159–164.

Ladd, B. (2003). It's all writing: Experience using rewriting to learn in introductory computer science. *The Journal of Computing Sciences in Colleges, 18,* 57–64.

Laird, J. (2007). *Arcade-style game review.* Retrieved from https://web.archive.org/web/20070207082206/http://ai.eecs.umich.edu/soar/Classes/494/gamereview.html

Leuf, B., & Cunningham, W. (2001). *The wiki way: Quick collaboration on the web.* Reading, MA: Addison-Wesley Professional Publishing.

Moeller, D. (2002).*Computers in the writing classroom.* Urbana, IL: National Council of Teachers of English.

Monfort, N. (2003). *Twisty little passages: An approach to interactive fiction.* Cambridge, MA: MIT Press.

Natale, M. J. (2002). The effect of a male-oriented computer gaming culture on careers in the computer industry. *SIGCAS Computers & Society, 32*(2), 24–31.

Nelson, G. (1995). *The craft of adventure.* Retrieved from http://www.ifarchive.org/ifarchive/info/Craft.Of.Adventure.T1.1etter.pdf

Newman, J. (2004). *Videogames.* London: Routledge.

Oblinger, D., & Oblinger, J. (2005). *Educating the net generation.* Washington: Educause.

Rouse, R. (2002). *Game design: Theory and practice.* 2nd ed. Plano, TX: Wordware.

Salen, K., & Zimmerman, E. (2003). *Rules of play: Game design fundamentals.* Cambridge, MA: MIT Press.

Sindre, G., Line, S., & Valåg, O. (2003). Positive experiences with an open project assignment in an introductory programming course. *ICSE '03: Proceedings of the 25th International Conference on Software Engineering,* 608–613.

Soloway, E. (1991). How the Nintendo generation learns. *Communications of the ACM, 34,* 23ff.

Spinellis, D. (2003). *Code reading: The open source perspective.* Boston, MA: Addison-Wesley Professional.

Toothman, B., & Shackelford, R. (1998). The effects of partially-individualized assignments on subsequent student performance. *SIGCSE '98,* 287–291.

Young, A. (1999). *Teaching writing across the curriculum.* Upper Saddle River, NJ: Prentice Hall.

17 Writing for Games

Brandes Stoddard

I n many types of games, writing is a great paradox. Though the game may demand large volumes of writing, and the game's quality suffers if the writing is rushed, the game cannot require that the player read or absorb the text in order to enjoy the game. A failure of any aspect of a game can doom it to the bargain bin, but once foundational elements such as user interface, graphics, and code stability reach an acceptable level, it is content that makes the rest of the difference in the game's quality. A rare few older games with outdated graphics and interface achieved cult classic status for the raw quality of their writing, such as Black Isle's *Planescape: Torment*, published in 1999. Games that have become household words, such as *BioShock* by 2K Boston or *Portal* by Valve Corporation, combine top-notch gameplay with all of the hallmarks of strong fiction writing: character, theme, tone, and narrative flow.

Writing for games, whether as a matter of design or development, consists of essentially five branches of composition. The importance of these branches varies for each individual role within a company, and for the type of game the company makes. With lots of room to dispute the boundaries between them, the categories might be identified as technical or instructive writing, brief evocative writing, dialogue, flavor text, and plot or overarching narrative writing. Though they demand quite different strengths, few writers can afford to neglect any of them in the long term.

Technical and instructive writing is the only kind of writing that is, or should be, completely universal in game creation. Every game, from the simplest to the most complex, requires design documentation and instructions on how to play. For the former, the common rules of technical writing apply: clarity and specificity above all, with the added understanding that design undergoes iteration just as much as any text changes through multiple drafts. It would belabor the obvious to further extol the virtues of clear communication between departments, and of documenting the game's features. The common term for an "undocumented feature," after all, is "bug."

The paradox of game writing emerges first in instructive text. Nearly every game comes with a tutorial, and often a manual as well. Ten or twenty years ago, the gaming community accepted that reading the manual was necessary to playing the game. More than that, they were at that time part of the whole experience, and further served as the game's insurance against piracy in the days before internet access rendered them obsolete. That was the idea, at least; in reality players have never wanted to read before they played and have expected to refer to the manual only at direst need. (But let's not be disingenuous; the manual is a tool of last resort for most projects, not just games.) Manual writers therefore designed text, images, and even physical presentation to attract interest, especially in the field of role-playing games. In the 80s and 90s, Infocom and its successor, Activision, were known for including "feelies" in their products; these might be books of game lore (part of or separate from the manual), maps, and so forth, luring the players into reading the instructive text by blurring the boundary between it and flavor text.

Though manuals are still in common use throughout role-playing and strategy video games, the huge expansion of game distribution through download (such as Steam) or Flash, Shockwave, and HTML 5 (such as Kongregate) has expanded the base of games for which there can be no physical manual. Any resistance players might have to reading a physical manual is redoubled in the face of an electronic manual. The heavy lifting of teaching players to play the game has thus shifted to the tutorial. This has the benefit of appealing to kinesthetic learners as well as visual and reading-preference learners. On the other hand, the writers of instructive text lose much of their available word count, and face the challenge of incorporating the early parts of the game's narrative into their teaching.

The difficulties of writing the perfect tutorial are subtle and manifold. Every storyteller has faced the problem of writing an exposition without letting it become so dense and dry that the reader sets it aside; the only difference for video game writers is that impatience has been bred into players even more deeply than readers. Furthermore, the video game must teach the player to access its content—that is, to proceed through the game's challenges—without overwhelming the player. Many games need for the tutorial to teach more features than the game intends for the player to have at the start of actual play. As the game also needs a higher tolerance for failure than later areas of play, games ranging from Icarus Studios' *Fallen Earth* to Ubisoft's *Assassin's Creed* series have decided to give the player a taste of power, with all of the experience, gear, or other game features of late-game play. The problem with this, of course, is that it is a blatant bait-and-switch. Thus the writer has gotten enmeshed in problems of design as well as user experience, and games keep solving the tutorial problem with different mechanical or narrative devices.

The next category of writing, listed above as "brief evocative writing," bears more explanation. A game's items, monsters, abilities, and quests all need names and at-a-glance descriptions. The writer's challenge is to communicate flavor with Hemingway-esque brevity, while still distinguishing that game element from others like it. Often there is a hard limit to the number of characters that the text string can display; at the same time, abbreviations look unprofessional. For example, Activision-Blizzard's *World of Warcraft* uses monsters with the same creature model from one zone to the next, but these creatures present differing degrees of challenge and wield different abilities against the player. Since the game has decided that players should be able to distinguish these creatures immediately, a writer assigns them different names. But then, "big ogre" and "bigger ogre" are rather unsatisfying. Naming creatures by region or tribe is a good start, but even this is often not enough distinction. The same problem extends to every kind of text that appears in the player's user interface. A gift for brief, evocative language is a strength in any writer, of course, but one who becomes accustomed to having at least a full sentence will be sorely disappointed when faced with user interface text.

Though space is tight for this kind of text, many games present worlds of fantasy or science fiction, where invented words are not at all out of place. The rest of the game acts as a text to which the player has access, by definition. Even if the player has not deeply absorbed that text, internal allusions carry as much weight for the game as Biblical references do for poetry. Perhaps more; this connection of ideas enriches both sides of the equation.

The third category of writing, dialogue, seems on the surface to be little different from dialogue in any fiction writing. This category of writing varies widely between different types of games. Flash-based puzzle games, and casual games as a broader category, often have no characters or spoken dialogue at all. At the other extreme, games such BioWare's seminal *Mass Effect* and *Dragon Age* franchises involved thousands of conversations, each with branching options based on the player's choices. *Mass Effect* in particular often presented the player with two to four distinct response options, each of which influenced the direction of the computer-controlled character's response. At the same time, each version of the conversation needs to circle back to the central thrust of the information that the game needs the scene to communicate. The writer's extraordinary challenge here is to write the same scene in three or more distinct versions. Moreover, the writer cannot allow any of those outcomes to so derail the flow of gameplay such that the character cannot proceed. BioWare's games are particularly known for encouraging the player to express his or her own vision of the protagonist, and these dialogue options are the primary means.

On the other hand, dialogue that is rapid-fire in the style of Aaron Sorkin, or twisting and ambiguous like David Mamet, currently has no home in game writing. The time required for player decision-making means that game dialogue cannot derive very much punch from pacing. While it may be possible to let one choice from the player dictate the player's choices in a few further salvos, eventually the conversation has to grind to a halt to let the player make another choice. The closest that player-chosen dialogue has come to this are the Quick Time Events of *Mass Effect 2* and *Mass Effect 3*, when the player's options are expressed as symbols for the Paragon and Renegade ethical paths, with a default (and valid) option of no key-press that represents an ethically neutral stance.

Games in the *Mass Effect* series also use overheard dialogue and radio snippets extensively. Particularly in the first game, the player frequently travels in elevators as a meta-fiction while the game loads the next area that the player enters. During these sequences, the player's computer-controlled squadmates talk to each other with character-establishing dialogue, or the radio in the elevator plays a news story. Considering how many possible arrangements of two squadmates there are in the game, the game holds a remarkable variety of potential conversations that may come up during this sequence. The radio segments, on the other hand, offer exposition about events going on in the galaxy, or reveal the consequences of the player's choices. This often opens a new side-quest in the player's mission log. The player also overhears conversations between characters in the environment while wandering around, even though the player cannot otherwise initiate interaction with these characters. These too often trigger new side-quests. In this way, *Mass Effect* uses dialogue that doesn't include the protagonist to avoid making the player interact with quest-giving characters. This lends a more naturalistic feel to the way that the player learns about new goals in the game, as compared to the quest-giving NPCs that stand still and request the player's aid in many other games.

BioWare's approach to dialogue-heavy games is hardly the only one, however. Games such as Rocksteady's *Arkham Asylum* and *Arkham City*, and Red Storm's whole line of tactical shooters, involve many hours of dialogue between computer-controlled characters that the player overhears while hidden. Red Storm writer Richard Dansky has commented extensively on the challenges of writing dialogue that communicates interesting, useful, character-revealing information, when the nature of the game is such that the player hears that dialogue repeated dozens or hundreds of times over the course of play. Known within the industry as "barks," this dialogue may range from a single word to a five-minute-long exchange between two or more characters. The game's AI chooses a conversation based on many factors, including minor or major decisions that the player has made up to that point and random rolls within the game's engine. With full control over all speakers in a scene, the writer's work regains some of the attributes of traditional screenwriting, and it seems at times that games set out to top one another in lengthy Tarantino-like digressions.

A still more limited form of dialogue—perhaps more properly called monologue—is found in the *Portal* franchise. In this series, almost all spoken lines come from GLaDOS or Wheatley addressing a completely silent Chell (the player-controlled character). Though one-sided, the writers of these conversations found ways to express the characters of GLaDOS, Wheatley, and Chell in remarkable depth. Lacking a second speaker, the dialogue derives its substantial emotional impact from a combination of pacing and heavy implication; the two games received extensive, industry-wide recognition for their success in communicating story and character.

Bastion, created by Supergiant Games in 2011, is relatively unusual in its style: a narrative voice-over that runs throughout the entire game and delivers almost all of the game's exposition, including extensive action sequences punctuated by a voice-over telling stories about the game's characters. Over the course of the game, the player discovers that the narrator is actually a character in the game, and personally responsible for some of the game's plot. The narrative style is even more unusual in that it responds to the player's choices without breaking the illusion of the narrator's omniscient perspective. A modest amount of additional exposition comes from the flavor text available for weapons, drinks, and shrine idols. Other than the narrator, the only voice in the game is a song with lyrics, which is again revealed to be the voice of a character in the game.

As with other categories of writing, the video game creators are compelled to assume that players ignore the game's dialogue. A player might miss audible dialogue, of course, by playing the game muted. More commonly, gamers assume that dialogue is keeping them from the action and hurry through it with whatever key presses the game allows, and few—if any—games have a mechanic for allowing the player the review previous conversations, skipped or otherwise. Information that presents a gameplay-blocking issue if the player misses it must always be available elsewhere, whether that is an automatic journal function, a detailed mission log, or elements of the user interface that point the character toward the next step along the way. This does not make the dialogue writer's job unimportant, any more than the technical writer's job is.

Writing flavor text is important as well. Flavor text is the writing that hangs out around the edges of the game, providing further context for those players who are motivated to engage with the game's setting more deeply. Of course, this only applies to games that present a setting in the first place; many puzzle games and abstract strategy games do not have even an implied setting. The games that do include flavor text vary widely in their depth of presentation. The media for flavor text vary likewise, from a sentence of two of description attached to an item in the world, to an in-depth journal function, to graffiti on the walls, to an entire library of readable books within the game. If carried far enough, the discovery of such flavor text ceases to be merely about the setting, and becomes a mini-game designed to appeal to completionists and explorers.

For example, *Fallen Earth* includes a few lines of description in the tooltip of almost every item in the game. Some items have text relevant to the game's mechanics, but the majority communicate the game's sense of gallows humor, which grows out of the game's setting, a post-apocalyptic wasteland in which all player characters are highly disposable clones. Much of this flavor text focuses on how the technology is jury-rigged, most food has spoiled, and the world has descended into chaos. Particularly in combination with the game's dialogue, this communicates a tone that takes its bleakness to a deliberately absurd level.

Similarly, *Portal* and *Portal 2* use graffiti as a primary vehicle for telling the game's story and building tension, often providing a counterpoint to the dialogue spoken by GLaDOS, who is presented as malicious and deceitful. Text and crude images presented in graffiti further reveal the story of other characters in the broader narrative—characters that are dead before the start of the narrative and never appear on-screen in any form. Much of this graffiti is hidden from plain view, so that players who care deeply about exploration are rewarded with additional aspects of the narrative or Easter eggs.

Three other franchises, though, have made extensive usage of flavor text in defining features of their games: *Mass Effect* and *Dragon Age* (also by BioWare), and *The Elder Scrolls*, by Bethesda Softworks. Each game of the *Mass Effect* series has had an in-game encyclopedia of the setting, with entries on every element of the setting: places, organizations, weapons, characters, and so on. The game reveals these entries after the initial mention of the setting element. Players who ignore the encyclopedia may do so without feeling that they have missed out on the game's narrative, but players who dive into it discover a staggering depth and breadth of writing invested in areas of the setting that are technically optional. While many players do choose to ignore the material, the text was a major factor in building the franchise's hardcore fan base. The flavor text gives the setting depth, from which it gains a sense of reality. For all that it is dense expository text, though, the action continues until the player decides to pause the game and read up. While there are business realities that provide a theoretical upper limit to how much writing of this kind a game's writers can include in the game, high-quality writing pays dividends for player investment in the setting.

Dragon Age follows a similar structure, with a character journal that also includes every in-setting text that the player comes across. These take the form of letters, journals, treatises, and so forth. The games of the *Elder Scrolls* series, most recently *Skyrim*, go still further, making all of their optional world exposition into in-setting documents, ranging from journals to one-act plays. Moreover, players collect these works and store them in quite large bookshelves, allowing characters to join in on their players' bibliophile tendencies. Many of the stories contained in these works touch only lightly on the action of the game or the parts of the setting that the player can experience directly. Such works become a kind of miscellaneous entertainment, a digression from the game's core activity.

The last category of writing for games is writing the overarching narrative. Unlike other categories, the player typically interacts with this text only indirectly. At the same time, this is the writing that gives the player something to do; in games with divergent narratives, the player's choices interact with this writing, often through the medium of dialogue. The player may not give extensive thought to the narrative, but it cannot be skipped. One may play a game—successfully or otherwise—without engaging the text of the user's manual, the tutorial, almost all of the dialogue (though that would be a challenge in guessing what to do next), or flavor text, but in games that possess overarching narrative, it is nearly nonsensical to speak of avoiding or rejecting the text. There are, of course, sandbox games without an overarching narrative, or games in which the player can diverge wildly from the path the designers intended. *Shadow of the Colossus* by Sony Computer Entertainment is particularly noted for at least raising the question of this kind of gameplay; the world is lushly rendered, but there is no action the player can take to move the game forward but to engage in violence, which the game's plot eventually reveals to be ill-considered; in a sense it is a story questioning the reader's submission to the imperative to engage the plot.

The paradox of game-writing, then, is its difference from writing for traditional, non-interactive entertainment. In a traditional narrative, the audience can end the experience by closing the book or leaving the theater, or perhaps watching a movie with the sound turned off. The text cannot usually be identified as unnecessary to the experience, and the audience does not demand that the experience be largely unchanged if they do elect to ignore large portions of the work. In games, players have been taught to shape the experience to their own tastes of the moment. The community does (broadly speaking) demand that the game remain comprehensible and enjoyable even when much of the text is disregarded, up to and including basic instructions on how to proceed in consuming the text. This is the guiding constraint of the game-writer's work: to make the writing compelling, but disposable; gripping, but easy to ignore.

18 Game Writing in Practice— MMORPG Quests

Joshua Peery

Writing in video games? Wait, aren't video games supposed to be computer programs or interactive movies? What writing? The fact is that even the simplest of games have written text even if it is only the title, the directions how to play, or just "Ready, Player 1." Opposite of this lack of written text were some of the earliest PC video games that were completely text-based games like Infocom's venerable *Zork*. Writing in (and around) video games is, at its root, used for the same purpose language is used: to convey information, be it technical or evocative.

Writing for video games is unique from other writing disciplines in that it is not a monolithic, singular, style. For example, screenwriting, by and large has a unified format and style that practitioners are taught or learn in order to conform to accepted industry expectations. Likewise, there are whole oceans of ink used to delineate proper academic writing and governing bodies, such as the Modern Language Association, that are custodians of these rules.

Much like the free-wheeling video games industry, the writing that goes into the games themselves is a new frontier that has only been practiced the past few decades. The study of such writing is even newer, where the only previous consideration of it has been largely through games reviewers and critics. Often, game writing was done out of necessity and the writing was rather organic, tasked to whomever had the penchant for the job. This first wave of video game writers were often the games' programmers and engineers. As the industry has gained traction as a reliable money maker, serving immensely more people than it had been in the small niche population of video game enthusiasts, firms have begun to hire individuals specifically to write for the games. If there is anything like "rules" for video game writing they are largely developed in-house at the firms that develop video games.

These video game writers have often matriculated from English, Drama, Film, and other Humanities programs. Just as often, these individuals have also practiced in other writing fields such as writing novels, comic books/graphic novels, technical writing, or tabletop/pen-and-paper game design. This influx of people that have specific writing training and experience have adapted their disciplines and methods into working conventions for video game writing.

Sometimes these conventions will travel as people who have used them take things learned at one firm to another. Recently, the volatility and lay-offs in the video game industry has stirred the pot of video game writing conventions, strategies, and methods. This has caused some homogenization of the process and methods of video game writing.

Focusing on one area of the industry, this has especially been the case for firms developing Massively Multiplayer Online Role-Playing Games. Since the huge success of *World of Warcraft*, many firms have sought to replicate the formula that brought such acclaim and profits to Blizzard Entertainment. One key area that made *WoW* stand out from precursors such as *Ultima Online* and *Everquest* was the concept of questing or missions. Beyond simply being a world populated by monsters to kill to pursue the "gear grind," *WoW* added new levels of story beyond what the players generated on their own. MMORPGs now had to tell a story and this new form of media, like film and televison before it, would require writing. Video Game writing, as mentioned above, is to impart information. The can be information for the players or for the video game designers themselves. This information can be divided into many different contexts and each of these essentially require a sub-discipline of video game writing.

THE READERS

Writing for an MMO is typically directed toward one or more of the following three distinct audiences:

1. Informed Insiders[1]
2. Exclusively Internal stakeholders
3. Game Players

The informed insider writing is directed at those who are close to a video game project but not necessarily a part of day-to-day writing or design. Documents written for these readers, who may or may not be employees of the developing firm, are often protected by Non-Disclosure Agreements. An example of this is a Game Design Document. The GDD is a high-level document that outlines a game's back-story, core mechanics, games systems, and important features. Often this document is used to outline a game's potential to investors, prospective and new employees, and outside consultants and contractors. An example of writing that does not require a non-disclosure agreement (NDA) for the informed insider are public relations materials to be disseminated to video gaming press, news websites, blogs, via fan kits, and advertising outlets.

The writing that goes into such documents is often equal parts creative, technical, and marketing techniques. Usually there is no single author of writing that is intended for the Informed Insider. Creative and Narrative Designers contribute to the writing with samples of stories from the game, Systems Designers outline, in a technical fashion, the core systems, and PR and marketing polish the package for the intended reader.

Writing intended for the exclusively internal reader often takes a very informative turn. The style is more technical, even when describing the fluff[2] of the game's story, locations, and characters.

The writing of this nature is often found in documents describing "best practices," data naming conventions, content development flow, zone briefings, iconic character bios and traits, style guides, and more. It is these in-house documents that are the source of what is the beginning of a coherent and recognizable writing method for video games. They act as a guide to unify design/writing styles and ensuring that anyone charged with writing text for the game has all the rules and advice as needed. Features of such documents include a collection of rules and tips to ensure consistent word choice, spelling, character count, etc. The ultimate goal is to ensure consistency in all text written for the game. The later part of this chapter, where common MMORPG writing methods are discussed, will largely be in this format.

Video game writing is mainly focused on the game player. This writing needs to convey everything from the story to how to play. It is this writing that will help pay the bills and ultimately be part of how a game will be judged and contribute to its success. This is especially true of MMORPGs. A game can have the most stunning visuals, an excellent end-game, etc., but if the writing does not engage and hold the player's interest from the beginning, through the leveling process, none of that will make a difference.

While the writing for the informed insider and the exclusively internal are vital parts of video games, these types of writing can be explored via the traditional studies of marketing and technical writing. The emerging field of writing for the game player is what will be the primary focus here.

VIDEO GAME WRITING IN MMORPGS

Probably the largest amount of writing that goes into the production of a video game is the writing and designing of quests[3]. Many quests in MMORPGs share a lot of similar basic components or elements. Often, besides using the correct dialects, editorial basics, and tone; each of these facets often will have unique stylistic needs and concerns. These can include the content of the text, user interface constraints, such as text-character counts, and the voice of NPC[4] speakers' dialogue, or the purpose of other UI story text.

In most MMORPGs, quests are often composed of similar basic pieces, in a basic structure that has become familiar to players. The quests are usually delivered to players as NPC dialogue or UI text panels in the game. Not all parts of the quest text are necessary for every quest, and often additional dialogue is added to be seen under certain circumstances. Many games also include before-and-after quest summaries that describe the quests in a longer format, usually in a virtual journal or log book UI.

One major concern that has arisen in MMORPG design is the dreaded "wall-of-text." This phenomenon often occurs when the designer is trying to relay too much in a single space. When players are confronted with these, they often by-pass the entire text, thus missing the quest information that was required. This in turn can lead to player frustration from not knowing exactly what they should be doing and decreased connection to the game via the missed story. This fallout is in opposition to the goal of succeeding in delivering to the player an enjoyable experience.

Methods by which writers can avoid the wall-of-text:

1. Text Character Limits
2. Interactive Dialogue
3. Cinematics

Managing character limits (including letters, numbers, punctuation and other characters as well as spaces) is important for consistent editorial style. In the past, characters were often limited by UI constraints and this can also still be a case due to UI aesthetics more than issues with the software. As the issue of "wall-of-text" grew, the character limit has became a more voluntary design decision.

In the age of Twitter, a popular target size for electronic text is the 140-character limit. This ballpark figure is often used for anything deemed "required text." Required text is usually any text that stays on the screen, requiring a player response. Short enough to read quickly, the idea behind this character limit is so players will not miss the most salient points of the narrative.

The use of interactive dialog can also be used to shorten any narrative elements that would normally far exceed character text limits. In practice, the text is divided up into a dialog between the player and the NPC. These can often be optional or require a decision from the player beyond "yes" or "no." These elements can also help to further player engagement in the storyline. Stylistically, the text will often resemble a screen-play or gamebook.[5] Furthermore, if these pieces of dialog are required text, then a text character limit and a text box limit may apply. For example, if a quest dialogue is limited to 140 characters, the overall dialogue should not exceed four, 70-character dialogue boxes. This would double the space of the narrative text without becoming too onerous on the player.

Cinematic representations of narrative, due to the investment of time and resources, are usually reserved for key moments of the story. However, the adage "a picture is worth a thousand words" works overtime for a MMORPG. The written preparation for implementing a cinematic is very similar to film screenwriting. To produce the desired cinematic, the same or similar screenplay elements should be used. Establishing shots, actions, character dialogue, parentheticals, etc., all necessary for a film, are useful for the design of a narrative cinematic.

QUEST TEXT

This writing element is the key support for most narratives in a traditional MMORPGs. The writing style however varies depending on the particular element of the quest that requires text. These elements range from the quest's title to the summary in the player's journal.

TITLES

Quest titles range in length from a single word to a complete sentence. The majority of titles should be relatively easy to understand and relevant to the goals of the quest. However, the title should not simply repeat the quest's objectives.

Many designers have succumbed to the temptation to add humor, puns, pop-culture, and other "real-world" references to their quest titles. There is a possibility for it to become too much, especially if the reference does not hold up well over time. This goes double for using the Internet meme de jour.

The following are good rules of thumb:

- The reference should at have at least some bearing or relation to the quest content.

- Do not specifically reference other intellectual property or trademarks.

- Spread a reference over several quest titles in short chain.

Two bad (and real) examples:

- "Baron's Chat" (a pun referencing the infamous *WoW* chat channel, but in a non-Blizzard game.)

- An entire quest chain featuring titles made up of out-of-context lines from Yeats, but spoken in a Yoda-like fashion.

Titles are the first bit of writing that can set the tone for the entire player experience and should be given more than cursory thought.

QUEST GREETING / OFFER / INTRODUCTION STRINGS

After the quest objectives and instructions, the introduction element is the second most important piece of writing the video game designer will use. This is the actual offer the NPC or other quest-delivering mob[6] is presenting to the player. The Greeting string, often in a limited amount of characters, has to convey a lot of information. The key thing to grasp is that the Intro does not stand alone and that the overall story is carried by the entire quest system and UI.

When writing Offers, the dialogue does not need not repeat specifics that will be found in the the quest objectives. The Greeting String exists to provide space for basic exposition, NPC flavor, and a bit of narrative. The main point is to mask the various quest archetypes that will be encountered many times over the course of the leveling cycle. "Kill ten rats in my basement." is an example of over-easy writing and can become a crutch where every task equals "Kill [x] [mob] [where]."

While this line can make an excellent quest objective, it fails to bring the quest alive.

A punched-up Intro could be:

> "Horrible! Those dirty creatures are eating all my grain! I shoo them out, but they come right back. Could you be a dear and take care of them for me?"

The primary role of the Greeting string is to present the quest objectives in a narrative fashion and to get the player invested. As shown in the "ten rats" example above, care should be taken not to use the same formulaic construction for every Intro line.

Important facets of a Greeting String should include the NPC:

1. Presenting a problem or conflict
2. Presenting a possible solution
3. Asks the player to solve the problem or conflict

Often the "presents solution" feature can be left out if it is obvious or easily inferred. This can save a lot time and as importantly, character space. Again, rigidly sticking to the above features will create patterns game writers will want to avoid. Also, not every quest need be presented in the form of a question. Commands and statements can work just as well for Intro elements.

For example, the above Greeting String could be written:

> "If this village wants fresh bread then you better get rid of the rats eating my grain!"

Thus, the Intro element should be the dramatic enticement to the quest rather than simply "go there, do this."

Player Response / Accept Strings

The next element of dialogue in a quest is most often spoken by the player character as they accept or decline a quest. For most cases, this line should be kept as a simple as possible without any dialect or exhortation.

In cases where player-character races exhibit a specific dialect, responses that are a normal part of their lexicon can be used.

The writing should try not force RP features onto what should mainly be an acknowledgment of the quest or a reiteration of what the NPC stated to reinforce the player investment in the quest.

INTERACTIVE DIALOGUE

Dialogue between the quest giver and the player can often go beyond the Intro and Accept elements of the quest. Often these sorts of conversations can offer chances to open longer quest chains and further cement the player's interest. Interactive Dialogue can also offer the player chances to role-play their character and elevates the RP in the MMO.

These dialogues can even provide for alternate avenues for the player to approach the resolution of a quest. For example, the quest giver could ask whether or not the player would like to attack a castle gate or to sneak in. How the player arrives at the next part of the quest chain is then decided by the player and further promotes player investment in the narrative by promoting ownership of actions.

QUEST ACCEPTED STRINGS

These quest elements can be written as further encouragement to the player or as a final piece of advice or clue about the quest. However, they should not be used to hold a vital piece of information. The writer may also use these to form a pseudo-dialogue where the NPC replies to the player's previous response. Also, the text could be used to provide small pieces of the big picture narrative.

Exit/Decline String

These written lines are the NPC's attempt to manipulate the player into reconsidering their choice to decline the quest offer. They are primarily for extending NPC flavor and narrative elements and should not be used to reveal any new information about the quest.

Possible roles the NPC can take when turned down:

Insulting: The NPC taunts the player about being turned down.
Pleading: Where the NPC expresses truly their need for the player to reconsider.

Stoically: The NPC accepts the player's refusal and re-offers the quest.

Examples of Exit Strings from a quest to fight Orcs:

(Taunt)
What's the matter? Afraid of getting your hands dirty? I've seen goblin children braver than you.

(Emotional)
If you won't help, I'm not sure the villagers will survive the next Orc attack! Please!

(Gracious)
Well, if you change your mind those Orcs will still be out there.

These little pieces of narrative, though they may go largely unseen, can further enhance the immersion and vitality of the game world.

QUEST ACHIEVED / REWARD STRINGS

Writing in these elements makes for a good time to hook the player's interest in the quest narrative even more. As a convention, the player can be conditioned to see if any clues to the next step in a quest chain or information about rewards will be written here. The format style for these string is often congratulatory, however a writer should not fall into the pattern of using similar expressions too often. Twist endings, if artfully done, are also communicated here and the quest giver could even be hostile because the player managed to survive the task they were set upon.

The elements, structurally, usually should restate what the player has accomplished. Also, this is where the writer can hint at the next step in the story or acknowledge the reward the player is about to receive. If the quest is of particular significance it may be a good place to use a cinematic that will render the same information that is found in the reward string, just on a grander scale.

REWARD / ACHIEVED STRING EXAMPLES:

(After the player was attacked unexpectedly while on a "simple" mission.)
You're telling me a Dark Energy Entity attacked? Unheard of! Take this chit, no time to debrief you. I must report this to Command. Stick around, you'll have new orders!

(After a quest to recover magical weapons.)

You have found them! We shall put them to good use in our fight. You have truly earned the right to wield one of Z'asha's blades. Be ready.

The reward strings above hit the three major points that should be present: restate the action, mention reward, and drops a hint to next quest. All of these serve to re-engage the player to the game and build the player's own sense of narrative and accomplishment.

Player Finish Strings

These sorts of strings should be written as a counterpoint to the Player Response/Accept Strings, and should be similar in style and rules. Since the previous NPC Reward / Achieved String usually restates what was just accomplished and rewards the player, then this text should be written as the socially appropriate way to respond. This usually will take some form of "Your welcome."

Also this string can be used to create a short conversational bridge between the NPC's Quest Reward/Achieved String and the NPC's Finished String.

Examples

> By your command, Sir.
> It will be an honor to wield Z'asha's Blade

These relatively small pieces of text are important as they help to build the game world's immersion and set a tone for the quests.

NPC "Busy" Strings: Not Yet, Incomplete, and Finished Strings

Busy Strings are pieces of conditional text the player will receive if they interact with the quest giving NPC at certain times. These strings help in rounding out the player's experience with the NPC and pragmatically cue the player to other information.

Not Yet Strings are seen when the player interacts with a quest giver prior to being able to take the quest offered. Circumstances such as being too low of level for the content, missing a certain factional standing or requirement, or anything other prerequisite the player is lacking should be communicated by the NPC here. These can take any sort of tone, from gruff and impatient, to gracious and helpful.

Examples

> (Not enough faction)
> Hey kid, I don't know if we can trust you yet. Maybe if you took out more bandits, we could talk.
> (Not high enough level)
> Darlin' aren't you just the cutest! But, I wouldn't want you to get hurt. Try back when you've seen more action.

Incomplete Strings are dialogue seen by the player when they interact with the Quest giving NPC when the quest has been accepted, but not yet achieved. Stylistically, Incomplete strings are free to focus on reiterating the objective, since they are not technically required for the player to read. However, since it may be safe to assume the player wants to read this text for that sort of information, any redundancy can be considered acceptable.

These lines should be written from the standpoint of familiarity with the player character. Thus, no reiteration of introduction information is required. The NPC could also be written in a confrontational tone as to express uncertainty that the player can finish the quest at hand.

Structurally, they should usually, though not necessarily, include a restatement of the objective.

Examples:

> The cellar door is around back, those horrible creatures are still down there.
> How goes the search? The battle will not be won until you have delivered the Blades of Z'asha.

Finished Strings often are used to cap a quest or chain of quests and are a final word from the NPC. These pieces of text should contain no essential information, but exist to enhance the game world and narrative. Also, these are often used as text the player will see if they interact with the NPC whose quests have been completed and can serve to further acknowledge, or depending on the NPC, denigrate the player's success.

Examples

> Sorry, I don't have any more work for you.
> The rats are still gone, thank the gods!

The Busy strings are often low priority to the video game writer, but the extra effort can really lend polish to the game world and make it a more living, less static place.

STORY/SUMMARY STRINGS

Story/Summary Strings are often written in two forms: present and past tense to reflect a active and completed quest. The active text should sum up the quest in a narrative fashion that is often termed a neutral GM[7] voice. The text, often located in the player's Journal, Log, or UI mission tracker, serves to sum up the quest situation for the player. Completed Summary Strings are available once the quest is over and are usually found in the player's Quest Journal or Mission Log. These may be viewed by the player for the rest of the game, forming an important part of the narrative record for the player.

These strings do not usually need to be in any particular NPC voice. However, they need not be sterile, either. The tone can be biased toward the player, applauding and stoking the fire of their triumph. The player's actions may be described as heroic and the enemies deeds to be derided and belittled. If the UI Journal aspect is taken in a literal sense the written voice could even be that of the PC and use the first person point of view.

Structurally, active summaries need to contain the pertinent information, reiterating the quest's goals and other important facts. The completed summaries can lose the "nuts-and-bolts" parts of the quest in favor of focusing on the key player actions and results.

GAME/GOAL/OBJECTIVE STRINGS

Goals and Objectives are the most important part of the quest. These strings must convert the entire quest into a simple text format. This is where game writing takes a turn from creative writing to something more akin to technical writing. Due to this the rules and style are radically different than in other areas of the quest element writing.

Game Strings needs to include all the information a player will require to finish a quest. This means the text needs to stand alone as if the player never read a single line of the dialogue or other elements of the quest writing. Where possible, the Game string should occupy only a single line in the UI using as few characters as possible. Style-wise the writer should use capitalization of people, places, and goals.

Word choice is the most important rule for writing a Game string and there must by consistent usage across all Game Strings of similar objective types. Below are some of the most commonly used objective words/phrases and examples of usage:

> Kill: Accomplished by killing a target or targets.
>
> Kill the Huge Rats
>
> Collect: Accomplished when the player has acquired the items in question.
>
> Collect Seed Pods from Hydra Weeds
>
> Use: Accomplished when the player interacts with a (usually) static object or by utilizing an item.
>
> Use the LifeNET Console
>
> Escort: Accomplished by protecting a NPC mob that is moving between points.
>
> Escort Mya Redfield back to Odenville
>
> Go to: Accomplished by moving to a particular location in the game world.
>
> Go to Bag End near Hobbiton.
>
> Talk with/to: Accomplished by the player interacting with one or more particular NPC(s)
>
> Talk to Lynn Anderson in Odenville
>
> Notable variants:
>
> Hunt: Accomplished by killing a target that moves across a large area or only spawns[8] only under certain conditions
>
> Hunt for One-Fang near Split-Paw
>
> Defeat/Fight: Similar to Kill, however with a less lethal outcome.
>
> Defeat the Midway Mutual Pain Society
>
> Defend: Similar to Escort, however the NPC (or location) being defended is static, or otherwise not moving.
>
> Defend Sheriff Darkwater from White Crow Soldiers
>
> Find: Similar to Go to, but could mean the area where the player must go is less defined by the game's map, could possibly

have a very small target area, or even no waypoints to guide
the player.
Find the Blessed Shrine in the Great Forest
Persuade/Convince: Similar to Talk To, but may require specific dialogue choices to be made by the player via interactive
dialogue.
Persuade Mayor Bancroft for the Refugees

It should be noted that these are just a small sample of quest types that
are used by various MMORPGs and as games become more sophisticated, the need for more word choices may arise.

GM Voice Quest Elements

Often the need arises for an inanimate object or quest giver without a
usual way to communicate, to "offer" a quest. Most GM Quest strings
are simply narration that takes the place of NPC dialogue.

Stylistically, the writing for these should often be neutral and matter-
of-fact. Unlike dialogue, which can be a little more flexible, GM Voice
should usually use a simpler structure:

Tell the player specific details of what they see. (Beyond what is
graphically on screen.)
Tell the player the meaning of what they see.
Tell the player what to do with or about what they've seen.

Examples

(A severed human ear near a chained up dog shows a Quest
Offer Icon)

Quest Intro String
There is a severed ear near Napalm's tether. Who did the dog
savage and where did they go?

Accepted String
You notice some blood and footprints leading out of town.

Reward String
The ear's owner was a bandit trying to sneak into town! Napalm
is good watch dog.

Busy Strings:

Not Yet String

Gross! The dog bit off someone's ear! Maybe you can track them later after gaining some experience.

Incomplete String

The ear has attracted some ants. The trail of ear's owner is getting cold.

Finished String

The ear is starting to smell.

The use of GM voiced quests helps break up the monotony of usual NPC quest givers and can add a notion of self-determined questing to the players.

Overall, quest writing in MMORPGs is a new and particular genre of video game writing. In this chapter, I have attempted to show how, even though relatively new, there are starting to be recognizable rules and conventions that are discernible to those who play, design and study games. By utilizing a unique hybrid of screenwriting, creative, and technical writing; video game writing is becoming its own, new area of expertise and study.

Notes

1. The term *insider* is used here as shorthand for someone who has more knowledge of the video game's details than the average enthusiast.

2. Fluff is a common pen-and-paper game industry term that has crossed-over to video games, denoting a back-story.

3. Quests or missions can be any sort of task or activity that the game designer uses to guide players through the game and leveling process.

4. Non-Player Character: a term inherited from pen-and-paper games. Here it denotes computer-controlled characters.

5. Branching narrative books made famous by Bantam Books' "Choose Your Own Adventure" book series.

6. Shorthand for mobile, or sometimes movable object in MMORPGs.

7. GM for Game Master: a term inherited from pen-and-paper games. Where the GM controlled the game and told players what they say, heard, and felt; the computer game program and graphics substitute for most duties.

8. Spawning is when a NPC or other game mob is available in the game world.

Contributors

Eric Alexander researches data visualization, with a particular focus on visual exploration of large text corpora. A member of the University of Wisconsin Graphics Group, his broader research interests include human-computer interaction, digital humanities, machine learning, and procedural rhetoric.

Phill Alexander has a deep interest in issues of technology/digital rhetoric, race and culture, social class, design and visual rhetoric, digital production and publishing, and gaming. His work has appeared in *World of Warcraft and Philosophy: Wrath of the Philosopher King, Multimodal Literacies and Emerging Genres*, and *Kairos: A Journal of Rhetoric, Technology, and Pedagogy*.

James J. Brown, Jr. is Director of the Digital Studies Center at Rutgers University - Camden, where he also teaches in the Digital Humanities program. His work has been published in *College Composition and Communication, The Computer Cultures Reader*, and *The Responsibilities of Rhetoric*. Jim is also an editor of *Enculturation: A Journal of Rhetoric, Writing, and Culture*.

Kym Buchanan is a professor in the School of Education at the University of Wisconsin-Stevens Point. Kym started his career as a high school teacher, and went on to earn his PhD in Learning, Technology, and Culture. His teaching and research include motivation, diversity, and technology. He's currently developing games for teaching civics.

Richard Colby teaches in the University of Denver Writing Program. He co-edited the collection *Rhetoric/Composition/Play through Video Games* and a special issue of the journal *Computers and Composition Online* on gaming and composition. His work on using games in teaching has been published in *Computers and Composition* and *Computers and Composition Online*.

Rebekah Shultz Colby teaches in the University of Denver Writing Program where she teaches courses that use games to teach rhetoric and disciplinary writing. She co-edited the collection *Rhetoric/Composition/Play through Video Games* and a special issue of the journal *Computers and Composition Online* on gaming and composition.

Sean M. Conrey teaches and coordinates the Project Advance program in the English and Textual Studies department at Syracuse University His poetry has appeared in *American Letters and Commentary, Cream City Review, Hayden's Ferry Review, Midwest Quarterly, Notre Dame Review* and *Tampa Review*, among others. He has also recorded an album of original songs, Hosmer and Ninth, recorded with The Mercury City String Band.

Andréa Davis, an aficionado and expert player of *World of Warcraft,* earned her PhD in digital and cultural rhetorics from Michigan State University. Andréa is co-editor of *Metamorphosis: The Effects of Professional Development on Graduate Students* and served as *Kairos* Praxis editor from 2006 to 2012.

Jessica Masri Eberhard studies the ways in which hospital ward teams encounter and teach medical ethics; her research theorizes a "Material, Networked Ethics" for geographically situated work-place locations. Her work on medical and health rhetorics and visual rhetoric has been published in *The Writing Commons* and *Present Tense.*

Douglas Eyman has previously published work on the digital ecologies and economies of video games. His most recent work, *Digital Rhetoric: Theory, Method, Practice* maps the growing field of digital rhetoric, including its relationship to the study of video games as platforms for the performance of writing and rhetoric. He is also the senior editor and publisher of *Kairos: A Journal of Rhetoric, Technology, and Pedagogy.*

Grace Hagood worked on the RPG *Fallen Earth* as a designer and voice actor; she She was completing her third year of doctoral studies in Composition and Rhetoric at the University of South Carolina, where she was pursuing her interests in Computers and Writing, Game Studies, and Digital Humanities. Grace passed away in April of 2013, and her friends and colleagues, Byron Hawk, Mary Fratini, and Stephanie Boone-Mosher completed chapter revisions for this collection.

Steven Keoni Holmes has published articles on a variety of digital interfaces, including videogames, trolling (Anonymous), digital humanities, code (and software studies), networked art, augmented reality apps, eBooks, and mobile media; his work has appeared in *Computational Culture, Rhetoric Review,* and *Enculturation.* He is a founding member of GEAR, a grant-funded project that supports undergraduate research on games.

Brian Ladd teaches computer science at SUNY Potsdam, where he is a member of an interdisciplinary team charged with bringing the arts into STEM curricula. Brian's work has appeared in *Connections,* and *The Journal of Computing Sciences in Colleges.* In 2003, he worked as a video game programmer for Epic Games (Scion Studios).

Jill Morris is involved in national research and service projects dealing with gaming and writing. She was one of the original lead designer and game masters of C's the Day, the annual conference game at the Conference on College Composition and Communication and currently serves on its Board of Directors. Jill is also Reviews Editor for *Kairos: A Journal of Rhetoric, Technology, and Pedagogy.*

Scott Nelson is executive director of a nonprofit for underserved teens and an education and multimedia consultant. He got his start in video games schooling his sisters in matches of *Combat* on the Atari 2600; this published statement serves as proof of his dominance in perpetuity.

Joshua Peery is a veteran video game designer who has worked in several genres and launched the MMO titles *Fallen Earth, Imagine Online,* and *WildStar.* Peery is currently working on the Prologue Games adventure title, *Knee Deep: A Swamp Noir* and is the Lead Game Designer for Serious Games at East Carolina University.

Lee Sherlock has recently published work in the collections *Computer Games and Technical Communication: Critical Methods and Applications at the Intersection* and *Rhetoric/Composition/Play through Video Games: Reshaping Theory and Practice of Writing,* as well as the *Journal of Business and Technical Communication.* His current interests include the roles of genre and activity systems in digital gaming; the design and assessment of serious games; race, class, gender, and sexuality in relation to gaming cultures; and the use of games in writing courses

David M. Sheridan directs the Language and Media Center at Michigan State University. Recent publications include *The Available Means of Persuasion: Mapping a Theory and Pedagogy of Multimodal Public Rhetoric* (2012), co-authored with Jim Ridolfo and Anthony J. Michel, as well as articles in *Enculturation* and *Computers and Composition*.

Wendi Sierra grew up playing NES and Super NES games with her parents and her sisters, although at the time she had no idea just how central these experiences would become to her academic future. She has been collaborating on a series of projects related to ethos in MMORPGs and co-authored "Ode to SparklePony: Gamification in Action" with Kyle Stedman, a winner of the 2011 C's the Day game. Wendi is the creator of BattleShirts™.

Brandes Stoddard is a freelance writer and designer of video, tabletop, and live-action games. Among many other projects, he edited the ENnie-nominated projects *Dawning Star: Operation Quick Launch* and *Helios Rising* for Blue Devil Games, designed the *Race Creation Cookbook* for Louis Porter Jr. Design, and wrote two chapters in *From Here to There* for Goodman Games.

Emi Stuemke researches the intersections of gaming and medical rhetoric. She is an avid digital archivist and disc priest. Emi was the PI on The Genre Project, a research endeavor from the University of North Carolina Writing Program.

Index

Aarseth, Espen, 309, 327, 336
abandonware, 244
Abbott, Rob, 138
ABET, 309, 313, 337
accent, 83, 85, 226
access, 44, 93, 120, 154–155, 161, 207, 211, 213, 219–220, 226, 244, 312, 315, 340–341
accessibility, 44, 151, 248
accountability, 249
achievements, 109, 261, 277
ACLU, 276
Activision, 24, 160, 176, 340
actor, 55, 66, 89, 156, 219
adaptation, 181
addiction, 231
add-ons, 43, 58, 185
Adobe, 92, 212
Aesica, 127–128, 138
aesthetics, 34, 152, 351
AFK, 191
agency, 7, 28–29, 35, 45, 78, 91, 123, 127–128, 135, 221, 258–259, 265, 268, 277
Agincourt, 191
Alberti, John, 64–65, 70
alchemy, 184
Alexander, Jonathan, 111, 216
Alexander, Phill, 232
algebra, 249
algorithm, 28–31, 33, 35–36, 38, 171–172, 282, 311
alternate reality games, 15, 255 –257, 259–263, 266–268

altruism, 63
amateurism, 38
Amazon, 25, 40, 53, 124
anagram, 261
analog, 238, 243
Anand, Pranav, 138
Angello, Anthony John, 69–70
animation, 6, 93, 199, 289, 316–317
animators, 175
anonymity, 138, 225–226, 229
Anthropy, Anna, 25, 33, 34, 38, 39
appropriation, 119–120, 126, 128, 136, 181
arcade, 140, 159–160, 162, 164–166, 168–169, 174, 273
archetype, 189, 191, 193, 353
Aristotle, 30, 285
Armstrong, Johanna, 59–60, 70
ARPAnet, 327
Arroyo, Sarah, 36, 39
artificial intelligence, 199, 249, 343
Asia, 181, 330
Ask, Kristine, 141, 157
assessment, 149, 186, 210, 215, 300
Asteroids, 337
Atari, 159, 167–169, 173, 176
attention, 7, 101, 185, 209, 220, 237, 239, 276, 279, 290–291, 294
attention economy, 101
Australia, 49, 108, 112

authorship, 43–44, 60, 62, 65, 69,
    141, 155, 158, 161–162, 166,
    169, 205, 207, 210, 286
autism, 231, 265
avatar, 24, 33, 47, 103, 198,
    202, 218, 220, 224, 228, 231,
    329–330, 332

Barab, Sasha, 137, 158
Barak, Azy, 122, 138
Barthes, Roland, 32, 39, 283, 299,
    306
Bataille, Georges, 21–23, 29, 31,
    37, 39
Bates, Marlin, 220, 231–232
Becker, Katrin, 333, 337
believability, 268
benchmarks, 83
Benkler, Yochai, 44, 63, 70
Bentley, Jon, 331, 337
Bergin, David A., 290, 306
Bernhardt, Stephen, 312, 337
Bethesda Software., 39
bias, 248, 283
Biesecker, Barbara A., 294, 306
BioWare, 43, 46–47, 49, 51–55,
    57–60, 62, 64–67, 69, 342, 343,
    345
Bitzer, Lloyd, 294, 306
Blair, Carole, 299, 306
Blaise, Furine, 164, 176
Blake, Bill, 9, 17
Blizzard Entertainment, 26, 123,
    125–129, 131, 135–136, 153,
    181–184, 194, 219, 233, 348
blogs, 55, 59, 66, 76, 87, 89,
    92–93, 206, 260, 264–265, 300,
    349
Bogost, Ian, 7–9, 17, 23, 25, 28,
    37–39, 98, 110, 112, 155, 157,
    197, 216, 251, 270, 272–273,
    285–286, 320, 337
Boyle, James, 64, 70

Braid, 255, 270, 272, 286
Brain, Robert, 159–160, 176
Britton, James, 289, 305–306
Brody, Marilyn, 171, 174, 176
Brooke, Collin, 26, 39, 271,
    283–286
Brown, John Seely, 16, 38, 169,
    176, 207, 216, 270
Buchanan, Kym, 16, 288, 305–306
Buddhist, 251
budget, 60, 275–276, 279, 280,
    302
Bui, Trung, 49, 52, 70
Burgess, Thomas, 306
Burghardt, M. David, 309, 337
Burke, Brian, 46, 70
Burney, Nabeel, 51– 52, 71

California, 260
camera, 200, 211
Campbell, Joseph, 212, 216
cancer, 57
canon, 91, 197, 271, 281–282,
    285
capital, 140, 181, 280, 295
capitalism, 26, 31, 63
Caplan, Scott, 225, 233
captions, 55, 265, 292
Cartegena, Antonio, 280, 286
Carter, Chris, 43, 71
cartoon, 80, 165, 201, 258
case studies, 5, 7, 17, 97
cassette, 161–162
Castronova, Edward, 4, 17
catastrophes, 23, 34, 59
CATTt, 36–37
cellphone, 200
Chanel, Guillaume, 232
Chang, Steve, 170, 172, 177
charity, 57, 63
cheating, 125, 128
Chien, Irene, 201, 216
China, 243

Chmiel, Marjee, 147, 158
chora, 36
Chun, Wendy, 26–27, 39
cinematics, 163, 168, 194, 198, 351, 355
circulation, 23, 25–27, 31, 34, 37–38, 55, 59–60, 150, 157, 209, 262, 289, 292–293, 299, 301–302
citizen, 22, 28, 236, 243, 248, 249, 276, 280, 293
citizenship, 304
Clarke, Nick, 108, 112
classical rhetoric, 7, 307, 308
classifications, 170
clickers, 267
climate, 81
cloudsourcing, 64
code, 26, 28, 155, 165–167, 198, 275, 282, 285, 310, 312–313, 315, 318, 321–323, 325, 328–329, 331, 333, 335, 339
    building code, 245–246, 251–252
    hermeneutic code, 283–284
    source code, 26, 169, 320, 322
code switching, 83
coding, 27–28, 166, 322, 331, 335–336
coercion, 47
cognition, 23, 29, 33, 36, 119, 140, 232, 279
Colby, Rebekah Shultz, 17
Colby, Richard, 17, 217
Coleridge, Samuel Taylor, 99, 101, 104–109, 111
collaboration, 51, 122, 132–134, 223, 232, 260, 296, 304, 312, 338
colonization, 47
Colossal Cave Adventure, 327, 337
comics, 80, 272
commons, 64, 172, 175

computer programming, 7, 11, 88, 272, 274, 282, 285, 286, 311, 312, 315
computer science, 309–314, 316, 320–321, 324–325, 327, 330, 335–336
Connors, Robert J., 97, 112
conscience, 249
consciousness, 29
Consigny, Scott, 294, 306
consoles, 159, 160, 162, 174, 219
consumers, 4, 25, 34, 43–45, 51, 57, 66–67, 69, 204, 207, 215, 315, 327
copia, 35
copyleft, 26
copyright, 14, 26, 44, 161–171, 173–175, 177, 210, 215
Costikyan, G., 268
Counter-Strike for Kids, 201–202
Crapart.org, 39
Crawford, Chris, 337
Crawford, Ilene Whitney, 112
credibility, 63, 67, 130, 136, 148, 155
Cross, Tim, 24, 40, 44, 45, 71
crowdsourcing, 25
Crowley, Sharon, 271, 286
Csikszentmihalyi, Mihaly, 290, 306
Culler, Mary Patricia, 166, 176
cultural studies, 5, 9, 98
Cunningham, Ward, 321, 338
curriculum, 15–16, 208, 262, 310, 323–324
Curtin, Pamela, 96
Cushman, Ellen, 301, 306
customization, 214
cybernetic, 176
cyberspace, 122, 137
cybertext, 327
cyborg, 256

Dahlberg, Lincoln, 122, 137
Danielewicz, Jane, 221, 232
Dasenbrock, Reed, 221, 232
database, 152
datamining, 153, 154, 158
Davidson, Cathy, 216
Davidson, Cynthia, 71, 216
Davidsson, Ola, 173, 175
Davis, Diane, 14, 35, 40, 181
Dede, Chris, 290, 306
Del Tufo, Stephanie, 232–233
Deleuze, Gilles, 25
delivery, 7, 209, 261, 267, 270,
    282, 302, 307
Der Untergang, 55
Derrick, T., 337
Derrida, Jacques, 100, 102, 112,
    221
DeVoss, Dànielle, 7, 17, 186, 194,
    301, 303, 306, 307
DeWinter, Jennifer, 6, 17
dialectic, 105
diaries, 10, 108
Dias, Patrick, 288–289, 294–295,
    303, 306
Dibbell, Julian, 122, 136–137
DigiRhet.Net, 7, 17
digital rhetoric, 7, 8, 11, 17, 21,
    23–24, 38, 140–141, 143–144,
    157, 271
Dinan, John S., 312, 337
diplomacy, 47
Disney, 207
diversity, 140, 154, 241, 296, 300
DIY, 12, 24–25, 27, 38
DLC, 43, 52, 57, 71–72
Dobrin, Sid, 295, 306
documentation, 11, 118, 141, 147,
    153, 156, 317, 339
Downfall, 55
Dragon Age, 342, 345
Duval, Erik, 206, 217

Eccles, Jacquelynne, 318, 330, 338
ecocomposition, 306
ecologies, 6–7, 12–13, 25, 99,
    100–101, 109, 117–120, 124,
    127, 132–133, 136, 141, 154,
    157, 219, 227, 241, 243, 285,
    290–292, 295, 301, 304–305
economics, 9, 45, 63–64, 112,
    181, 197
economy, 22–24, 26, 28–31, 33,
    35–36, 38–39, 62–64, 66–68,
    73, 173, 243, 248
ecosystem, 7–8, 117, 121, 123,
    135, 295
Edbauer, Jenny, 27, 40
Ede, Lisa, 152, 157
Educause, 338
Ekman, Inger, 232
Elbow, Peter, 221, 232
Elder Scrolls, 24, 45, 90, 99, 106,
    112, 345
electracy, 36, 39
Elitist Jerks, 144–146, 148,
    150–151, 157–158
embodiment, 143, 220
emotion, 31, 60–61, 68, 109, 203,
    290
Entertainment Software Associa-
    tion, 5, 18, 121, 137
entropy, 296
Epicus, 212–213, 216
epistemology, 29, 99, 242
epitexts, 118
Erasmus, 35
ergodic literature, 327
Estell, John, 314, 337
ethics, 17, 29, 44, 46, 60, 63, 236,
    248, 250–251
ethnicity, 252
ethnography, 5, 9, 108, 186
ethos, 52, 55, 58, 63, 69, 119,
    127, 136, 144, 155, 193, 218,
    227, 231

Etter, Katherine, 229, 233
Everquest, 219, 228, 233, 348
exigence, 197, 274, 289, 294–302, 304–305
expertise, 111, 136, 156, 157, 171, 361
Eyman, Douglas, 3, 111, 117, 135, 137, 141, 157, 256

Facebook, 44, 57–58, 137, 261, 264
Faigley, Lester, 7, 17, 289–299, 306–307
failure, 33, 35, 46, 54, 84, 131, 192, 224, 313–314, 317, 339, 341
fandom, 52
fanzines, 293
FDA, 263, 264
feedback, 45, 51, 61, 67, 93, 111, 123, 126–128, 154, 186, 258, 261, 331, 333–334
Feenberg, Andrew, 235, 252
Feldman, Stuart, 321, 337
feminist, 137
Ferrari, Simon, 39
Fincham, Ben, 108, 112–113
Flanagan, Mary, 25, 40, 98, 110, 112
flashbacks, 60, 255
flashforwards, 255
Flikr, 205
Flowerday, Terri, 290, 307
football, 90, 110
Fosk, Kate, 199, 203–204, 216
Foucault, Michel, 64, 71
Freedman, Aviva, 288, 306
freeware, 26–27
frequently asked questions, 118, 137, 145–146, 150, 155, 157, 199, 214, 216

Gabrieli, John, 232, 233

Gagnon, Rebecca, 312, 337
Game Maker, 24
Game Salad, 27
gamification, 46, 261
Gardiner, Josh, 11, 18, 96, 154, 158
Gaudiosi, John, 58, 71
Gauld, Alan, 105, 112
Gee, James Paul, 3, 5, 17, 23, 40, 46, 71, 75–76, 79, 96, 98, 112, 120, 137, 145, 157, 229, 260, 268, 290, 295, 307, 337
gender, 9, 183, 226, 252, 318
Genette, Gérard, 118, 137
genre, 6, 8, 10–11, 16, 35, 38, 44, 45–46, 50, 65, 92–95, 106, 117, 142, 146, 150, 154, 156, 168, 173, 182, 189, 196, 200, 257, 267, 272, 297, 309, 318, 327–328, 361
Gere, Anne, 305, 307
gesture, 154, 162, 227
Ghosh, Shubba, 170, 176
gift economy, 21, 32, 175
Glasser, Alan, 164–165, 176
globalization, 9
Glorious Trainwrecks, 12, 21, 24, 40
Goldberg, David Theo, 207, 216
Grabill, Jeffrey, 301, 305–306
graffiti, 344–345
griefing, 134
Gross, Kyle, 5, 159, 170, 172–173, 176, 361
Guattari, Félix, 25
guild charters, 10
guilds, 10, 78, 84, 106, 118, 181, 183, 185, 188, 190, 192–193, 223, 230–231, 292
Gurak, Laura, 65
Guzdial, Mark, 316, 337

Habermas, Jürgen, 39, 252

habit, 37
Hacker, Michael, 309, 313, 337
Halflife, 45
Halo, 4, 90, 204, 210, 260, 268
Hardaker, Claire, 122, 137
hardware, 162, 170, 172, 207,
    319, 333
Harrigan, Pat, 217, 257, 268
Harris, Roy, 221, 232
Harrison, Anthony, 159, 256
Hawhee, Debra, 271, 286
Hawisher, Gail, 5, 9, 18, 96, 158
Hawk, Byron, 30–32, 40, 104–
    105, 111–112
Hayes, Elisabeth, 23, 220, 232
Hayles, N. Katherine, 281–282,
    286–287
Haynes, Cynthia, 291, 307
Heidegger, Martin, 30, 238–239,
    251–252
hermeneutics, 38, 283–284
Herring, Susan, 123, 137
heuretics, 36–37
heuristic, 9, 23, 29–31, 33, 36, 38,
    41, 98, 102, 208
Heuvelman, Ard, 122, 138
Hindmarch, Will, 258, 268
Holmevik, Jan, 291, 307
holocaust, 40
Homo Ludens, 102, 112, 137
Hufford, Patrick, 188, 194
Huizinga, Johan, 102, 112, 137
human-computer interaction, 194
humanities, 3–4
Hunt, Andrew, 310, 337, 359
Hunter, Rik, 132, 155, 158
Husserl, Edmund, 238, 251–252
hyperreal, 31
hypertext, 36, 77, 312, 322

I Love Bees, 260

identity, 5, 15, 60, 64, 94, 95, 102,
    122–123, 126, 145, 157, 181,
    186, 218–221, 224–231
ideology, 23, 29
imagery, 203
iMovie, 211
imperialism, 109
infrastructure, 109, 118, 171, 281,
    295, 301
intellectual property, 14, 43, 64,
    159–161, 164, 166, 169–170,
    174–175, 352
Interactive Fiction Awards, 327
interface, 10–11, 76–78, 80, 92,
    117, 156, 182–185, 187, 218,
    222–223, 227, 245, 247, 259,
    285, 301, 319, 324–325, 328,
    331, 339, 341
intertextuality, 303–304
invention, 12–13, 16, 23–24,
    27–33, 35–38, 41, 97, 99,
    101–102, 105, 111–112, 159,
    169, 186–188, 271, 273–274,
    277–279, 281–286
invisibility, 138
iPhone, 25
irony, 62, 304

Jackson, Zoevera Ann, 46, 71, 112
Järvelä, Simo, 231–232
Jenkins, Henry, 14, 119, 120–121,
    126, 128, 130, 137, 192,
    204–207, 213, 216
Job-Sluder, Kirk, 137
Johansen, Joseph, 17
Johnson, Matthew S. S., 6, 17,
    119, 127, 136, 138
Johnson-Eilola, Johndan, 65, 75,
    96, 208, 216, 308
Jones, Sydney, 121, 138
journalism, 44, 166, 282
Juul, Jesper, 37, 255, 268

Kain, Erik, 62, 67, 72
kairos, 191, 193, 297
Kambe, Charles, 229, 233
Kameen, Paul, 104, 105
Karcher, Mary, 255–256
Katz, Steven, 40
Keating, Elizabeth, 226, 232
Kernighan, Brian, 337
Kerr, Aphra, 310, 338
Kiesler, Sara, 318, 330, 338
Kinect, 52, 72
King, Joseph, 124, 131, 138
Kinneavy, James, 298, 307
Kitchens, Marshall, 46, 72
Kivikangas, J. Matias, 232
Klinger, Shana Lieberman, 229, 233
Klopfer, Eric, 196, 197–198, 216
Kongregate, 340
Koster, Ralph, 258, 268
Kravchenko, Alexander, 221, 232
Kress, Gunther, 6, 17, 208, 216, 299, 307

labor, 9, 26, 208, 214, 279
labyrinth, 72
Ladd, Brian, 11, 16, 309, 313–314, 338
lag, 192
Laird, John E., 320, 338
LAN, 227
Land, Nick, 40
Lanham, Richard, 101, 112
Lapidot-Lefler, Noam, 122, 138
laptop, 94, 211, 244
Latour, Bruno, 68, 72
lawsuits, 14, 175–177
Layar, 27
leadership, 5, 47–48
Leeroy Jenkins, 14, 181–182, 188, 193–195
Left4Dead, 45
legislation, 4, 161, 250

Lehdonvirta, Vili, 45–46, 72
Lehman, Stephen, 290, 307
Lenhart, Amanda, 121, 138
Lessig, Lawrence, 44, 207, 216
Leuf, Bo, 321, 338
Lindquist, Julie, 186, 194
Line, Steinar, 317, 338
LinguaMOO, 291
linguistics, 220
Linux, 26
Lipson, Ashley S., 159–160, 176
listserv, 120
literacy, 3, 6–11, 13, 46, 74–79, 81, 84–85, 87, 89–92, 94, 97, 111, 118–120, 122–124, 128, 130, 132, 136–137, 140, 145, 150, 154–157, 186, 206, 209, 216, 222, 227, 260, 295
literacy narratives, 109
litigation, 170, 173
lobbying, 248
logocentrism, 220–221
logos, 143, 168, 193
Longman, Huon, 229, 231–232, 286
lore, 107, 340
Losh, Elizabeth, 23, 40
Lowood, Henry, 199–200, 203–204, 211, 216
ludology, 255, 258, 266
Lunsford, Andrea, 152, 157
lurkers, 206–207

Macgill, Alexandra, 121, 138
machinima, 194, 196, 198–205, 208–216
macros, 151
magic circle, 134
mainframe, 327
Mallory, Jordan, 73
manifesto, 34, 72
Manovich, Lev, 163, 176

Mareck, Anne, 11, 18, 91, 96, 154, 158
marketing, 4, 46, 259–260, 349, 350
markets, 6, 26, 70, 175
Martin, Nancy, 30, 44, 71, 306
masks, 56, 66, 81, 353
materiality, 41, 209, 220, 225, 299–301, 306
Maton, Nathan, 260, 268
Maya, 27
McCloud, Scott, 272, 286–287
McCorkle, Ben, 272, 287
McGonigal, Jane, 25, 28, 40, 228, 233
McGuinness, Mark, 108, 112–113
McKee, Heidi, 17
McKenny, Craig, 46, 72
McLeod, Alex, 306
Mead, Corey, 40
mechanics, 107, 127, 142, 144, 146–147, 152, 160, 170, 172–173, 175, 202, 223–224, 276, 288, 293, 295–296, 344, 349
Medway, Peter, 288, 306
meme, 55, 72, 119, 126–127, 135, 352
memorial, 306
memory, 7, 165, 242–243, 282, 323
mentorship, 206–207, 213
Merleau-Ponty, Maurice, 242, 252
Metacritic, 51, 53–54, 72
metaphor, 23–24, 105, 160, 163, 167–168, 207, 220–222, 291, 293
metaphysics, 220
metaprogramming, 333
Metcalf, Chelsey, 286
Michel, Anthony, 26, 40, 300, 307
microphone, 223, 225
Miis, 198
MiLK, 198

Miller, Carolyn R., 294, 307
Minecraft, 163
Minesweeper, 337
Mitchell, Matthew, 290, 307
MMORPG, 12, 16, 45, 72, 74–75, 94, 111, 117–118, 128, 144, 152, 181, 185, 187, 192, 202, 252, 266, 291–292, 308, 347–351, 354, 360–361
moderators, 145
mods, 25, 45, 64, 185, 327
Moeller, David, 6, 17, 314, 338
Moeller, Ryan, 6, 17
monetization, 33
money, 57, 66, 68, 92, 241, 248, 250, 276–278, 280, 298, 301, 347
Monfort, Nick, 327, 332, 338
monologue, 343
monomodality, 209, 300
monopoly, 168, 171
monuments, 10
Moor, Peter J., 122, 138
MOOs, 291, 307
Morran, Chris, 62, 73
Morrowind, 90
Morton, Kenneth, 204, 211, 217
MoveOn.org, 300
Moxley, Roy, 221, 233
Muchkin, 167
Muckelbauer, John, 99, 101–105, 107–109, 112
multiboxing, 124–126, 128, 131–132, 138–139
multiliteracies, 18
multimedia, 6, 11, 14, 17, 27, 193, 215, 322, 324
multimodality, 6, 10–12, 14–15, 24, 27, 38, 40, 109, 154, 156, 182, 193, 197–198, 208–210, 217–218, 220, 222, 227, 229, 232, 299, 307

multiplayer, 9, 46, 73, 117, 138, 141, 144, 147, 155, 157, 188, 218–219, 222, 231–232, 288, 295–296
multitasking, 119, 182, 185, 186, 187, 188, 195
murder mystery, 283
Murray, Lesley, 108, 112–113
music, 44, 164–165, 206, 212, 242, 306
MySpace, 87–89, 91, 205
mythology, 10, 35, 72, 81, 137, 141, 232, 308

Nardi, Bonnie A., 117, 138
narrative, 11–12, 16, 43, 46–50, 53–55, 59, 61–62, 64–65, 69, 76, 81, 109, 120, 157, 185, 198, 202, 204, 212, 231, 255–258, 262, 266–268, 283, 293, 309, 319, 328, 339–341, 343, 345–346, 351, 353–358, 361
narrator, 255, 343
Natale, Marc, 318, 338
Nelson, Graham, 14, 159, 328, 338
networks, 3, 6, 10, 13–14, 24, 26, 31–32, 35–36, 44, 51, 57, 68–70, 78, 96–97, 108, 111–112, 150, 156, 158, 260, 301, 312
Neuwirth, Christine, 18
Neverwinter Nights, 88
New London Group, 6, 18
new media, 3, 14, 17, 26, 39, 68, 72, 120, 163, 176, 200, 204, 209–210, 212, 215–217, 281, 284–286, 308
Newman, James, 320, 338
newsgames, 25, 39
Nintendo, 170, 176, 316, 320, 337–338
Nissenbaum, Helen, 63, 70

nonplayer characters, 10, 11, 75, 110, 184, 198, 256, 343, 350–361
Norman, Christina, 70
Nyberg, Amy Kiste, 138

Oblinger, Diana, 315, 338
Oblinger, James, 315, 338
Obst, Patricia, 229, 231–232
Ochoa, Xavier, 206, 217
Ong, Walter J., 233
ontology, 29, 99, 251
open source, 26, 27, 73, 206, 338
orator, 8
Orland, Kyle, 170, 177
Osterweil, Scot, 196–198, 216
Ozymandias, 203, 217

Paese, Anthony, 286
Palmeri, Jason, 208, 217
PALS For Life, 188, 192, 194
paratext, 12–13, 25, 73, 118–119, 121–124, 132, 136, 144
Paré, Anthony, 288, 306
parody, 202
Passage, 13, 99, 101, 103–104, 107, 113
patents, 14, 159–60, 169–177
Paul, Christopher A., 46, 73, 75, 98, 104, 144, 158, 195, 229, 260, 286
Pearce, Celia, 117, 138
pedagogy, 3, 8–9, 11–14, 18, 40, 97–98, 108, 112, 157, 182, 186, 197–198, 217, 229, 236, 238, 240, 265–267, 282–283, 289, 294–295, 299–300, 303, 305, 307, 309, 333, 337
Penner, Jeremy, 24, 32–33, 35–37, 40
peripherals, 170
Perrachione, Tyler, 233

persuasion, 8, 10, 25, 28–31, 35, 40, 103, 109, 127, 131, 188, 193, 197, 210, 214, 223, 271–274, 278, 286, 291, 304, 307

phenomenology, 39, 65

photographs, 109, 206, 300, 303

Photoshop, 92

photoshopped, 55

piracy, 171, 340

pixel, 103, 163

pixelated, 104

plagiarism, 318, 324–325

platform, 6, 14, 25–27, 38, 45, 198, 214, 272, 324, 329

Plato, 30, 36, 101–102, 105, 111, 113

player vs. player, 123, 133–134, 138

playthrough, 50

poetics, 36

poetry, 31, 267, 341

Polaroid, 38, 161

politics, 6, 16, 28, 37, 39, 67, 70, 109, 200, 204, 235–236, 238, 240, 249, 264, 270, 273–275, 277–280, 282, 286, 291, 300, 306

Pong, 14, 159–163, 165, 169, 174–175

Portal, 262, 339, 343, 345

Porter, James, 17, 44, 63, 72–73, 295

postcardware, 32

postmodernism, 112, 200

potlatch, 21–24, 26, 31, 35, 39

PowerPoint, 267

praxis, 68, 77, 157, 307

Prensky, Marc, 187, 194

prewriting, 283, 314–315, 317

Priestly, Chris, 51, 58, 73

printing, 161, 302

prison, 248, 298

proairesis, 16, 271, 283–285

procedural literacy, 155

procedural rhetoric, 8, 13, 16, 98, 155, 197, 270–272, 275, 278, 282, 285

procedurality, 7, 13, 40, 98–99, 101, 110, 113, 270–271, 273

programming, 16, 166, 168, 270, 277, 282, 310–318, 320–324, 326–328, 331, 334, 336–338

prosumer, 25

protests, 42, 57, 59, 275–276

prototype, 110–111

pseudonyms, 95

psychology, 5, 9, 29, 55, 232, 290, 304

public domain, 26, 70, 174–175

pun, 343, 352

quest, 47, 107, 131–132, 182–184, 202, 261, 341, 350–361

race, 9, 47–48, 93, 141, 252

raiding, 123, 129, 141–143, 145–149, 151, 156, 158, 189, 191

Ravaja, Niklas, 232

realism, 266, 277–278

recomposition, 296, 307

Reed, Scott, 221, 256

Reid, Alex, 97, 113

remake, 57, 157

remix, 15, 126, 206, 209, 284

Remley, Dirk, 46, 73

replayability, 163, 255

repository, 322

reproduction, 22, 28, 48, 170, 301, 305

reputation, 48, 292

revision, 58, 151, 265–266

rhetoric, 4, 7–9, 11–14, 16, 23, 26, 28–31, 35–38, 46, 65–66, 68, 91, 98, 109, 143, 153, 155–157, 196, 220, 227, 270, 272–274, 276–277, 285–289,

294–295, 297–299, 301, 303–305
rhetorical situation, 40, 63, 102, 120, 153, 181, 186, 228, 273–274, 286, 294–295, 300, 306, 308
rhetorician, 7, 16, 28, 36, 111, 221, 271–272, 282, 285, 294, 297, 300–302, 304
Rice, Jeff, 155, 158
Rickert, Thomas, 36, 40
Ridolfo, James, 26, 40, 300, 303, 307
Rigney, Ryan, 25, 40
Ritchie, Dennis, 336–337
Robinson, Erick, 46, 65, 177, 252
robot, 83, 95, 161
Rohrer, Jason, 99, 103, 113
roleplaying, 80, 89, 354
roleplaying game, 46, 49–51, 90, 231
romanticism, 34
Root-Wiley, Mark, 73
Rosen, Harold, 306
Rouse, Richard, 320, 338
Rowsell, Jennifer, 209, 217
rubrics, 214, 227
Rude, Carolyn, 301–303, 307
Ruszkiewicz, Sheryl, 256

Salen, Katie, 196–198, 216, 320, 332, 338
Salminen, Mikko, 232
Sample, Mark, 37, 40
Samuelson, Pamela, 170, 177
Saper, Craig, 32, 40
sarcasm, 124, 126–127, 133, 135, 192
satire, 189–191, 193
Scalpel, 24, 27
scandal, 40, 42, 62
scapegoats, 181
scarcity, 22

Scheckler, Rebecca, 137
Schneider, Emily, 286
Schrader, P. G., 290, 308
Schraw, Gregory, 290, 307
Schweizer, Bobby, 25, 39
science, 11, 16, 99, 171, 194, 217, 281, 307, 311, 321, 323, 325, 341
Scratch, 198, 270
screenshots, 131, 327
screenwriting, 343, 347, 351, 361
scripts, 199
Seamon, David, 238, 252
Second Life, 71, 198, 205, 211, 214, 292, 305
Sega, 173
Selber, Stuart, 73, 76, 77, 96, 307
Selfe, Cynthia, 5, 9, 11, 17–18, 91, 96, 154, 158, 209, 217, 308
sexuality, 23
Shackelford, Russell, 338
Shadow of the Colossus, 346
Shaffer, David W., 186, 188, 195
Shakespeare, William, 191, 195
shaman, 150
shareware, 32
Sheridan, David, 16, 26, 40, 288, 300, 302, 305, 307
Sheridan-Rabideau, Mary P., 209, 217
Shin, Jiwon, 122, 138
Shipka, Jody, 113, 208–209, 217, 300, 307
Shirky, Clay, 73
Sicart, Miguel, 40, 98, 113
Sierra, Wendi, 14, 196, 255–256
simulation, 119, 141, 143, 151, 160, 201, 231, 250, 277, 288, 304, 332
Sindre, Guttorm, 317, 325, 338
Sirc, Geoffrey, 97, 113, 308
skins, 45, 270

Skyrim IV: The Elder Scrolls, 13, 24–25, 39, 45, 99, 104, 106–107, 112, 118, 137, 345
smartphones, 299
Smith, Leonora, 194
Smith, Richard, 96
Socrates, 102
soldier, 48
Soloway, Elliot, 316, 337–338
Sophist, 101, 105, 113
sophists, 99, 101–102, 105, 111
Sotomma, Olli, 217
sound, 6, 32, 34–35, 93, 154, 162–165, 203, 211–213, 225, 281, 299, 346
soundtracks, 93
spectacle, 22–24, 37
speeches, 276, 278
Spiderman, 95
Spinellis, Diomidis, 328, 338
spoof, 5, 194
Sproull, Lee, 318, 330, 338
Squire, Kurt, 5–6, 18
Starcraft, 198, 219
stasis, 100–101, 109
Steinkuehler, Constance, 46, 73, 147, 158
Stewart, Mary Amanda, 233
Stickney, Anne, 153, 158
storytelling, 71, 258, 268, 340
Strange Company, 198, 203, 217
Sunakawa, Chiho, 226, 232
surveillance, 138, 158
sustainability, 248
Swalwell, Melanie, 46, 73
Swarts, Jason, 158
Szulborski, Dave, 259, 269

tabletop games, 259
tactics, 146, 148–149
Taylor, Jennifer, 337
Taylor, T. L., 138, 158, 233

teamwork, 10, 49, 51, 59, 60–61, 66, 79, 89–90, 96, 128, 145, 147, 156, 182, 188–189, 191–193, 213, 219, 223, 225, 267, 305, 322
Tebeaux, Elizabeth, 76, 96
techne, 28–29, 30, 35–37
television, 3–5, 91, 159–161, 165, 169
terrorism, 264
Testerman, Doyce, 58, 65, 73
Tetris, 168, 177, 258
The Academy of Machinima Arts and Sciences, 216
The Burning Crusade, 127, 139
The Sims, 214
theorycraft, 13, 129–130, 141–150, 152–153, 155–158
Thomas, David, 337
Thomas, Rebecca, 268
TINAG, 259
Tobin, Lad, 97, 113
Tolkien, J. R. R., 73
tooltip, 344
toon, 79, 82, 84–85, 87–90, 93–95
Toothman, Brian, 338
topoi, 29–30, 36–37, 73, 307
tournaments, 140
trademark, 170, 352
transmedia, 119–120, 122, 133–134, 136
Tree, Jean E. Fox, 138
Trimbur, John, 26, 41, 261, 265, 269, 299, 301, 307–308
troll, 74, 122–123, 125, 127, 138, 173
trolling, 13, 118, 122–128, 132–135, 137
trope, 66, 155
tutorials, 44, 75, 246, 340, 346
Twitter, 58, 261, 264, 351
tyranny, 240

Ubisoft, 341
Ulmer, Gregory, 32, 36, 37, 41
Ultima Online, 348
unicorns, 264–265
Urban Dictionary, 194–195
Urbanski, Heather, 185
usability, 212
user interface, 143, 151, 324, 326,
    334, 339, 341, 344, 350–352,
    358–359
USPTO, 176–177
utopian, 28
utterance, 294

Valåg, Ottar, 317, 338
Valve, 45, 339
van Dijck, José, 205, 207, 217
van Leeuwen, Theo, 208, 216,
    299, 307
Vatz, Richard E., 294, 308
Vee, Annette, 166, 171–172, 175,
    177
Ventrillo, 185
Verleur, Ria, 122, 138
videotape, 108
Vietnam, 109
villain, 58, 93
violence, 28, 31, 37, 181, 202,
    317, 336, 346
virtual reality, 194, 229, 233
virtue, 21, 30, 63, 70
virus, 194, 256, 261, 263–264
visualizations, 143, 154
vitalism, 36, 104
Vitanza, Victor, 23, 28–31, 35–36,
    41
voice over IP, 14, 218–219,
    222–223, 225–229, 231
Voorhees, Owen, 24–25
Vygotsky, Lev, 233

Wallis, Claudia, 187, 195

war, 23, 39, 40, 47, 76, 90, 130,
    157, 318, 338
Wardrip-Fruin, Nick, 217, 257,
    268, 281–282, 287
warlock, 126, 136, 183
warrant, 165
Warren, Stanford, 170, 172, 177,
    282
warrior, 81, 153, 183, 190
WASD, 33
waypoints, 360
web browser, 27, 292–293
webzine, 207
Weidner, Hal Rivers, 29, 40
Weisser, Christian, 295, 306
Welch, Kathleen E., 308
Welch, Nancy, 308
werewolf, 106
Wesch, Michael, 214, 217
Whalley, Peter, 186, 195
whistleblowers, 263
White, David, 17–18, 113, 205,
    207, 217, 359
Wii, 170, 176
Wikipedia, 37, 194–195
wikis, 44, 156, 158, 268, 321, 338
Wiley, Steve, 46, 73
Williams, Dmitri, 18, 233
Williams, John C., Jr., 17
World of Warcraft, 10, 13–14,
    26, 42, 62, 67, 97, 118, 121,
    123, 125, 133–134, 141, 142,
    144–147, 153, 155–156, 158,
    181–185, 188, 192, 194–195,
    197–199, 202, 207, 210, 219,
    223, 228–231, 255, 291, 341,
    348, 352
World of Workcraft, 199, 217
WoWWiki, 142, 155, 158,
    188–189, 195
writing across the curriculum,
    311–312, 314, 320, 322, 338

writing studies, 3, 6, 11–12, 14,
285
Wysocki, Anne Frances, 209, 217,
299, 308

Xanatos, 216
Xbox, 25, 52, 94
Xiong, Li, 219, 225, 233
XYZZY Awards, 328

Yeats, William Butler, 352
Yee, Nick, 5, 18
Young, Art, 338

Young, Michael, 308
Young, Richard E., 41
YouTube, 131, 138, 194, 205, 207

Zhang, Schuming, 286
Zheng, Dongping, 290, 308
Zimmerman, Eric, 204, 217, 320,
332, 338
zines, 25
zombies, 29, 256, 261, 263–265,
267
zombification, 263
Zork, 327, 347

CPSIA information can be obtained
at www.ICGtesting.com
Printed in the USA
LVHW042123070723
751748LV00001B/114

9 781602 357310